27 MEN OUT

Also by Michael Coffey

THE IRISH IN AMERICA *(with Terry Golway)*
87 NORTH *(poems)*
ELEMENOPY *(poems)*

27 MEN OUT

BASEBALL'S PERFECT GAMES

MICHAEL COFFEY

796.3572
COF

ATRIA BOOKS

NEW YORK LONDON TORONTO SYDNEY

ATRIA BOOKS
1230 Avenue of the Americas
New York, NY 10020

Library of Congress Cataloging-in-Publication Data
Coffey, Michael, 1954–
27 men out : baseball's perfect games through history / Michael Coffey.—
1st Atria Books hardcover ed.
p. cm.
ISBN: 0-7434-4606-2
1. Perfect games (Baseball) 2. Pitchers (Baseball)—United States.
3. Baseball—United States—History. I. Title: Twenty-seven men out.
II. Title: Baseball's perfect games. III. Title.

GV871.C64 2004
796.357'22—dc22   2003063779

First Atria Books hardcover edition April 2004

1   3   5   7   9   10   8   6   4   2

ATRIA BOOKS is a trademark of Simon & Schuster, Inc.

Manufactured in the United States of America

For information regarding special discounts for bulk purchases,
please contact Simon & Schuster Special Sales at 1-800-456-6798
or business@simonandschuster.com.

FOR GABE

CONTENTS

FOREWORD BY BILL JAMES

Let me tell you a secret. I almost never read my own books for three or four years after they are published, or even look at them. On a certain level, they disgust me. They are so far from perfection. Whenever I write a book, it begins in my head with some idea of a wonderful book—complex, profound, unique, inspiring, with every phrase sanded smooth, every figure of speech wedged in without a seam, every anecdote documented. Real books, like real life, are nowhere near so satisfying. They are filled with issues that I didn't quite have time to research, with phrases that I took a liking to and shouldn't have, with awkward conjunctions, tired images, and blind detours. In the process of writing each book, I must come to terms anew with my own many limitations and I come to dislike the book, for a time, for forcing me to face myself.

When I go to a baseball game, I go through the same process. I think we all go through a similar process, and it is this process that makes Michael's book so appealing. If there is a walk in the first, I think, "Well, he still has his no-hitter." If there is a hit in the second, I think, "Well, he still has his shutout." If there is a run in the third, I think, "Well, he could still get a complete game." If he is knocked out in the fourth, I think, "Well, he could still avoid a loss here."

I think this is a common thought pattern; I know I have talked to other fans who said they did much the same thing. We start looking everywhere with the idea of perfection, and we cling to that hope, in a sense, by adapting it. We negotiate with God for as much perfection as we can get. When I get up in the morning, I so often promise myself that I will make this a perfect day; I will do my exercises, I will not spend four hours at work playing various kinds of solitaire on my computer, but will focus on my task list, I will answer all of my e-mail, I will be nice to everyone I meet. In reality I am rude, lazy, and obsessed with amusing myself, but I forget this while I sleep, and arise with the first-pitch potential of perfection shining brightly from the east.

Dating, I suppose, is a perfect image of a perfect game. Every generation is born naïve. Every man begins the rituals of mate selection as a pur-
suit of perfection—every woman, too, I suppose, although I really know
nothing about women except that there probably aren't very many of
them reading this book. We get slapped down by beauty queens, and
think, "Well, maybe I could still wind up with someone who is kind of
cute." Two weeks out of any relationship, we begin to fantasize anew, not
so much about flawless beauty but about flawless . . . what? Tolerance,
perhaps; endless patience with our foibles, endless interest in our interests, endless support for our ambitions.

God didn't make too many perfect women, and so far She has made
only fourteen perfect games. The odd thing is that, when someone actually throws a perfect game—or even a no-hitter—I always feel let down
somehow, disappointed. It is as if the author has marred perfection by
attaining it. In time, I come to terms with the new name on the list of
perfection, the new chapter that will have to be added to Michael's second edition. I have the same reaction when I read a book if the book is
too good, too close to perfection. I get depressed if I read a book that is too
good; it makes me feel like such a wastrel. In time, I come to terms with
my own books; I eventually reach the point, with each book, that I can
look at it without feeling those twinges of regret. If I were ever to write a
perfect book, I would celebrate without end, and I would never write
another. Perfection should be celebrated, and we are blessed that such a
skilled and seamless writer as Mr. Coffey has taken up the challenge of
the celebration.

Let's just hope he made enough mistakes that he'll have to write
another one someday.

—Bill James

INTRODUCTION

If you skip to the end of this book—the closing pages of chapter 13—you will find where and when it started: at Yankee Stadium on a summer Sunday in 1999.

To a baseball fan, witnessing a perfect game is a little like glimpsing Heaven on Earth (complete with beer vendor and a good seat). Or, more genteelly, like sitting one day at the keyboard, hearing some lost celestial chord that links "all perplexed meanings/into one perfect peace," as in the Arthur Sullivan hymn. Blessedness itself? Nirvana? An extended moment in which Yeats's center *does* hold? We will admit that it is hard to describe.

Fortunately, the perfect game, like some elegant mathematical theorem, can be objectively posited and proved. Something either is or is not a perfect game. It is 27 men out in a row. You can add it up. You can look it up. Officially, according to Major League Baseball, a perfect game occurs when a pitcher pitches at least nine innings of a complete-game victory and allows not a single runner to reach first base.

There are, by one measure, 23 legal ways for a batter to make it to first base, the most common being a base hit, followed by base on balls, error, or hit batsman. The rest involve various forms of interference and obstruction (by catcher, fielder, umpire, fan) or require a runner already to be on base (fielder's choice, for example). With these many roads to first, the chances of foiling batters, one after the other for an entire game, are slim—try taking 1 minus a pitcher's opposition's on-base percentage and raising it to the 27th power. You get a very small number no matter how bad the pitcher. For someone like the great Addie Joss, who threw a perfect game in 1908, you get a probability that in 10,000 starts he'd pitch a perfect game eight times. Don Larsen, with a considerably less distinguished career, would have to start more than 100,000 games to get his one perfect one (of course, he got it in less than 200 career starts).

While well over 150,000 games have been played in the modern era, which began in 1903, when the National and American Leagues agreed to play by the same rules, only 14 have ended in perfection (the two perfect games thrown in 1880 in the pre-modern era, when pitching was under-handed and from 45 feet away, are not covered in this book). Before I began researching these wonderful instances of baseball perfection—thrown by pitchers from great to good to average to bad—I had a sense that there was no secret to their occurrence, nothing that these games or pitchers shared exclusively with each other. I was correct in this—nothing did link these games, from Cy Young's in 1904 to David Cone's in 1999, beyond extremely effective pitching and excellent control, but these two things were hardly exclusive to these games.

But the one fact shared by these fellows (Cy Young, Addie Joss, Charlie Robertson, Don Larsen, Jim Bunning, Sandy Koufax, Catfish Hunter, Len Barker, Mike Witt, Tom Browning, Dennis Martinez, Kenny Rogers, David Wells, and David Cone)—their singular, record-book outings—paled next to what they shared with all ballplayers: the struggle to make it to the top of their profession. For all of them, this struggle involved the uncertainty of youth and young manhood embarking on a chancy career in a professional sport controlled by a cartel of businessmen and ruled by the vagaries of luck, the verities of gamesmanship, and the roar of the crowd.

The distribution of these games over time, sprinkled throughout the 20th century as they are, suggested to me early on that one could get a good survey of baseball itself—its history, its place in the culture, the life of players in it—by detailing the contexts in which these wonderful performances occurred. In treating the games this way—historically—I felt I could add to the work already done by Ronald A. Mayer in *Perfect!* (1991) and James Buckley, Jr., in *Perfect* (2002), both of whom focused on the games and seldom strayed to the larger game itself.

The larger game itself is a business. It is so much a business that, when looking in depth at any of these pitchers, what surfaces is a story involving agents, contracts, trades, grievances, injuries, and that which unites them all—money. And these stories seem central to understanding each player, and each player's time; and they just may shed a little light on the great accomplishment on the field.

To fully understand the impact of Cy Young's perfect game in 1904, I would argue, you have to understand why he was pitching in Boston, in the new American League, and not in Cleveland, where he had become baseball's best pitcher; you have to understand the critical role he played in forging the peace between the two leagues. To appreciate Addie Joss's perfect game in 1908, you should know how this player, plagued by ill health, pushed himself beyond his physical limits in a great pennant race, only to die shortly thereafter, at age 31, leaving a destitute wife and family, and fellow players both mournful and embittered. Before getting to Charlie Robertson's perfect game in 1922 for the White Sox, you have to understand owner Charles Comiskey's continual purging of talented ballplayers in order to keep payroll down, and how Robertson, of underwhelming talent, tried to catch on by dint of illegal pitches. With Don Larsen in 1956, you have a talented but undisciplined pitcher pitching a huge game for the dynastic Yankees with baseball on the verge of enormous change. That enormous change—the Dodgers and the Giants moving to California after the following year—brought more change. And in 1964, Jim Bunning, traded by Detroit for his activities in the nascent player's union and soon to be instrumental in the hiring of Marvin Miller, found himself facing the lowly expansion New York Mets on Father's Day, and he was perfect that day. Sandy Koufax, who was nearly perfect for five years, was absolutely perfect against the last-place Cubs in 1965, and by the next spring was dancing in top hat and tails at the Hollywood Palace on national TV, singing "We're in the Money" with co-holdout Don Drysdale—an early two-man union that terrified the owners. In 1968, with America writhing with social unrest, Jim "Catfish" Hunter pitched a perfect game for Charlie Finley's A's, even then plotting his escape from the Finley farm. He became baseball's first free agent. After Hunter's perfect game, the third in four years, Major League Baseball, which had heightened the mound and widened the strike zone in 1963 in response to Roger Maris's assault on Babe Ruth's home-run record two years earlier, reversed itself. There would be no more perfect games till Len Barker's in 1981, during a strike-bifurcated season that dashed the hopes of Cleveland fans. Mike Witt was perfect in a meaningless, end-of-season outing against the Rangers in scorching heat, as teams without established traditions played out the string before family and friends. Meanwhile, a new commissioner was preparing to strangle free agency via collusion, victimizing Witt and many others. The Reds' Tom Browning threw another in 1988, the summer in which baseball owners were found guilty of stacking the deck against free agency and Reds manager Pete Rose began his last season of gambling on his team—he was suspended for life before the next season. In 1991, the first perfect game by a Latin American was thrown by Dennis Martinez, hurling heroically in the midst of seven years of Montreal mediocrity, battling his own alcohol demons, and with the business of baseball in complete disarray as the owners tried to shed yet another commissioner; in 1994, baseball's most ignominious year, Kenny Rogers set down the Angels, 27 in a row, on the very day the Players Association set its fateful strike date. In 1998, as the Yankees were back in the saddle with the most money and the best team, David Wells mowed down a lowly Minnesota team and a year later, David Cone ran through a Montreal Expos squad in 88 pitches—each pitcher performing by dint of medical interventions that Sandy Koufax could only have dreamed of.

What I have found in my two years of research is that baseball can't be looked at for long in isolation from the business that it is. We may wish to, and allow our children to do so for as long as possible, quite understandably: everyone's heart sinks seeing op-ed pieces on baseball's economics and charts citing ticket prices, media contracts, and financial losses. Would that baseball were a world contained in a box score.

Today, it is increasingly a challenge to be a fan, to invest hopes, interest, time, and money in watching swarms of millionaires cavort on your field of dreams in an effort that is meant to enrich media moguls and men and women who made their fortunes dealing cars. But baseball is a great game—beautifully designed, ingeniously scaled, and full of magnificent achievement. It would be a shame to turn away. By understanding the story behind the game, the imperfect struggle that is behind those instances of perfection, is to perhaps find a way to salvage a measure of respect for those who have fought to make a living or a thriving business in a game that children play.

CHAPTER ONE

The Cyclone

Denton True "Cy" Young
May 5, 1904

Cy Young didn't know what to tell his young wife. After all, Ohio had always been their home. They had grown up together in the neighboring townships of Peoli and Gilmore, in the central part of the state. For nine years Young had thrived as the best pitcher on the Cleveland Spiders team, perhaps the best pitcher in all of baseball. Now, on the eve of a new season, after a winter of uncertainty, Young and his entire cast of teammates were being shipped to St. Louis.

Cy and Robba Miller had been married going on seven years that spring of 1899. By all accounts they were extremely close, with the big, quiet Cy dependent on the tomboyish and outgoing little pepperpot he called "Bobby." Robba would accompany her husband to his spring training sessions down in Hot Springs, Arkansas, and she would, on occasion, go with him on the road to see American cities at a time when Americans were moving in droves from the farms. In the post–Civil War decades, the country was bursting with change; assembly-line motor cars and the birth of American aviation were just a few years away; the movie industry was born; the century's last war—the Spanish-American War—ran its course in a year's time, and the country added to its territorial possessions, finishing the great work of dominion that would make the next century an American one.

The pace was both exciting and exhausting, as the many lurid entertainments and crack cures of the day would attest. For relaxation, Cy and Robba Young liked nothing better than the diversions provided by the novels of Charles Dickens, William Makepeace Thackeray, and the homegrown Mark Twain. To while away the time on the long trips, Robba would read aloud to her husband, whose sixth-grade education had left him a little shy in literacy skills. Second cousins (Cy's mother was Robba's aunt), the two had played together often as children, and as adults they had a natural and contented ease.

The Youngs were comfortable enough on Cy's baseball salary, which was tops in the league at about $2,400 a year—they lived about three times better than the average steelworker. Young's success on the field, however, was anything but run-of-the-mill. A dozen years later, he would retire with more wins, 511, than any other pitcher is likely to get (as well as more losses). In 1898 he was already an established star and a hugely popular figure not only in "The Forest City," as Cleveland was rather incongruously known, but around the country. People were even beginning to refer to him fondly as "the G.O.M."—the Grand Old Man. And he was only 31.

Cy had spent nine seasons with the Cleveland Spiders, playing for owners Frank Robinson and his brother Stanley. He had won 25 games in '98, his eighth straight season with more than 20 wins; his career victory total already stood at 241. The Spiders managed to finish in what used to be called "the first division," taking fifth place, in the upper half of the 12-team league. The team had in fact been more than respectable for years, playing in the Temple Cup (which passed for a World Series before there was such a thing), and posting competitive second- and third-place finishes as well. The Spiders had one of the league's best hitters in Jesse Burkett, a future Hall of Famer who would finish with a lifetime .338 batting average, and Bobby Wallace, another Cooperstown-bound player, who would play for 25 years in the bigs. But all of a sudden, during spring

training for the 1899 season, Young and Burkett and Wallace, virtually
the entire team—including the manager—were traded to St. Louis. Not
really traded to St. Louis, but traded *for* St. Louis, as an equal number
from the Browns came to be Spiders in the same swift move.

It was a long way from Ohio to St. Louis, close to 600 miles. Cy tried
to sell his wife on the splendors of the big river there. After all, Twain had
made much of it, and was a fan of the game. "Baseball," Twain wrote, "is
the very symbol, the outward and visible expression of the drive and push
and rush and struggle of the raging, tearing, booming nineteenth century."
So the Youngs moved west.

BASEBALL HISTORIAN Bill James has called it "the greatest disgrace in
the history of baseball," bigger than the notorious Black Sox scandal of
1919, when eight embittered players threw a World Series. In 1899, two
owners gutted a whole team and threw an entire season away. The reason
was money.

Home attendance in League Park, Cleveland, which had been in the
150,000 a year range, fell to 70,000 in 1898; the Robinson brothers were
convinced that Sunday baseball was the answer to their problems, but
that was a liberty not allowed in their rather patrician city. The Robinsons publicly mused that perhaps another city—how about Buffalo?—
would be more roundly hospitable to the game of ball and the likes of
Young and Burkett and Wallace. With attendance dropping in midsummer, the Robinsons started converting home games to road, and ended up
playing in places like Weehawken, New Jersey, and Rochester, New
York. As the club became demoralized ("We could have won it by playing
all our games at home," Cy later lamented; the Spiders arguably weren't
out of the pennant race till mid-August), the Robinsons set their sights
on the franchise in St. Louis, where the lowly Browns plied their trade in
front of surprisingly energetic fans. But their ballpark, poorly maintained, caught fire, sparking lawsuits; the team, poorly skilled, finished
last. Over the winter, the rest of the league's owners, not to mention the
city fathers of St. Louis, worked to separate the Browns' owner—brewer
Chris van der Ahe—from his franchise. They did, buying him out for the
sum of $33,000. They sold it in a day to the circling Robinson brothers
for $40,000, and all this accomplished during spring training, 1899.

The Robinsons now owned two teams, one in a baseball-mad city
that loved beer and Sunday ball, the other in a morally straitened Cleve-

land. So, just before opening day, they transferred the Cleveland players to St. Louis, and the losing St. Louisans from the banks of the Mississippi to the Cuyahoga. Such a situation—where men own more than one club—is known as syndicalism, and was common in the early days of baseball. In theory, it is impermissible today; in practice, as was evidenced in the recent convoluted purchase of the Boston Red Sox by John Henry, who financed his acquisition by selling his Marlins to the owner of the Expos, who financed his move by way of a buyout of his beleaguered club by all of Major League Baseball, it is still going on.

The St. Louis fans couldn't have cared less about syndicalism. In the spirit of both renewal and alliteration, the fans and press ditched the name "Browns" and began calling their team Pat's Perfectos, after Tebeau, the new manager, late of Cleveland.

It was a different story for the Spiders, who managed to win but 20 games of the 154 played, good for last place, 35 games out of next-to-last place and a mind-boggling 83.5 games out of first place. The team's .130 winning percentage remains the game's low-water mark. They drew 6,000 fans for the entire season. The Spiders folded the next year, as part of the first contraction in Major League Baseball.

CY YOUNG WAS NOW 32 years old; he posted 26 wins for his new club, or rather, new locale. But he wasn't happy. He and Robba didn't care one bit for being shuttled off to the west bank of the Mississippi, to a town known for its un-Methodist ways and stifling summer heat. Neither were they thrilled to have Cy's salary capped by league fiat at $2,400. Nonetheless, Young gave it his all, as did teammates Burkett, who hit .396, second in the league, and Wallace, the brilliant shortstop, who drove in 108 runs. The team finished fifth, just as the Spiders had the year before. Little wonder: It was the same team.

As it turns out, Cy Young was not the only unhappy player in baseball. On an off-day early in the 1900 season, when most of the Western teams were in the East, the players held a meeting at the Stuyvesant House in New York City. They emerged newly organized, as the Players Protective Association, denouncing the language of the standard player's contract as "unfair, illegal, and too one-sided." They objected in particular to the so-called reserve clause, in which a team reserved exclusive rights to a player's services in perpetuity, if it wished, and also the right to terminate the player's service on only 10 days' notice. The players also proposed the establishment of a grievance committee. Cy Young was one of three St. Louis delegates.

In the early days of baseball, wherever there were unhappy ballplayers, there were entrepreneurs ready to use that as a wedge to get into the baseball business. And the founding of the Players Protective Association prompted another run. Almost immediately, a man named Ban Johnson, president of the Western League, a professional league without major league status, with teams in cities such as Indianapolis, Grand Rapids, and Sioux City, rechristened his circuit the American League, and moved ball clubs into three National League towns—Chicago, St. Louis, and Cleveland, the last city, as we know, now without a club. Plans for Boston, Philadelphia, and Washington, also National League towns, followed. The National League owners knew a threat when they saw one. They had already absorbed a competing league or two, including one that was run by players. In the face of Johnson's announced intentions, they axed four teams and instituted a salary freeze. But that couldn't stop Ban Johnson, and hardly seemed designed to placate the ballplayers.

On January 28, 1901, Johnson walked out of Chicago's Grand Pacific Hotel and announced a 140-game schedule for his eight-team American League, consisting of the Baltimore Orioles (to be managed by John McGraw), the Boston Somersets (nicknamed after their owner, Charles W. Somers, a coal magnate who was a league vice president), the Chicago White Stockings (with onetime Johnson mentor Charles Comiskey as owner), the Cleveland Blues (so named for the color of their uniforms), the Detroit Tigers, the Philadelphia Athletics (whose part owner/manager Cornelius McGillicuddy, aka Connie Mack, was about to begin a 50-year term on the bench), and the Washington Nationals. Johnson also announced roster size—14 players—and, most important, asserted that his league would recognize the recently formed Players Protective Association and accept their work-rule demands. The National League had already rebuked the association ("I do not believe in labor organizations or unions," said one owner who would come to regret it, Arthur Soden of the Boston Beaneaters. "When a player ceases to be useful to me," he went on, "I will release him.") But Ban Johnson and his merry band of owners, for their own purposes, welcomed the union.

Meanwhile, the Robinsons were feeling the pressure, too. The possibility of a new American League team sitting in St. Louis, siphoning off their fan base, did nothing to ease things. Frank Robinson sent a letter to all his players telling them that he was withholding their last paycheck because of general drunkenness and gambling, and warning them one and all to expect pay cuts for 1901. The honorable, disciplined, and nongambling Cy Young vowed never to play for the Robinsons again, and he didn't. Young jumped to the new American League, and he was not alone. More than 70 active National Leaguers from 1900 were in the new league the next year—Young, Nap Lajoie, Hugh Duffy, Joe McGinnity, and Jimmy Collins all jumped. Every great player except Honus Wagner was lured by the new league's promise of no salary cap, even under the threat of permanent blacklisting by the National League. And Mrs. Young would surely prefer Boston's summer weather, and Cy's $1,100 raise.

Young would play for eight seasons in Boston, win 192 games, throw the first pitch of the first World Series game, and lay claim to being the greatest pitcher of all time. He would also, fittingly, throw the first perfect game of the modern era.

CY YOUNG WASN'T born Cy but Denton, and his middle name wasn't Tecumseh, as his original Hall of Fame plaque had it, but True: Denton True Young, born March 29, 1867, in Gilmore, Ohio.

His father, a farmer by the name of McKinzie Young, served as a soldier in the Union army (under Gen. James B. True), fought at Gettysburg, and then came home after Appomattox and married Nancy Miller, the daughter of a neighboring family. They set about having their own family, and began with the one they called Denton, which was a common surname in the Young family.

"All of us Youngs could throw," the long-retired Cy Young told a New York reporter, Arthur Daley, in 1947. "I usta kill squirrels with a stone when I was a kid and my grandad onct [sic] killed a turkey buzzard on the fly with a rock." Young, from the first time he was seen by whatever hungry, bewhiskered pipe-smoking sort passed for a baseball scout in the late 19th century, was from another era, always a farm boy, always "strapping," always "honest as the day is long." And the name Cy was attached to the boy called Denton because he could break things—backstops—with his humming fastball, and leave boards splintered as if a cyclone had swept through: the Cyclone, or Cy for short.

By the time Denton Young was two years old, Candy Cummings had thrown the first curveball, Ned Cuthbert had instituted the practice of base thievery, and a fellow named Bob Addy had been the first to slide. And a group of businessmen had put together a team of barnstorming professionals, the 1869 Cincinnati Red Stockings. By the time the boy was nine, the National League had been founded, with teams in Chicago, St. Louis, Hartford, Boston, Louisville, New York, Philadelphia, and Cincinnati; the first minor league, the International League, would be founded the next year, 1877; when Young was only 12, the owners, on September 29, 1879, invented the reserve clause, which bound players to owners—15 years after the Emancipation Proclamation. But that meant little to a kid tossing a ball in a meadow; his job was to get the hay in and figure out why in the world Mike Kelley would leave his Red Stockings for Chicago. Baseball was in Ohio in a big way, and though Denton Young grew to manhood on a farm and in a farm community, by all accounts following a path of discipline and self-control and piety, he couldn't get enough of the game.

By the age of 18 he'd become a local legend. At six feet two inches and 200 pounds, Young was a hitting and pitching dynamo. Team organizers would pay his expenses—"and sometimes, a little extra," according to the biographer Reed Browning. Young was paid a dollar a game to play for a team from Carrollton, before moving on, at age 23, to became part of a full-fledged minor league team, in Canton, which is where he signed to play ball for $60 a month in the spring of 1890. And it was in Canton where "Cy" Young was, if not discovered, at least named, doing his backstop destruction in front of a crowd that spread the word.

There was a good reason the young farm boy's talents were attracting attention, a reason that goes beyond the appeal of his natural talent. In 1890, a new professional league had started up, the Player's League, which was an organization owned and run by players unhappy with their treatment at the hands of the National League and the American Association. As players jumped to the player-owned league, spots opened up elsewhere, and Canton was hoping to develop talent that it could sell to the highest bidder. And indeed, at the end of the Canton season, Cy Young was sold for $300 to the Cleveland Spiders of the National League. Young would be paid $75 a month for his services. It was still midseason for the Spiders, and Cy Young made an immediate impression in his major league debut on August 6, 1890, beating the Cap Anson–led Chicago White Stockings and besting the great Bill Hutchinson, who would win 42 games that year. Legend has it that Anson—who struck out twice—tried to buy Young's contract right then and there for $1,000 but was rebuffed by the Spiders ownership. Cleveland knew what they had, and Young would be a Spider until the Robinson brothers made their move to St. Louis.

———————

IT WAS A DIFFERENT game in 1890, when Cy Young first turned pro, than the one we know today—pitchers threw from a flat, squared off area, like a box (hence the still-current phrase "back to the box" to describe a ball tapped back to the pitcher). They'd only recently started throwing overhand, underhand delivery being the rule till the mid-1880s. The front of the pitcher's box was 50 feet from home plate, which itself was square and not five-sided. Pitchers were not confined by a rubber, allowing them to run, hop, jump, and skip before releasing the ball. The catcher was bare-handed and stood far behind the batter to field and return the pitch, unless runners were on base. There was one umpire, who moved to the infield when there were men on base, the better to adjudicate across the big pasture. Players wore all-woolen uniforms, though you wouldn't say they were uniform, settling mostly for the same colored sock or top jersey; gloves were for protecting the palm (and some players wore one on each hand, and some, like Young, wore none); bats were more like long clubs (some over three and a half feet long); the ball was rubber, yarn, and leather; the ballparks were made of hazardous wood, risking fire and collapse; the outfields were more likely ringed by spectators and horse carriages than walls or fences.

Young's abbreviated rookie season went well enough, considering he was pitching for the lowly Spiders, who managed to win only one in every three games that year. During the next eight years, Young would win 232 games. The increasing of the pitching distance to 60 feet 6 inches in 1894 didn't faze him much; after dipping to a "mediocre" 26 wins that year, Young won 35 the next. By 1898, Young had begun to add pinpoint control to his already impressive arsenal of blazing fastball and sweeping curve. He walked no one in 13 of his 41 starts that year, never walked more than three in a game all season, averaging less than a walk per nine innings. As we know, it was Cy's last year as a Spider.

CY YOUNG WAS 34 years old when he jumped leagues. The team, known then as the Boston Somersets, or Pilgrims or Americans or Plymouth Rocks—nicknames variously bestowed by sportswriters—would share the city with the crosstown Boston Beaneaters of the National League. But early on, it was the Somersets who won the heart of the Boston faithful (this is the team that would eventually become—officially—the Red Sox).

The team's owner, Clevelander Charles Somers, saw to it that the city's charter entry in the new league would be distinctive. First off, he lured the best third baseman of the time, Jimmy Collins, away from the Beaneaters. He offered Collins a whopping $5,500 a year, 10 percent of the gate, and the role of player-manager. Beaneaters' owner Arthur Soden, he of the "I do not believe in unions," could only sit and watch as Collins and others of his teammates signed up to play for Somers.

Collins was the instrumental pickup. He not only knew Boston well enough to help scout the location for the building of a ball yard—they settled on the Huntington Avenue Grounds, hard by a handy trolley line and some Irish taverns—he was also such a respected player that the new club had instant credibility. Cy Young and his batterymate Lou Criger fled St. Louis in a heartbeat to join up with Collins. Somers also signed players with some local appeal—Freddy Parent of Maine, Hobe Ferris of Rhode Island. He also enlisted a man to work a megaphone at the ball grounds, announcing batters up and the official scoring.

The team was an immediate success. Drawing crowds twice the size of those drawn by the rival Beaneaters, the new American League entry, after a slow start, roared to a second-place finish, behind the Chicago White Sox. Young led the league in wins with 33 and posted a league-best ERA of 1.62. The next year, the Somersets grabbed yet another ballplayer from across town, the pitcher Bill Dinneen, who would post 21 wins for the club. And in 1903, with the addition of Long Tom Hughes to the starting rotation, the Somersets won the pennant by 14.5 games over Connie Mack's second-place Philadelphia Athletics.

By now, the National League was looking for peace with the Americans, who continued to outdraw their rivals in every city in which each had a franchise. With owners in both leagues interested in stability, a "National Agreement" was signed before the start of the 1903 season, in which all clubs promised not to raid each other for players and to insert and enforce the reserve clause in all player contracts. Additionally, the agreement standardized the game on the field, with the American League consenting to a National League rule that foul balls would be counted as strikes until there were two strikes. There was no mention in the agreement, however, of postseason interleague play. But by mid-September 1903, with the pennant races settled in each league, Pittsburgh owner Barney Dreyfus and the new Boston president Henry J. Killilea signed an agreement for a best-of-nine series at season's end. This is now known as the first World Series. Fittingly, at least from the long historical view of more than a century, Cy Young threw the first pitch of the first World Series game, October 1, 1903, at the Huntington Avenue Grounds, in front of an overflow crowd of 16,242. Young was the loser in that game, but came back to win his next two starts, and Boston shocked the venerable National League by defeating its champion Pirates, five games to three. It was akin to Joe Namath leading the American Football League New York Jets over the NFL's Baltimore Colts 66 years later, and it effectively had the same result—the peaceful coexistence of two once-rival leagues.

"THIS OLD PURITANICAL town is in for a lot of good base ball from now on," wrote *The Sporting News* on May 1, 1904, previewing the prospects for baseball in Boston after that championship season. "Captain Collins and the boys arrived in town this afternoon and all were congratulated by John I. Taylor, the new owner, for their remarkable showing at Philadelphia and Washington. . . . The Americans have lost but one game since their bad start in New York on the first day of the season. . . . The only criticism one can make today is that the boys should brace up their batting and this will come now that they are at Huntington Avenue and that Cy Young is not at his best." Young was indeed just rounding into form, having suffered a bout of tonsillitis in spring training followed by a severe cold. As *The Sporting News* presciently noted in the early May dispatch, "It is dollars to doughnuts that Cy will be doing his share at an early date in 'bringing home the goods.' "

In the year previous, in capturing his 362nd career win, Young had surpassed Pud Galvin as the all-time leader in victories, a crown he still wears. In his three years since jumping to Boston, Young had posted 93 wins against only 30 losses, and he owned the town. His wife liked Boston, Boston liked his wife and her agreeable and durable and nearly unbeatable husband. Young has become so popular, with a reputation of honesty and civility on and off the field (in a game filled with wild miscreants, hard-drinking noggin knockers, and an encirclement of gaming men), that he was routinely cheered, on the road as well as at home, and on those not-so-rare occasions when an umpire was delayed in coming to the game, he would, by mutual agreement between the two clubs, call the balls and strikes.

By early May, both the team and Young were on a roll. Boston got off to a hot start, standing in first place with a record of 12-3 on May 4. Young was on a bit of a streak of his own, which would reach record proportions before it ended, and have at its heart a gemstone of perfection.

Young had dropped the season opener, 8–2, to New York's Jack Chesbro (who would win 41 games that year, still the modern-era record). Young's first win of the year, and 380th of his career, came four days later, a 3–2 victory over Washington. And although he would be bested, 2–0, by the A's quirky left-hander Rube Waddell, on April 25, Young finished the game with seven shutout innings, the last two being hitless, finding a groove that would take him into the history books. Five days later, Young entered a game in relief of starter George Winter with two on and no one out in the third in a game against Washington. Young set down the next three hitters, and, in all, set down the opposition without a run or a hit for the final seven innings, getting the 4–1 win.

So on May 5, Young, on a run of 14 scoreless innings and 9 hitless innings, took a somewhat misleading record of 2–2 into his rematch with Waddell, the man who perhaps single-handedly inspired the common baseball wisdom that left-handers are by nature eccentric. Consider one-time Hall of Fame historian Lee Allen's unimprovable description of George Edward Waddell's 1903 season: "Rube began that year sleeping in a firehouse in Camden, New Jersey, and ended it tending bar in a saloon in Wheeling, West Virginia. In between those events he won 21 games for the Philadelphia Athletics, played left end for the Business Men's Rugby Football Club of Grand Rapids, Michigan, toured the nation in a melodrama called *The Stain of Guilt*, courted, married and became separated from May Wynne Skinner of Lynn, Massachusetts, saved a woman from drowning, accidentally shot a friend through the hand, and was bitten by a lion." Among the activities Mr. Allen chose to gloss over: chasing fire engines, leading parades, and wrestling alligators. Evidently a free spirit and a terrific pitcher, now in the Hall of Fame, the six-foot-two-inch, 195-pound Waddell from Bradford, Pennsylvania, north of Pittsburgh, would lead the league seven times in strikeouts, six in succession; his 349 Ks in 1904 would stand as a modern-era season record until another left-hander, more enigmatic than eccentric, Sandy Koufax, struck out 382 in 1965.

The Athletics, with the high-collared Cornelius McGillicuddy in the dugout, were struggling in the early going. But Cy Young would be facing a solid lineup indeed, one that, without much alteration, would come to dominate the American League in but a few years, winning five pennants and three World Series from 1905 to 1914. Topsy Hartsel, the left-handed-hitting leadoff man, stood only five feet five inches tall, but had led the league in steals in 1902 and hit .311 in 1903, and was perhaps the A's toughest out. Ollie Pickering was in center, a wily veteran though perhaps

on the down side of his career (today he is remembered by cognoscenti for
hitting seven straight bloop singles, in the Texas League, inspiring the
general use of the term Texas Leaguer to refer to such a hit). Harry
"Jasper" Davis, a Philadelphian, was the team's slugging first baseman.
Davis would lead the league in homers in 1904, the first of his four consecutive home-run titles, a feat equaled only by Frank "Home Run"
Baker, Babe Ruth, and Ralph Kiner. Lave Cross, christened Lafayette
Napoleon Cross, out of Milwaukee, was a catcher converted to an
infielder; despite a rule in 1895 limiting the size of gloves for all but the
catcher, Cross lugged his catcher's mitt to his infield positions. Cross was
an excellent hitter who would play 21 years in the big leagues and finish
with more than 2,600 hits. Playing right field and usually batting fifth
was Socks Seybold, who had some pop in his bat. He'd led the league in
home runs with 16 in 1902. Danny Murphy, another Philly native, was a
superb second baseman who hit a grand slam in his professional debut
and would go on to play 16 years in the majors. Monte Cross played short,
and though he was a good fielder, his lifetime batting average of .234
ranks him second lowest at the position, just ahead of Eddie Brinkman.
Batting eighth was Ossee Schreckengost. Ossee roomed on the road with
Waddell, but not before insisting on a clause in his contract forbidding his
roommate to eat crackers in bed. A great handler of pitchers, he was one
of the last catchers to don shin guards and among the first to catch one-
handed. He would figure prominently four years later in the modern era's
second perfect game. And batting ninth was Waddell, a good-hitting
pitcher.

For Boston, pesky Patsy Dougherty led off and played left field;
Dougherty was the first player to hit two home runs in a World Series
game, which he had done in Game Two the previous year; earlier in the
week he had opened against Waddell with a bunt single, making him the
only batter to reach base against the overpowering A's ace. Player-
manager and third baseman Jimmy Collins batted second; a native of Buffalo, New York, Collins would become the first third baseman inducted
into the Hall of Fame, appropriate for a man who was considered to have
revolutionized the position by playing bunts with a bare-handed pickup
and throw. Charles Sylvester "Chick" Stahl batted third and played center. Like Collins, a jumper from the Beaneaters, Stahl had turned in a
great World Series performance the previous year, batting over .300 and
hitting three triples; he would replace Collins as manager in 1906 but
come to a tragic end during the next year's spring training, committing

suicide by swallowing carbolic acid in despair over a woman. (Young, his roommate, would find him in death throes.) Buck Freeman was the cleanup-hitting right fielder. He'd also jumped across town along with Collins and Stahl; back in '99, with the Washington Senators, he'd led the National League in homers with a whopping (for the time) 25. Freddy Parent, of Biddeford, Maine, was a very popular player in Boston, a slick fielder coming off a year in which he hit over .300. Candy LaChance was perhaps the league's best-fielding first baseman, and his arrival allowed Collins to move the stone-handed Buck Freeman to the outfield. Possessed of a sour disposition, the six-foot-one, 183-pound LaChance once challenged Waddell to a wrestling match, which lasted for an hour. Waddell finally pinned the exhausted LaChance and then went out and pitched a shutout. Hobe Ferris batted seventh and played second; he'd distinguished himself in the 1903 Series by batting in all three runs in the final game, a 3–0 Boston win. Lou Criger was the catcher, batting in the eighth spot. Despite a career batting average of .221, he remained Young's favorite batterymate, as they had been together in Cleveland and St. Louis. Quick-footed and with a strong arm, Criger was famous for being base-stealing Ty Cobb's greatest nemesis. Young, a crafty hitter and good bat handler, batted ninth.

The two teams were set to square off in the final game of a six-game series. The weather was warm for early May in Boston. More than 10,000 fans showed up, half of them, according to a *Sporting News* commentator, attracted solely by the promise of a classic pitchers' duel. Young, of course, was always a draw, but the 28-year-old Waddell was enjoying the kind of fan interest that such eccentrics as Mark Fidrych and Spaceman Bill Lee would attract decades later. The year before, he had recovered from a rather rare ailment for a pitcher: an alligator bite, suffered in Florida during spring training while wrestling. Waddell recovered and went on to win 21 games, with a sparkling ERA of 2.44 and a league-leading 302 strikeouts. His mastery had carried into the 1904 season. Just three days earlier, but for the Patsy Dougherty bunt single to start the game, he was perfect against this very team, besting the tough Jesse Tannehill.

Waddell was not a man lacking in confidence. Before the game, he sauntered over to Young and informed him of his plans for the day: "I'll give you the same what I gave Tannehill." Waddell also took the time to taunt his former wrestling foe Candy LaChance, who, this time, declined the invitation to grapple.

Both pitchers breezed through the first two innings. The A's nearly got a man on base in the top of third, when shortstop Monte Cross blooped one over the head of second baseman Hobe Ferris, but Buck Freeman raced in from right field ("like a deer," Young would later recall) and made a lunging catch. In the fourth, nearly the same thing happened, as the A's Ollie Pickering looped one into the no-man's-land beyond the second-base bag—in a bid for the kind of hit he made famous—only to have center fielder Chick Stahl make a fine running catch. Pickering was almost the spoiler again, with one down in the top of the sixth, when he tapped a slow roller to short, but Freddy Parent charged the ball and nipped Pickering by half a step at first.

Waddell was rolling through the Boston lineup with equal dispatch. As Boston came to bat in the bottom of the sixth, there was no score. But the Pilgrims broke through when Chick Stahl slugged one over Socks Seybold's head in right and into the crowd—a ground-rule triple—and Buck Freeman plated him with a three-bagger of his own to put Boston up 1–0 after six. In the top of the seventh, the crowd held its collective breath when Danny Hoffman, a second-year man who had replaced lead-off hitter Topsy Hartsel after an injury, sliced a ball far down the left-field line, only to have Patsy Dougherty race into foul territory and make the catch, banging into the fence. It would be the last close call till the final batter.

In the bottom of the seventh, Boston added to its lead, on a Hobe Ferris triple and a double by catcher Lou Criger, making it 2–0. Young followed with a grounder to third, which turned into an error on first baseman Jasper Davis, who mishandled the throw, bringing Criger home with what would be the game's final run.

Young breezed through the eighth, and got the first two batters in the ninth—Monte Cross, leading off, became Young's eighth strikeout victim, and then Ossee Schreckengost grounded out, Parent at shortstop to LaChance. Rube Waddell stepped to the plate. Odd as it might seem today, the hometown crowd booed A's manager Connie Mack for letting Waddell hit; they wanted Young to crown his performance against a tougher out. But Mack did not relent, perhaps counting on Waddell's irascible, troublemaking nature, or perhaps his flair for the dramatic, to put a dent in Cy Young's so-far-perfect day. Commenting on Waddell's off-season career as an actor in a traveling drama, the *Philadelphia Inquirer* had pictured him standing graveside, in a dark fog, intoning, "Alas, poor baseball . . ." Would he render a tragic end to Young's bid for perfection? Waddell took two strikes and then hit a drifting fly ball to center that seemed to keep carrying, but Chick Stahl made the catch going away for the 27th and final out.

Boston first baseman LaChance, at game's end, was the first to reach Young at the mound, and told him, "Nobody came down to see me today," which indeed no Athletic had done. Only then, it is said, did Young realize what he had accomplished. Huntington Avenue may have had a megaphone, but it had no scoreboard recording hits.

Young would later say that it wasn't until a fan rushed to the mound at the game's end and pressed money into his hand that he realized he had done something special. The *Boston Daily Globe* reported that the ever-modest Young returned one bill to his benefactor. In a mere 83 minutes, he had beaten the tough Rube Waddell; he had retired 27 men in order, no walks, no hits, and no errors committed behind him, a feat that had been achieved only twice before, five days apart, in 1880, by Lee Richmond and John Montgomery Ward, back when the pitchers threw from 45 feet, it took eight balls to walk a guy, and the pitcher's hand could not rise above his hip on the delivery. Young's was the first perfection of the young modern era. The term perfect game wasn't even around yet—the headline the next day in Boston read, "Athletics Lose in Unique Game."

The New York Times was even more nonplussed by the event. It's entire notice the next day read:

> BOSTON, May 5.—Not one of the Philadelphians made a run, a hit, or reached first base in to-day's game, by reason of Young's superb pitching. Young's feat is a record-breaker in the major leagues. While the champions batted Waddell hard, sharp fielding by the visitors kept down the runs. Attendance 10,000."

Over time, Young would come to appreciate what he had accomplished. In 1945, at the ripe old age of 68, he would say, "Of all the 879 games I pitched in the big leagues, that one stands out clearest in my mind. I was real fast in those days but what very few batters knew was that I had two curves. One of them sailed in there as hard as my fastball and broke in reverse"—this would be called a tailing fastball today—"and the other was a wide break. I don't think I ever had more stuff."

Young's good stuff continued. His perfect game of May 5 brought his consecutive scoreless inning streak to 23 and his hitless inning streak to 18. Six days later he would pitch a 15-inning, 1–0 shutout, holding the Detroit club hitless until the seventh, closing out his consecutive hitless innings streak at 24. On May 17, he would hold Cleveland scoreless into the eighth, before giving way in a 3–1 loss, finishing with 45 straight scoreless innings.

Cy Young biographer Reed Browning makes the point: "Although others can equal the performance, nobody can surpass the excellence of a perfect game. But there was an even more impressive accomplishment during these five great games. For the 45 straight scoreless innings that link the games constitute a feat that has occasionally been exceeded [it has since been eclipsed by Doc White, Jack Coombs, Walter Johnson, Carl Hubbell, Don Drysdale, and Orel Hershiser, the current record holder at 59 innings], and if his perfect game represents an achievement that has sometimes been equaled, there was a third record that emerged from these games that Cy Young—over 90 years later—still holds all by himself. [His] 24 consecutive innings without yielding a base hit—no one has ever equaled that mark. Not even Johnny Vander Meer, who managed 22 hitless innings around his consecutive no-hitters in 1938."

YOUNG WOULD FINISH with another banner year: 26 wins, 1.97 ERA; Waddell would finish with one less win, and would just barely lose out the ERA title to Cleveland's up-and-coming "twirlologist" Addie Joss. Boston would win the pennant on the last day of the season but there would be no World Series: John Brush, new owner of the National League champion New York Giants, refused to play against a league that was run by Ban Johnson, who had moved an American League franchise, from Baltimore, onto his turf. (They would be known as the Yankees.) The World Series would survive two world wars and the intervening Depression, Red scares, Korea, Vietnam, social upheaval, not to mention disco and five-cent beer nights and double-knit uniforms and Bowie Kuhn and Bob Uecker and drug scandals and even an earthquake before being canceled again, in 1994, during a players' strike. By then it was a different game, because the rules of play between owners and players had changed, but the measurement of perfection on the field—so objective and inarguable—remained the same: 27 up, 27 down, no one reaching first base safely; perfection not as an abstract ideal, but as 27 things to do right and in a row. And Cy Young, as seems appropriate, showed the way.

CHAPTER TWO

The Twirlologist

Addie Joss
October 2, 1908

H ERE COMES RUBE Waddell again, walking into someone else's story, that of Adrian "Addie" Joss, of Wisconsin. Lots of guys walk through lots of guys' stories early on in baseball, when careers were long and rosters small. There were about 200 major league ball-playing jobs, year to year, in baseball's first decades, as compared to about 750 now. There wasn't a lot of player movement. Thanks to the reserve clause, there weren't as many revolving doors or "cups of coffee." Rooks and interlopers got the cold treatment. So, familiar names will troop through from the Cy Young story to the Addie Joss story—Ban Johnson, Connie Mack, Jesse Burkett, Freddy Parent, Patsy Dougherty, and Charles Comiskey, not to mention Ossee Schreckengost, who caught Waddell against Young in 1904, and will catch Big Ed Walsh against Joss four years later.

Traded for a cigar in 1901 from the Pittsburgh Pirates to the Chicago Orphans (pre-Cubs), Rube Waddell pitched erratically, at times brilliantly, but was often among the missing—letting the lure of good fishing get the better of him on occasion, and then, of course, suffering the aggravating assaults of train wrecks and other disasters of similar kind to further extend the duration of his unexplained absences. Toward the end of the 1901 season (Rube would win 14 games), he disappeared altogether—left the team—for the remainder of the schedule. Turns out he had joined a ball team, in early September (prime fly-fishing season!) in Gray's Lake, Wisconsin. He negotiated a contract that allowed him to fish six days a week and pitch on the seventh day. No more idling on the bench while trout were jumping elsewhere. He got five dollars a game.

Although Waddell's official biographer more or less loses track of him during this period, picking up his scent only in late fall when the wayward left-hander barnstorms to California for warmer weather and more ball (and where Connie Mack will track him down and sign him up for the A's in the new American League), Addie Joss's biographer finds Rube in Racine, on October 20, playing in a big game for the Kenosha nine.

At the turn of the century, America was baseball mad. At the local level—town ball, church teams, grade-school nines, sandlot squads, college ranks or men's clubs or whatever—the game was hot. The people couldn't get enough of it.

In Wisconsin, as throughout the Midwest and Northeast, the ball-playing season was extended to the limit by tournaments and showdowns from Labor Day till the first snows. When the professional and semipro leagues had all concluded their seasons, proud nines representing various towns continued to skirmish while the weather permitted. In October 1901, a team from Racine was involved in a grudge match with a team from Appleton for the informal state championship. Racine enlisted a young hurler from the little hamlet of Juneau to do their pitching, a former schoolteacher with some college in him named Addie Joss. Joss, long and lanky, long-armed, long-haired, with soft, doelike eyes and a baleful look, had mesmerized the opposition while pitching for Toledo in the Western Association, which was what was left of the Western League once Ban Johnson made out for his brand-new American League. Joss's Toledo season was done, he'd been the league's best pitcher; now, with the weather still fine and light still long enough, he was taking on all comers.

Joss took the train from Juneau down to Racine, a good-sized town sitting on the western shore of Lake Michigan. He whipped Appleton; in fact, he and the Racine men had whipped them twice, since Appleton insisted on a rematch. They'd agreed that that settled the issue of state champ, until a team from Kenosha, another good-sized town just south of Racine, brought themselves to town with their own ringer, fly fisherman Rube Waddell, ready to make a challenge.

So, on October 20, 1901, two future Hall of Famers, one of them a 21-year-old son of a cheesemaker, the other just turned 25 with stardom awaiting him the next year (he'd win 24 games for Mack and the A's), squared off on a dusty sandlot in Racine.

As 5,000 fans looked on, with perhaps the state's best pitcher and a bona fide major leaguer battling it out for pure entertainment and the glory that is Wisconsin, the nervous Joss gave up two early runs on a long triple by the wild-man Waddell, who was given to waving his cap to the crowd and flipping an occasional cartwheel during dead time. Racine looked overmatched and outshone, with Waddell fanning the first nine men to face him. But some sloppy fielding behind Waddell allowed Racine to tie the score in the bottom of the fourth, and the young Joss settled down. In the sixth, Racine pushed across two runs to take a 4–2 lead. In the top of the ninth, the score still 4–2 in his favor, Joss got the first two outs, but then gave up two successive singles, bringing up the cocky Waddell. With the crowd roaring, Addie Joss reached for something extra and fanned Rube on three pitches. Pandemonium in Racine, and Addie Joss was a major leaguer the next year.

ADDIE JOSS WOULD come to be called many things during his lifetime, most of them colorful, none of them mean, and most of them, more or less, true—"the Swiss Whiz from Wisconsin," after his origins; "The Human Corkscrew," after his funky pitching delivery; "The Maestro of Twirlology," for his dazzling assortment of stuff—curve, fastball, fade-away and the curious "jumpball." Whether he was "the best sportswriting ballplayer ever" (as baseball historian Bob Broeg has suggested), owing to his weekly column in the *Toledo Bee*, is a question for the Sabremetricians and the MLA to sort out. But that Joss pitched the "clutchest" game in history, that being his perfect game during the heat of the greatest pennant race of all time, in October 1908, is not worth denying. And there's another thing best left alone: At Joss's sudden death at the age of 31, in

1911, Cy Young, who roomed with Joss, said he'd "never met a fairer or squarer man than Addie." The death of Addie Joss (Lou Gehrig, Ray Chapman, Thurman Munson, Ken Hubbs, Lyman Bostock, and Darryl Kile notwithstanding) stunned the baseball world like no other.

Joss was born April 12, 1880, in Juneau. His Swiss father, Jacob, was a cheesemaker, and his mother, Teresa Staudenmayer, was a learned woman from a prominent political family. The Josses prospered early on, as Jacob sold his cheeses and dabbled in town politics. But financial reversals in the late 1880s, and perhaps Jacob's predilection for drink, brought severely diminished circumstances to the family. In 1890, Jacob died of a liver ailment, leaving behind Teresa and the 10-year-old Addie. It was a turn of events that would eventually instill in the adult Addie a grim determination to establish solid ground for his own family. But at the time, he was just a midwestern boy with a taste for book learning and baseball. And he excelled at both.

The legend of Addie Joss the ballplayer began when he was around 14; he supposedly knocked a brick loose from the side of his aunt and uncle's farmhouse with a baseball. The tall and gangly kid with an easygoing manner and a studious bent was all of a sudden more than that. He was a real thrower; he had made his mark, so to speak. He would make more.

Kids grew up fast back then, especially in rural areas, where the incessant need for farm labor didn't put much of a premium on academics. But Addie Joss finished high school and was teaching school himself by the age of 16, lessening the burden on his widowed mother, no doubt, and leaving summers free to play ball.

Addie was such a sensation playing town ball that he was offered a scholarship to Sacred Heart College in nearby Watertown. In those days, colleges would often field teams of not necessarily matriculated students, but the industrious Addie took the tuition and attended engineering classes.

He took his baseball seriously, too, plunking the first three batters to face him in a bitterly fought local contest, just to show he feared no one and that the plate was his. He also hit a long home run that day on the way to a big 18–3 win. Sacred Heart became a regional powerhouse. Watertown's city fathers got so excited about Sacred Heart's great team that they signed up the entire roster to represent the city on a semipro circuit.

In 1898, Charles Comiskey brought his Western League professionals to play Watertown in an exhibition game, and to take a look at the long-limbed, sidearming Joss. Comiskey's club clobbered the 18-year-old, but Joss's speed, assortment of pitches, and bizarre windup—hiding the ball behind arms and legs and hip till the last instant—intrigued the professional onlookers.

Connie Mack, who ran the Western League club in nearby Milwaukee, sent a man to see young Joss. He offered him a contract—to play in Albany, New York, with the possibility of later moving up to the Milwaukee club. Joss, a practical man, knew that Albany was not the shortest route from Juneau to Milwaukee, nor to big-time baseball. He declined.

Instead, he bounced to a team from Oshkosh, for $10 a week, then to Manitowoc, where a scout for the Toledo Mud Hens spotted him. For $75 a month, Joss became a Mud Hen.

Joss won 19 games in his first year, and by 1901, it was clear he was the best pitcher in the league. Ban Johnson's American League was in its first season, hungry for ballplayers and willing to pay. The Boston Americans, led by Jimmy Collins and Cy Young, offered Toledo $1,500 for Joss's contract at midseason; St. Louis of the National League matched the offer. But the Toledo owners held out for more. Joss won 27 games by season's end.

In the autumn, Joss barnstormed around his home state, displaying his baseball skills. The Cleveland club offered him a contract to play in the American League, and they did so by first making his Mud Hens manager, Bob Gilks, a scout, and then giving the Hens $500. By baseball's rules, this made Toledo more or less a farm team—an enhanced status— and they consented to sell Joss.

In 1902, things were good for baseball and good for the players. The raid on National League talent by the new American League jacked up salaries all around, the average pay going up 50 percent or more, to nearly $3,000. The A.L. franchises were outdrawing their counterparts, which were nonetheless rebounding after some tough years at the end of the nineties, when the American economy spiraled downward, in part due to monopoly seekers who were on a collision course with a trust-busting Teddy Roosevelt. But most important, the American public seemed to welcome two strong leagues, well stocked with talent, and playing in new stadiums that could accommodate larger crowds—Huntington Avenue Grounds in Boston, South Side Park in Chicago, Bennett Park in Detroit, and Hilltop Stadium in New York, all built in the first three years of the new century.

With the arrival of the American League, baseball got clean. Ban

Johnson put forth a product that was more disciplined, more respectful of authority; the league insisted on more gentlemanly play, in hopes of attracting women and children to the games. The ballparks were more commodious and less likely to go up in flames or to collapse in a heap— another nice marketing angle. And when Barney Dreyfus of the Pirates and Henry J. Killilea of the Boston Club inaugurated the first World Series in 1903, the people loved it. Addie Joss was arriving into a game that was just beginning to blossom as an American spectacle.

And he arrived with a bang: In Joss's first start, April 26, 1902, he gave up only one hit—a disputed one at that—to Jesse Burkett, who was now toiling for the St. Louis Browns. Joss finished with a shutout. Two starts later, Joss took a legitimate no-hitter into the ninth inning in front of a menacing Detroit crowd, which pressed close to the foul lines in an attempt to intimidate the young pitcher. There were loud and lisping references to his long curly hair. Joss lost his no-hit bid in the last frame, but finished with a 2–1 win.

Although the year wasn't a great one for Cleveland, good things did happen. For one, the great Nap Lajoie joined the club. Lajoie was one of the famous jumpers, from Philly of the National League to Philly (and Connie Mack) of the new A.L., where he hit a league-leading .426 in 1901. But a judge ruled that the jumping wasn't legal and that Lajoie could not play ball anywhere in the state of Pennsylvania, so the owner of the Cleveland club, Mr. Somerset, who had loaned Mr. Mack money, inveigled the latter (with the persuasive assistance of league president Ban Johnson) to unload Lajoie to Cleveland.

Cleveland would finish in the middle of the pack in 1902, two games over .500, but Joss would mightily impress, winning 17 games and finishing all but one of his starts. Joss, feeling somewhat established, married Lillian Shinivar, a Toledo steno girl—and rabid baseball fan—in the off-season.

Joss's job was made a little easier in 1903 when the American League, as part of the National Agreement it signed with the N.L., adopted the rule that made a foul ball a strike. Joss thrived: His walks were cut in half, and the league batting average dropped from .280 to around .240. He won 18 games for a club that was leaving mediocrity behind, finishing 14 games over .500, but 15 games back of the Cy Young–led Boston Pilgrims. Just before the season ended, though, calamity visited Joss, and not for the last time. A train from Cleveland to St. Louis with the whole club aboard suffered a derailment, and although Joss and the others were pulled unharmed from the wreckage, Joss grew gravely ill with a fever—whether coincidentally or not no one ever knew—and missed the last month of the season.

In 1904, Addie fell victim to fever again, missing five weeks of the season and winning only 14 games, although he pitched five shutouts and led the league with a minuscule 1.59 ERA, just ahead of—guess who?—Rube Waddell. But the Blues continued their improvement, much assisted by Lajoie, who tore up the league again, leading in batting average, hits, doubles, and RBI in one of the more dominating years a hitter has ever had. Cleveland finished two dozen games over .500, in fourth place, just 7.5 games behind Boston, which won again, though there would be no World Series in 1904, because Mr. John Brush and Mr. Johnson despised each other.

Prospects were high for the next season; Addie was a healthy 215 pounds in spring training. The pallid face and gaunt build of his feverish previous year seemed long gone. And with big Napoleon Lajoie clearly a legend in the making, team ownership appointed him player-manager. The Blues were immediately dubbed the Naps, in his honor.

Joss came out roaring in 1905, winning 9 of his first 10 starts. He fought hard for victory number 10, pitching a complete game, 16-inning win over Chicago, but it cost him. Once again, fatigue or stress seemed to usher in sickness—in this case, an extreme head cold, and Addie missed several starts. Then more trouble for the club—Lajoie went down for a month with blood poisoning from a spike wound, and the Naps lost momentum. In a year when the Boston Pilgrims seemed vulnerable, Cleveland finished under .500, 19 games behind the new league champs, the A's, led by a wacky left-hander who won 27 games, and led the league in strikeouts and ERA, and alligator subduing. Still, Joss excelled, winning 20 games and earning a $500 bonus, with which he and Lillian bought a house in Toledo, the only house he would ever own.

The Naps got back on pace in '06, finishing only five games out of first. Joss won 21 games, had nine shutouts and a 1.72 ERA. He was also developing a reputation for stifling the phenomenal young Ty Cobb (Cobb, a lifetime .367 hitter, would manage to hit only .253 in 25 games against Joss during his career). Joss survived the year without serious physical incident; only a sore arm wearied him toward season's end, more from playing center field on his off-days than from pitching. In the fall, Lillian and Addie would have their second child, Ruth; a son, Norman, had been born two years earlier. Although life was fairly good for the Josses, Addie's father's quick flameout never left his mind; now, with two children of his own, he began to think about life after baseball. He cast around for off-season employment ideas. Waddell found his calling, tending bar and chasing fire engines; Nap Lajoie ran a smoke shop in Cleveland; Christy Mathewson read Shakespeare to theater-house crowds, Turkey Mike Donlin would try his hand at acting, having met an actress. Addie took a different route: He approached the local newspaper, the *Toledo Bee*, and talked his way into writing a regular column and serving as the Sunday sports editor. His reporting was a great success, not only bringing expanded readership to the paper, but spreading the byline of Addie Joss across the land as his dispatches were picked up by UPI.

Emboldened by apparently having secured a postbaseball career, Joss dug in his heels when offered a contract for the 1907 season that he didn't care for: a $400 raise, to $3,100 a year, but a deletion of the $500 bonus clause for winning 20 games. Since he very much intended to win 20 games or more, Joss felt he was being asked to actually take a cut in pay. He returned the contract unsigned and took the Cleveland ownership to task in the best way he knew how—in his Sunday column. The owners responded unwisely though not irrationally, disparaging Joss's durability. But the public—the poor Cleveland public, which only eight years before had a club destroyed by its ownership—took the columnist's side and, in the end, a meeting was held in Cleveland. Joss made the trip from Toledo, the owners acquiesced and gave him $4,000, but still without a bonus provision.

With the Cleveland fans feeling that this might be their year, the prideful Joss flew out of the gate and won his first 10 starts, the 10th being a victory over his jovial nemesis, Waddell. Cleveland held second place deep into the summer, drawing large crowds to League Park. Joss continued his hot pitching, throwing three straight shutouts in July. But the Naps wilted in the hot pennant race, finishing in fourth place, eight games behind pennant-winning Detroit. Joss, despite a great year that saw him tie for the league lead in wins with 27, post an era of 1.83, and not miss a start, got to see the Fall Classic from the press box, as a newsman for the *Toledo Bee*.

THERE HAVE BEEN many great pennant races in baseball, and generations and loyalties can be pinned from which ones a fan might chose to cite: the 1978 Yankees and Red Sox race, or the '67 four-way A.L. race in which Boston, Minnesota, Detroit, and the White Sox all had a shot in the last weekend of the season; or the '46 Cards-Dodgers, the first playoff ever, won by the Cards in a best-of-three series; or the Giants-Dodgers playoff of 1951. It would be hard to argue, though, that the pennant races of 1908 weren't truly the best and most competitive of all time. Four teams in one league and three in the other had clear shots at the pennant entering the last weekend of play—that's nearly half of all teams playing. In the end, the National League championship had to be decided by the addition of a makeup game, as a result of what is now known as Fred Merkle's boner, and on the A.L. side, one of the greatest pitching duels ever waged figured in the scramble for glory: Addie Joss's 1–0 perfect-game win over the White Sox and Big Ed Walsh.

Detroit was the defending A.L. champ; the Tigers had the best out-field in the game, with Cobb, Sam Crawford, and Matty McIntyre; the White Sox had excellent player-manager Fielder Jones and the rubber-armed hurler Ed Walsh, now a Hall of Famer with the lowest lifetime ERA on record; the St. Louis Browns, somehow, were in the race till the bitter end, with that guy Rube Waddell anchoring the staff and the forgotten George Stone from Lost Nation, Iowa, who led the league with a .358 average in 1906 and who was coming off another good year, hitting .320. But the Naps had Nap and Joss and they were red hot in September.

The four teams jockeyed for top spot all month, but with Joss unbeatable, winning five games in September (four by shutout), Cleveland finished the month 21–9, and stood a half game behind the Tigers on September 30, a game ahead of the White Sox, and four in front of the fading Browns. These four teams had two series left among themselves. This is how it looked:

Team	W	L	Pct.	GB
Detroit	87	61	.588	—
Cleveland	87	62	.584	.5
Chicago	85	62	.579	1.5
St. Louis	82	65	.558	4.5

After a universal off-day, on Thursday, October 1, all four contending teams had five games remaining. Detroit had a two-game set with the Browns and then three with the White Sox to finish out the year. The Naps had to face the White Sox first, for two games, and then close with the Browns, in a three-game set.

On October 2, the Tigers pounded Waddell early and then held on for an 8–7 win, eliminating St. Louis, putting them 5.5 back with four to play. In Cleveland, Joss squared off against Ed Walsh of the White Sox, with but a game separating the two clubs, and the Naps trying to keep within a half-game of the Tigers. And what a game it was.

For Cleveland, this was the closest they had ever come to winning— one game out in the loss column with five to play. They hoped to dis- patch the heel-nipping White Sox on their own, and then, if things worked out, trounce a dispirited St. Louis Browns while the angry Sox took on Detroit and beat them twice, which would give the Naps the crown, enabling Addie Joss to play in the World Series rather than just write about it.

On a Friday afternoon, 10,000 Cleveland faithful showed up at League Park to see the start of what they hoped would be a historic turn by their Napoleons. The league's two best pitchers were set to go, Joss and Walsh. Earlier in the week, Walsh had won both games of a double- header to keep the White Sox in the race; he would finish the year with 40 wins; he would hurl more than 460 innings; he would pitch in 7 of his team's last 10 games; he would never pitch better than on this day.

Adrian Joss, too, was on a roll; his sizzling September had kept his team's hopes alive, and the turn into October found him still at the top of his uncanny form. A historic pitching duel was about to unfold. It would be over in 89 minutes.

BIG ED WALSH was among the cockiest of ballplayers; he was said to strut while standing still. The youngest of 13 children of an Irish coal miner from Pennsylvania, he had been discovered by Charles Comiskey, who bought his contract for $750 in 1903. At six feet one and nearly 200 pounds, young Walsh was a fireballer. In his rookie year he roomed with another rookie, Elmer "Spitball" Stricklett, whose nickname rubbed off on his bunkmate; Walsh learned the spitter. By 1906, Walsh was a key member on a strong staff that led the famous "hitless won- ders" to a World Series victory over the heavily favored, 116-game- winning crosstown Cubs. Comiskey, whom history would come to know as the biggest tightwad to call himself a baseball man, was so pleased to win the battle of Chicago that he showered the Pale Hose with a total of $15,000 in bonuses, only to count it against next year's salary pool, once his head cleared. Walsh won 24 games the next year, as the Sox finished just behind Detroit. By 1908, he was carrying the White Sox on his back.

Because of the prospect of no one scoring anything against these two great hurlers and the game going into extra innings, the starting time of the game was moved up half an hour, to 2:30, but there was nothing doing as far as the visiting team was concerned. The wily White Sox player-manager Fielder Jones (a great fielder, by the way, though Fielder was his real name) refused to return to the dugout until he made a fine point or two about one ground rule or another, in all likelihood just giving the fatigued Walsh—who wasn't told till just before game time that he was pitching—a little more time to limber up.

Jones, trained as an engineer, was one of the greatest young managers of all time—he was only 35 when he led the Sox to the World Series upset two years earlier. Once the game began, he continued working the umpires. He argued the very first out, contending that his leadoff man Ed Hahn's tapper down the line was foul. He argued hard with future Hall of Fame ump Tommy Connolly, as if everything were at stake. All that came of it was the first of Addie Joss's 27 outs. Jones himself made the second out, popping to short, before White Sox first baseman Frank Isbell flew out to left fielder Bill Hinchman to end the inning.

In the bottom of the first, Walsh got a strikeout (of leadoff man Wilbur Good), an assist on a grounder back to the box by Naps third baseman Bill Bradley, and a putout, when Isbell ranged across the line to take a double away from Hinchman and toss to Walsh covering the bag.

In the top of the second, Chicago's fleet-footed left fielder, Patsy Dougherty, formerly with Cy Young and the Boston Pilgrims, tapped weakly to Joss, a good-fielding pitcher, who would help his cause with five assists on this sunny, 50-degree afternoon. George Davis, batting fifth for the Sox and near the end of a 20-year career that would earn him a Veteran's Committee ticket into Cooperstown, flied routinely to left. And Nap rookie shortstop George Perring nearly derailed Joss's perfect effort, throwing high to first on Freddy Parent's ground ball, but Cleveland's steady George Stovall leaped in the air and came down on the bag for the out.

In the home half of the second, Nap Lajoie went down looking, Stovall grounded out to short, and "Nig" Clarke (so-nicknamed for his dusky complexion) struck out swinging. The Walsh wet one was working well.

Joss would only throw 74 pitches on this day, the fewest thrown in any perfect game. And he kept mowing down the Sox with a very Swiss

efficiency, like clockwork. In the top of the third, the man known universally as "Schreck," Ossee Schreckengost, whom we have met once before
as the battery- and roommate of Waddell back in '04, popped out to his
opposition catcher. Then the weak-hitting Lee Tannehill popped to Nap
Lajoie at second for out number two. Walsh, batting ninth, nubbed one
past the mound, where Lajoie, the great Hall of Fame second baseman,
turned it into an out, as he would do often this day, recording eight
assists in addition to two putouts. Not bad for a fellow who supposedly
got out of his sickbed to play.

The bottom of the third saw the only action in a day nonetheless
chock-full of drama. Joe "Dode" Birmingham, the Naps fast center fielder,
got the game's first hit, a single to right. In the dead-ball era, with runs hard
to come by, a steal or a sacrifice bunt was virtually automatic here. With
Birmingham a known practitioner of the delayed steal, Walsh eyed him
closely at first base. Birmingham eyed back. But when Walsh wheeled and
threw over, Birmingham was caught leaning and had to take off for second
and pray for luck. Prayer answered: First baseman Frank Isbell's throw to
Parent glanced off Birmingham's shoulder and Birmingham steamed all the
way to third, nobody out. E-3. With the infield drawn in, the weak-hitting
Perring grounded out to short, Birmingham holding at third. Walsh then
fanned Joss for out number two, and seemed ready to escape without damage. The Cleveland leadoff hitter, Wilbur Good, was up next, and soon was
in the hole, 0 and 2. But a spitball got away from Walsh, and Schreck, who
had been with the team for only a week, acquired because the team's regular catcher went down with an injury, could not handle the pitch. It sailed
outside and Schreck thrust out his bare hand in an attempt to knock it
down. "A bone being broken and ligaments torn loose" is what he got for
his efforts, according to a newspaper account. As the ball rolled to a stop
near the Cleveland bench, Dode Birmingham came across with an
unearned run to put Cleveland up 1–0. Good then struck out.

The top of the fourth was all Nap Lajoie on defense, retiring the side
by tossing out Hahn routinely and Fielder Jones spectacularly on
grounders and drifting back to corral a pop off the bat of Frank Isbell. For
the Naps in the bottom of the fourth, Bill Bradley and Hinchman became
strikeout victims six and seven for Walsh; skipper Lajoie singled to center, stole second, but was stranded there as Walsh made a fine grab of a
shot back up the middle by Stovall and threw him out.

In the Chicago fifth, cleanup man Dougherty (who, the reader may
recall, hit leadoff when he was with Boston, showing just how hitless

were these wondrous White Sox) struck out swinging, Joss's first K of the game (he would finish with three, the lowest in any perfect game). George Davis then made it o for 2 for himself by grounding back to Joss, as did Freddy Parent, ending the inning. In the bottom of the fifth, Walsh was just about untouchable, striking out the side—Nig Clarke, Dode Birmingham, and Joss (for the second time), although little Freddy Parent, at five-seven, worked out a two-out walk, only to be left stranded.

As our account rolls into the sixth inning, I feel compelled to remind the reader that such games, from early in the century, are patched together from various box scores, game summaries, and postgame and often postcareer interviews. Not only is much of the color faded from these accounts, as compared to what today would be a full digital capture of sights and sounds, but much of the faded color was often, originally, *added* color, sportswriters ornamenting a skeletal teletype account with the mischievously odd "the ball lodged in Lajoie's right armpit and fell into his open right hand and he was able to nip the runner at first." So let us say that in the Chicago sixth, "Schreck was thrown out by Lajoie, Joss handled Tannehill's grounder, Walsh gave Good a long fly. No runs." It was reported as such in a clipping that sits in the Joss file at Cooperstown, and in this fashion we are left to more solemnly imagine how Ossee Schreckengost might have handled a bat with a finger broken.

In the bottom of the sixth, Cleveland's Wilbur Good, on his way to a pretty forgettable day, struck out for the third time; Walsh handled Bill Bradley's hopper to the mound and threw to Isbell for the out. Hinchman hit perhaps the hardest ball off of Big Ed Walsh all day, a sharp liner the other way, to Hahn in right field, who caught it in his tracks for the third out.

By the start of the seventh, the crowd was in thrall to the contest's quickly unfolding precisions. The game was barely an hour old, their Naps led 1–0; Ed Walsh had given up two hits, struck out 11, walked no one; only the throwing error by Isbell, followed by a passed ball, gave Cleveland its margin; Joss had been not untouchable, but unhittable, striking out only one, but retiring all 18 men to come to the plate.

The seventh went smoothly for Joss but for one near hiccup. After throwing out Hahn for his fifth assist of the game, Joss threw three straight pitches out of the strike zone to Fielder Jones. The White Sox looked to get their first runner on base all day. With the crowd sensing the possibility of Chicago breaking Joss's spell, they fell silent—not exactly what we'd expect in today's hyperactive venues, where the crowd would be standing and roaring and some kind of canned drumbeat would reverberate throughout an entire ZIP code. But in League Park, Cleveland, silence reigned; even cigars went unlit, said one report, as everyone watched intently, riveted upon Addie Joss and the opposing hitter. Joss fired two strikes right down the middle to Jones, who was taking. As Jones stood in with the count full, ready to hit away, Joss threw a gutsy sinker. Thinking and hoping it was low, Fielder Jones let it go. Tommy Connolly, perhaps recalling Jones's earlier argumentativeness, rung him up—too close to take. The crowd vocalized its displeasure with Jones as he stood there jawing with Connolly. Isbell then grounded one to the very busy Lajoie, and Joss was making it look easy.

In the bottom of the seventh, Walsh seemed to have plenty of spit left in him. Lajoie "whiffed the atmosphere," for strikeout number 12; George Stovall popped to second. Nig Clarke went down on strikes for the third time, ending the inning. It is not recorded what the Cleveland crowd made of Ed Walsh's effort this day; perhaps they permitted themselves to admire his great effort. He was pitching a masterpiece that not even Joss's total mastery could overshadow.

In the eighth, with six outs to go for a Cleveland win, and six *consecutive* outs for a very rare "no runner reaches base" game, Patsy Dougherty almost upset the apple cart, hitting a shot up the middle that caught the edge of the infield grass and took a weird hop. But Lajoie, playing, as was the fashion in those days, close to the second-base bag, was in position to glove it, eye level, and throw out Dougherty at first. Five outs to go. George Davis then hit a high infield pop, which the avaricious Lajoie grabbed for the out. Freddy Parent then hit a routine fly to left for the third out, number 24 of 27.

Unlike some other perfect games played at home (only 4 of 14 were thrown on the road), the crowd wasn't in a hurrying mood when it came time for the bottom of the eighth. This was a pennant race, this was a 1–0 game, and the Naps could surely use more of a cushion, despite Joss's brilliance. And they almost came through. Joe Birmingham got his second hit of the day, the only man to do so, beating out an infield grounder. When Perring lined a single over the head of the shortstop, things looked promising for the Naps; then a double steal was perfectly executed, and it was apparent at this time that Schreck, the Sox catcher, playing with a split finger since the third inning, could not go on. Time was called and he was replaced behind the plate by Al Shaw, with runners at second and third, no one out, still 1–0 Cleveland.

There was no question that Joss would take his turn at bat; Walsh fanned him. Then poor Wilbur Good completed his bad day with his fourth strike out, Walsh's 15th and last. Bradley then rapped one to Parent for out number three. Walsh had slammed the door, and the game moved into the ninth.

When Joss took the mound, the crowd was "eerily silent," according to a local account. Shaw, the new catcher, was due up but would not bat. Instead, a good-hitting White Sox pitcher, Doc White, was sent up to hit, the first of three pinch-hitters Fielder Jones would throw up there to try to break through Joss. The spindly White (six feet one inch, 150 pounds) won 18 games that year, and wasn't a bad hitter, for a pitcher. A lefty swinger, he could manage only what seven other Sox had done, a ground ball to Lajoie at second. One down. Jiggs Donahue, a poor hitter on a poor-hitting team, stepped in to hit for Lee Tannehill, and fanned weakly, for Joss's third strikeout.

And then it came time for Ed Walsh to hit; we'll never know what kind of reception he would have gotten had he stepped to the plate—the third and final pinch-hitter of the inning stepped forward instead. And this one could hit. "Honest John" Anderson, born in Norway, of all places, but raised in Worcester, Massachusetts, was in the final year of a 14-year career that he would finish with a solid .290 average. He'd hit as high as .330 one year and over .300 four times. Technically a switch-hitter, Anderson nonetheless stepped in right-handed to try to get something going against Joss. He slashed the first pitch he saw down the line in left, where it fell foul by inches. Joss threw the next pitch by him for strike two. Wasting no time, Joss whirled and fired a fastball that Anderson was able to turn on, grounding it hard down the third-base line. Bill Bradley, an excellent fielder, was playing Anderson to pull and snagged it behind the bag. His throw to George Stovall at first was low and in the dirt, but Stovall made a clean scoop and the game was over. Joss had done it. More important, at the time, the Naps had done it: kept pace with the Tigers, who stood only a half game ahead of them; and a nail was driven into the coffin of the tough White Sox, now two and half games out with four to play.

On the following day, a Saturday, the Cleveland faithful came out in double strength—nearly 21,000 showed up to cheer their boys' vault into first place, but it didn't happen. Not only did Detroit win its game against St. Louis, but the Naps lost a heartbreaker, 3–2, when Lajoie struck out with the bases loaded in the bottom of the ninth against none other than Big Ed Walsh, who'd come on in the seventh. The Naps were now a game and a half behind Detroit, with Chicago at two and a half back, and St. Louis out of it. Then it was on to St. Louis for the Naps, for a three-game set that could get them back in it; the White Sox, meanwhile, had no margin for error heading home into a season-ending three-game set with the first-place and defending champion Tigers.

When the Naps pulled into the St. Louis train depot in the morning, Addie Joss fell faint. Although Lajoie said later he would never have asked Joss to pitch that day—"His eyes were sunken, his expression dull, he looked like a man in a severe illness"—Joss volunteered to relieve in the second inning before the crucial game got out of hand. He pitched 6⅔ innings of two-hit, scoreless relief, but the game was called due to darkness, tied at 3–3, a contest that many contend the Naps would have won in the ninth if a) Bill Hinchman had hustled and beat out an infield grounder, which would have scored Joss with the go-ahead run, or b) an ump named Egan hadn't blown the call, since everyone thought Hinchman had beaten the throw anyway.

In any event, the game was suspended, and up in Chicago, the Sox beat Detroit 3–1 to move within a game and half with two to play. Cleveland was forced to play a doubleheader the next day, to make up for the suspended game. An error by Lajoie cost Cleveland the opener and brought them to the point of mathematical elimination; a win in the second game meant nothing. For Chicago, however, Big Ed Walsh wasn't done with his work; his 6–1 whipping of the Tigers, for his 40th win of the year, brought them to within a half-game with one to play.

Despite still another appearance by Walsh, Detroit managed a shutout behind Wild Bill Donovan on the final day, and the chance to play the winner of the Merkle-inspired makeup game between the Cubs and the Giants.

FOR ADDIE JOSS, it was yet another World Series to cover for the *Toledo Bee*. The Naps officially finished in second place, a half-game back; Addie posted a 24-11 record, with a league-leading 1.16 ERA; he walked only 30 men in 325 innings. The following year, 1909, he was joined by the great Cy Young, returning to the city of Cleveland, where his professional game had begun 19 years earlier. Joss didn't have much of a year, as a general physical malaise seemed to hang over him. He finished with a 14-13 record, and Cleveland finished in 6th place, 27.5 games behind Detroit.

The following year, 1910, showed further decline for Joss; despite pitching a no-hitter in April, his arm broke down in June; he finished the year 5-5, gave up writing his sports column, and bought a pool hall in Toledo. In the winter months he worked in his new establishment, and frequently felt ill, losing his appetite. Spring training, 1911, found Joss with a swollen arm and a weak constitution; he collapsed in Chattanooga before an exhibition game: heat prostration. The team doctor sent him on a train home to Toledo, but by Cincinnati, Addie was complaining of chest pains, and was seen by a doctor, who diagnosed "congestion in his right lung with a bad attack of pleurisy" and an "affection of the brain." Spinal fluid was drained via lumbar puncture when he reached home, and a definitive diagnosis of tubercular meningitis was given. There was no cure. Addie Joss died at home on April 14, two days into the season, which would have been his 10th. The doctor attributed the contraction of TB to the wintry months in the pool hall, but, clearly, Addie had long been prone to infectious maladies and respiratory problems. And TB was taking a heavy toll all over the country.

ADDIE WAS MAKING $5,500 a year when he died, working with a one-year contract. He left no will, being only 31 years old. The baseball world was shaken by the premature death of such a great pitcher and fine fellow, well liked by all. His Cleveland mates were devastated, and, led by first baseman George "Firebrand" Stovall, determined to attend Addie's funeral. The problem was that there was a game scheduled that day in Detroit and league president Ban Johnson said the game must be played. The team threatened to strike and take a train to Toledo; the opposition Tigers supported them. Still, Johnson would not relent: "The Cleveland-Detroit game will be played Monday as scheduled." Stovall called a team meeting; he distributed a petition. Despite the threat of a game forfeit, a team fine, and even league suspension, the players stood together. At the last moment, Johnson granted postponement of the game.

"Every Train Brings Flowers" reported the *Cleveland Plain Dealer*. "Floral tributes by the wagonload are hourly arriving at the Joss home from all sections of the country . . . a mammoth wreath of pink roses on an easel from John I. Taylor, owner of the Boston Red Sox . . . a spray of red roses from the owners of the Cleveland club . . . a nine-string harp with one string broken . . . the harp made wholly of white Easter lilies . . ." And baseball, its players and fans, did more to honor Addie.

Wisely choosing a travel day for both leagues, a group led by Cleveland owner Charles Somers and Cy Young organized a fund-raiser for Lillian Joss, the first All-Star Game ever, featuring the Cleveland club versus the likes of Tris Speaker, Eddie Collins, Ty Cobb, Frank Baker, Sam Crawford, Bobby Wallace, and Walter Johnson; along with Lajoie and Cy Young from the Naps, that makes nine Hall of Famers. And a guy named Joe Jackson suited up for Cleveland, to show his respect, a would-be Hall of Famer but for the Black Sox scandal eight years later. More than $13,000 was raised for the Joss family.

At the time of Addie's death, Lillian said "I don't believe I can ever look at a ball game again and the recollections the game would bring back would be miserable." Their son, Norman, was nine years old and intent on following in his father's footsteps; seven-year-old Ruth still believed her Daddy would come home.

If Joss had thrown just one pitch in the 1911 season, he would have officially played in the "10 championship seasons" required for Hall of Fame induction, and would have been an early inductee, perhaps in the very first class. It wasn't until 1978, however, that Joss was granted the exception that opened the doors at Cooperstown to a pitcher most richly deserving. Under the brick proscenium on Main Street in Cooperstown, there were no Josses present. Addie's widow had long been gone; their daughter Ruth as well. Norman had lived to the age of 75, but died just two months before Addie's election by the Veterans' Committee. Comment was left to Mrs. Norman A. Joss, back in Toledo. "My husband always felt his father belonged in the Hall of Fame, but didn't believe he should push it. My husband was only a boy when Addie died, but he remembered him as a wonderful father."

Perhaps no Josses were present, but plenty of familiar company awaited Addie's induction in Cooperstown—Ed Walsh, Nap Lajoie, and Cy Young, not to mention Rube Waddell, who, like Addie, had succumbed to meningitis in his 30s. They're all in bronze now.

CHAPTER THREE

The Mystery Guest

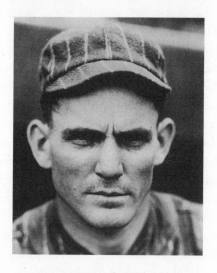

Charlie Robertson
April 30, 1922

O N A JULY NIGHT in Cincinnati in 1954, Carl Erskine retired the first 21 Reds he faced. When Ted Kluszewski stepped to the plate leading off the eighth, the press box buzzed with questions. Who was Charlie Robertson? Was it -ie or -ey? Did he play for the White Sox, the Red Sox, or was it the Cubs? What the guys in the press box were trying to pinpoint was just exactly who the last pitcher was to throw a perfect game, since Erskine was only six outs away.

Big Klu's single to left made the question moot for the time being and C. Robertson dipped below the surface of common knowledge once again—or at least you don't see any more clippings in the Robertson folder at the Hall of Fame for a while, and then only one. A few years later, when Don Larsen stunned the baseball world with his performance in Game Five of the 1956 World Series, Charlie Robertson was back in the news, sort of: He got a few mentions; an AP reporter reached him. It was the man's ultimate and final due in a game he never much loved.

Charlie Robertson's reign as the "last man to have thrown a perfect game" came to an end after 34 rather silent years, the silence surrounding his accomplishment nurtured by his own reticence and perhaps baseball's willed amnesia about a dark and confusing period in its history, filled as it was with spit, scandal, a fatal beaning, and a crusading commissioner armed with a mandate to clean up the game. Still, in any extended contemplation of pitching perfection, the ghost of Charlie Robertson skulks at the edges, defying almost everything.

Charlie Robertson was not a great pitcher; he was not even a good pitcher, and he wasn't around that long. Somewhere far south of mediocrity is where Robertson toiled for about eight years, winning only 49 games, losing 80, retiring from the game in 1928 to become a pecan broker. He was one of those ballplayers with an undistinguished career and an everyday name who was forgettable before he was forgotten. But in 1922, with the help of (take your pick) "Lady Luck," liberal applications of a foreign substance to the ball, or the cooperation of some betting men in the crowd, the tall Texan pitched one very impressive game and got into the record books forever. He also proved an important thing about perfection: It's not always all about talent; it's also about luck or the law of averages (some law!) or any other of the mysterious things that permit grace to alight where it will. As awesome as the accomplishments of Cy Young and Addie Joss were—and this pertains to their careers as ballplayers and gentlemen—the lowly, the profane, the regular Joe or Charlie can, on a given day, have things roll his way.

CHARLES COMISKEY ONCE said that crookedness and baseball don't mix. He should have said they don't mix well, because they certainly mixed. In the decade of the 1910s, baseball seemed to get very dirty—meaning it got dishonest. The boom of the first decade of the modern era, with two leagues playing in bustling cities, featuring big stars and colorful owners of great wealth, the whole pageant leading to a World Series, had lost some of its appeal to the American public. By 1912, Cy Young and Addie Joss were gone, along with a certain innocence. The incorruptible and loyal Honus Wagner, still beloved in his Pittsburgh, had been superseded as the game's greatest performer by a player almost universally loathed, Ty Cobb. And the game featured another twisted citizen, Hal Chase, who went by the ironic nickname of Prince Hal—this prince was ugly and pockmarked and crooked, "laying down" for games and recruiting conspirators. Owners, having squashed employee threats to their right to run the game, became increasingly penurious, fueling the worse instincts in men.

On the field, the dead-ball era, which had seemed to come to an end in 1911 when the A. L. Reach company introduced a livelier cork-centered ball, made its return, thanks to what many contend was the canny doctoring of the ball by pitchers. Run production fell once again. Fan interest waned. With war brewing in Europe, everyone was a little tentative, especially with his or her dollars. The American economy was entering its Wilson era—unsteady, defensive, protectionist. Attendance continued to plummet; the owners panicked. Connie Mack, for his part, cashed in, dismantling a World Series team and selling his best players for cash.

Such tough times inspired a renegade league. It lasted only two years, 1914–15, but it had a huge impact on the game. It was a brief rebellion consisting of disgruntled players and entrepreneurial businessman. Although the new league's challenge to Organized Baseball was, in the end, successfully fought off, the owner of the Baltimore Federal team would not go quietly; he sued, under the terms of the recent Sherman Anti-Trust Act. And a federal judge, whose name was Kenesaw Mountain Landis, would earn the thanks of baseball ownership for his deft steward-ship of the lawsuit—dragging it out until the plaintiffs ran out of money—and he would stay involved in Organized Baseball for a very long time.

BY 1919, WITH THE WAR over in Europe and the Federal League chal-lenge put behind it, baseball enjoyed a seeming revival, with fans return-ing to the ballparks in droves. Who could have known the game was entering one of its darkest periods?

The World Series that fall featured the Chicago White Sox versus the underdog Cincinnati Reds. The White Sox were heavy favorites, and few sensed an upset until Chicago ace Eddie Cicotte hit the very first Cincin-nati batter in the first game. Wiseguys knew what that meant: It was a signal to certain gamblers that the fix was in.

The guys of note on that White Sox team were the eight men out, in Eliot Asinof's term—Eddie Cicotte, Chick Gandil, Buck Weaver, Lefty

Williams, Swede Risberg, Happy Felsch, Fred McMullin, and, of course, Shoeless Joe Jackson, the unschooled millhand from Georgia who finished with a lifetime BA of .356 but who would be out of baseball at age 31. The great Eddie Collins, the Chicago second baseman, was not tainted, and is in the Hall of Fame. So is Collins's best friend on the team, catcher Ray Schalk. Early in the season, before the White Sox were at full strength, Charlie Robertson was called up to pitch, got a start, took a loss, and didn't come back to the Sox for three years.

The lid didn't blow off the Black Sox scandal until the next year, during the 1920 World Series. When it did, desperate owners, faced with the prospect of their entire game being discredited, offered the friendly Judge Landis the commissioner's job. Landis refused to give up his judgeship, asked for $50,000 in salary, and complete authority to rule "in the best interests of baseball." He insisted there be one conscience for baseball, and for a quarter-century thereafter he was it. On his office door in Chicago, stenciled into the frosted glass, was the word "Baseball." Therein sat the conscience.

Landis first gave voice to his conscience in the spring of 1921, a day after the Chicago ballplayers were acquitted in the public courtroom: He banned them all for life. He showed no forgiveness and no notion that there were degrees of guilt. They were all equally damned, from ringleaders Chick Gandil and Swede Risberg to those who were merely in the know and who played to win, like Buck Weaver. Nothing happened to owner Charles Comiskey, who kept secret his knowledge of the fix, who destroyed evidence, and routinely reneged on salary and bonus commitments to his players, daring them to find their money some other way.

The common wisdom is that baseball was saved in the 1920s—either by Judge Landis restoring integrity to the game, by Babe Ruth making himself the world's most famous athlete, or simply by a livelier ball. And true enough, from our vantage point, eight decades after the fact, the 1920s look like a roaring, jitterbugging decade with an honest game as its major pastime and a near-mythical Sultan of Swat leading the way.

But back in 1922, things weren't yet so clear. First of all, baseball wasn't clean. Gambling was still rife in and around the game. As Steven Riess say in his *Touching Base*, "Fans gambled on the outcome of a game, the total number of hits and runs, the call of the pitch, and even the possibility of a batted ball being caught." Even though Landis's unforgiving show of power in banning the Black Sox in 1921 must have struck fear in the heart of any player making even the friendliest wager on a game, the practice continued. As *The Sporting News* lamented in the summer of 1921, "The truth is that there is still loads to be done to eradicate bad actors in baseball, magnates as well as players. The bad ones may have been scared into keeping straight, but baseball should not be satisfied with men in it who have to be frightened into honesty." And any casual reading of the sports pages of the time will turn up weary acknowledgments of the fact that certain teams have "sympathies" with other squads: "We have met the enemy," observed a beat writer for the Cincinnati team after a woeful performance against the Giants, "and we were theirs."

Landis drove the owners hard to weed out gambling at their stadiums: Signs prohibiting gambling were posted in all the ballparks; spies reported on bet-taking in the stands; owners were asked by the stern commish to give up horse-racing interests and not to consort with the gambling crowd. More tellingly, there were well-known gambling sections throughout baseball: Burkeville at the Polo Grounds, Gambler's Patch at Shibe Park, and Corktown, the Irish rooting section at Navin Field in Detroit.

With fans customarily crowding the sidelines and the outfields, it was possible to vocally express more than a rooting interest to a ballplayer. Owner Weeghman at Wrigley Field, as well as Frank Navin at Detroit, when faced with an overflow turnout, would allow paying customers to stand on the field of play, "shortening the foul lines and giving some lucky spectators an excellent chance of catching either a ball or an outfielder," says Michael Gershman in *Diamonds*. On April 30, 1922, such fans at Detroit's Navin Field got lucky, or maybe just Charlie Robertson did.

By 1922, THE WHITE SOX were a sorry mess, their pennant-winning teams of 1917 and 1919 a thing of the past. With six regulars and two starting pitchers banned from baseball just before the 1921 season began, the team floundered and finished next to last. With the future Hall of Famer Red Faber anchoring the White Sox rotation and winning 25 games in 1921, Comiskey felt there was no need to bargain with another up-and-comer, the little left-hander Dickie Kerr, who had pitched brilliantly in the 1919 Series, winning two games against the Reds, and then winning 40 games over the next two seasons. Kerr held out for more money in 1922, asking for a $500 raise; Comiskey said no. Kerr moved back to Texas, during which time he played in an exhibition game with a few of his banned former Sox teammates, earning Kerr, one of the "Clean Sox" of 1919, his own banishment from the game. Comiskey, in 1922, was going with youth, and presented three new pitchers to join spit-balling Red Faber. *The Sporting News,* which seemed to take some plea-sure in chiding the tight-fisted "Commy" about his reluctance to invest in his team, reckoned that the three newcomers "were old enough to lie about their ages." One of them was Charlie Robertson.

Robertson, in 1921, had completed a long season of toil with the Minneapolis Millers of the American Association. He threw 300 innings in what was his third year with the club, putting a lot of miles on his still young arm, which had clocked 322 innings the year before. Along the way, Robertson had developed into a pretty good Double-A pitcher, with an ERA of 3.48, sixth in the league; he gave up about a hit per inning (312), struck out 175, and walked 116. Was he ready for the major leagues? It didn't much matter—Comiskey needed bodies.

ROBERTSON WAS BORN in 1896 in Dexter, a small town in East Texas, just across the border from Oklahoma. He was a serious, sober-minded fellow who studied to be a minister at Austin College. Solidly built at six feet and 175 pounds, Robertson was also a natural athlete, playing three sports at Austin until he signed to play with the minor league team from Sherman in 1917, when he was 21 years old. Things get a lit-tle vague here amid the sparse clippings: Robertson played with Sher-man of the Texas League; or was it Hutchinson of the Western League? According to a clipping in March of 1917, he somehow was a "veteran" who might be quitting the game, intent on finishing college and starting a business. It seems that the Chicago White Sox were willing to buy his contract for $2,000 ($250 down and the balance if Robertson worked out) from a team from Sherman, although later, there was no longer a team from Sherman when the White Sox tried to return him. A few things are somewhat more clear, such as the fact that, early on, Robert-son had a reputation for doctoring the baseball (the *Paris Texas News* summarized him as "a college recruit and shine ball expert"), that he spent most of 1918 in the Army Air Corps, and upon his return, the White Sox decided to give him another look-see for the 1919 season since they still had his contract. On May 13 of that year, manager Kid Gleason gave Robertson his first major league start, against the Browns.

Robertson was removed after two innings and sent out to Minneapolis for more seasoning.

Three years' seasoning, as it turned out, and nearly 700 innings pitched. Eventually, new commissioner Landis looked into the matter of the White Sox contract with Robertson and ordered the balance of the $2,000 purchase price paid to the team in Sherman, or somewhere, and it apparently was. And in the spring of 1922, "newcomer" Robertson, as *The Sporting News* said, still technically a rookie at 26 years of age, got his chance. Within a month he would make history.

At the start of the 1922 season, Landis had seen fit to suspend Babe Ruth for playing in exhibitions. As the fans buzzed about the absent Babe and the unaccountably hot start by the St. Louis Browns, talk also turned to how oddly, and ineffectively, the Tigers, now in their second year with Tyrus Raymond Cobb managing, were playing. The poor execution, mental errors, and general witlessness of the previous year, when Detroit finished 27 games behind the Yankees, was continuing in the new season. They had managed to lose games ingeniously—"Fielding plays that win and lose ball games are quite frequently plays on which no scoring is done. A play to the wrong base, a late throw, failure to play the batsman, slow starts, slow finishes, a wrong turn, bad judgement, all these things are errors that do not go into the records," agonized *The Sporting News*. "In all frankness," it added painfully, "it must be said that the Tigers have the unhappy facility of sagging on defense at critical moments." Cobb was forced to bench veteran shortstop Donie Bush after "an inglorious exhibition at Cleveland," in which he made seven "bad plays," although he was charged with only one error. "Peculiar scoring and peculiar playing," mused *The Sporting News*. What was going on? To make things worse, in April 1922, Cobb was recovering from a nasty spike wound, Harry Heilmann was sick, and Bobby Veach was in a slump. One of the great outfields of all time was broken down.

As for the White Sox, no one gave them much of a chance in 1922. With their depleted roster and skinny payroll, it's hard to imagine hopes ran high even in the owner's box. Their season began with a 3–2 loss to St. Louis. The game, played in Chicago, had Commissioner Landis in attendance, ensuring the game's sanctity. Three days later, St. Louis completed its sweep of the White Sox, with a 14–0 drubbing, in which Charlie Robertson mopped up. Counting his two-inning start back in 1919, it was his second major league appearance.

Winless Detroit then came to town, and the Sox got their first win of the season, 4–3, in 10 innings in a game whose start was delayed by the funeral of Cap Anson, the great White Sox player who had died two days earlier, making nearly complete the severance of the White Sox from a glorious past. On April 21, Robertson pitched well enough against the Browns—giving up five hits and two runs in a six-inning start—but didn't get the decision in a 10–5 White Sox win. On April 26, Robertson "was hit freely, but pitched airtight ball in the pinches," said *The Sporting News* of his effort against Cleveland. But it was Robertson's first major league win, a complete-game victory in which he gave up only three runs despite being touched for 12 hits. It was a workmanlike effort, the kind he'd been accustomed to having with the Minneapolis Millers. Perhaps he was finding his way. Next up was a trip to Detroit and a start, the fourth in his career. His lifetime record stood at 1-1.

The White Sox were starting to show signs of life. They took the first two games in the Detroit series, on a Friday and a Saturday afternoon, bringing them to 8-6 and third place, behind St. Louis and the Yanks. On Saturday, Cobb, with his team truly on the skids—his team was 4-11, already 7.5 games out of first place—put himself back in the lineup; he'd been out since April 13. But he went hitless in a 4–0 White Sox win.

ON THOSE FEW OCCASIONS when Charlie Robertson's performance on April 30, 1922, is mentioned, it is often pointed out that he pitched his perfect game against an impressive suite of hitters. But some numbers lie. It is true that Detroit's eventual 1922 team BA of .306 is higher than that faced by any other perfect-game hurler. And that Cobb finished the year at .401; that Cooperstown-bound Harry Heilmann hit .356, fourth in the league; and that Bobby Veach hit .327. But these numbers don't tell us just how poorly (and indifferently) the Detroit team was playing at the time, because of injuries, inexperience, and a good player taking the day off. The team numbers do say this: Through April, Detroit as a team was hitting in the .270s, fifth in the eight-team league.

In fact, neither of these teams was much to look at, the occasional gaudy number notwithstanding. The Detroit lineup was this: One Luzerne Atwell Blue, known as Lu, batted leadoff and played first. In his second year, he was not a favorite of Mr. Cobb, though later Blue would attribute much of his improvement as a ballplayer to Cobb's gruff tutoring. Although he lacked power, Blue became prodigious at drawing walks (he can be found at number 44 on the list of all-time on-base percentage leaders). At second, and batting second for the Tigers, a reliable fielder named George Cutshaw at the tail end of a long career, which tells you all you need to know about his hitting—he was average, hitting around .265 every year. Batting third and playing center was the still monstrously talented Cobb, in his 18th season with a dozen batting titles to his credit. The Kentuckian Bobby Veach played left field with great skill and wielded an explosive bat in the cleanup position. Harry Heilmann, tall and rangy, roamed in right, batted fifth, finished with a .342 lifetime BA and a bronze plaque in the Hall. After that, the Tiger lineup thins. Bob Jones, nicknamed Ducky, was in his sixth year; he'd hit .303 the previous year, but was basically a .265 hitter with no power and no speed. Played third, batted sixth. In the seven hole was a curiosity: Emory Elmo "Topper" Rigney. A rookie, Rigney would go on to hit .300, and improve to .315 in 1923, filling the hole in Cobb's infield left by the departed Donie Bush. But just as quickly, Rigney's offensive skills eroded and he was out of baseball at age 30. Clyde Manion was the catcher that sunny Sunday in Detroit, filling in for the regular receiver, Johnny Bassler, who was given the day off. Manion was a career backup backstop, and we're talking about sitting on the bench a lot—250 hits in a 13-year career and a lifetime BA of .218. And on the mound, a rookie pitcher named Herman Pillette, a six-foot-two-inch 190-pound junkball pitcher with fine control and the middle name of Polycarp. He would win 19 games in 1922, with a sharp ERA of 2.85, but, the Wally Bunker of his time, he would be out of baseball in two years.

The White Sox, two seasons removed from the scandalous 1919 team, had very little going for them. The light-hitting Eddie Mulligan batted leadoff and played short. Mulligan, who had played two years with the Cubs back in '15 and '16 before the war interrupted, had turned up again in 1921, but on Chicago's North Side, replacing the banned Buck Weaver at third. He was playing short this day, in place of Ernie Johnson, who inherited short from Swede Risberg. Mulligan will play out the year and then, but for a short stint with Pittsburgh, leave the game. Covering for Mulligan at third was Harvey McClellan, another light hitter who came up in 1919, played only seven games and little more than that in the 1920 season, but was seeing more playing time by 1922 with Weaver gone.

The team superstar was Eddie Collins, batting third and playing second base, at which position he is considered perhaps the best of all time (or right behind Joe Morgan). Collins played on four world championship teams, hit .333 lifetime, was a great base-stealer, and endured a dozen years in Chicago, albeit as a Comiskey favorite, earning twice as much money as any teammate. A one-time captain of the Columbia University baseball team, Collins was a polished and intelligent fellow despised by the rougher Chick Gandil/Swede Risberg crowd. Harry Hooper batted cleanup and roamed right field. Hooper was a veteran and one-time star in a great Red Sox outfield that featured Tris Speaker and Duffy Lewis. Hooper had batted leadoff for the Red Sox, and it's testimony to the punchlessness of the White Sox that the aging Hooper is in the number-four spot for Chicago.

Johnny Mostil was batting fifth and playing left field on this day—for the first and only time in his career; he had basically won the starting job in center from Amos Strunk, who'd played full-time there the year before. A Chicago native brought up to the club with much fanfare to help restock the depleted outfield (Happy Felsch, Joe Jackson gone), Mostil was fast, compact, and a good hitter who would go on to be the fielding hero in the game. He would play his entire 10 years with the Sox and hit .301 lifetime. Known to be plagued by hypochondria and fleeting ailments, Mostil, right in keeping with the sensitivities of the time, was known as "Bananas." (Sadly, years later he would slash his wrists in a Boston hotel room.)

Amos Strunk, who'd joined the team in mid-1920, batted sixth and, as stated, played center field. One of the finest defensive center fielders of all time, he was also quick on the bases—nicknamed "Lightning," as in Lightning Strunk—known for scoring from second on a sacrifice bunt. Strunk hit .332 in 1921, his best year ever, at the age of 32. He was getting less and less playing time, though, and he would be out of baseball in two years. Earl "Whitey" Sheely batted seventh and played first base. Sheely, like Mostil, was another local boy. He came up to the Sox the year before, a rookie at 28 years of age, replacing the disgraced Chick Gandil. Whitey had been thrown right into the breach, playing 154 games that year and proving to be deft defensively and clutch with the bat, and steady, hitting around .300. He played the position nearly as well as had Gandil (who was terrific), hit better, and didn't have the unfortunate inclination to resent people more intelligent than he.

Ray Schalk, the catcher, batted eighth. Fast for a backstop, Schalk, like Eddie Collins, was one of the Clean Sox from the 1919 squad. A local boy who came up in 1912 at age 19, Schalk signed with Comiskey's club and (legend has it) was turned away from the ballpark—they thought he was just a kid trying to sneak in. He possessed a good arm and soft hands and would end up catching four no-hitters, one perfect game, and a piece of eternity in Cooperstown, to which he was inducted in 1955.

There was a fine crowd of about 25,000 at Detroit's Navin Field on Sunday afternoon, April 30, 1922. When the name of the Chicago pitcher was announced, few were likely to have recognized it. This was only the third start of the year for Robertson, fourth lifetime. And, with a rookie going for the Tigers, it was hardly a marquee matchup. So it was a surprisingly fine crowd for the event.

One can only wonder what the buzz was as game time approached, what the talk was in the stands, in the areas of the capacity crowd that spilled into foul territory and into the outfield. Was there action on the contest? Had the ballplayers been seen around town the night before (Robertson would later say of his mastery, "I just caught a bunch of players with the blind staggers")?

Robertson breezed. He breezed through the whole game. He fanned Lu Blue to open the game and got a pop-out to Collins at second by George Cutshaw, bringing Cobb to the plate dragging his lumber, still trying to get untracked after coming back into the lineup only the day before. He slashed a ball the other way but third baseman McClellan handled it cleanly and threw out the no-longer-swift Ty at first.

The White Sox half of the second would feature the game's only scoring. Chicago cleanup hitter Harry Hooper drew a walk from the left-handed Herb Pillette. Johnny Mostil, playing the small ball of the previous decade still favored by manager Kid Gleason, tried to bunt Hooper over and ended up beating it out, as the ball rolled slowly down the third base line. That left only one thing for Amos Strunk to do: bunt also, which he did, sacrificing himself, for the inning's first out, but moving Hooper and Mostil to third and second, respectively. When Whitey Sheely's grounder skipped off third baseman Bob Jones's glove into left field for a single, both runners scored, and Chicago led, 2–0.

In the bottom of the second, cleanup hitter Bobby Veach hit a fly ball to deep left. Johnny Mostil, new to the position, moved back and over and back toward the scoreboard in left-center. Still tracking the flight of the ball, he found himself wading against the rope that held back the overflow crowd, until the Tiger crowd made way for Mostil and let him make the catch clean. A local clipping noted that the crowd "spread out to make his feat easier to perform" just inside the ropes in front of the scoreboard. Given the fierce partisanship that the Detroit faithful were capable of (recall the crowding of the field that Addie Joss faced in only the third start of his career), one has to wonder why the opposition was being so generously accommodated. The next two batters, Heilmann and Jones, flied out the other way, to right, with Harry Hooper making a fine running catch of Jones's drive.

In the third, Robertson had little trouble, getting Topper Rigney to pop out to Eddie Collins at second and Clyde Manion to foul out to catcher Schalk before the pitcher Pillette grounded out to short. Nine up, nine down. In the fourth, the first two batters went just as they had in the first—Lu Blue fanning and Cutshaw popping to Collins. Cobb again went the other way against Robertson, this time getting the ball out of the infield, lifting a fly that left-fielder Mostil put in his mitt, his second putout of the day.

With the game nearly half over and their Tigers seeming asleep, the crowd at Navin Field, or so it is reported, grew ornery. They gave Robertson what they had given Addie Joss 14 years before: boos and uncivil invective. Cobb showed evidence of being riled, too. He began riding home-plate umpire Dick Nallin, claiming that Robertson, the shine-ball expert, was plying his trade—the spitball had been illegal since 1920. It didn't help Cobb's mood when Veach, who'd managed to work Robertson to a full count, swung at what would have been ball four and hit a fly to right, which Hooper grabbed. Harry Heilmann was up next and he asked Nallin to check the ball; then he asked him to check Robertson, and Cobb got into it even more. The game was stopped and Robertson's uniform was gone over by Nallin. Nothing turned up. To worsen things, Heilmann tapped back to Robertson, who got to throw him out at first. Then Cobb had Nallin check the first baseman's glove. Whitey Sheely was clean. Then Ducky Jones popped out to third, for out number three. It was Robertson's 15th consecutive batter retired.

The Tiger pitcher Pillette, for his part, was handling the White Sox with ease, but for the two cheap runs they pushed across in the second. (He would finish with a neat seven-hitter.)

In the sixth, Robertson seemed to get even sharper. His fastball and curve were both hitting the corners, and if he had a trick pitch it was hard to distinguish from his regular repertoire, all of which seemed, on this day, untouchable. Topper Rigney led off the sixth with an infield fly to Collins, Clyde Manion flied out to Hooper in right, and Pillette struck out. The Tigers went more meekly in the seventh: Blue, finally managing to put the ball in play, rolled out to Collins; Cutshaw did the same, but to McClellan at third. And Ty Cobb, reportedly fuming, went down swinging.

The game was hustling along. The April sun was sinking some, and only right field remained in bright sunlight. Cobb continued to holler at the home-plate ump, who would periodically take a ball out of play; these balls were hoarded by the Tigers, for future reference. The crowd got involved as well: This was one of the kinds of shows you could expect when Ty Cobb was present—he brought with him an air of violence and deceit. The fans hollered at Robertson, now trying to rattle him. But the Tigers went quietly again in the eighth. Veach struck out, Heilmann popped out, and Ducky Jones grounded out to Collins.

The Detroit crowd, which had seemed to make way for an enemy outfielder, and then turned to vociferous booing of Robertson, now, faced with the possibility of being witness to something extremely rare, began to root for him. Charlie Robertson had three outs to go.

Cobb was having none of this. At the start of the inning, brandishing balls he claimed had oil on them, he demanded that Ump Nallin inspect Robertson again. Nallin did so, and found nothing. Cobb stomped back to the dugout flinging bats and epithets. He called for a pinch-hitter.

Danny Clark walked to the plate to hit for Rigney. Clark, in his rookie year, was a left-handed-hitting utility man who would play three years with three different teams. He took a mighty swing at Robertson's first offering, and missed. He complained to Ump Nallin after the next pitch, a called strike. He wanted the ball checked. Clark was a hard-headed Mississippi boy; Cobb's type. But to no avail this day. He looked at strike three, and Robertson was two outs away from a big, big day.

The right-handed-hitting Clyde Manion, the backup catcher, batted for himself. He waved at a pitch that seemed to have something extra on it. And then he popped out to Collins. Cobb was down to his last out. He sent Johnny Bassler up to hit. Bassler was a fine hitter, the team's regular catcher who had been given Sunday off. Bassler came up in 1913 with Cleveland, then sat out 1915 through 1920; he returned to the game in 1921 with the Tigers. He would hit .323 in 1922, hit as high as .346 (in 1924), and finish with a lifetime batting average over .300 and the second-highest on-base percentage, lifetime, among catchers. On this day, at about four o'clock in the afternoon, pinch-hitting for the pitcher Pillette, he stood in against Robertson from the left side, a stocky, five-foot-nine-inch, 170-pound hitter with a sweet stroke, looking to break up Robertson's improbable run.

Robertson could feel the pressure. Literally, he could *see* the pressure as both squads pressed closer to the playing field, up off the benches. Robertson walked off the mound toward shortstop Eddie Mulligan; reportedly, he said, "Do you realize that little fat man up there is the only thing between me and a perfect game?" Mulligan didn't have a response.

Bassler tried some tricks. After taking a ball and a strike, he decided his bat wasn't right. He called time and went to the bench for another stick. Robertson waited him out. The crowd actually booed Bassler's stratagem. Perhaps the most seductive aspect of a rare sporting event is that all witnesses feel that they are part of history. That's how the Tiger fans felt. They wanted Bassler out.

On the third pitch, Bassler swung and looped a fly ball the opposite way, down the left-field line. Johnny Mostil had a long run to catch up to it. The ball seemed to be dropping just foul just before it landed in Mostil's glove. The crowd converged around him, raucous at what they had just seen. Mostil emerged without the ball, but the game was over.

But there were plenty of balls, presented as evidence of tampering, in the Detroit dugout. From *The American*, May 1:

TIGERS PROTEST STAR CHISOX HURLER

It is a pity that such a magnificent game as that pitched by Charlie Robertson yesterday—perhaps the best game ever pitched in the history of the world—may be barred because it is tainted.

Nallin threw out balls perfectly clean. After a few were pitched a Tiger player would call for a ball, and lo, its pristine beauty had been destroyed by a great splotch of black oil, it is declared. Robertson denied tampering with the ball. . . .

Dr. Keene, the Detroit physician, is the authority for the statement that balls had been discolored by crude oil. He would not charge Robertson with it, but he did assert that oil was smeared on almost every ball pitched.

The balls were sent to league president Ban Johnson's office but no action was taken. Cobb would always insist that Robertson had something illegal on the ball. It didn't matter. Robertson had thrown what was being called at the time the sixth perfect game in history (after the two in 1880 by Lee Richmond and J. M. Ward, Cy Young's, Addie Joss's, and the one by Babe Ruth and Ernie Shore in 1917 later deemed to not meet the perfect-game standard). Interestingly, Robertson's seems to be the first to which the term "perfect game" was applied.

For Robertson, April 30, 1922, was the highlight of the best year of a less-than-stellar career. He would have some bright spots later—in May, he beat Carl Mays, 2–1, in 10 innings, holding the Yankees hitless for seven innings. But there were more downs than ups for Robertson— "Robertson driven from slab as White Sox start to slump"; games featuring lots of walks and balks and runs scored against the often overmatched White Sox, who would finish at 77-77, 17 games behind the Yankees. Robertson would have his best year, winning 14, losing 15, and having a better-than-league-average ERA of 3.64. He would get in a losing squabble about money with Comiskey the next winter. Worse, he developed a bone chip in his elbow, and though he would pitch three more years for Chicago, he would be traded to St. Louis and then to the Boston Braves, where he finished his career. In Boston, Robertson had the distinction, in 1928, of being the first pitcher to have his glove taken away from him, when the opposition's manager, Wilbert Robinson, suspected that Robertson was doing "odd stunts with the ball with the aid of his glove."

Robertson won only two games that year, his last. His career totals: 8 years, 49 wins, 80 losses, 4.44 ERA. Hands down, Robertson is the least-accomplished pitcher to have thrown the most accomplished of games. Whether he had help or not, via petroleum or an accommodating left-field crowd that "spread" for Johnny Mostil's catch, it doesn't really matter. The game is in the books.

BY THE TIME an AP reporter tracked down Charlie Robertson the day after Don Larsen's perfect game in the 1956 World Series, Robertson, then 59, had been driving all night on business. He didn't have much good to say about baseball.

"If I had known then what I know now it would never have happened to me. I wouldn't have been in baseball. It isn't sour grapes or anything like that. Baseball didn't give me a particularly bad break. But I went through it and found out too late that it is ridiculous for any young man with the qualifications to make good in another profession to waste time in professional athletics."

Five days later, on the Sunday evening of October 14, 1956, Robertson surfaced for the last time. Viewers of the popular television program *What's My Line?* got to see a mystery guest sign in as "C. C. Robertson." To the celebrity panel—"star of stage and television" Arlene Francis, the "charmer who had just been around the world in 80 days" David Niven, "pride of the press box" columnist Dorothy Kilgallen, and "our Random House publisher" Bennett Cerf—fell the task of guessing Mr. Robertson's current occupation, revealed to the viewing audience as "Nut Broker." Right off the bat, the urbane, tuxedoed Mr. Cerf, a lifelong baseball fan, remarked that "there was a fellow named Robertson who did what Don Larsen just did, pitched a complete perfect game. Is that the Mr. Robertson?" The show's host, John Daly, was delighted. "Yes, indeed!" he enthused. "Right here, yes. Charlie Robertson!" Mr. C. C. Robertson, of Fort Worth, Texas, dressed in an ill-fitting suit, struggled unsuccessfully to suppress a shy smile.

It took six questions from the panel before Robertson's current occupation was, rather anticlimactically, disclosed. He won thirty dollars, five dollars a question. Robertson died in 1984, but his rare feat lives on, a testament to how luck of the most extraordinary kind can fall just about anywhere.

CHAPTER FOUR

Gooney Bird

Don Larsen
October 8, 1956

"I T CREPT FORWARD like a scout on his knees, but it admitted no revolutions and no upheavals." That's Bill James on baseball from the 1920s to 1960. As usual, James has it exactly right, more or less.

Baseball did hang on through some very tough times during the period cited by James—the Depression, a world war, the Korean conflict. Along the way, it managed to suppress some potentially disruptive forces by vanquishing yet another rival league (the Mexican League), narrowly avoiding a test of its antitrust exemption, and quelling a player revolt by rounding up beloved veterans like Frankie Frisch and Honus Wagner to serve as strike-busters. Although baseball famously integrated its player ranks during this period, it was owing more to the vision and guile of one man, Branch Rickey, than to baseball as a whole. For Rickey, there was

never a wrong time to be the first to dip into a pool of undervalued baseball talent, and he took the passage of a fair employment act in New York
State in 1946 as sufficient cause to find and sign the right black man to
break the game's 75-year-old color barrier. For the most part, the rest of
baseball was slow to follow Rickey's lead, with the Red Sox—the last
team to integrate—waiting 12 years to find exactly the right man: Pump-
sie Green. Baseball was far from the forefront in integrating its workforce:
Truman had integrated the entire U.S. military by 1948. In matters of
race, Mr. Rickey was surely an innovator, but baseball was not.

That's not to say that baseball didn't do anything surprising or bold
between the wars or up through the 1950s, and this is where one can say
perhaps that James has it just a little bit wrong. Baseball didn't move only
when forced to; it wasn't wholly reactive in nature. The men who ran the
game, and even those who played it, anticipated, in the immediate post-
war years, broader changes in the culture that would in a few decades
remake the sport—namely, television, expansion, and unionization. It
was the moving of a franchise, for the first time in half a century, that
was a harbinger of things to come. Baseball, then, was indeed admitting
of no revolutions, creeping slowly, but nonetheless, it moved.

SPECIFICALLY, IT WAS the Boston Braves who moved, in 1953, to Milwaukee. Until then, the same 16 teams had played in the same 10 cities
for 50 years—Boston (2 teams), Cincinnati, Cleveland, Chicago (2),
Detroit, New York (3), Philadelphia (2), Pittsburgh, St. Louis (2), and
Washington. Baseball may have held steady all that time, but Americans
had not. Between World War I and the end of the Korean War, there was
an unprecedented relocation under way. Increased mechanization of
farming equipment in the teens and twenties forced southern fieldhand
labor, mostly black, to move north to cities like Chicago, Detroit, New
York, and Pittsburgh, where there were hopes of manufacturing jobs.
During the Depression, people of all colors went in search of anything
other than what they were left with, moving from East to West in *Grapes
of Wrath* desperation. In the 1940s, the wartime economy poured money
into aviation, munitions, and shipbuilding, much of it on the West
Coast—San Diego, Los Angeles, Seattle—and people flocked there for
work. After the war, the peacetime economy helped itself to cars;
Detroit, its capacity enlarged by its wartime efforts, ran them off the line;
and President Eisenhower saw to it that America would be laced with a

modern interstate highway system. Empty fields became suburban tracts of affordable, prefab housing; the culture, looking for solid Republican comforts after the sheer madness of world war, found them—in the Sunbelt, in Levittown and Houston City; concomitantly, downtowns started to become known as inner cities, with the poor moving in. "Urban blight" entered the vocabulary.

In the early years of the century, it was an advancing web of telegraph wire that carried news of baseball to all corners of the United States, enabling reenactments of a game's progress by a variety of methods— child actors on a stage moving around in simulation of reported action on the field, or odd contraptions called Playographs, which were erected in town squares or outside newspapers offices, and by which a system of lights and magnets conveyed to the assembled viewers what was happening in the far-distant contest. In 1921, in the second year of commercial radio and the first summer of Pittsburgh's KDKA, engineer Harold Arlin broadcast a ballgame from Forbes Field. Already, four companies—Fox Movietone, Pathe, Hearst, and Paramount—were delivering twice-weekly newsreel coverage of baseball to movie houses. Baseball had found a key partner—entertainment technologies. The game could now travel at near the speed of light from ballpark to home or theater. You didn't need to be in a certain city to see baseball: You could be on a farmstead and hear it, and if you waited till Saturday afternoon down at the picture show, you could see the great Babe Ruth himself, uncoiling his quick, powerful stroke and sailing off on dainty ankles around the bases in the grainy shade of some distant stadium. As mass communication took its early, pioneering steps, baseball was able to deepen its hold on an American public that itself was on the move. Radio, which at first was thought to be a threat to ballpark attendance, was soon embraced. In 1937, Larry McPhail, then directing the Dodgers, even traded a player for a radio announcer, Red Barber, who he felt could help the team's bottom line from the booth just as a hitter might from the batter's box.

What McPhail could see in radio was that it helped spread one ingredient of the game's magic—its sound. Gathered around an Imperial Capehart Radio console on a hot summer's evening, listeners were offered an experience of baseball that was both full in itself and yet begged for frequent refreshers of the real thing. You might want to see that crowd you could hear over the airwaves, or see for yourself the coil of Stan Musial's stance, or get a view of just what a "cat bird seat" looked like. Television would be another matter. In the 1950s in New York, then television capital of the world, the men who owned great entertainment franchises—Horace Stoneham of the Giants, Walter O'Malley of the Dodgers (he had bought out Rickey), and the duo of Dan Topping and Del Webb of the Yankees—didn't have a clue how to handle TV. Rickey feared it the most. "Radio," he said, "created a desire to see something. Television is *giving* it to them." Rickey worried that if the habit of going out to the ballpark was broken, "a great many fans will never acquire it." In the 1950s, Rickey seemed to be right on the money. Fans stayed home more and more. But, uncharacteristically, Rickey couldn't see that there was big money hidden in the picture tube.

Rickey wasn't alone. All of management got a wake-up call in 1950, courtesy of Gillette, the razor company, which talked Commissioner Happy Chandler into selling them broadcast rights to six World Series for $1 million a year, and then turned around and sold those rights to NBC for $4 million a year.

Chandler was quickly replaced by Ford Frick, who knew enough to welcome television revenue but couldn't see it as more than a way to get money to throw at the players, who had been agitating for a pension plan ever since Ernie Bonham, a 10-year veteran and one-time 20-game winner for the Yankees, died during an emergency appendectomy with no money in the pension plan for his widow. To the owners, television was nothing more than the means to appease a minor grievance from their employees.

SINCE THE MID-1940S, the players had been pressing for pension contributions from their employers. The owners reluctantly listened. With the advent, in 1954, of the Players Association, which neither side wanted to call a union during the Red-baiting fifties, the players had at least managed a united front, and their lawyer, J. Norman Lewis, was able to keep the pressure on, with the added leverage being that the owners never, ever wanted to have their antitrust exemption tested in court. Consequently, they could be scared into at least token concessions, anything to keep their shaky arrangement out of the courtroom. When the six-year Gillette deal ended in 1956, baseball renewed the deal for one year for $3.25 million. Lewis managed to secure 60 percent of the proceeds for the pension fund. Other employment issues, however, remained.

Geoffrey Ward and Ken Burns, in their elegant *Baseball: An Illustrated History,* title their chapter on the 1950s "The Capital of Baseball," by which they execute a neat double entendre. For the capital in the 1950s is New York, where, in the decade, 14 of the 20 league titles were won by New York teams, and 8 of the 10 World Series (6 of them being subway series). This New York dominance may have had something to do with the declining attendance in the game generally, though it does not explain attendance drop-offs in New York itself. But it is the drop in gate revenue and the rise of television that lend "capital" its second meaning for baseball in the fifties: The money was shifting, the profit centers were shifting, the owners and players were beginning to jockey. And it was television—the ingenious contraption made practical in the late 1920s by Philo T. Farnsworth that, 20 years later, had launched a hundred commercial stations, made celebrities out of Milton Berle and Arthur Godfrey and John Cameron Swayze, and brought America to its living room—that held the key to capital not only in baseball, but in all the major sports in America. And in those 1950s, baseball in New York did its best to make sure that whatever the medium, baseball was the message.

IT WAS PERHAPS the most famous rivalry that ever existed in any American sport—the New York Yankees versus the Brooklyn Dodgers. Its heyday was a 10-year span, from 1947 to 1956, when the two clubs played each other in six World Series. The myth is large, indeed, and like most things of mythical proportions, it contains those wonderfully simple oppositional elements that can lend themselves to cheap sentiment, Parnassian revery, and the occasional insight. In the Yankees and Dodgers we have two mighty forces, one spectacularly successful and self-assured, the other haunted, insecure, and terribly charming; together, they are locked in a battle for the rights to a single kingdom. On the periphery, a conniving third force (the Giants) plays one off the other and presumes, at least once, to steal away as victor. Epic wars are fought, fierce innings of colorful and awful conflict follow one upon the other; dirt mixes with blood, bitter oaths and ecstatic ovations fill the air of a great city. In the end, though, and this seems a signature of all myths, too, the outcome is fated, the losers—lovable, flawed—lose; they withdraw from the contested ground and escape to a new kingdom of their own in the West. They even bring their conflicted co-conspirator, the Giants, with them. The Yankees will reign alone in their city until an upstart offspring of the two vanquished foes, sporting a mix of the parental colors and a name taken from another century—the Metropolitans—will start learning to play ball in the empty grounds below Coogan's Bluff.

THE 1956 WORLD SERIES represents the last time those two great, storied teams would ever play each other—that is to say, the last time the Dodgers *from Brooklyn* would ever play the Yankees, for they would do so from their Los Angeles address three more times before the century was out. But as combatants with ballparks reachable by subway, they squared off six other times—in '41, '47, '49, '52, '53, and the year before, in '55, which was the only time the Dodgers of Brooklyn ever won. That was perhaps the borough's finest hour, and one of baseball's, as a 23-year-old miner's son named Johnny Podres, from Mineville, New York, shut out the Yankees in Game Seven at Yankee Stadium to bring a world championship to the everyman Dodgers. Bells rang out in the Borough of Churches in October 1955. There was a spontaneous parade down the canyons of bums—Flatbush Avenue and Ocean Parkway—caravans of cars honking and trailing streamers and signs with "Wait Till Next Year" exuberantly crossed out.

IN 1956, THE YANKEES broke spring training and came north by train. They opened the season on the road against the Senators, with Don Larsen, acquired the year before in a mammoth 18-player trade, doing the pitching. Manager Casey Stengel was saving his ace Whitey Ford for the home opener against the Red Sox. This was Casey's team, and had been since he came in 1949 and silenced his many detractors by winning the World Series. Casey's team made up of Casey's boys—the rabble-rousing producers, Ford, Mantle, Martin, Hank Bauer, along with the ranking veteran Yogi Berra. Casey's view of abstinence from alcohol: "It only helps them if they can play."

In the Washington opener, Mantle hit two huge home runs and Larsen picked up the win in a 10–4 victory. By mid-May New York had opened up a 3.5-game lead over the Indians. Mantle was hitting close to .500 and leading the league in homers with 11, Berra had 10, and Whitey Ford, judiciously used by Stengel, hadn't lost a game. Only Billy Martin, the scrappy heart and soul of the club, was struggling; he even got benched for a while as the unsentimental Stengel tried playing the young, clean-

living, born-again South Carolinian Bobby Richardson, and then Jerry
Coleman, at second base. To no avail—the Yanks began to lose; they fell
out of first place on a night when 40-year-old Enos Slaughter beat them
with a late-inning hit in Kansas City. Casey put the aging Phil Rizzuto
back in the starting lineup, to shake things up. But nothing seemed to
help until Martin took matters into his own hands, pummeling Tommy
Lasorda, then a left-handed pitcher trying to catch on with the A's,
prompting a bench-clearing donnybrook (Lasorda had been released by the
Dodgers in favor of another young lefty named Koufax). The Yankees
came back to life, winning six straight and taking over first place again.
Mantle remained on a torrid pace that would end in his winning the
Triple Crown. In early June, with 27 homers, he was 18 games ahead of
Babe Ruth's 1927, 60-homer pace. Young right-hander Johnny Kucks was
surprising everyone, winning 11 games (to Ford's 10) by the All-Star
Game. But the Yanks got roughed up in Cleveland by the great Indian
hurlers—Early Wynn (three-hit shutout), Bob Lemon (six-hitter), and Herb
Score (four-hit shutout), and the Yankee lead dropped to seven games.
Then the Yanks got swept in Detroit and moved on to Fenway Park for a
tough and crucial series. Stengel pulled the right strings: He called up a
young Ralph Terry to face the Red Sox, and he beat them 4–3 to end a six-
game skid; it was Terry's only win of the year. But the Yanks recovered
their equilibrium and started planning for the postseason. For $50,000
they went out and got Enos Slaughter from Kansas City to give them
some experience and clutch hitting; to make room they unceremoniously
released Phil Rizzuto after 13 years in pinstripes. On September 18, Mantle hit one out of Comiskey Park in the 11th inning, his 50th of the season, giving Whitey his 19th win of the year. It also gave the Yanks their
seventh pennant in eight years under "The Old Perfessor," Mr. Stengel.

The Dodgers were pretty much the same team in 1956 as they were
in '55 when they'd finally bested the Yankees, except for the fact that
Johnny Podres was in the Navy and everyone was a year older. Robinson,
who'd lost a step, was now a third baseman being regularly spelled by
"Handsome" Ransome Jackson, who drove in more runs and played in
more games than Jackie. Reese was in his 14th year and was 38 years old;
Campanella hit .219; but Duke Snider was at his peak, having hit a
career-high 43 home runs during the regular season, as was Gil Hodges,
who hit 32. Still, the team's productivity was in significant decline. After
scoring 857 runs in their triumphant 1955 season (and 955 in '53, the
most since the '39 Yanks), Dodger totals dipped to 720 in 1956. Only con-

tinued strong pitching from Don Newcombe, who won 27 games, and the midseason addition of former Giant (and Mexican Leaguer) Sal Maglie ensured that Brooklyn could fend off the young and driving Milwaukee Braves of Warren Spahn, Lew Burdette, Eddie Mathews, and a young, astounding Henry Aaron. The Dodgers played hot and cold throughout the year, but prevailed, in the end, winning the pennant on the last day of the season, behind Newcombe.

Warren Spahn once said that he played for Casey Stengel "before and after he was a genius," having played for Casey in 1942 in his rookie year, with the Boston Braves, and in his last year, with the New York Mets, 23 years later. Indeed, over the course of Stengel's first nine years as a manager, for the Brooklyn Dodgers and the Braves, his teams never finished higher than fifth and only once played over .500 ball (.507); and in the final four years of his quarter-century of major league managing, he posted four last-place finishes with his Amazin' Mets. But those middle 12 years were surely years of genius. From 1949 till 1960, Stengel ran the Yankees, winning 10 pennants and seven World Series titles.

Hired by his old friend George Weiss to replace Bucky Harris after the 1948 season, in which the Yankees finished third behind Cleveland, Stengel's first move was to insist on the hiring of Jim Turner as pitching coach. Turner had pitched with modest success for Stengel in Boston, and finished out his career as a reliever during the war years for the Yanks. Together, Turner and Stengel, with the help of the front office, would convert seemingly jerry-rigged pitching staffs into a force good enough to win and win repeatedly.

Stengel had learned platooning from the great New York Giants manager John McGraw. Stengel played for McGraw for three years, three pennant-winning years, and Stengel starred in two World Series triumphs. But by the 1940s, platooning had nearly become a lost art. Everything was long ball and no percentages. But Stengel was old school, something that must have brought a warm flush to a young Mickey Mantle when he was called up in 1951; his father had insisted he learn to switch-hit in the belief that platooning would one day rule again.

Stengel went beyond platooning position players; he even platooned pitchers, making starters into relievers and back again as he played his inscrutable hunches. Spahn in his comment may have been hinting that Stengel's success had more to do with players than managerial strategy, but no less a strategist than Leo Durocher put a finer point on his Stengel assessment: "He was a *fucking* genius."

That's not to say that Stengel wasn't managing with some great ballplayers and some good arms: he had Vic Raschi, Allie Reynolds, and Eddie Lopat through the early fifties, but they would be abetted by contributions from pickups like Johnny Sain and Bob Grim, Tommy Byrne and Spec Shea. When the Queens native Ed "Whitey" Ford showed up, he was handled delicately by Stengel and never overpitched, and from the mid-fifties on, Ford was surrounded by the likes of Johnny Kucks, Bob Kuzava, Tom Sturdivant, and Bob Turley. And Don Larsen.

After the 1954 season, and another second-place finish to Cleveland, even though the Yankees won 103 games, the team engineered an 18-player trade with Baltimore. A lot of marginal and over-the-hill ballplayers were involved, but what the Yankees wanted was a shoring up of their pitching. Amidst it all they got Bob Turley, who had gone 14-15 with the O's, and Don James Larsen, who had managed to lose 21 games while winning 3. In 1955, Raschi and Reynolds were gone. Ford was there, anchoring the staff. Turley won 17 games in 1955, and Larsen went 9-2, starting and relieving, with an ERA of 3.06.

Larsen seemed to be a raw talent just awaiting the kind of handling that Stengel and Turner could minister. After bouncing around in the minors in the late forties and doing two years of military service (mostly playing ball for the service team in Hawaii), he was brought up to the St. Louis Browns in 1953. He started 22 games, pitched nearly 200 innings, and finished 7-12 for the last-place Browns, who drew fewer than 300,000 people and moved the next year to Baltimore. There, Larsen was a workhorse for the next-to-last-place Orioles, who drew more than a million but kept searching in vain for a way to play better than the Yankees.

The Yanks bounced back nicely from their Series loss to Brooklyn in '55, unfazed it seemed, and won the A.L. pennant in '56 by nine games. It would be Yankees-Brooklyn once again. Stengel named a well-rested Whitey Ford to pitch the opener at Ebbets Field, a dangerous spot for a left-hander, what with the short porches in left and left-center and a Dodger lineup stacked with heavy-hitting right-handers—Campy, Hodges, Reese, Robinson, Furillo. The last time Ford had pitched in Ebbets Field he made it through only one inning and took the loss in Game Four of the '53 series. In the '55 series, Stengel managed to pitch Ford only in the Bronx. Dodger manager Walter Alston called on Sal Maglie for the opener: Acquired in May from Cleveland, "The Barber" went 13-5 and by the end of the year was the team's best pitcher. Newcombe, their 27-game winner, was worn out and would never return to top form.

Brooklyn jumped on Ford for five runs early, behind home runs from Robinson and Hodges. Stengel immediately started to scramble; it almost looked like panic. He sent Ford to the showers after three innings' work and brought in Johnny Kucks, who was scheduled to pitch Game Two, and went to Bob Turley, another starting pitcher, in the eighth, but to no avail. Despite home runs by Mantle and Martin, the Dodgers, in front of 34,479 fans, won the first game 6–3. Maglie went all the way and struck out 10.

The next day brought a driving rain, and it looked lucky for the Dodgers, as it allowed Newcombe—who had to pitch on the last day of the regular season to clinch the pennant—another day of rest. Stengel, having run through three starting pitchers in the opening-day loss, gave the ball to Don Larsen. Larsen had been pitching particularly well since early September, when Jim Turner allowed him to adopt a no-windup delivery. (Larsen felt he was tipping his pitches.) He went 4-0 in September, besting the Red Sox in his last start of the year, after which Ted Williams said Larsen was the toughest pitcher in the American League. Larsen threw a heavy fastball, dense with topspin, that dropped down and away from left-handed hitters, and a rising four-seamer; his slider was his out pitch; he would show the curve as a change of pace. He was tough to hit, giving up only 133 hits in 180 innings; control was his major challenge, as he gave up, on average, a walk every other inning. Larsen was 27 years old and pitching as well as he ever would for any sustained period. In two years with New York, he had won 20 and lost only 7.

But when the sun shone on Brooklyn on Friday, October 5, neither Newcombe nor Larsen had anything. Yogi Berra hit a grand slam in the second inning, giving the Yanks a quick 6–0 lead and knocking out Newcombe. But Larsen had trouble finding the plate, walking two without incident in the first, but no such luck in the second. An error by first-baseman Joe Collins on a routine grounder rattled Larsen; two more walks and a sacrifice fly brought out Stengel. He'd seen enough. Johnny Kucks was the choice once again; the right-hander gave up a two-run single to Pee Wee Reese. Stengel then tapped lefty Tommy Byrne to pitch to the left-handed slugger Duke Snider. Snider hit the ball over the 40-foot screen in right field, a three-run shot, and the game was tied, all six runs officially unearned. The parade of Yankee pitchers continued, as Stengel struggled desperately to avoid going down two games to none, but Tom Sturdivant, Tom Morgan, Bob Turley, and Mickey McDermott could not stem the tide. Gil Hodges hit a pair of two-run doubles. Dodger pitcher

Don Bessent pitched seven innings of stout relief and Brooklyn won the game, 13–8.

As it turns out, the rainout of Game Two had a benefit for the Yanks: Whitey Ford, with two full days of rest after his brief Game One stint, took the ball for Game Three at Yankee Stadium. And in front of 73,977 fans, he pitched a complete-game win over Roger Craig, who took a 2–1 lead into the bottom of the sixth, only to have Enos Slaughter launch a three-run shot to right center. The Yanks won 5–3 and were back in it. In Game Four, Stengel gave the ball to Tom Sturdivant, a 16-game winner. Behind home runs from Mantle and Hank Bauer, Sturdivant stifled the Dodgers on six hits, besting Carl Erskine. The series was tied.

Game Four had been on a Sunday afternoon. There are more than a few versions of what transpired that night among the Yankees. Bob Cerv, a reserve outfielder, claims he was drinking with Don Larsen till four in the morning. Bob Turley said Larsen got half an hour's sleep before arriving at the ballpark, where he snoozed in the trainer's room till noon. Mickey Mantle said he "caught up with Larsen and his friends" at nine o'clock at Bill Taylor's saloon on West 57th Street and stayed for about an hour and a half. Larsen, said Mickey, was drinking ginger ale. Mantle added that he was told by others that Larsen left shortly after he did and returned to his room across the street at the Henry Hudson Hotel with a pizza box under his arm. Maybe Mantle, who says in his book *My Favorite Summer 1956* that, after the Game Four victory, "word went around the clubhouse" that Casey had told Larsen he was starting Game Five the next day, saw what he wanted to see, a Yankee getting ready to give his best.

It seems Mickey had a few things wrong. First of all, Larsen claimed he was never told he was pitching the next day, although since no starter had been named, it was a distinct possibility that he would pitch. He had two full days of rest after facing only 10 batters in the disastrous second game. Second, he didn't live at the Henry Hudson Hotel. In Larsen's account, he and a longtime friend, the Yankee publicist Arthur Richman, had steaks and a few beers at Bill Taylor's and then took a long cab ride to the Bronx, where Larsen had a room at the Concourse Plaza Hotel (other Yankees lived in the Henry Hudson; what did Mantle know? He lived more luxuriously at the St. Moritz). Larsen says he was dropped off by midnight; along the way, realizing that another Sunday had passed without his going to church, he gave Richman a dollar and asked him to give it to his synagogue. Larsen, born a Lutheran, was not exactly a churchgoing man, but perhaps he was trying to cover his bases by currying a little favor with greater powers than he. The gadfly restaurateur Toots Shor tells yet another story about that night, claiming that Larsen was at his joint, and was introduced to Chief Justice Earl Warren. Maybe alcohol is a factor in all these addled memories, but let's take Larsen's word. He showed up at the ballpark at 10:30 in the morning, Monday, October 8, and found a warmup ball in his shoe in the locker, a sign from coach Frank Crosetti, on instructions from Jim Turner based on a decision by Casey, that he was starting Game Five.

Larsen was a wild character, so the stories about his carousing the night before the game are not so shocking. During spring training that year, he rammed his Olds 98 into a telephone pole at 5:30 in the morning, hitched a ride back to the hotel, and then fessed up to Stengel at the Yankee training complex. Larsen stood before Casey with a headache and a chipped tooth and feared the worst, but Stengel just shook his head for 30 seconds and told Larsen to get out to the field. When reporters got wind of the Yankee early morning crash, they besieged Stengel, asking for consequences—fine, suspension, dismissal? Stengel said he could not decide what to do, since perhaps Larsen had not been out too late but rather up too early. Stengel stood by his big, good-natured kid.

IF ANYONE EVER epitomized the old saying that it is better to be lucky than good, it was Don Larsen. Born just before the stock market crash in 1929, in Michigan City, Indiana, home to 35,000 people and a big state prison, Larsen was delivered by his father and a neighbor when the doctor was late in arriving. He weighed 10 pounds. His father bought him a bat when he was four years old. His older sister Joyce took him under her wing; a great sports fan, she carted him to South Bend to see Notre Dame football games and to Chicago to see the Black Hawks. When Don was 15 the family moved to San Diego, where the big six-footer began to excel in basketball and baseball. Although he received college scholarship offers to play basketball, baseball was his first love. At 18 he stood six feet four inches, and major leagues scouts where impressed by this kid who could hit, throw hard, and run. He was scouted by a man named Arthur Schwartz and, over dinner with Larsen's father, signed with the Browns organization for $850. He progressed through the minors, then was drafted in 1951 into the Army. When he got out, the Browns brought him to the big leagues. Entering major league baseball at the lowest level—the

Browns were perennial doormats—didn't phase the unflappable Larsen;
he was simply happy to be there. Two years later, he's drinking with
Mickey Mantle and Billy Martin, on his way to earning the nickname
"Gooney Bird," after a clumsy, flightless species the Yankees had seen on
a tour of Japan.

SAL MAGLIE, WHO had stymied the Yanks in Game One, had been
tabbed as the Brooklyn pitcher for Game Five. On Sunday, Gil
McDougald had mused, "What if Maglie pitches a no-hitter?" to which
Larsen supposedly said that he just might throw one himself, if he
pitched. Maybe that's why he offered the indulgence of a dollar to Richman, to cover the rare show of hubris. Or perhaps it was the ginger ale
talking.

It was a "must" game for the Yankees, the last in the Series to be
played at the Stadium. Games Six and Seven were set for Ebbets Field,
where the Yanks had won only 8 of 18 games played since the 1947
Series; they were 13-5 at home.

It was 60 degrees, with a slight wind to left field, at game time. There
were 64,519 fans in the ballpark. NBC broadcast the game on television
nationally, Mel Allen and Vin Scully at the mike; the Mutual Broadcast
System did the radio, with Bob Wolff. Lots of New York kids skipped
school (including a 16-year-old Brooklyn kid named Joe Torre, who wan-
gled a ticket) and many a grownup never returned to the office from
lunch.

Larsen was sharp from the get go. He caught the careful-eyed Junior
Gilliam looking with a slider at the knees. With the count full on Pee
Wee Reese, Berra, showing a world of confidence in Larsen's stuff, called
for the slider in. Reese let it pass and Babe Pinelli, umping his last game
ever behind the plate, rang him up. Duke Snider, who had led the
National League in home runs and slugging percentage, flied out to Hank
Bauer in right field. In the Yankee half, 39-year-old Sal Maglie, making
his first appearance ever at Yankee Stadium, heightened the drama
almost immediately, putting his second pitch behind the head of tough-
guy ex-Marine Hank Bauer. Bauer glared at Maglie, who looked inno-
cently at his hands, in mock bewilderment. Bauer then popped to short.
Joe Collins, having a rough series in the field and at the plate, tried to
bunt his way on, but Jackie Robinson, playing third, jumped on it and

threw him out. Mantle, who had had a monstrous year, leading the majors in home runs, RBI, and batting average, faced a shift: Shortstop Reese moved to the right side of the infield. Trying to go the opposite way, Mantle flied out to left.

Jackie Robinson, batting cleanup for Brooklyn, had endured an injury-plagued year, though he was having a fine Series. Berra counseled Larsen to pitch him hard stuff away, but Larsen got his second pitch up and in and Larsen's date with destiny was nearly canceled right there. Robinson hit a scorching one-hopper to third-baseman Andy Carey's left. Carey managed to just tip the ball with his glove, but as fortune would have it, the ball caromed about 40 feet to where shortstop Gil McDougald caught it on the fly in the hole and threw out Robinson on a very close play. Gil Hodges, enjoying a big Series at the plate with eight RBI in the first four games, including a home run, stepped in. Berra called for sliders and Hodges went down swinging, Larsen's third K. Speedy Sandy Amoros, whose great running catch in the seventh game the year before had saved Johnny Podres and the Dodgers, got more sliders from Larsen. He popped weakly to short right field. Bauer couldn't get there but Billy Martin made a tumbling catch for the third out. The Yankees went quietly in their half of the second—Berra popping out to Reese, left-fielder Enos Slaughter flying to left, and Martin striking out on a big Maglie curveball.

Larsen settled in and had a third inning without any thrills: Furillo, being pitched away, flew out to right field. Campanella took a called third strike. Sal Maglie came to the plate and hit the first pitch to straightaway center, where Mantle made the catch. In the Yankee third, Gil McDougald, coming off a great year in which he would finish second to Mantle in the MVP voting, couldn't do much with Maglie, who was razor sharp. He grounded out to Robinson. Andy Carey fouled out to Campy, and so did Larsen. Three perfect innings from both pitchers.

Larsen got economical in the fourth. He was now challenging the Brooklyn hitters the second time through the lineup. Gilliam and Reese were each retired on one pitch, both grounding to Martin at second. When Duke Snider stepped in, Larsen had recorded 11 outs on 35 pitches. With that kind of efficiency, the Yankees, if they could solve Maglie, could all be at Bill Taylor's well before cocktail hour. Against the tough Snider, however, Larsen's focus seemed to waver. Two fastballs missed the outside corner and Larsen found himself in a 2-0 hole. He would have to challenge Snider with a pitch in the strike zone, and did so. With a mighty swing from Duke and the ensuing crack, it seemed that Brooklyn had the lead. But the ball sailed high and far and just foul into the stands down the right-field line. Right-field umpire Ed Runge immediately signaled foul ball, and later said it was clearly foul, "by six inches." Larsen then bent a low slider across the corner for a called strike two, evening the count. Snider fouled off the next but was caught looking for strike three to end the inning and keep perfection alive.

Maglie kept up his mastery as he faced the Yankee lineup for the second time. Bauer grounded out to Robinson; Joe Collins, looking more and more hapless, looked at strike three, bringing Mantle to the plate. As Larsen had with Snider, Maglie made a mistake. But whereas Larsen got a bit of luck when Duke smashed his 2-0 delivery half a foot foul, Mantle pulled a hanging curveball down the right-field line; it landed in the crowd, half a foot fair, just inside the foul pole 296 feet away. It was 1–0 Yankees. Snider made a fine running catch of a drive off Berra's bat to end the inning.

The Dodgers came out swinging in the fifth; there had been too many called strikes. Mantle said "you could see the determination" flashing in Jackie Robinson's eyes when he dug in against Larsen to lead off. Larsen started him off with a curve inside for a ball, then sailed a slow curve off the plate that the aggressive Robinson lunged for and hit foul. Robinson fell behind 1-2 when he swung mightily at another curveball. Berra was crossing up Robinson, shifting to slow breaking stuff. But Robinson was still looking fastball, and got one, and hit a wicked shot down the left-field line, but foul. Trying to wait a little, Robinson then drove the next pitch, another fastball, to deep right, but Hank Bauer hauled it in. Hodges came up, and Berra and Larsen were careful with him, as they were all day. They went with hard stuff, and Larsen jumped out in front 0-2 with two fastballs on the corner. Then the sharp-eyed and selective Hodges watched two more fastballs just miss. Larsen then blundered. Berra called for 2-2 slider and Larsen hung it. Hodges pounced and ripped a drive to deep left-center. Mantle, who had been shading Hodges that way, took off. He ran and ran and caught the ball with his left arm at full extension, his legs in full stride. He was more than 400 feet from home plate. A home run in Ebbets Field, a long out in Death Valley, the Bronx. Amoros followed. Berra wanted to pitch the diminutive Cuban low and away, but Larsen, struggling with his pitch placement a bit, got a 1-1 fastball up and Amoros hit a long fly ball into the stands in right, again, just foul. Ed Runge, sprinting down the right-field line, again made a crucial call, and said after the game that Amoros's hit was foul by "that much," making a space with his thumb and forefinger. Home-plate ump Babe Pinelli said he saw it as fair, and was glad Runge was down there. On a 2-2 pitch, Amoros grounded out to Martin for Larsen's 15th consecutive out, though the last four—Snider, Robinson, Hodges, and Amoros—were true adventures. The Yankee fifth featured Enos Slaughter, one year older than Maglie, working him for a walk. Martin, trying to move up the runner, instead bunted back to Maglie, who got the force on the still-hard-charging Slaughter at second. Then Pee Wee Reese turned in a great play against Gil McDougald, who hit a line drive that seemed bound for left-center field. Reese leaped and clipped the ball straight up and caught it himself for the out, then doubled Martin off first to retire the side.

Before coming out for the sixth, the loosey-goosey Gooney Bird tried to break the growing tension on the bench, joking with Mickey: Wouldn't it be something if he threw a no-hitter? Mantle wanted nothing to do with it. Larsen then stood on the hill; he still had four long innings to go, and not much to work with, a 1–0 lead. He seemed to have recovered from his shaky fifth inning; perhaps the bottom of the order was just what he needed. Furillo was out on two pitches, popping to Martin in shallow right. Campanella did the same, on the first pitch, with Martin corralling it behind second. A three-pitch inning with the pitcher due up. No way Alston was going to pinch-hit for a guy throwing a one-hitter. And this time, Maglie gave battle. He swung and missed the first two pitches, then fouled off a couple, worked the count to 2-2, but couldn't catch up to a good Larsen fastball and went down swinging, Larsen's 5th strikeout, 66th pitch, and 18th consecutive man retired.

Andy Carey, in his fifth year as a Yankee and second as their regular third baseman, was coming off a tough year in which he hit only .237. He was the weak link in an infield anchored by McDougald and Billy Martin. But he gave the Yankee fans hope for some breathing room when he led off the sixth with a line single up the middle. Arguably, a better hitter was coming up next in Larsen, who hit 14 home runs in his career, and on occasion would bat eighth in the lineup. Batting in the customary pitcher's position on this day, Larsen was up there to bunt. He failed on his first two attempts to move Carey into scoring position, but Stengel had him bunt even with two strikes, and Larsen laid down a beauty, moving Carey to second. Hank Bauer followed with a single to left and the

Yankees had their run and a little insurance. Joe Collins reached Maglie for a single, moving Bauer to third with only one out. It looked as if the Yanks might really breathe with relief, because Mickey Mantle was coming up. But Mickey hit the ball so hard right at Gil Hodges at first that Hodges was able to just step on the bag to get Mantle and throw to home to Campanella before Bauer even got close. He was caught in a rundown and Robinson applied the tag. Inning over.

For Larsen, it was back to the top of the order for the third—and he hoped last—time through. Nine Dodgers to go. Starting with Junior Gilliam, o for 2 with a strikeout and a grounder to Martin. This time, Gilliam worked the count to 2-2. Larsen has said he got away with a terrible slider "that didn't have a lot of zip on it." Gilliam took it for a ball. On the next pitch, he short-hopped McDougald at short with a low liner, but McDougald stayed with it, made the backhand stab, and turned it into out number 19. Larsen faced Reese next. Berra was familiar with all these Dodgers, and Larsen was told that Pee Wee was selective at the plate if Gilliam got on before him, but otherwise he was aggressive. No time to groove one. Sure enough, Reese went after the first pitch and fouled it off, and he turned the next pitch around and drove it deep to center. But deep was something Yankee Stadium had plenty of, 463 feet all the way to a wall so distant they could safely put granite monuments—of Ruth, Gehrig, and Miller Huggins—right on the warning track. Mantle ranged back a bit and made the catch. Snider was next and Larsen, having almost been taken for a home run by Duke in the fourth, pitched him low and away and got a fly out to Slaughter in left. The Yanks, in their half, kept the pressure on Maglie. After Berra and Slaughter flied out, gritty Billy Martin singled and McDougald worked out a walk. But Carey grounded out to Reese to end the inning. As the shadows lengthened at Yankee Stadium, the hometown crowd was anxious to see Larsen out there, getting six more Dodgers out.

Bob Wolff, doing the Mutual Broadcasting radio call, was struggling hard not to mention what Larsen had going. "The crowd this afternoon is interested in runs as well as totals," he said. The crowd was extraordinarily silent, at least compared to the crowds of today. On the radio, despite more than 64,000 fans, you can hear the hot dog vendor and Bob Shepard in the background. "Batting for the Dodgers, number 42, Robinson, number 42." How was Larsen going to get Robinson out again? He had had a sure single, possible double, turned into an out in the second, when his liner glanced off Carey's glove right to McDougald; in the fourth he had been just out in front of a Larsen delivery and hit it deep, but foul, down the left-field line, and then had adjusted and rocketed one to right that Bauer nonetheless was able to gather in. Now Robinson was up there with a little gamesmanship on his mind. Larsen got the first pitch in there for a called strike, what he later called "a good, hard-moving fastball." It was Larsen's 75th pitch and showed he still was in command. Robinson called time as Larsen was about to throw him another. Robinson picked at something in his eye. Then he walked to the on-deck circle, took one of the two bats Gil Hodges had there, took a practice swing with it. The crowd roused itself into thunderous booing at Robinson's tactics. Larsen looked away, as he would do often in the last two innings, staring into center field, taking off his cap, then going to the resin bag. The crowd's booing, he said later, comforted him. Robinson hit the next pitch right back to Larsen, and the crowd roared its approval. Hodges was next. Berra and Larsen worked him away, knowing how powerful a pull hitter he was. The count went to 2 and 2 when Larsen threw what he recalled as a "mediocre" fastball; Hodges jumped on it and hit a shot just to Andy Carey's left, low to the ground. Carey flinched and caught this one; unsure of what he'd done, he threw to first just in case the drive he hardly saw might have hit the ground. It hadn't, and there were two down in the eighth. And now the tough Amoros was up. Larsen fooled him with a rare curveball and Amoros hit a lazy fly to Mantle in center. And now there were three to go.

The affable, sociable Don Larsen had never been as alone as he was in the dugout in the bottom of the eighth. No one wanted anything to do with him, no one wanted to jinx the unconscious zone in which Larsen was living for a day. He may have been on his own, but when he came to the plate to take his hacks against Maglie, the crowd let him know that they were behind him. Larsen, understandably, doesn't remember anything about his at-bat, other than considering and then rejecting the possibility that Maglie would brush him back. He struck out, as did Bauer and Collins. Maglie had struck out the side, as if he, too, were in a hurry to see if Larsen could do it.

Bob Wolff was not alone in skirting mention of the perfect game unfolding. Neither Scully nor Mel Allen mentioned it either. They remembered the guff Red Barber got for mentioning the no-hitter Yankee Bill Bevens had going back in the 1947 Series against the Dodgers, and being blamed by Yankee fans when Cookie Lavagetto broke the spell, and won the game, with a double in the 10th. But the scoreboard told most of the story—no runs or hits for the Dodgers, no errors for the Yankees. And when you see the bottom of the order due up in the ninth, you are reasonably sure that no one has reached first base.

Carl Furillo, "the Reading Rifle," as he was called for his throwing arm and his Pennsylvania city of origin, was the first man up. Larsen admits to being unnerved by Furillo, his mean look, his sculpted, ready-to-rumble build. Berra visited the mound and reminded Larsen not to lose focus. "If he walked one guy and the next guy hit one out the game was tied," Yogi figured, and told him so. Furillo was aggressive as usual. He swung hard at the first pitch, and fouled it off. It was Larsen's 17th first-pitch strike. Furillo swung hard at the second pitch, and fouled it off. Berra wanted nothing but sliders and hard stuff from Larsen. He threw a third consecutive slider but it was way high; Berra changed to a fastball, not wanting to give up the advantage in the count; Furillo flicked it away foul. He got a slider next, but fouled that off. It was a tough at-bat, but Larsen was giving no ground either. He was maintaining a kind of discipline that escaped him for his entire career. The crowd was insane with the tension. Larsen fed Furillo another slider, low and away, resulting in a lazy fly to Bauer in right. One down, two to go. The great Campanella, nearing the end of his effectiveness, was gone in two pitches: a liner foul and a weak ground ball to Martin. The pitcher's spot was next and of course Maglie would not bat. No 27th at-bat fighting against any perfect game had been as important as this one—the fifth game of a World Series, a close game in a Series tied at two. Dale Mitchell was sent up, an Oklahoma boy who had played most of his career with Cleveland. A good hitter, he would retire with more than 1,200 career hits and a batting average of .312.

It was a little after three o'clock when Mitchell stepped in. A left-handed hitter who batted out of a slight crouch, he took the first pitch for ball. Larsen then nicked the corner to even the count. Larsen then threw a low, hard slider, out of the strike zone, but Mitchell waved at it for strike two. An outside fastball was flicked back foul by Mitchell, who was wisely guarding the plate. Wisely, because Larsen has said he could see ump Pinelli rocking to throw his right hand up for strike three. Larsen took a moment to compose himself, then prepared for another try to bring this unprecedented adventure to a close. Larsen threw a fastball, pitch number 97. Mitchell checked his swing, the ball looked high. Yogi

Berra and 65,000 people in the stands and millions more watching on TV thought otherwise—even the radio listeners thought it was at the letters. And Babe Pinelli agreed. Bill Coram, doing the quick wrap-up on Mutual radio, said the unsayable with great eloquence: "Tremendous, superb, gorgeous, wonderful, magical. Perfect. You supply the adjectives. . . ."

Famously, little Yogi Berra, at five feet eight inches, leaped into the lap of the huge Larsen. In the sharp autumn shadows, the achievement of perfection was framed: the perfect-game pitcher and the perfect-game catcher ("I shook him off a couple of times, but that was just to confuse the Dodger batters," Larsen said later).

But the brilliant, thrilling Series wasn't over yet. The Yanks had done what they could—won the three middle games at home—to turn a 2–0 game deficit into a 3–2 lead. But this Series would end in Brooklyn, one way or another. The next day, it was the Yankees getting on the team bus in the Bronx, driving into Manhattan to pick up brass, a few writers, and Mantle and Martin at the Yankee offices in the Squibb Building on Fifth Avenue, and then over the Brooklyn Bridge to Ebbets Field.

Brooklyn didn't quit. Because there was no off-day, Stengel couldn't go back to his ace, Whitey Ford. He named Bob Turley to start, keeping up his surprising pitching selections. Alston surprised a few himself by naming reliever Clem Labine as his starter for the do-or-die (for Brooklyn) Game Six. Both men turned in spectacular performances in an incredible pitchers' duel that was scoreless after nine. Each pitcher was allowed to bat for himself in the 10th; neither Stengel nor Alston was willing to blink as long as Turley and Labine weren't. But a one-out walk to Junior Gilliam and a sac bunt by Reese put Brooklyn in a position to win the game and tie the Series. Stengel wanted nothing to do with Duke Snider, who was walked intentionally, bringing up Robinson. Robinson hit a line drive right at Enos Slaughter, but the 40-year-old took a step or two in and the ball sailed over his head. The game was over.

Mantle says that Billy Martin was so ticked off by Slaughter's flub, and by Joe Collins's desultory play at first, that he went right to Stengel after the dispiriting loss and suggested two changes: Moose Skowron to first, Elston Howard to left. "Give them a shot," he told Casey. "They're young and hungry. You won't be sorry."

Stengel did shake up the lineup for Game Seven, getting Collins out, putting Skowron in, moving Martin to bat second, and playing Howard in left rather than Slaughter. Whether it was Martin's idea or Stengel's or both, it was counter to logic. Big right-hander Don Newcombe was pitching, Howard and Skowron batted right, replacing left-handed hitters. But that was Casey.

Skowron had played a lot during the regular season, but took an o-for-4 collar against Maglie in Game One and hadn't played since. Howard had yet to get into a game. Stengel again chose to keep Ford out of Ebbets Field and named 23-year-old Johnny Kucks to pitch. He would go to Whitey if he had to. He didn't. Yogi hit two-run homers in the first and third innings, Howard ripped one over the scoreboard in right-center in the fourth, chasing Newcombe, and Skowron hit a grand slam off Roger Craig in the seventh. Kucks was sharp, going all the way on a three-hit shutout, as the Yanks won the game, and the Series, 9–0. Jackie Robinson struck out to end the game. It was Robinson's last at-bat, and it was the last postseason game in Brooklyn, ever: The team would finish in third place in 1957, 11 games behind Milwaukee, and attendance would drop another 200,000.

Walter O'Malley, who had wrested control of the Dodgers from Branch Rickey, was anxious to make changes. He envisioned pay TV ("coin-box" TV, he called it) to help finance a domed stadium in Brooklyn. He wanted to float a bond backed by the Dodgers. He wanted air rights over the Long Island Railroad station, over which he would build his stadium, with the tracks below delivering his fans from the suburbs. He was more visionary than he's been given credit for. Commissioner of Parks Robert Moses nixed the idea; he offered the Brooklyn ball club a site in Flushing, Queens, and that was that. Beaten in New York by tradition and power, O'Malley convinced Horace Stoneham that new ideas flourished better in the West. After the 1957 season, the Giants and the Dodgers left New York to the Yankees. They took with them a marvelous Willie Mays, an undiscovered Sandy Koufax, Vin Scully, Russ Hodges, an admirable past, and the future of baseball.

As for Larsen, he's a man who kept landing on his feet. Despite having the morning-after headlines describe both his perfect game and his estranged wife's court action requesting part of his World Series share in lieu of delinquent child-support payments, he carried on. He sent Vivian Larsen $420 that very night, perhaps anticipating a bonus from the Yankees for pitching such a historic game (it never came). But Larsen would appear in two more World Series; he would get divorced and meet the woman who would become his second wife, Corinne. He would be traded to KC, where Corinne had many friends. He would get some revenge on his former team by beating them at Yankee Stadium in the 1962 Series, when he pitched for the San Francisco Giants. A man of few regrets and famous good cheer, Larsen would even be lucky enough to be seated in the press box at Yankee Stadium in 1999 on Yogi Berra Day and see the century's last perfect game.

CHAPTER FIVE

The Senator

Jim Bunning
June 21, 1964

PAY TV WAS WALTER O'Malley's idea, and then it was Horace
Stoneham's idea, but first it was the idea of Matthew Fox, president
of a company called Skiatron.

Matt Fox lived in a Park Avenue penthouse and had had a string of
pretty remarkable successes. Born and raised in Racine, Wisconsin, Fox
rose from an usher and doorman in a theater to become the "wonder
boy" of the motion picture industry, making it to vice president of Universal Pictures by the age of 25. When World War II broke out, he at first
took civilian charge of the national scrap metal collection program, and
then simply enlisted. Entering as a private, he emerged at war's end a
major. He also came away with extensive business connections in

Indonesia and parlayed those into very serious wealth. *The New York Times* called him the "economic godfather" of the region.

At five feet eight inches tall, and 200 pounds, Mathew Fox, Esq., living in Los Angeles, was considered quite the desirable catch at the time. He married Miss America, 1951, and then moved to New York. Always a baseball fan, he saw the possibilities for the game and the new, onrushing commercial medium—television—and he bought Skiatron, still a young company. Although a Giants fan, Fox sought out Dodgers owner Walter O'Malley, a fellow world-class businessman. "Don't give it away," he told O'Malley. Fox had a plan for laying coaxial cable to households and bars and then providing a "gadget" installation that would provide baseball programming, for a fee, on a game-by-game basis. IBM punch cards would be used for billing and descrambling.

Free TV, thought Fox, was killing baseball. He wasn't alone in this. Editorialists fulminated about it; owners wrung their hands; *The Sporting News* kept its eye on television, looking for signs of the game's future but fearing it would find its end. Fox made the point to O'Malley that the Braves, who had drawn more than two million fans a year every year since moving to Milwaukee from Boston, broadcast no home games on television. The president of ABC Television, Thomas Moore, had already warned Major League Baseball of "overexposure." Playing on weekends only, and diminishing the season to 60 games, would "put the game on a much sounder financial basis," he said. Moore was explaining why his network was not interested in a proposal by Detroit owner John Fetzer that had the majors offering a TV package of Monday night games. As far as Moore was concerned, CBS and NBC, which each broadcast a national game on the weekend, had the good stuff locked up. Many teams had their games on local television but there seemed to be no money in it. In any event, the real sports jewel for television was not local but national, as in National Football League: CBS had just bid $28.2 million for the rights to broadcast the games.

O'Malley didn't need to hear this. He knew his team was overexposed. He was making money, sure enough. In fact, in figures presented to the House Subcommittee on Sports Monopolies, chaired by New York Democrat Emanuel Celler, the Dodgers, from 1952 to 1956, were shown to have made more than 40 percent of all profits taken in the National League. But O'Malley wanted more. And TV was standing in the way.

"One night," he told Celler in his testimony in Washington, "we had

15,700 people in Ebbets Field and I asked a radio-wise man who was with me to try and get me some idea how many TV sets were tuned in on the particular game. After some phone calling, he came back and said: 'Walter, there are about 2,400,000 sets watching this game.' That made me a convert right away."

With three brand-new Buicks as prizes for randomly selected participants, O'Malley distributed a questionnaire to Ebbets Field patrons, asking if they would object to paying a "reasonable" fee to watch games at home. Fifty-two percent said they would not object. Not a ringing endorsement, but good enough for O'Malley. He started talks with Fox about Skiatron.

No one knew for sure what O'Malley would do. The Celler committee, it seemed, was determined to withdraw baseball's antitrust exemption, but it all really looked more like an attempt to get O'Malley to say what his intentions were with respect to his Dodgers: Was he taking them to Los Angeles? Abe Stark, president of the New York City Council (and the clothier with the famous "Hit sign and win suit" ad in right field of Ebbets Field), was allowed to testify. He rolled out the emotionally sound but otherwise dubious claim that "a franchise morally belongs to the people of a community" and "is not the personal property of any individual."

O'Malley finally felt compelled to update the committee members, not to mention Celler and Stark, both Brooklynites, about their "community," as he saw it. "Look what's happening. We've lost our last newspaper [the *Brooklyn Eagle*]. We're losing our department stores and there hasn't been a hotel or theater built there since 1929." What O'Malley left unsaid was said by others: "The white families were moving out of Brooklyn," one man told Peter Golenbock in his *Bums: An Oral History of the Brooklyn Dodgers.* "And they were the backbone of Ebbets Field."

Even when pressed about his intentions about possibly relocating the club, the clever O'Malley would not show his hand. "I'm just crazy enough to stay," he teased. When confronted with a magazine article in which he said he had no interest whatsoever in staying in Brooklyn, he responded that "half the lies they tell about the Irish aren't true." The committee members had a good laugh at that one. O'Malley, large, well dressed, bespectacled, with hair slicked straight back, puffed on his cigar and laughed, too.

Giants owner Horace Stoneham was also called to the table to testify. In possession of none of O'Malley's smooth moves or nice suits, the graceless Stoneham resorted to the blunt truth. "Our current location is such that it is impossible for us to operate profitably," he said of the Polo Grounds, located at 155th Street and Eighth Avenue in northern Manhattan, along the Harlem River. Stoneham cited everything he could think of: lack of parking, lack of suitable public transportation; the missing $100,000 a year he used to get from the New York football Giants, who had moved to Yankee Stadium the year before; he even mentioned Yonkers Raceway as drawing away attendance. "If only they could bet on nine innings rather than nine races," he lamented, as half-seriously as a serious gambler might. He didn't mention the changing demographics of the Washington Heights section of upper Manhattan, not unlike what was happening in Brooklyn. San Francisco mayor George Christopher had $10 million available for a new stadium, he said. Three other teams were also interested in the Bay Area. Stoneham felt he had to move. The Giants were all but gone. By August 18, 1957, it would be official.

Stoneham also admitted his interest in Skiatron, telling the committee that he had 1,000 shares, and that O'Malley had shares, too. He was glum, however, over a recent report that wiring New York had enormous hurdles and that wiring the West Coast might cost $60 million. Still, Stoneham had done the same math as O'Malley with the same optimistic projections. They dreamed of hundreds of thousands of dollars in pay TV revenues—*for every game.*

One of the Celler committee members thought to ask Stoneham if ballplayers would participate in the pay TV bonanza, if it ever came to pass.

"No, sir," said Stoneham.

THE CELLER COMMITTEE hearings adjourned in the summer of 1957 for the All-Star break. A phenomenal young Detroit pitcher named Jim Bunning started that game for the American League. He was 10-2 at the break, with an ERA of 2.08. In the All-Star Game, he pitched three perfect innings and got Willie Mays swinging. "That first guy had the most," said Mays afterward. When the hearings reconvened, committee members felt the heat of Bob Feller, now retired, but blazing with disdain for baseball's owners—for their claiming credit for starting the player pension plan and their refusal to grant fundamental freedoms to their employees. Feller, who had become the first head of the Players Association when it was founded in 1954, added that Commissioner Ford Frick was in the owners' pocket.

Congress—and America—were not ready for such radicalism from ballplayers. Although unions were firmly established throughout the land, the Cold War and Red-baiting and Joseph McCarthy were fresh in everyone's mind. Feller was politely dismissed from the committee, but got the third degree by Mike Wallace, then a quiz-show host. "Why is a man who has collected approximately a million dollars from baseball so bitterly critical of some of its policies?" he asked Feller, who enlisted in the Navy the day after Pearl Harbor and spent three and a half prime years serving his country. Feller replied: "It's not the money, it's the principle." Incredulous, Wallace pressed for ulterior motives. "Do you want to one day be the players' commissioner?" Feller just shook his head.

Seven years later, things had changed. Ironically, congressional inaction might have had something to do with it. The Celler hearings never moved a scrap of legislation out of committee regarding baseball's antitrust status. When O'Malley struck his deal with the city of Los Angeles and broke all those Brooklyn hearts, following Stoneham's lead-footed departure to San Francisco, the city of New York didn't sit still. Mayor Robert Wagner appointed lawyer Bill Shea to head a committee to return National League baseball to New York. Shea enlisted 77-year-old and no-friend-of-O'Malley Branch Rickey to lead the way. Rickey announced intentions to start a third league, the Continental League, with teams in Minneapolis, Houston, Denver, Toronto, Buffalo, Dallas, and, yes, New York. Worried, Major League Baseball agreed to expand and invited representatives from the Continental League to figure out how. That killed the Continental League, but the threat had done its work. In 1961, the American League added a team in Los Angeles (the Angels) and put a new club in the nation's capital and called them the Senators, while allowing the old Senators, an original American League club, to relocate to Minnesota as the Twins. The National League agreed to add two teams as well: the Colt .45s in Houston and the Mets in New York, playing in the old Polo Grounds.

Meanwhile, although pay TV was not yet realized, broadcast television revenues tripled between 1956 and 1960, and tripled again by 1964. Back in 1947, when the first World Series game was broadcast, 3.9 million viewers, mostly in bars, checked in. When Sandy Koufax completed the sweep of the Yankees in Game Four of the 1963 Series, 57 million people, mostly at home, checked in. Players, however, were getting very little of this revenue windfall, as Stoneham had predicted, and slowly they were becoming radicalized. Ralph Kiner, Robin Roberts, Bob Friend, and Jim Bunning were instrumental as vocal player representatives in seeing the need for at least a part-time executive director for their association. Up till then, except for the pension issues, their grievances centered on workplace concerns like poor lighting at night games, dugout odor, and "more toilet facilities in Cincinnati." The players would learn to ask for more.

Increasingly, club owners at contract time were finding themselves talking across the table to a different kind of ballplayer. Although owners still refused to deal with any agent or lawyer representing a player, it was getting harder to outfox or intimidate the new breed of ballplayer, who, like Allie Reynolds or Robin Roberts or Hank Greenberg, had attended college. Jim Bunning was this new kind of ballplayer.

JAMES PAUL DAVID Bunning was born October 23, 1931, in the heart of the Depression in Southgate, Kentucky, the second of three sons of an executive in a stepladder manufacturing company. The family moved to Fort Thomas, a residential town about 10 minutes from downtown Cincinnati, when Jim was in grade school. He attended St. Xavier, a Jesuit high school, where he excelled at basketball and baseball. His father initially refused to allow Jim to sign a major league contract and insisted he take a basketball scholarship to Xavier University. By the time Bunning graduated in 1953, he had married his high-school sweetheart, Mary Theis, received a degree in business administration, and signed a no-bonus contract with the Detroit Tigers.

Bunning, a six-foot-three-inch, 195-pound right-hander, had a wild delivery, coming from the side in a style more reminiscent of the turn of the century, when Cy Young, Walter Johnson, and Addie Joss turned their backs from the plate in their delivery and then whipped the pitch round. Bunning had a peculiar finish to the process, ending up almost pole vaulting over his stiff landing leg and then nearly tumbling headlong as he tried to catch his balance with a sweep of his glove hand. He would be peering sidewise beneath the bill of his cap as the pitch reached the plate.

Bunning needed some seasoning, which he got in exotic locales like Richmond and Davenport and Little Rock, learning to control his hard fastball. He got his "cup of coffee" in Detroit in 1955 and didn't do much with it, winning three games and losing five. But he spent the winter in Cuba and picked up a good breaking ball. He was much more effective in his second callup, '56, going 5-1. That was the year the Briggs family sold the Tigers to a syndicate led by radio pioneer John Fetzer. In 1957, Bunning was the best pitcher in the American League, getting the All-Star Game start, leading the league in wins (with 20) and posting an ERA of 2.69.

Unfortunately for Bunning, the Tigers were a picture of mediocrity during his early years, posting second-division finishes every year from 1955 through 1960 under a succession of managers—Bucky Harris, Jack Tighe, Jimmy Dykes. Bunning continued to excel, winning 17 games twice and never missing a start. The Tigers came closest in 1961 under manager Bob Scheffing, but fell off the pace late as the country watched Mantle and Maris duel toward Babe Ruth's season home-run record. The Tigers won 101 games but still finished eight games back of the Yankees. Still, the fans and Fetzer had high hopes that their team had arrived. Despite Bunning's winning 19 the next year, however, and hard hitting by Rocky Colavito, Norm Cash, and the great Al Kaline, the Tigers dropped back to fourth place in '62. A slow start in '63 got Scheffing fired, and former Brooklyn Dodger manager Charlie Dressen took over in June.

The team improved a little, but nonetheless managed only a fifth-place tie with Cleveland. Attendance had fallen to half of what it was when the Tigers finished second to the Yankees two years earlier. Still, there was much talent in the Tiger ranks, thanks in part to the efforts of GM Jim Campbell. They had two promising rookies worked into the starting rotation, Mickey Lolich and 19-year-old Denny McLain. A 20-year-old slugger named Willie Horton reminded Dressen of a young Campanella with his low-riding, compact power; the catcher was 21-year-old Bill Freehan; Dick McAuliffe, at 23, played short; Al Kaline was still only 28. Norm Cash played first; Gates Brown and Don Wert were under 25 and very talented. Bunning, at 32, found himself in the bullpen at season's end. Sensing that the time was now, Campbell made an off-season trade, dealing Rocky Colavito to Kansas City for solid second baseman Jerry Lumpe.

Bunning hadn't had a great year, finishing 12-13. And he didn't get along with Dressen, although he hadn't gotten along that well with Harris or Dykes or Tighe or Scheffing before him. High-strung, voluble, and opinionated, Bunning didn't mind being a pain in the ass; he was quick to voice a disagreement. On the field, he had a reputation for throwing at hitters. Off the field, he was just as aggressive and uncompromising. If he didn't care for the way the players were generally treated, he spoke up. Seeing team executives' wives on the team plane while players' wives were excluded, he told management in no uncertain terms that his wife would be sitting next to him on the next flight out. In 1960, he became an official voice for player concerns, being named Tiger player representative.

At his first meeting with the other team reps, this businessman's son with the sharp tongue and a business degree was elected pension representative for the American League, opposite the Phillies' Richie Ashburn, the N.L. rep. By the end of the disappointing 1963 season, the Detroit newspapers began to call Bunning a "brief-case ball player." When Joe Falls, a prominent sports columnist for the *Detroit Free Press*, suggested that Bunning "might have done better last year if he had concentrated on only one job instead of two," the writing was more than in the morning paper; it was on the wall. Or as *The Sporting News* put it, Bunning "did not improve his personal image with the front office in his role as player representative." So Campbell made yet another off-season deal. On December 4, 1963, nine-year veteran Bunning was traded to Philadelphia, along with catcher Gus Triandos, for hard-hitting Don Demeter and reliever Jack Hamilton.

JUNE 21, 1964, was a hot, muggy Sunday in New York. The newspapers were filled with the news that a young senator Ted Kennedy, along with Indiana senator Birch Bayh and his wife, had gone down in a small plane in an apple orchard in Western Massachusetts the previous Friday night. Kennedy's back was broken, the pilot was killed. In Vietnam, General Paul Harkins was stepping down as U.S. commander, to be replaced by Lieutenant General William C. Westmoreland, with the promise of a change in policy. On Sunday morning, a sports story also made the front pages: Golfer Ken Venturi, playing two rounds in 95-degree heat in Washington, D.C., had fought off fainting spells and a case of the shivers to win the U.S. Open. June 21 was the first day of summer, the longest day of the year, and Father's Day to boot. It would prove to be a very long day for the New York Mets, and a memorable day for Jim Bunning, father of seven.

The Phillies were coming off their finest season in a decade. They had finished one game out of third place in 1963; only the Dodgers, who won it all that year, had a better record from late June on. Dodger pitcher Johnny Podres said of the Phillies: "They are no longer a coming club. They've arrived."

The acquisition of Bunning had only strengthened the team, as had the hitting of rookie third baseman Richie Allen. In June, the Phillies, managed by Gene Mauch, were in first place. Oklahoman John Wesley

Callison, acquired from the White Sox, was turning into a star in right field; steady Tony Taylor was at second; good-hitting Cookie Rojas played short; and Wes Covington, who had been an integral part of the Braves' championship teams in '57 and '58, was a good bat patrolling a little dangerously in left field. In center was Tony Gonzalez, giving the team three Cubans in the starting lineup (along with Taylor and Rojas). The Phillies, one of the last teams in the National League to integrate, were fully there by 1964. Bunning and lefty Chris Short anchored the rotation, which thinned out somewhat thereafter—with Dallas Green, Art Mahaffey, and Dennis Bennett. Screwballer Jack Baldschun served as the closer.

Bunning was 6-2 going into the game. It was his second time through the National League schedule after spending his entire career in the American League. But he would take the mound with a couple of other advantages. Major League Baseball, stunned by Roger Maris's toppling of the great Ruth home-run record in 1961, instituted some changes that took effect in 1963. They raised the height of the mound 50 percent, to 15 inches, and they lengthened the strike zone to where it was in 1887—top of the shoulder to bottom of the knee. "I would even like to see the spitball come back," said Commissioner Ford Frick. "Take a look at the batting, home-run, and slugging records for recent seasons and you become convinced that the pitchers need help urgently." As a result, overall ERA in the N.L. in 1963 dropped to 3.29, the lowest since 1920, the year the spitball was outlawed.

The timing of this significant rule change proved disastrous, and it had to be reversed five years later, after the 1968 season, when ERAs in both leagues dropped below 3.00 for the first time since 1918 and only one player in the American League batted over .300. Pitchers got help, for sure, not the least of it, coming via baseball's first expansion.

The American League added two teams in 1961, and the National League followed suit in 1962. That's 100 more players on major league rosters who wouldn't perhaps have made the cut in 1960. A few of that sort were facing Jim Bunning and the high-flying Phillies.

On that Mets team, in its third year but first in the brand-new ballpark named after lawyer Bill Shea, there were maybe four legitimate major leaguers—Jim Hickman, Ron Hunt, George Altman, and Frank Thomas—and no stars. Hickman had one great year in his 13-year career, and this wasn't it. Hunt was a below-average second baseman, but he had a good eye and he crowded the plate, so he was always a danger to get on base one way or the other—slap single, walk, or HBP. Altman, who had twice been an All-Star with the Cubs, still knew how to hit, but at the age of 31, he was on the downside. Same with Frank Thomas. In his 14th year in the bigs, Thomas's best year—34 home runs for the Mets in their inaugural season—seemed long ago. Today, he is best remembered for not knowing what "Yo lo tengo" meant, mowing down then-center-fielder Richie Ashburn, who had hollered the Spanish phrase to call off no-English shortstop Elio Chacon on a short fly. No-Spanish Thomas, all six feet three inches, 210 pounds of him, thundered in from left field, flattening Ashburn. With the Mets playing their second doubleheader in three days in the heavy heat, neither Thomas nor Altman was in the starting lineup. Ashburn was safe in the Phillies broadcast booth, calling the game for WFIL in Philadelphia.

The Phillies had swept the Mets in a Friday night doubleheader to open the series, making it eight straight losses for Casey Stengel's Amazin's. But on Saturday, the Mets pounded out 16 hits against Bennett, Baldschun, former Dodger Ed Roebuck and future Philly (and Met) manager Dallas Green, exposing a weakness in the Philly pitching that would come back to bite them in September, and that haunts the Philly faithful to this day.

It was to be another doubleheader on Sunday, Bunning versus Tracy Stallard in the opener, with more than 32,000 rabid Mets fans, dubbed by prickly New York *Daily News* columnist Dick Young as "the new breed." They loved their losing Mets, who were headed for their third-straight last-place finish. Bunning was coming off his only bad outing of the year, an early shelling courtesy of the Cubs. He was looking to get quickly back on track. He had faced the Mets once before, beating them 4–1 in Philadelphia in April, a complete-game seven-hitter in which he struck out 11. Three weeks earlier, in late May, Bunning had near-total mastery over another expansion group, the Colt .45s, pitching perfect ball into the seventh. Manager Gene Mauch, perhaps remembering how a young Bunning had mowed down National Leaguers in the 1957 All-Star Game, kept him under wraps during spring training, at least as far as showing him to N.L.ers. "If you can hold out a pitcher until the season starts," he said, "it might give him a slight edge." Bunning also had his wife and daughter in attendance, dressed in matching madras dresses; they had driven up from Philadelphia in the morning to honor husband and father. Bunning had everything going for him.

The game began in 91-degree heat with clear skies and no wind. The fleet-footed John Briggs was playing center field for the Phils in place of Tony Gonzalez, who was getting a rest. Briggs was batting leadoff. With Briggs hitting a scorching .358, Met pitcher Tracy Stallard pitched him carefully to start, and walked him on a 3-2 pitch as the Met crowd continued to file in. John Herrnstein, playing first base, executed a perfect sacrifice, as Gene Mauch, with his ace pitching, went for the early lead. Callison, hitting an even .300, missed a Stallard sinker for strike three. But the rookie phenom Richie Allen, hitting .294 and batting cleanup, rifled a single to left, scoring Briggs, giving Bunning a 1–0 lead.

For the Mets, Jim Hickman was leading off and playing center. Casey Stengel was trying anything he could to generate some offense. In this case, he put his best two hitters, Hickman and Hunt, at the top of the order. Hickman was really more of a power hitter, but he was nothing more than a .250 hitter overall; he would have his one great year (32/115/.315) batting cleanup (between Williams and Santo) for the Chicago Cubs in 1970. In this, his third year, he was hitting .239. He came out swinging against Bunning, whose first two pitches were hanging curveballs. Hickman ticked them both foul. "Then he laughed at me," Hickman would later say. Pitch number three broke sharply with deadly purpose over the outside corner and Hickman was out looking. Triandos, Bunning, and radio voice Richie Ashburn would later mention those two opening pitches to Hickman as the most serious mistakes the pitcher made all day. Second-baseman Ron Hunt followed. Bunning later named Hunt as one of his toughest outs because of his compact swing and good eye and penchant for getting hit by the pitch. He started him out with a fastball on the corner. Hunt, hitting .333 and bound for the All-Star Game, took it for a strike before grounding the next pitch to second-baseman Tony Taylor for the out. Big Ed Kranepool, a tall, left-handed, native New Yorker who had debuted with the Mets at age 17 two years earlier, was pitched aggressively by the veteran Bunning: chin music for a ball, fastball down the middle for a called strike, then slider away. He popped up to shortstop Cookie Rojas for the third out. A tidy, eight-pitch inning for Bunning on a hot day.

By the top of the second, Met pitcher Stallard had already changed his shirt. Facing Tony Taylor, the excellent Philly second baseman, Stallard made his own day harder by walking him on a 3-2 pitch. Following the form of inning one, Mauch ordered up a sacrifice from Rojas, who was hitting a gaudy .354 (he would finish the year at .291). Rojas did his job, and Taylor moved to second. Gus Triandos, the big catcher, who in

1955 was traded by the Yankees to Baltimore in the Don Larsen deal, and who came over from the Tigers in the Bunning deal, ripped a double to left that Bob "Hawk" Taylor had trouble corralling. Tony Taylor scored to make it 2–0. Bunning, a good hitter for a pitcher, lined out to short and Johnny Briggs popped to Kranepool at first to retire the side.

Joe Christopher, the Met right fielder, was batting cleanup. The Virgin Islands native had come up with Pittsburgh and had played sparingly, before landing with the Mets in the expansion draft, where he played considerably more. Nineteen sixty-four would be his best year as a pro— he would finish with 16 home runs and a .300 average. And he was hot, having nailed two homers the night before in the Mets' 7–3 win. He was seeing the ball well, and Bunning needed to mix pitches and not rely on just the breaking stuff. He got a fastball in for a strike. Christopher laid off a curveball high—not a good place for a curveball. Christopher chopped the next one foul before hitting a long drive to center that Briggs ranged back on and grabbed for the out. Next up was Mets catcher Jesse Gonder, a decent enough hitter but a master of the passed ball. Gonder, like Hickman leading off the game, may have gotten some pitches he thought were very hittable, given his reactions. A left-handed hitter, Gonder popped a foul out of play, chopped another foul, and then fouled out to Triandos. Richie Ashburn, calling the game with Jim Gordon on WFIL, remarked that Gonder seemed "a little burned up at himself." Hawk Taylor stepped in next. He was just an awful ballplayer coming off the best day (two homers) he would ever have as a professional; in his 11-year career, which would end in 1970, he would hit only 16 home runs. We should forgive him the cockiness he would show throughout the day. Bunning, leery of something, went 2–0 on the Hawk, who, with his average now up to .250, decided to take a cut at the incoming fastball, which he drove the opposite way to Johnny Callison for the third out.

The Phillies went easily in their half of the third, although the Mets were clearly pitching Allen carefully—with one on and two out, Stallard walked him on four pitches, then induced Wes Covington to fly out to Christopher. For the Met half, it was the bottom of the order up against Bunning, whose jersey was gray with sweat. He started Charley Smith, the Mets' third baseman, with a fastball for a strike; Smith fouled off the next fastball and breaking pitch and then swung for strike three at a ball low and away. Amado Samuel was batting eighth, and the only Met fans who recognize that name are probably from the broadcast booth and confined to two: Bob Murphy and Ralph Kiner. Just 23 years old and from the great shortstop town of San Pedro de Macoris, Dominican Republic, "Sammy" Samuel is not one of the people the town is known for; this would be his last year in major league baseball. Like Hawk Taylor, he had his career day the day before, with three hits—his average was up to .178. After taking a fastball for a strike, he stroked a sinking liner that Rojas grabbed for the out. An almost hit. Stallard, the pitcher, followed—"hitting .219, with seven hits on the season, hitting better than some of the Met regulars," Richie Ashburn reported to his listeners. And Stallard did make contact, a long drive to left, always an adventure with Covington out there, but he made the grab near the foul line. Nine up, nine down.

Twenty-six pitches for Bunning for those nine outs. He'd keep this up pretty much all day.

The Phillies came up empty in their half of the fourth. The red-hot Rojas picked up another hit, a single, but with the number-eight hitter, Triandos, up and Bunning to follow, Mauch had him run, and Jesse Gonder uncharacteristically caught Cookie, who probably wondered why he was on the move. In his 16 years, he'd only manage 74 stolen bases. Triandos grounded out. Bunning would lead off the fifth.

In the Mets fourth it was the top of the order again, starting with Hickman, who was no doubt looking for those fat pitches he saw his first time up. Instead, he got a sharp fastball for a strike, followed by a ball just missing. And then Hickman swung and missed at two sliders and went back to the bench. Hunt, who had bounced to second his first time up, got ahead in the count 2-0. Hunt, always aggressive, swung through Bunning's 2-0 fastball; the next pitch, he hit down the right-field line. "Fair or foul?" asked Jim Gordon on WFIL (he had replaced Richie Ashburn in the fourth inning, in the style of old, where broadcast partners would alternate three-inning stints). "Foul!" he got to cry, evening the count at 2-2. Bunning told his biographer, Frank Dolson, that, as the game progressed, Hunt was his "biggest fear" because he thought the scrappy Met might "stick an elbow in front of a pitch" just to get on base. Bunning recalled that he pitched him away all day so that Hunt "would've had to run across the plate to get hit." But Bunning either made a mistake on the 2-2 pitch or misremembered his strategy, because he backed Hunt off the plate with an inside curveball, throwing it with a nasty, exaggerated sidearm motion. The count was full for the first time all day. Hunt, looking perhaps for the Bunning slider on the outside corner, now that he'd been brushed back a bit, could only flail at a letter-high fastball in the middle of the plate for strike three. Kranepool was next, and took a fastball high for a ball, missed another one, and then popped to the catcher. Kranepool didn't run, the ball was fair, and Triandos caught it for the out.

The Phillies, with their 9-1-2 hitters up, went quietly on three ground balls in the fifth, and Bunning went back to work in the steaming heat. Cleanup hitter Joe Christopher led off. He'd hit the ball well his first time up, rapping a drive to center that Briggs hauled in. Bunning started him off with a fastball for a strike. It was apparent now that not only was Bunning throwing hard, but he had fantastic control; he was finding a machinelike rhythm. He dropped down for a sidearm curve, and Christopher took the nasty pitch for a strike, which he didn't like, and he let ump Ed Sudol know about it. Bunning came in with a fastball, high, and then another, which Christopher popped up to the infield. Rojas pocketed it behind the pitcher's mound. Bunning paced about the mound as the ball went around the horn. Gonder was next and Bunning drilled a fastball in for a strike. Then, the Bunning-Stallard game on the first day of summer, 1964, almost became like all but 14 of the 156,000 games played since 1903—imperfect. This is Jim Gordon's fifth inning call: "There's a . . . stopped by Taylor! Throw. He's out! Gonder made a bid for a hit and little Tony Taylor went all out, got that glove on the ball, knocked it down as he made a dive to his left and throws him out. What a play by Tony. Bunning looks out there and says thank you."

Gonder had hit perhaps the last Bunning mistake of the game. "A straight change, right down the middle," Bunning would say later. "I thought it was a hit." When Hawk Taylor tapped weakly to Richie Allen at third, making it 15 in a row for Bunning, that sense of being more than halfway to something remarkable began to dawn on participants and witnesses alike.

The Phillies came out blazing and put the game away. Callison homered over the 371-foot sign in right field. After Richie Allen went down swinging—which he would do a lot of in his next 15 years, currently ranking 19th on the all-time list in strikeouts—Wes Covington worked out a walk, and Mauch pinch-ran for him with utility man Bobby Wine. Stallard suddenly looked spent. Tony Taylor singled to center, Rojas flied to Christopher in right, and Triandos lined a two-out single to left, scoring Wine and making it 4–0. Bunning stepped to the plate with the Met bullpen warming but not ready. He doubled to left-center, the ball glancing off Hickman's glove as left-fielder Hawk Taylor was a latecomer to the action; two runs scored, and that was how it would end, 6–0. Bill Wakefield of Kansas City, in his only year in the majors, came

on in relief and got the only out he had to get, Briggs flying to left. Stallard, who three years earlier gained some degree of infamy by giving up
Roger Maris's 61st home run over in the Bronx, trudged to the cool of the
clubhouse.

Bunning, meanwhile, strode back to the mound, aware that history
was his to make. It was after Taylor's play in the fifth, Bunning has said,
that he began to think he "might have something special going. I became
aware of what we were doing." Seeing that Mauch, in pinch-running
Bobby Wine for Covington, had now, in the bottom of the inning, kept
Wine in the game, at short, and moved Rojas to left, getting the unsteady
Covington out of there, must have given Bunning the sense that Mauch
could feel what was possible as well. Only three weeks earlier, in Houston, Covington had misplayed a fly ball into a double, ruining a Bunning
perfect-game bid in the seventh inning. Mauch later said he wanted to do
all he could to help Bunning, who was busy moving his fielders around as
the game progressed, waving Taylor into the hole, moving Allen in at
third, knowing just how he was going to pitch these Mets. Bunning
became animated, energized, "jabbering like a magpie," Triandos
recalled. And he was becoming even more relentlessly efficient. Having
thrown 47 pitches, 10 of them balls, through five innings, he spun
through the bottom of the Mets order in only seven pitches in the sixth: a
fly ball to center by Charley Smith, a pop-out to the shortstop from
Sammy Samuel, and pinch-hitter Rod Kanehl's slow roller to Wine. Bunning was two-thirds of the way there.

Knuckleballer Tom Sturdivant took a turn for the Mets, in what
must have seemed like a comic interlude within the grander drama. The
34-year-old Kansan, once a reliable cog in the Stengel rotation with the
Yankees in '56 and '57 (and a witness to Larsen's perfect game), was in his
last campaign and it wasn't too pretty. As Richie Ashburn put it, "He's
been belted around, no won and lost record." But "Snake" Sturdivant had
his game today, and the Phillies would do no more damage against the
Mets, not that they had to. Only a single by Callison would mar his three
innings of relief. But no one cared this day about Tom Sturdivant.

As the Met fans rose for the seventh-inning stretch, the scoreboard
told the story: goose eggs for the Mets through six, no runs, no hits—and
no errors for the Phillies. At Shea, a breeze finally began to stir as Jim
Hickman stepped to the plate. Showers were predicted for later in the
day, but for the moment, all they got was a hot wind. Bunning went right

to work, striking out Hickman on three pitches. Hunt fouled a pitch back and then pulled a sharp grounder right at Allen at third, who dug it out and threw to John Herrnstein for the out. Ed Kranepool, who had popped up twice, gave a little better show of himself this time—fastball for a strike, pop foul out of play, fastball fouled back, ball just outside, another pop foul out of play—but then swung and missed for strike three, Bunning's fifth K. His control—10 out of 11 pitches in the inning for strikes—seemed unconscious.

In the Met eighth, the crowd's sympathies began to shift. Rooting for the Mets was never about winning anyway, it was about style and heart. Bunning was showing lots of both, whipping his pitches with all his might, right leg turning at a 90-degree angle as he followed through, himself falling off the too-high mound, his hat askew, and each pitch lasering where he wanted it, inning after inning. The sunshine, relentless, was unable to make Bunning wilt. The Met fans began to cheer him on.

Joe Christopher, however, was yet to convert. He took a slider for a strike to start the eighth, and barked at Sudol and pounded his bat on the plate. He'd argued with the home-plate ump earlier and wasn't having a nice day. He lunged at an outside curveball. The canny Bunning, known in the American League for coming inside on hitters, came inside on the distressed and anxious Christopher, who laid off it for a ball. But a 1-2 curveball dipped away and Christopher was out on strikes, swinging. Gonder hit the next pitch easily to Taylor, who didn't have to leave his feet to field this one, and there were two down. Hawk Taylor then stepped in. Taylor, like Christopher, didn't seem the ballplayer today he had been the day before. A two-home-run game followed by, so far, a fly out and groundout against Bunning, who seemed, indeed, to be laughing on the mound. His excitement had widened into a grin, the slash of a grin that had perhaps earned him his nickname, The Lizard. Taylor squared to bunt. Two out, down 6–0, eighth inning, perfect game going: the crowd immediately got on the audacious Taylor for such an act. Suddenly, what had simply been a rising crowd noise, urging the Mets to rally, was clearly on Bunning's side. Hawk changed his strategy and took a full swing and chopped one foul to even the count at 1-1. He missed a curveball and then took a ball way outside to even the count, 2-2. The ball went all the way to the backstop. Was Bunning getting rattled? He missed with a slider just off the plate; the crowd groaned, the count now full. Bunning rocked and wheeled and fired a fastball and Sudol punched out Taylor, strike three, on the corner. Perhaps off the corner, or low, because Gus Triandos didn't handle the ball cleanly. Taylor started to jaw with Sudol and then realized he might best be served by running to first. But Triandos threw him out. Three outs to go.

Bunning led off the top of the ninth and the Met fans gave him a standing ovation. He quickly got off the stage with a fly to right. He was more concerned with firing up his teammates to go all out for the perfect game. "I'd like to borrow Koufax's hummer for the last inning," he said to no one in particular in the dugout. "He was going up and down and telling everybody what was going on," said Callison afterward. "Everybody tried to get away from him, but he was so wired he followed us around." Bunning had no fear of jinxing himself by talking about the game in progress. "I don't believe in jinxes," he would say later.

It would be the bottom of the order and surely some pinch-hitters up for the Mets in the last of the ninth. Charley Smith was first up; he had a strikeout and a fly ball to center for his day's efforts. He popped the first pitch foul, took a fastball high for a ball from the fast-working Bunning; a foul just behind the screen gave Bunning the edge in the count, 1-2. Smith then lifted a short fly to shallow left, which Wine grabbed. George Altman, a rangy left-handed hitter, came out on deck during Smith's at-bat, to pinch-hit for Samuel. As he dug in at the plate, Triandos was summoned out to the mound by the hyperkinetic Bunning. Bunning asked his old catcher to tell him a joke, but Triandos came up empty. Bunning looked elsewhere for diversion—to the resin bag. And he glared in for the sign. Nothing but strikes to Altman—two foul balls and a swing and a miss at a curveball low and away and the Mets were down to their last out.

Stengel sent up rookie catcher, left-handed-hitting John Stephenson, hitting .074 with two hits on the season. He'd bat for Sturdivant. Bunning knew enough about a rookie hitting .074 to know that he was not hitting the major league curveball, and that's all he gave him. With the Mets fans cheering on every pitch, Bunning put up a curveball that Stephenson missed; bent another over for called strike two. Bunning was chewing gum hard, popping the ball in his mitt, and repeatedly punishing the resin bag. He missed with two curves to even the count. But curveball number five was the one: Stephenson swung and missed, and 215-pound Gus Triandos ran to his pitcher and just tapped him on the shoulder. His teammates gathered round.

COLUMNIST DICK YOUNG put the final touch on the game in the *Daily News*, and left us with a joke:

> The people roared at the final out, and as Bunning's mates ran
> onto the field, and pounded him from the infield to the dugout,
> the New Breeds stood and clapped and finally chanted: "We want
> Bunning . . . we want Bunning." After a couple of minutes he
> made his reappearance to do a TV show with Ralph Kiner near
> home plate. Bunning tipped his hat warmly to the cheering
> crowd, then tossed his cap to the ground for the interview.
>
> Kiner, just before chatting with Bunning, shook the hand of
> Ed Sudol off-camera, and congratulated him on umpiring the per-
> fect game.
>
> "I knew it was a no-hitter," Sudol said to Kiner, "but I didn't
> realize it was perfect. Do you mean I umpired a perfect game?"
>
> The old ballplayer in Kiner couldn't resist saying: "No, you
> didn't, but it was."

Indeed, it was. And it was the first National League perfect game of
the modern era, and Bunning became only the second pitcher, after Cy
Young, to throw a no-hitter in each league. Back in the clubhouse, Frank
Scott, a onetime Yankee traveling secretary and now a kind of roving
player's agent, worked the frenzied New York media on Bunning's behalf.
Bunning had asked Kiner, "how much," before agreeing to do the
postgame interview. Scott worked a $1,000 deal with Ed Sullivan's peo-
ple for Bunning to appear for 30 seconds that night. Bunning was not
alone in thinking that ballplayers were unfairly expected to give things
away. Owners never did. They certainly were giving away no television
money, not even to each other. Of the $895,000 contract with CBS for its
game of the week, the money went to the only five clubs CBS wanted to
show—Yankees, Cubs, Cards, Phillies, and Orioles. And the Yankees got
$550,000 of the total. In a few weeks' time, CBS would pull a neat trick:
They would buy the Yankees and, in a sense, pay themselves to put their
own team on national TV. Meanwhile, Bunning sold insurance and studied to become a stockbroker; Robin Roberts sold cardboard boxes in the
off-season; Yogi Berra sold suits. Overall, player salaries in 1964 were
about where they were in 1947. You pitch a perfect game, you have to
look for the payday in it.

To celebrate his perfect day and his 30-second appearance on the Ed

Sullivan show, Bunning treated his wife and daughter to a dinner at a Howard Johnson's off the New Jersey Turnpike.

AFTER WINNING THE second game of the doubleheader, 8–2, behind rookie Rick Wise, the Phillies went two games up over the Giants in a tight National League race; the Cardinals, in sixth place, were only eight games off the pace. Although disbelief in jinxes worked well for Bunning, the poor Phillies may have jinxed themselves with a shady maneuver in midsummer.

In early August, the Phillies were flying high. They were to face the Dodgers and Sandy Koufax in a Monday night game concluding a four-game set in Philadelphia. The Phillies had seen enough of Koufax, as had the rest of the National League. He was in the middle of the most dominant run a pitcher has ever had in baseball, four years of brilliant artistry and matchless courage. The Phillies had seen Koufax back in June, sort of: They struck out 11 times and sent up only the minimum 27 batters. Richie Allen walked in the fourth and was caught stealing. That was it. Near perfection, Koufax's third no-hitter in three years. So Gene Mauch got together with his general manger, John Quinn, on the morning of the game and availed himself of rule 3.10(a): "The manager of the home team shall be the sole judge as to whether a game shall be started because of unsuitable weather conditions." Mauch saw rough weather ahead, all right; a Jewish cyclone. So, in the early afternoon of a sunny day, Mauch informed the league that due to "threatening weather," the evening's game between the Phillies and Dodgers would be canceled. The Phillies offered a makeup for the Dodgers: September 8. A Jewish holiday.

The Phillies kept rolling through August, going 19-10 for the month. They started September five and a half games in front. A late-season acquisition—veteran Frank Thomas of the Mets—had given the club added spark, with Thomas hitting seven home runs in a short span. But on September 8, making up the "rainout" against the Dodgers, Thomas hit a double, rounded second a little wide, dove back, and broke his thumb. The Dodgers won 3–2, and Thomas went on the disabled list. "He carried us for two weeks," said Bunning. After his demise, the team began to swoon, and they couldn't buy a break. Willie Davis beat them in L.A. with a 16th-inning steal of home. Reds rookie Chico Ruiz stole home to beat them 1–0. With Mauch mismanaging his pitching rotation down the stretch, the Phillies lost a 6.5-game lead with only 12 to play.

Mauch had confidence only in Bunning and Short, Short and Bunning—the two started nine times in the final two weeks—and the season was a few games too long for Mauch and the Phils. The Cardinals won the pennant and went on to beat the Yankees in seven games. Bunning's old team, the Tigers, the new youthful Tigers, finished 14 games behind the Yankees, but Dressen's squad would mature into world champions in another four years, although he'd not be around to see it.

On July 17, 1964, the O'Malley-Stoneham dream was about to come true. On that evening, more than 3,000 miles and seven years beyond Brooklyn, the Dodgers would face the Chicago Cubs in a game available for viewing over a special box installation via an automatic phone dialup. Giants games were expected to be available in August. That night, it was Dodgers-Cubs on one of the three channels available to those who paid the $7.50 installation charge and agreed to the $1.00 per month fee. For another $1.50, the price of the Dodger Stadium bleacher seat, you could dial up the game; for $0.75, you could get a surfing film, *Gun Ho*, on Channel C. A Broadway dance was available on Channel A. The company delivering the programming was no longer called Skiatron, it had become Subscription Television, a more prosaic name that hewed closer to what the whole scheme was about—money, not celestial transmissions. Matt Fox, alas, was gone. He'd dropped dead of a heart attack at the age of 53 in New York, just a few weeks before Bunning's perfect game and six weeks before STV's debut on the Coast. A prominent CBS executive, Sylvester "Pat" Weaver (father to a toddler named Sigourney), was now president. The campaign to sign up subscribers in L.A. and the Bay Area had not gone well. Needing 70,000 enthusiasts to break even, STV ran into public opposition to pricing the air waves, and managed about 4,000 customers all told. A petition in favor of free TV ("This may be the last time you see the Rams on free TV!") began to circulate. Nonetheless, every one of the few thousands who watched the Dodgers beat the Cubs that night, 3–2, lauded the fine color and sharp picture delivered by the coaxial cable. The broadcast team, which consisted of two Dodger executives, received more tepid reviews—most folks opted to listen to Scully on the radio. In November, Proposition 15 was on the ballot, calling for the banning of pay TV in California, at least for the time being. The measure passed by more than a 2–1 margin with more than five million votes cast. Operation of STV would suspend the next day. Although the experiment had received extraordinary press coverage, the model wasn't right, and the technology for wiring was insufficient. It was a bold idea from Matt Fox and Walter O'Malley and Pat Weaver, ahead of its time but nonetheless dead. The money in TV was elsewhere, in free TV, national and local. Even the ballplayers were aware of that.

In 1964, Yankee shortstop Tony Kubek raised some hackles, and a warning, when he declared, "Players want a fair share of any extra money" that television promised to generate. "We are unified on this thing, though not formally. I think we are closer now to a ball player's union than we've ever been before."

Judge Robert Cannon, who at the time represented the players' interests in a part-time post, reprimanded Kubek: "Hardly the time to pose a threat," he said, not indicating when the proper time might be. The players recognized that they needed to hire a full-time executive director of their organization and fund a full-time office to keep up with the changing economics of the game. In 1965, they began the process of interviewing candidates for the job. Judge Cannon wanted it, but the players were a little suspicious of Cannon's cozy relationship to the owners.

Bunning, Robin Roberts, and Harvey Kuenn interviewed Richard Nixon in the law offices of John Mitchell in New York. Nixon took them all to lunch, invited former New York governor Thomas E. Dewey along, but managed to talk himself out of contention. A friend of Robin Roberts's recommended they talk to Marvin Miller, a union lawyer for the United Steel Workers. The interview went well, but Bunning and the others were a little leery of hiring "the union type," as Bunning put it. They offered the job to Judge Cannon, who was delighted. But then he blew it by insisting that he stay in Milwaukee, where he ran for his judgeship every six years unopposed, and his constant questioning about the kind of pension *he* would get proved irksome to some of the players. They needed a man in New York to fight for them. They withdrew the offer and turned to Miller, who grew up as a Brooklyn Dodger fan and lived in Manhattan.

The players who, like some of the owners, saw television spreading the game and generating revenue, were right on the money. Skiatron and STV didn't make it, but soon enough, national network deals would be overwhelmed by the "superstation" reach of some ostensibly "local" deals. This would change the economics of the game. As far as player participation in the rapidly growing wealth of the game is concerned, Marvin Miller arrived just in time.

With the perspective of years, Bunning is still proud of the Miller hire. "When we had Judge Cannon represent us, we argued about mounds at Yankee Stadium. We worried about whether we were going to have a split doubleheader, all kinds of little, penny-ante stuff. As soon as Marvin took over we got into the meat of the thing. We had two basic things to negotiate—a pension agreement and a basic agreement." And Miller surely did negotiate well. Bunning, who spent the last dozen years of his career as the league representative to the pension committee, now enjoys a pension of close to $50,000 a year. In the late 1960s, it was less than $722 a month for a 20-year vet. After retiring in 1971, Bunning spent five years managing in the Philadelphia minor league system before being fired at the Triple-A level. By then the father of nine children, Bunning pursued stockbrokering before running for public office in his home state of Kentucky. He is now a U.S. senator of a particularly conservative bent, especially on labor issues (he is given a 12 percent approval rating on his voting record by the AFL-CIO). In the months following the September 11 terrorist attacks on the United States, he even voted against giving firemen and police officers the right to collective bargaining in the states where it was prohibited. Although Bunning developed a fierce distrust of baseball management—"They very seldom tell the truth"—he is worried that the game is being ruined by player greed.

Two years after his election to the U.S. Senate and four years after the cancellation of the 1994 World Series, Bunning found himself in Cooperstown, elected to the Hall of Fame by the Veterans Committee after his 15 years of eligibility had run out. He chided baseball in general in his acceptance speech: "For god's sake and for the game's sake, find a rudder. Pick a course and stick with it, and get your internal problems resolved before the Congress of the United States gives up on you. The only thing worse is if the fans give up on you."

By now, "baseball" is too complex a set of competing interests to be chided into "picking a course" and sticking with it, unless there be some form of grand partnership among players, owners, and networks—a most unlikely thing. Perhaps Bunning, as a senator, is sitting just where baseball issues need to be heard and resolved. At least then there's a chance that the public's interest could also be heard. In that way, Bunning and his colleagues could make a much-needed and long-overdue contribution to America's game.

CHAPTER SIX

The Great One

Sandy Koufax
September 9, 1965

J UST NORTH OF THE intersection of Hollywood and Vine in L.A. is a landmark building called the Hollywood Palace. The ornate, theatrical showplace still plays host to movie premiers and wrap parties, the odd rock concert and the occasional politician (Clinton gave his treatise on gays in the military there in 1992), but its identity is rooted in its past. The venue opened in 1927 and was known then as the Hollywood Playhouse. Ibsen's *An Enemy of the People* opened there. In the 1930s, it changed its name to the WPA Federal Theater, and produced plays by George Bernard Shaw. Then came radio and the likes of Fanny Brice doing her *Baby Snooks* show and a young Lucille Ball with her loopy *My Favorite Husband*, both for CBS radio, which broadcast live from the theater. Burlesque took over in the 1940s and the theater took on a new name—El Capitan—before television entered the picture. As an NBC-TV facility, El Capitan housed such classics as *This Is Your Life, The Bob Hope Chesterfield Special,* and *The Colgate Comedy Hour.* But the theater got its lasting name when ABC, in 1964, began to broadcast an hour-long variety program called *Hollywood Palace* from the theater on Saturday nights at 9:30. The show, with a different host each week, featured the kind of diverse entertainments that Ed Sullivan was doing so successfully from New York on Sunday nights. But this was Hollywood.

The burgeoning television industry and abundant California sunshine were a potent combination. American entertainers came running. The Catskills were one thing. In the summer, the resorts boasted a few good rooms to play. But in California, summer weather was a year-round thing, and at least one room, the Palace, provided a national audience. Milton Berle, Jack Carter, Shecky Green, Wally Cox, Vic Damone, the McGuire sisters, Alan King, Alan Sherman, Joan Rivers, and other acts well known at Kutchsher's and Grossinger's found work on the show. And the show was a hit—funny, fast moving, and a little more California hip than Sullivan could manage. More Sonny & Cher, more Smothers Brothers, more Rowan & Martin, less Topo Gigio and the Marine Precision Marching Band.

On April 9, 1966, two guys who used to live in Brooklyn, one of whom was born there, sang a number and performed a skit with Milton Berle. After Gene Barry (that week's host) told a few jokes, and Wally Cox told a few more, and between the Mamas and the Papas and the Maguire Sisters, the nation got to see Dodgers Sandy Koufax and Don Drysdale, in top hat and tails, caterwaul their way through "We're in the Money" before offering up a few punch lines to Berle and exiting the stage. It was a gutsy performance. They had danced, these big rangy ballplayers. They had looked in the camera and sang through grins unnaturally wide. They were nervous; they talked rather than sang some of the lyrics, but their nervousness couldn't hide their glee. Not exactly light of foot, they nonetheless moved with a powerful, athletic grace. Their shoes gleamed. The crowd at the Hollywood Palace applauded their moxie. The crowd at the Palace also knew it as a local story—that Sandy and Don had put it to Walter and Buzzie. The national television audience, however, was less enthusiastic. These two great pitchers were ruining baseball. As far as the regular Joe in Toledo was concerned, these guys were rich guys sporting California tans—in April. Sandy and Don may have flopped as a song and dance team, but as a force in the game of baseball, they had just taken the first steps in a kind of partnering that would change the game forever.

THE DODGERS' O'MALLEY and his sidekick Buzzie Bavasi were notorious for their handling of players at contract time. Pee Wee Reese and Duke Snider both tell of receiving contracts in the spring with no figures written in; the idea was that they should get in shape, sign the blank contract, and then come north to Brooklyn and see what they were going to get. Relief pitcher Phil Regan recounts going to Bavasi's office, intent on asking for $40,000 after having a great year. Bavasi threw five pieces of crumpled paper across the desk and told him to choose one. Each supposedly held a different salary figure. Regan chose one and opened it up: $37,000. Bavasi then cursed his luck while sweeping the other four wads of paper into his drawer. Tommy Davis tells of a contract meeting in which he saw Maury Wills's contract on the desk. He spied the figure and reckoned he had better lower his salary request, if that's all Wills was getting. Davis found out later that Bavasi had gone to the trouble of drawing up a phony contract and planting it where Davis couldn't miss it. There was no appealing these kinds of shenanigans. With one-year deals the rule, agents and lawyers were not even allowed in the room while salaries were under discussion. Clause 10(a) of the standard contract stated that if the player and the owner couldn't agree on a salary by March 1, the owner had 10 days in which to insist that the player play the next year for last year's salary. The common understanding was that this renewable option applied in perpetuity; that is, a player had no option but to quit. He could work for no one else.

But E. J. "Buzzie" Bavasi made a mistake. He lied to two smart guys who were the best pitchers in the league, old Brooklyn Dodger teammates, and good friends. In the winter of 1965, after a world championship year for the Dodgers, Drysdale went to talk to Buzzie about money, only to have his request for a raise sternly rebuffed. He was told that Koufax—who had won 26 games to Drysdale's 23—wasn't even asking for that much. When Koufax went to talk to Buzzie about money and had his request for a raise rejected, he was told that Drysdale wasn't even asking for that much, and that Drysdale had been a Dodgers workhorse longer. When Drysdale and Koufax had dinner together, they compared notes and had to bitterly laugh at Bavasi's tactics, playing one off the other like that. But Drysdale's wife, Ginger, had an idea sharper than bitter laughter and bolder than resignation: "If Buzzie's going to compare the two of you, why don't you just walk in there together?" Presto, a union of two.

DRYSDALE AND KOUFAX *were* the Dodgers, they were *all* of the Dodgers, from Brooklyn to L.A., from Jackie Robinson and the Duke of Flatbush and the thundering, hard-hitting Bums to the telegenic Wes Parker and the fleet and mercurial small-ball game sparked by the impassively larcenous Maury Wills and the five-yard-striding Willie Davis. Sandy and Don had been there for it all. Victory, defeat, Campanella's tragic car wreck, Ebbets Field, "hit sign, win suit," O'Malley, the whole New York scene, the controversy, the move West, the new ballpark, the sunshine, laid-back L.A., Grumman's Chinese. They were not so much the heart and soul of the team, these two stalwart fellows, as its muscle and meanness and memory.

Drysdale, the cocky, blond, almost too-handsome Californian, and Koufax, the dark, reserved, more intriguingly fine-featured native Brooklynite, had met as teenage ballplayers wearing Dodger blue.

Koufax didn't play much organized baseball—a little in high school, one year at the University of Cincinnati (he pitched in four games), and then some sandlot ball in Brooklyn the summer after his freshman year. He mostly played basketball, a game in which he was, at 18, a playground legend, making the New York papers for showing up Harry Gallatin and Al McGuire of the Knicks in a scrimmage. Still, whenever Sandy threw a baseball, people noticed. The Yankees were interested but bungled their chances by upsetting Sandy's adoptive father, Irving Koufax, who took offense at the Yankees presumptiveness in sending a Jewish scout. When Branch Rickey, a bona fide Methodist then running the Pirate organization, saw Koufax throwing so hard in a tryout that he broke the catcher's thumb, he wanted him at all costs. Well, not quite—owner John Galbraith would only offer $15,000, which Irving Koufax deemed insufficient to sidetrack his son's ambition to become an architect. But then the hometown Dodgers got a look at Sandy throwing off the mound at Ebbets Field. They may have been alerted to Koufax by a high-school stringer for the *Brooklyn Eagle* named Jimmy Murphy, or it may have been author Ken Auletta's father, Pat, who ran a sporting goods store in Coney Island. Or a man named Milt Laurie, a one-time major league prospect now delivering papers and coaching an amateur team in the Coney Island summer league. He'd seen Koufax play first base on the Lafayette school team and had his sons, who also played at Lafayette, recruit the tall lefty to pitch on his Parkviews team. In any event, it was Rube Walker who caught Koufax at Ebbets Field on a September morning in 1954. At session's end, Walker said give the kid "whatever he wants." Al Campanis, a Dodger official, wrote up a sparkling report, whilst new Dodger manager Walt Alston looked on. Bavasi, the general manager, offered Irving Koufax, acting on behalf of his son, $20,000—which was the minimum first-year salary of $6,000 plus a bonus of $14,000, which would cover a college education, just in case. The total was 33 percent more than the Pirates had offered. Koufax became a Dodger. The world lost an architect but found perhaps the greatest practitioner of throwing baseballs past hitters that it would ever see.

However, over the next two years, 1955 and 1956, the most ardent and perceptive fan could be forgiven for not knowing that greatness was growing in Brooklyn, and could even be forgiven for not knowing that a guy named Koufax was on the team. As a "bonus baby," Koufax was covered by a major league rule that forced the Dodgers to keep him on the roster for two full years, a measure adopted by the owners to discourage big spending on college players at the expense of investment in minor league player development. Too bad for Koufax, who, at the age of 19, needed serious seasoning and coaching. In his first two years combined, he pitched fewer than 100 innings, won four of six decisions, walked a lot of guys, and played not a lick in either World Series against the Yankees.

Drysdale, who was about seven months younger than Koufax, was a quicker study and showed significantly more polish as a pitching prospect. Signed out of high school in Van Nuys when he was 17, Drysdale played only one year of Class-C ball in Bakersfield before joining the big club in 1956. The six-foot-six-inch right-hander then took his apprenticeship under Sal Maglie and learned all he would need to know about barbering—that is, pitching inside—with a baseball. "It was part of the game," he would say later. "I watched Maglie, I listened to Maglie, and it all sunk in." Eventually, Double D would hit 154 batsmen in his career, right up there with Bunning's 160 and ahead of Bob Gibson, two other intimidators.

That first year, Drysdale went 5-5 as a spot starter. Entering Game Four of the World Series in the seventh inning against the Yankees, he had the honor of giving up a two-run homer to Hank Bauer in a 6–2 loss.

But by 1957, Drysdale was a 20-year-old star, winning 17 games for the Bums in their last year in Brooklyn, and becoming an anchor on the staff.

Through 1960, Drysdale had won 66 games as a Dodger, while Koufax had won 30 fewer. Equally, however, the two were finding their stride in L.A., traveling in celebrity circles, for one thing, but finding, too, that not being in Brooklyn, that is, not pitching in hitter-friendly Ebbets Field, was enjoyable. The Memorial Coliseum, where the Dodgers played from 1958 through 1961, was huge—425 feet to center, 440 to right-center, and 301 down the line in right. The weirdly shaped park was only 250 feet down the left-field line, but a 30-foot-high fence helped keep cheap shots in the ballpark. It all helped the hometown pitching, and the move to Dodger Stadium didn't hurt either. The rock-hard infield suited the quick-footed team put together by Campanis, and the unusually high mound—said to be 16 inches or more above the playing field—cruelly added to the stature of Drysdale and the six-foot-two-inch Koufax. At night, the air in Chavez Ravine was often thick and the ball didn't carry well. In the four seasons from 1962 to 1965, the Dodgers finished second to the Giants (losing a playoff), seventh (way behind the Cardinals), and won the World Series twice. During those four seasons, Drysdale went 85-54 and was an All-Star every year, while Koufax, following some sage advice from catcher Norm Sherry (basically, "Don't throw so hard"), had become nearly unhittable, going 84-24. He was a perennial All-Star, too. In the winter of 1965, they were at the very top of their profession and the Dodgers were on top of the major leagues. Yet Walter O'Malley treated them like he treated Brooklyn: I can do without you.

In 1965, Koufax made $85,000 and Drysdale around $80,000. They thought they were worth more. Salaries generally were on the rise in baseball, as expansion from 16 teams to 20 and the longer schedule—162 games rather than 154—and handsome national radio and television contracts fed the coffers of the owners. A few players made more than the Dodger duo: Williams, Musial, Mantle, and Mays were supposedly the only ones allowed to break the magic $100,000 barrier. But Koufax and Drysdale were at their absolute peak in earning power and, they figured, in negotiating power as well. Koufax's advisor, a lawyer named Bill Hayes, worked up the numbers on their behalf. Drysdale, in nine seasons, averaged 275 innings a year, 40 or more games eight seasons in a row, more than 300 innings pitched in each of the last four years, 40 starts or more in those years as well. According to *The Sporting News*, Drysdale possessed an "indestructible constitution, which has enabled him to take his regular turn despite broken ribs, shingles, a broken thumb on his pitching hand and a trick knee that popped out on him six times in 1965." Koufax was coming off five straight All-Star selections, four straight ERA titles, two Cy Young Awards (when only one award was given for both leagues; he'd go on to win a third), a regular-season record of 102-38 in those five years; 4-1 in five World Series starts.

What was all this doing for Walter O'Malley? The Dodgers were booming. The beloved team that had drawn a million people a year in the Borough of Churches was drawing more than twice as many in the City of Angels. From 1959 through 1964, the Dodgers were the only team in either league drawing two million a year. Who needed pay TV anyway? O'Malley had a nice big ballpark that he paid for (with shrewdly acquired help) and a good team. But Bill Hayes put a finer point on all this success, just so O'Malley and Bavasi wouldn't miss it. He figured that, on average, Koufax brought roughly 8,000 extra fans per game to Dodger Stadium, and Drysdale attracted an extra 3,000. At $3.50 a ticket, Hayes figured, and with 40 home starts between them, the Don & Sandy show meant a million extra bucks a year for O'Malley, at the very least.

So they asked Buzzie for $1,000,000 between them, over three years, guaranteed, or about $167,000 a year for each guy. In retrospect, perhaps Bavasi was happy to face the unorthodox negotiating team of Drysdale and Koufax. It saved him from pricing singly what Sandy Koufax had done in 1965. In all fairness to Drysdale, a superb Hall of Fame pitcher, the year that Koufax had can only be diminished when lumped with anyone else's. By itself, Sandy's '65 stands as one of the most impressive accomplishments in baseball history. Let's leave aside for the moment how he emboldened and made proud American Jewry by declining to pitch a big World Series game on Yom Kippur—his on-the-field exploits were brilliant enough. There, he not only almost single-handedly won a pennant and a World Series for the Dodgers, he also pitched the most perfect of the 14 perfect games ever pitched, striking out the most (14), and doing it with the least offensive support of any—one hit. We know now that he also did so with an arm that was killing him and that he stood one year away from retirement at age 30. In 1965, Koufax may have had the best year a pitcher has ever had. And his perfect game, thrown on September 9, stands as the culmination of pitching mastery that began in

1962 and reached its ultimate form on a comfortable Thursday evening in Los Angeles.

THE DODGERS, AS ALMOST always seemed the case, were in a tight pennant race. This time it was with the Giants; the Reds, contending all year, faded badly. A commanding first-place Dodger lead had also evaporated in the face of a 15-game Frisco winning streak. And the club was coming off dropping another pair to the Giants, who were a hard-hitting ball club featuring Willie Mays (on his way to a 52-homer season), Willie McCovey, Orlando Cepeda, Jim Ray Hart, and the high-kicking Dominican right-hander Juan Marichal. The Giants were a half-game in front, and a tension bordering on hatred had developed between the two teams, and it seemed to reflect society in general. On August 22, Marichal had hit Ron Fairly with a pitch, and Johnny Roseboro, the Dodger catcher, took care of things by buzzing a throw right by Marichal's ear when the latter was at the plate. Marichal infamously took exception and turned to Roseboro and beat him over the head with the bat. Koufax, on the mound for the Dodgers, rushed in to awkwardly pull the dazed-looking Marichal away. Meanwhile, in Watts, a poor, black section of L.A., racial tensions had erupted on August 12, sparking a spate of looting and police crackdowns. Five hundred square blocks were burned, 15,000 police and National Guardsmen were called in, 34 people were killed and a thousand were arrested. America had never seen such urban turmoil, and they watched it on TV. On September 9, the city still smoked in the distance beyond Dodger Stadium. With the tensions high in the city, and after having struggled to focus on a just-ended series with the Giants, it was a bit of a relief to have the placid Cubs, led by Mr. Baseball, Ernie Banks, come to town for a rare one-game set.

Koufax was in a bit of a pitching funk at the time, if a guy who is on his way to a 26-8 year can be said to have actually had one. He had been stuck at 21 wins for nearly a month. He and the Dodgers seemed to lose themselves as the city of Los Angeles writhed in self-immolation. In that night's game, he would be pitching once again to young Jeff Torborg, who was filling in for the recovering Roseboro, who in any event would probably have sat against the left-handed Bob Hendley. Over in San Francisco, Marichal would be making his first appearance since serving out his suspension for the gruesome bat-wielding incident.

Koufax writhed, too. Jane Leavy, in her wonderful biography, writes of his pregame preparation, which involved lathering his arm and shoulder in a hot chili pepper concoction, oral doses of Butazolidin—which was illegal in race horses—cortisone shots, and codeine. His postgame ritual was a tub of ice for the elbow and three beers for the head.

Still, he was facing the Cubs, a lousy team with three very good players in the everyday lineup—future Hall of Famers Ernie Banks and Billy Williams, and a third, Ron Santo, for whom there is considerable Cooperstown support. Amazingly, the three played a total of 51 years as Cub regulars, 11 full seasons together, and never swung a bat in postseason play. The Cubs were in a slump that spanned decades; they hadn't finished in the first division since 1946. As a team, only the expansion Mets and Colt .45s had lower batting averages. On September 9, surrounding 3-4-5 hitters Williams, Santo, and Banks were five rookies and the sore-armed, up-and-down pitcher Bob Hendley, acquired earlier in the year from the Giants. If Gene Mauch were managing the Cubs, you can imagine he'd find a way to get this game canceled. As it turns out, the Cubs didn't have a manager. They instead had adopted a system of revolving coaches serving as field managers. It was Lou Klein making out the lineup for the Cubbies on this night.

With the civic unrest in and around L.A., the weeknight crowd was slim—for a Koufax outing, that is, around 29,000. Still, Milton Berle and Doris Day were in attendance. Part of being a Dodger in those days was chatting with movie stars. Brooklyn was so far away. . . .

The game began a little after 8 P.M. Vin Scully did the call on KFI radio. As was the fashion in Dodger Stadium, most of the crowd carried transistors, so that what Vin Scully said reverberated throughout the crowd. Players would know if Vin had told a joke, as tens of thousands in the stands would be laughing.

If Scully had been a crueler man, rather than the soul of courtliness, the fans might have found themselves laughing over the unfortunate predicament of the Cubs leadoff hitter. As Jane Leavy put it, "There's a special place in heaven reserved for guys who face Koufax in their first major league at-bat." That would be Don Young, a late-season callup, starting in center field. Koufax bounced a curveball in the dirt on the first pitch—early evidence that it would be mostly a fastball night. The anxious Young, too anxious to dream he might be walked, popped the second pitch to the Dodgers' rookie phenom at second base, Jim Lefebvre. Don Young's two hits for the 1965 season would come on some other day.

Another rookie, Glenn Beckert, stepped in. He lined the second pitch, a lollipop of a curve, down the left-field line for what looked like a sure double, but it skipped just foul. It was the best shot the Cubs would take all night. Beckert struck out, as did Billy Williams. Koufax walked off to what Scully astutely claimed was "applause, not cheering," befitting a maestro.

In the second inning Ron Santo, the 25-year-old third baseman out of Seattle, coming off a 30-homer, .312 year, freshly bloomed in a stardom that would last for another decade, was dispatched so utterly that he later confused his at-bat, recounting to Leavy in great detail how he had struck out looking at three diabolical fastballs—"Whish. . . . Whish. . . . Whish . . . ," he recalled. He actually fouled out to the catcher. Ernie Banks was up next. The veteran Banks had seen more of Koufax than most batters, facing him since he first came up with Brooklyn in 1955 (Banks would end up tied, with Frank Robinson, Aaron, and Felipe Alou for most career homers against Koufax: seven). Koufax had recently developed something new for the likes of Ernie Banks. Having been struck out himself earlier in the year by an Elroy Face forkball, the long-fingered Koufax started fooling with the pitch, tried it out on Henry Aaron on August 8 (inducing a grounder to third), and in this instance showed it to Banks on a two-strike count: strike three, swinging. For the third out, another fellow bound to see Don Young in that special heaven stepped in: Byron Browne, a 22-year-old, six-foot-two-inch, 200-pound Missourian who on this day would register half of his six at-bats for the year. After looking at a curve and listening to a fastball, Browne got a hanging curve to hit on 0 and 2, but managed only to punch the ball to center, where Willie Davis moved in for the catch. Side retired.

The Dodgers were doing their usual nothing on offense. Two years earlier, they had hit .251 as a team, finished eighth in slugging percentage, but stole twice as many bases as the league average and won the pennant by six over the Cardinals and swept the Yankees in the World Series. Of course, Koufax and Drysdale were awesome. Again, in 1965, the Dodgers played a game right out of the dead-ball era—singles, walks, sacrifices, stolen bases, good defense, and stingy pitching. Through two innings, their brand of ball produced nothing against Bob Hendley, who entered the game with a 2-2 record. Hendley was a hulking left-hander out of Macon, Georgia. Only 26 years old, he'd pitched well early in his career with the Braves. But arm troubles had slowed him, and Chicago was his third team in three years. His career was bound for a terminus common to many of the mediocre players in the mid-sixties: the New York Mets. But Hendley was sharp on this day, and after two innings, he was matching Koufax out for out.

In the Cubs third, rookie catcher Chris Krug, a native of L.A., took his lumber to the plate. Krug was a big fellow, six-feet-four-inches and more than 200 pounds. After his 79-game, three-year career came to an end, Krug would go on to become a landscape architect and enter baseball legend by building the famous ballfield in the Iowa corn featured in the Kevin Costner film *Field of Dreams.* But against Koufax on this Thursday night, he, like the rookie before him, would serve an 0-2 pitch on a soft line into the glove of smooth Willie Davis. The number-eight hitter was the fifth of the Cubs rookies in the lineup, Don Kessinger, who would go on to have a long and defensively distinguished career. The tall, slight, switch-hitting Arkansan would hit only .201 as a rookie, and would finish his career 15 years later as a lifetime .252 hitter. Facing Koufax with one out and the pitcher up next in a tie game, Kessinger flew out on the first pitch. Hendley fanned to make it nine straight for Koufax.

In the fourth, Don Young managed only a sky-high pop to first-baseman Wes Parker; Beckert then cued one to right, where Fairly ran in for the easy grab. Williams, getting steady doses of Koufax's "yellow hammer," struck out looking at a curve, Sandy's fifth K. The Dodgers continued to go quietly, as Hendley found the big mound distinctly to his liking.

In the Cubs fifth, Koufax fanned Santo and then had full counts on both Banks and the rookie Browne, before retiring each. The game was clipping along into the evening. How quickly nothing happening happens. But in the home half of the fifth, the Dodgers broke through, in typical Dodger fashion. Journeyman Lou Johnson had spent eight years in the minors and now, at 31, found himself, in his first year as a Dodger, a crowd favorite. Brought up in May from the Dodgers' Triple-A Spokane club when two-time N.L. batting king Tommy Davis broke his ankle, the easygoing Kentuckian filled a void the team didn't know it had. Johnson was affable and ribbable—perhaps he reminded a few of the players of the old Brooklyn days. Koufax and Johnson, in any event, became fast friends.

Johnson had only modest power, but he was positively Ruthian in this Dodger lineup. Hendley lost him on a 3-2 pitch to start the fifth, and Hendley's night of perfection was over, not that anyone was keeping track. Fairly, going by the book of Alston, bunted Johnson over to second and into scoring position for Jim Lefebvre, the eventual N.L. Rookie of the Year. On the first pitch, Sweet Lou took off for third, as Hendley didn't pay him much mind, and the rookie catcher Krug threw the ball high to third. Santo, caught by surprise, didn't get there in time anyway, and the throw ended up in left field. Johnson leaped to his feet and ran home with the game's first run. He'd scored on a walk, a bunt, a stolen base and a throwing error, that is, a run without a hit. With Lefebvre still at the plate, the inning hadn't even seen an official at-bat yet.

In the sixth inning, Don Drysdale emerged from the training room, in full uniform, and sat in the dugout. His presence may just have signaled that something special was afoot. Koufax was perfect through five, Hendley had a no-hitter going, and, miracle of miracles, the Dodgers had a lead. (The story goes that Drysdale, given a night off in 1964, received a call saying that Koufax had thrown a no-hitter, and he responded, "But did he win?")

The young man wearing the goat horns in this unlikely affair, Chris Krug, led off the sixth and rapped a grounder to short. Maury Wills's throw was low but slick-fielding Wes Parker made the play. Kessinger almost ran a penny nail across the perfect surface of the game by dribbling one down the third-base line. But the baked and rolled Dodger dirt and the nimble footwork of Junior Gilliam, at 37 years of age playing in his 13th season as a Dodger, conspired to nail the young Kessinger by half a step at first. No way the out-of-contention Cubs were going to pinch-hit for Hendley, who had a no-hitter of his own going. So Koufax struck him out.

Hendley kept up his mastery, too. He set down Torborg, Koufax, and Wills to get through the sixth.

It was to be the third time through the order for Koufax as Young, Beckert, and Williams were due up in the seventh. Young, now advanced all the way to his third career at-bat, got to experience his first strikeout. Beckert, a good contact hitter all his career, made contact again, as he had in the fourth, with the same result: a fly to Fairly in right field. Up came Billy Williams, the smooth-swinging lefty who had struck out twice. Koufax bounced one in the dirt; he fell behind 2-0 but battled back. On Koufax's third 3-2 count of the evening, Williams fouled one straight back before lifting an easy fly to left. Twenty-one up and down.

There has only been one nine-inning double no-hitter in major league history, in 1917, when Fred Toney of the Reds and Hippo Vaughan of the Cubs twirled nine hitless innings against each other in Wrigley Field, to no end. The end did come in the 10th, when Larry Kopf singled and scored on an infield hit by the legendary Jim Thorpe. In this game, it was the legendary Lou Johnson who broke up the double no-hitter, dunking one behind first base where it dropped and scooted into foul territory—a double on a ball fielded by the first baseman. Hendley's unlikely run was over. Ron Fairly then bounced out to end the inning, leaving Johnson at second, the game's only man left on base.

Little did the Cubs know how over it was for them. Koufax has admitted to thinking about the perfect-game possibility as he walked off the mound at the end of his seventh inning of work. After that, he left little to chance. In the eighth he blew Santo away with high heat and a wicked curveball. Banks went down swinging, for the third time, for out number two. The rookie Byron Browne met the same fate as the great Ernie Banks: down swinging.

Koufax had 11 strikeouts through eight innings. He was on pace to set a National League record for strikeouts in a season, at 382, breaking the record for left-handers, held by Rube Waddell since 1904. And the ninth inning would be no different than the eighth. Leading off was Chris Krug—poor Chris Krug, he of the errant throw into left field that allowed the only run of the game. But Krug now had a chance at redemption of a sort. It was during this at-bat that Scully did his famous setting of time and place, and managed to calibrate a communal nervousness by elevating a cliché into poetry:

"It is 9:41 P.M. on September the ninth, 1-2 pitch on the way. The Dodgers defensively, in this spine-tingling moment, Sandy Koufax, and Jeff Torborg, and the boys who will try to sop anything hit their way, Wes Parker, Dick Tracewski, Maury Wills, John Kennedy [who had replaced Gilliam at third], and the outfield of Lou Johnson, Willie Davis, and Ron Fairly. There are 29,000 people in the ballpark and a million butterflies."

Back to poor Krug. He swung through a 2-2 fastball. Next, veteran Joey Amalfitano was sent up to pinch-hit for the overmatched Kessinger. Wiseguy all the way, Amalfitano, a onetime Giant, heard one whistle by for a strike, and had to say to ump Ed Vargo that the ball "sounded high." Koufax got him swinging on another fastball, his fifth straight strikeout. And now, for the 27th out, Koufax would have to get veteran Harvey Kuenn, playing in the next-to-last year of his 15-year career. Koufax had gotten Kuenn to end a no-hitter two years before, when Harvey was with the Giants. He had bounced out then. No such contact on this night. Koufax was smoking the ball in, whipping the ball so hard his hat flew off. (Once, his hat flew so far that his catcher retrieved it.) Scully thought Koufax was forcing it; he obviously wanted it, wanted the perfection he had come so close to before.

Harvey Kuenn went down swinging and Koufax had what he wanted.

It was Koufax's fourth no-hitter in four years; he'd reached the perfection that, in retrospect, seemed inevitable. He had walked five in his '62 no-hitter against the Mets, two in his no-hitter versus the Giants in '63 (he was perfect into the eighth); one in his gem against the Phillies in '64; and now none versus the Cubs. No pitcher of any era has flirted so extensively with utter invincibility.

IN BEATING THE CUBS, the Dodgers had stayed on pace with the Giants, who had also won, behind Marichal's 10th shutout of the season. But in the next week, things began to slip for the Dodgers. With only two weeks to go in the regular season, they found themselves 4.5 games back of the Giants, and Milwaukee had sneaked into second place. But Koufax and the Dodgers, just like that, turned it on, winning 15 of their last 16 games. Koufax threw three more shutouts to make it four in September and eight for the year. It looked like it might be the Giants and the Dodgers in a playoff once again, but Alston asked Koufax to pitch on two days' rest in the season's next-to-last game. He struck out 13 Milwaukee Braves, and the Dodgers were in.

Their opponent in the World Series would be the Minnesota Twins of Harmon Killebrew, Tony Oliva, Bob Allison, curveball specialist Camilo Pascual, league MVP Zoilo Versalles, a young crafty left-hander named Jim Kaat and 21-game-winner Jim "Mudcat" Grant. Game One, in Minnesota, fell on a high holiday for the Jewish faith—Yom Kippur. There was never any question for Koufax: He would not pitch. Instead, Drysdale opened for the Dodgers and didn't have it; meanwhile, Mudcat had no trouble with the light-hitting Dodgers, one-hitting them. Koufax pitched Game Two. Exhausted, he lost 5–1 to Kaat, and the Series shifted to L.A. Claude Osteen gave L.A. life with a five-hit shutout in Game Three, and Drysdale brought them even in Game Four, twirling another five-hitter. Koufax, fresher, nailed the Twins to the wall with a four-hit shutout in Game Five, and it was back to the Twin Cities to settle things. Osteen was bested by Grant, who had himself a field day, allowing only six hits and hitting a three-run homer. And then the classic Game Seven. Walter Alston conferred with Drysdale, who got his drift. Dandy Don agreed to be ready in the bullpen should Koufax falter. It was really Drysdale's turn, but could the Dodgers turn to anyone else? Sweet Lou Johnson hit a home run off Jim Kaat, which was all Koufax would need, though the game was so tight Drysdale was up six times in the bullpen. But Koufax never wavered. He gave up three hits, no runs, and struck out 10, atoning for any inconvenience his religious observance may have foisted upon the Dodger faithful, all of whom would forgive him anyway. Dodgers 2, Twins 0. Koufax brought to a dramatic and fitting close an incredible year. He finished as king.

IF YOU DIP INTO *The Sporting News*, January 1, 1966, you find a touching innocence. You wouldn't know that the war in Vietnam was escalating or that Watts had burned in late summer or that tensions in Cleveland and Chicago were coming to a boil or that the Civil Rights Act, enacted in 1965, was not going over well in the Deep South or that the National Organization of Women had just been founded. Of course, we are talking about a baseball publication, not *The New York Times*. Still, you wouldn't even know from *The Sporting News* that the very foundation of the baseball business—the indenturing of players to owners—was under assault. Instead, the year's first issue was full of the glory of a new American hero, Sandy Koufax. Ironically, it was Koufax and his buddy Drysdale who were spearheading the assault.

During the dead of winter, as the year turned into 1966, the main baseball news was of Koufax's triumphant tour around the country, picking up prizes. "Koufax in the middle of a cross-country safari, collects awards everywhere," said *The Sporting News*. Although it was his record-setting 15-strikeout performance in Game One against the aging Yankees in the 1963 World Series that vaulted Koufax to national prominence, his performance down the stretch in 1965, including his dominating perfect game, his bold, principled refusal to pitch on Yom Kippur, and his brilliant pitching throughout the rest of the Series put him at another level in the sports pantheon. He seemed perhaps the greatest pitcher who had ever lived, and on December 30 he had just turned 30 years old. Koufax received 224 of 303 first-place votes for Athlete of the Year from AP; he was acclaimed *Sporting News* Player of the Year. He won the Hickock Belt and the Van Heusen Award, the World Series MVP Award, the National League MVP Award, the Cy Young Award, the league ERA title. Ironically, or is it forebodingly, he was named honorary chairman of the

National Arthritis Foundation. *Life* magazine put Koufax on its cover. Everywhere he went he was treated like a Hollywood star or a visitor from a distant and brilliant civilization. Always, he was humble and kind. When honored at a Boy Scouts of America banquet, he made a speech and handed the organization a $15,000 check. Walter O'Malley told *The Sporting News,* "We are so proud of him and his accomplishments and we hope he's only starting his collection of awards. He's coming into his prime as a pitcher . . . I'm saying all this before contract time, too."

O'Malley had been told by Bavasi that his star pitchers had come into his office together, asking, as Drysdale later put it, "for the moon"— three years guaranteed, a million dollars between them. O'Malley had always been able to count on Buzzie. But change was in the air—in the streets, in the bedroom, in the music world, and in the sports world, too, where no working professional ballplayer could help but notice what a little competition for services had done for the likes of a young fellow named Joe Namath. Coming out of the University of Alabama in 1965, Namath was drafted by the St. Louis Cardinals of the NFL and by the New York Jets of the AFL, which had just signed a hefty TV contract with NBC. The two leagues were warring for talent. Four hundred thousand dollars later, the Jets won Namath, who as a rookie quarterback would make five times the salary of baseball's best pitcher, an 11-year veteran.

Bavasi said, "No way, boys."

But the boys had a few cards to play. They were intelligent, savvy veterans who could already see a life after baseball. Drysdale had a little acting career underway, appearing in the television show *The Lawman.* And both had agreed in principle to appear in a movie called, somewhat prophetically, *Warning Shot.*

As the winter rolled along, Koufax and Drysdale watched as one after another of their Dodger teammates came away with new contracts for whatever it was Bavasi and O'Malley felt they had to pay: Fairly got a $7,000 raise to $34,000; eight-year veteran Roseboro signed for $46,000, while his backup and heir apparent Jeff Torborg got one grand up from the minimum, to $8,000; Rookie of the Year Jim Lefebvre had his pay doubled to $15,000; Al Ferrara got $11,000; reliever Jim Brewer $15,000. Meanwhile, team captain Maury Wills, unpredictable and seldom happy, wouldn't sign and took off for Japan on a banjo-playing tour.

In early March, the team flight from L.A. to Vero Beach for the opening of spring-training camp was rough in spots, with several players getting airsick. Perhaps it was because O'Malley and Bavasi were aboard, or because Koufax, Drysdale, and Wills were not. Meanwhile, the rumor was afloat that Jimmy Hoffa was looking into organizing major league baseball players as part of the United Brotherhood of Teamsters. Cincinnati catcher Johnny Edwards, head of the National League player reps, rushed to assure the public that "the players aren't interested in becoming part of any union." *The Sporting News* excoriated the labor boss, whose "covetous glance" had put him on every sports page in America. Then the holdout news went public in the *L.A. Herald Examiner*: "Sandy, Don Salary Rumor—$600,000 for Sandy, $450,000 for double D."

C. C. Johnson Spink was moved to editorialize thus in his *Sporting News*. Quoting an obscure economist named Ralph Andreano, he said that ballplayers are "folk heroes" who should be "above the din of the average guy who works for weekly or hourly wages . . . he is expected to be satisfied with his moderate financial status . . . to try to reap the material benefits of his status means necessarily to destroy the myths."

One might wonder what part of the myth the great Frank Robinson wanted to preserve. In March, he was traded, against his wishes, from Cincinnati to Baltimore. Tough F. Robby was in tears at the news.

Koufax and Drysdale remained behind in L.A., calmly plotting their futures without baseball. Bavasi and O'Malley declared an impasse and were ready to call the players' bluff or do without them. But then O'Malley, through a friend of his, film producer Mervin Leroy, heard that Bill Hayes, representing the pitchers, was preparing to take legal action against the club. Hayes had found some pieces of legislation passed by the California courts in response to disputes between the movie studios and actors. Bob Cummings and Olivia de Havilland had used the statute to escape onerous studio contracts. Motion picture stars, like ballplayers, had been held as the property of one studio for life until the ruling, which stated that personal service contracts were illegal after seven years and had to be renegotiated. In other words, Hollywood's version of the reserve clause had been overturned for employees in the state of California. Hayes unearthed the statute in late March, and shortly thereafter Leroy told O'Malley. Koufax and Drysdale were prepared to sue, and the law was on their side.

O'Malley held forth with his annual St. Patrick's Day party in Vero Beach—corned beef and cabbage, green biscuits, shamrocks, shillelaghs, streamers and balloons and lights. New commissioner William Eckert (a one-star general whose feckless efforts soon would earn him the nickname "the unknown soldier," courtesy of the viper-tongued New York *Daily News* columnist Dick Young) volunteered that he would be "available" if needed to help break the impasse. Bavasi assured everyone that he was planning to "make every effort to bring in the Dodgers' two big men."

During the month of March, as the impasse wore on and thoughtful men worried about the future of baseball, Marvin J. Miller, nominated by the players' executive committee to be the new executive director of the Players Association, was touring the camps. Players, managers, and coaches were the members of the Players Association, and they had to ratify by vote Miller's selection: He won them over. As Jim Lefebvre told Jane Leavy, after Miller visited Dodgertown, Bavasi grimly informed the players, "We can't have this guy." That meant Miller was in, said Lefebvre. "Anybody Buzzie was that scared of had to be good for you."

After Miller had toured all the camps, the player reps met in Miami to approve Miller's selection. Each rep had to render his team's vote. The Dodgers weren't represented; their new representative, who replaced Wally Moon, was in phone range if his vote was needed to break a tie. That was Koufax, way back in Sherman Oaks, and his vote wasn't needed. Miller, indeed, was in.

All told, it was a 32-day holdout. On March 30, Drysdale and Koufax signed new one-year contracts, $115,000 for Koufax, $105,000 for Drysdale. They had won far less than they had asked for but more than they were offered. And they had made a point that, with the appointment of Marvin Miller, was rather timely. There is strength in any number greater than one.

Drysdale and Koufax caught up with the Dodgers in Arizona, as the team headed west for opening day. Koufax no-hit the Indians for seven innings in his first outing, striking out nine. The next night, he and Drysdale were in top hat and tails and bright red cummerbunds, singing a song on *Hollywood Palace.*

Koufax won 27 games the next year. The Dodgers lost in the World Series in four straight to the upstart Baltimore Orioles, led by Triple-Crown-winning Frank Robinson. Koufax was in tremendous pain throughout the year. After each outing his elbow grew discolored, swelling to melon size. He was tired of the pills and the shots and the pain. At the time, he had no surgical options. He called it quits at the top of his game, but with nothing left to give to baseball on the field.

———

KOUFAX WAS A LATE bloomer; he won 18 games as a 25-year-old, but it was his seventh year in the big leagues. He then went on to win 111 regular-season games over the next five years, losing only 34, a phosphorescent burst of brilliance that will never be matched. At 31, Koufax's career as a pitcher was over. Five years later, he became the youngest inductee into the Hall of Fame, younger than the ill-fated Gehrig by five months. Today, he moves at baseball's edges with a lanky mystery. Jane Leavy's bestselling biography of Koufax, published in September 2002, painted him as a man of great integrity. When rumors about his private life surfaced in a New York tabloid newspaper, and Leavy's credibility as a journalist was impugned, Koufax and Leavy kept their silence. Koufax waited till spring training 2003 to indirectly condemn the newspaper report by notifying the Dodgers that he would no longer make his customary visit to Vero Beach to speak to their young pitchers. After all, the Dodgers and the gossiping tabloid—the *New York Post*—were owned by the same man, Rupert Murdoch. For once, the *Post* retracted a scurrilous item and apologized to both Koufax and Leavy. Koufax had made the perfect pitch. At age 68, he remains untouchable.

CHAPTER SEVEN

Name of Jimmy

Catfish Hunter

May 8, 1968

O N DECEMBER 16, 1974, the telephone rang at the home of Jimmy
and Helen Hunter in the small town of Hertford, located along
the coastal plain in the northeastern part of North Carolina, about 60
miles from Norfolk, Virginia. It was J. Carlton Cherry on the line, the
family lawyer, calling from New York City with big news. Jimmy, for
that is how he was known around Hertford, listened, nodded, and then
said "Okay," and turned to Helen, his wife. "We don't belong to anybody," he told her matter-of-factly.

It was now indeed a matter of fact that James Augustus "Catfish"
Hunter, aged 28, after 10 years of consecutive service as a major league
ballplayer in the employ of Charles O. Finley and the Oakland Athletics
Baseball Club, was now free to play baseball for whomever he wanted.

Given what Catfish Hunter had done during those 10 years, everyone figured the phone would be ringing pretty good, as other teams made their
offers. Carlton Cherry had called to give Catfish word of the final verdict
of an arbitration panel, headed by Peter Seitz and including two addi-
tional members—Players Association executive director Marvin Miller
and the owners' negotiator John Gaherin. The three were adjudicating in
the matter of a complaint filed by the players union on Hunter's behalf,
claiming breach of contract on Finley's part. The panel had decided in
favor of the ballplayer—Hunter was now free to offer his services wherever he wished, to whichever bidder he chose. Catfish was right; he
didn't belong to anybody.

Understandably, Catfish was a little scared. Pitching for the A's had
been the only job he'd ever known other than the farm chores; he'd been
drawing a check for playing ball since he was 18. Professional baseball
had taken him a long way from Hertford, from his father's farmstead to
the bright, jazzy downtown of Kansas City in 1964; he'd seen Florida,
Caracas, and eventually Oakland, not to mention every baseball city in
America, traveling first class with money in his pocket (if only meal tickets). Along the way, he'd made a lifetime's worth of good friends, ball-
playing friends, men his own age trying to win and get along in the crazy
world of the professional athlete, and men older than him, coaches and
managers, trying to teach him how winning was done, or even how to
lose. He'd feuded with just about no one other than Mr. Finley, but Mr.
Finley, one of the last great eccentrics in the game, had been good to Catfish. It was hard to dislike a man who was proud of you and who had
given you your start, who had given you what seemed like a king's ran-
som even after you'd gotten yourself shot in the foot.

Catfish didn't know what, or where, his future would be, hence his
trepidation. But he was excited too. He was healthy, he was in love with
his wife, he had two lovely children. Professionally, he was at the top of
the heap. His team had just won its third straight World Series, something that had been done only twice before and only once since. He'd led
the league in wins with 25 and earned run average (2.49) and won the Cy
Young Award. He'd won 88 regular-season games in the last four years.
He'd been an All-Star six times. He was the best pitcher in the American
League. In his last year as an Oakland A, his contract called for $100,000.
He only got half of it; that was the disputed matter. Now he was unem-
ployed. No one had a clue what such talent would be worth on the open

market. In 1974, the concept of free agency was but a glimmer in Marvin Miller's eye.

JIMMY HUNTER WAS BORN on April 8, 1946, the youngest of 10 children. His father, Abbott, was a tenant farmer who made a habit of carrying a thousand dollars cash around with him; he'd buy nothing on credit. Hunter's mother, Lillie, was long-suffering—she'd lost two of her children in infancy—and a little sickly, but by all accounts a kind woman. She was the historian in the family, keeping scrapbooks and records of births and deaths and the athletic exploits of her five boys. The Hunters, through the Depression and the war years, had managed nonetheless to establish a happy home. The boys—Marvin, Pete, Ray, Edward, and Jimmy—worked the farm hard alongside their father, up at 4 A.M. to do the chores—feeding the hogs, milking the cows, spraying the peanut crops. They hunted the woods, fished the streams, and played baseball and football with skill and great energy in the tiny town. When the boys needed extra money for a new ball or some sort of equipment, they sold frogs to a local restaurant or loaded melons on a truck. The world of young Jimmy Hunter, seen from today's perspective, is almost aching with innocence. In his autobiography, Catfish marveled at his own idyllic upbringing:

"It was, I must confess, a beautiful way of life, one full of simple pleasures. Work and play. Play and work. My brothers and me piling into our '59 Ford for trips up north to see my childhood hero, Robin Roberts, pitch for the Phillies. Singing country tunes along with Grandpa Jones and Hank Williams on the way back home."

Catfish would have a professional career spanning 15 years. The shadow of an averted tragedy at its very dawning, in 1963, would persist through his playing days, assuming various forms. Though he would endure life in three different cities, enjoy great success during a time of social upheaval in America, in the end, Catfish Hunter suffered most of his hurt and most of his happiness in Hertford. He always belonged to Hertford.

HUNTER WAS A STAR athlete at Perquimans High School, which was named after the river that flowed through Herftord into Albemarle

Sound. He stood an even six feet tall and weighed 175 pounds, and was fleet afoot, as he proved by winning the state title in the 440-yard dash. On the baseball diamond, he could run and hit and throw. He was the ace of the staff, going 12-1 as a junior, leading Perquimans to the state title. During the summer between his junior and senior years, he pitched brilliantly for the American Legion team, throwing a perfect game and never losing, as his team took the area championship. All summer, according to Hunter, there was one constant: the presence of a man named Clyde Kluttz from nearby Salisbury. Kluttz was a lot like Hunter's father—a farmer with a crew cut, a weathered face, and a certain taciturnity. Kluttz had been a major leaguer for nine years, and was retained as a scout by the Kansas City Athletics. He was at all Hunter's games and visited the family with regularity, sitting down to dinner, talking national politics, local weather, and food prices.

As young Hunter's on-the-field exploits continued, Kluttz began to get company in the grandstands: gentlemen in straw hats making notes. But a mishap on Thanksgiving Day began to dilute the interest in Jimmy Hunter.

Thursday, November 28, 1963, was a rough holiday in America. Six days before, John Kennedy had been assassinated on a sunny day in Dallas; three days later he was buried in 30-degree weather at Arlington National Cemetery. The country was numb with grief. It struggled with its mourning, not knowing quite how to do it. The Thanksgiving Day football game featured the Green Bay Packers versus the Detroit Lions; the crowd at Tiger Stadium was solemn but the seats were filled. The game flickered into crepuscular living rooms across the country, as Americans sat down to grim midday dinners.

In North Carolina, the day was warm and cloudy, temperatures in the low 70s, with rain expected in the evening. People sought comfort in the regular rituals and the scheduled events. Hunter and his Perquimans High School football team (Jimmy was a linebacker) played and won a championship game that morning, and in the afternoon, he and his brothers Ray and Pete, along with a cousin, went bird hunting. Along the way, Pete's Remington shotgun accidentally went off, with birdshot peppering Jimmy's right foot. He looked down at his shredded boot spouting blood; he and Pete both passed out. Eventually, Jimmy was carried out to the road and taken to the hospital, where the doctors counted at least 45 pellets in the foot; his little toe was gone.

The scouts took flight as quickly as the ducks did at the sound of the shot. Jimmy's right foot, the one with which he drove off the rubber toward home plate, was disfigured. Jimmy told his father that he thought his career was over. Abbott Hunter agreed, but kept it to himself. He encouraged his youngest boy to get well. Even better tonic arrived in the person of Clyde Kluttz. "Can you still play?" Jimmy couldn't tell him no. He wasn't sure himself; he was only 17. Clyde seemed unfazed.

Clyde Kluttz loved this kid. Jimmy Hunter was quiet, self-effacing, well mannered, from a solid family; he knew hogs, cows, and peanuts and could dress a deer, skin a rabbit, and play some very serious country hardball. He had remarkable control for a young pitcher, good velocity and a nasty slider; more important, perhaps, he seldom lost. The country had a lot of healing to do, and so did Jimmy Hunter. Why not have hope?

Indeed, the young man healed quickly. About a third of the pellets were removed from his foot, and he was soon walking without a limp. His senior year was even more brilliant than his junior year. He was 12-0 going into the state playoffs. Kluttz had company again as the scouts returned to watch the young farm boy with the hopping fastball and pinpoint control. Charley Finley came down to watch him pitch for the championship. He liked what he saw.

Finley had bird-dogging scouts like Kluttz working the mid- and Deep South looking for ballplayers. He had just signed Johnny Lee Odom out of Macon, Georgia, for $75,000. Finley visited the Hunter household. His recollection of the visit, as told to Armen Keteyian, who helped Hunter with his autobiography, shows Finley's predilection for the mythical, with a coat of the blarney:

"I went down to Hertford to visit him and his family in June of '64. He lived in a sharecropper's home with a tin roof. His mother was out in the field with a bonnet on her head and a hoe in her hand, hoeing weeds in the peanut patch. His father was in the smokehouse turning the bacon and hams. The water for the house came from a pump with a long handle."

Finley made a busily working farm seem like something out of Dogpatch, but he did visit. And Jimmy showed Mr. Finley his foot. Finley was aghast, and couldn't believe the kid was asking for $75,000. But, said Finley, "I fell in love with him and his parents and his brothers and sisters after seeing what mold they came from. I was impressed with him as a person."

Catfish got what he asked for, minus the Thunderbird he proposed at the last minute. Finley right away began to market his new product, angling for a nickname for his country boy hurler. "Jim" Hunter was a little too forgettable. He told Hunter that to play baseball you needed a nickname. What do you like to do, he asked. Hunter had to admit to hunting and fishing, no doubt with a bit of a wince. Fine, said Finley, and he made up a story on the spot: "When you were six years old you ran away from home and went fishing. Your mom and dad had been looking for you all day. When they finally found you, about, oh, four o'clock in the afternoon, you'd caught two big fish . . . ahh . . . catfish . . . and were reeling in the third. And that's how you got your nickname. Okay?"

Hunter told that apocryphal story to the AP right after his signing became public. It was repeated as gospel by sportswriters for the next decade, till Hunter was free of Finley and could afford to abandon the fish story. But "Catfish" stuck and seemed perfect, just as the Finley-inspired nickname "Blue Moon" for Johnny Lee Odom stuck.

THERE WAS A LITTLE OF THE Barnum poet in Charles O. Finley. Raised in Birmingham, Alabama, Finley sold eggs on the street during the Depression; he made wine from wild grapes and sold his hooch during Prohibition. He also worked as a batboy for the Birmingham Barons of the Southern Association, making half a dollar a game and all the baseballs he could spirit away. Eventually, through his father's steelworker connections he found work at U.S. Steel in Gary, Indiana. He married Shirley McCarthy and looked for a better life. He began to sell insurance on the side, but tuberculosis got hold of him and he spent more than two years in a sanitarium. When he emerged he had a full-blown idea: Doctors as a group could be sold disability insurance. Finley made his first million on the back of this idea within two years. In 1960, after trying to buy the nearby White Sox and the not-that-far-away Tigers, he bought the Athletics from the heirs of Arnold Johnson, who had passed away in March 1960. Finley's 1961 A's team finished in last place, tied with the expansion Washington Senators and behind the expansion Los Angeles Angels. His '62 team improved to next to last, thanks mostly to a huge year by Norm Siebern, who drove in 117 runs. In '63 and '64, KC and the Senators battled for the right to be last. Still, the hard-driving Finley kept trying. New ideas, new managers, new gimmicks.

Catfish was lucky in several respects. Nineteen sixty-four was the last year before the amateur draft was instituted. This meant that Hunter had the luxury of signing with whomever he chose and was not subject to the rights to his services going to whichever team chose *him*. There was also a rule still in effect that young players signed to big bonuses had to stay on the major league roster or be available to any other team. This is the same rule that confined a young Koufax to two years of inactivity on a very talented Dodger team. It would be the rule that would throw Catfish right into the middle of major league play, since he was on a team that would never be mistaken for the 1955 Dodgers. He was allowed to learn his craft in the relative obscurity of Missouri and the second division. Hunter was lucky in one other respect as well: Finley was a hands-on owner. In his early 40s, he was a self-made man with lots of energy. He took early and immediate care of his new phenom.

As soon as Finley signed his wounded bonus baby, he had him out to his huge farm in Laporte, Indiana, for a little relaxation; he then sent Hunter up to the Mayo Clinic in Rochester, Minnesota, where surgeons removed almost all of the buckshot from his foot and some of the bone, and generally cleaned the whole mess up. Catfish was on the disabled list for the rest of the 1964 season, but went to the instructional league over the winter, where he got back in shape, ready for his rookie year in the bigs.

A man named Mel McGaha was Hunter's first A's manager. McGaha was a southerner who had bounced around the minor leagues for two decades; he was a strict disciplinarian, but it didn't bother the unflappable Hunter. He was developing a taste for scotch-and-water at the Apartment Lounge in Kansas City, where he often repaired with his bonus baby buddies—Paul Lindblad, Blue Moon Odom, and Dave Duncan. Each of them felt pretty secure, which may have made the whiskey flow but also let them work on their games without the gnawing fear of being released. These kids, if sent down to the minors, were open to any team that wanted to pay $25,000 for them. But Finley had his investment to protect, so the A's stayed young and bad and on the roster. And everyone got to play.

Catfish arrived just as Finley was finding his creative stride as a salesman. The canary yellow and Kelly green uniforms debuted in '65; so did Charley O., the 1,200-pound mule that relievers had to ride in from the bullpen; and there were the white shoes and—almost—the orange baseballs that Finley felt night baseball was waiting for. The 19-year-old Hunter made 20 starts, appeared in 32 games, and finished with an 8-8 record. He pitched two shutouts. The Cuban-born Bert Campaneris established himself as an exciting player with tremendous potential, hitting .270 and stealing 51 bases. Ken Harrelson, in his third year as an Athletic, hit 23 home runs. For his part, Catfish began to accumulate the experiences that would make him among the savviest of players by the time he matured. One example here may suffice. It's his Ed Runge story.

As Catfish prepared for a start early in the season, a teammate mentioned that the day's home-plate ump, Runge, was someone Hunter should find to his liking. "He gives you everything," he was told. But for a rookie, nothing comes easy. Hunter started the game by throwing two balls right down the middle that Runge, with not a little attitude, declared balls. It continued through the game—periodically Runge would look for the perfect strike to call a ball. Hunter said nothing, even though a few times Runge whipped off his mask ready for some lip. But nothing. A few weeks later, Hunter ran into Runge in a hotel lobby. "I see you don't argue with umpires, kid," said Runge.

"No, sir," said Hunter.

Runge smiled. "It's a good thing."

From then on, according to Catfish, he was a "card-carrying member of the Ed Runge Club. Anything close was a strike." Catfish had passed the test.

At the conclusion of the otherwise miserable '65 season, in which the A's finished in last place, 43 games behind the Twins, with the worst attendance in baseball, A's executive and former White Sox ace Eddie Lopat found something good to say about Hunter: "He has more aptitude for pitching than anyone I've ever seen at his age."

Alvin Dark, hired by Finley after having lost his job as manager of the Giants due to some racist remarks about the lack of "mental alertness" among "Negroes and Spanish players" and an embarrassing adultery scandal, was the opening-day skipper in 1966. In his autobiography, Hunter called this period "the Dark ages." Nonetheless, Dark, newly minted as a born-again Baptist, took a liking to the young Hunter's effort in spring training. "Another Robin Roberts," said Dark, the highest praise Hunter could possibly hear. Dark gave Catfish the opening-day pitching assignment. Catfish pitched well but lost 2–1, and it would be a very long year for the A's. Although attendance jumped 50 percent, the team still managed to outdraw only the Senators and the White Sox; the A's finished not in last place but in seventh, as the aging Yankees found themselves in the cellar for the first time since 1915. Catfish finished 9-11, but was the Kansas City representative to the All-Star Game. The team was coming along, though, and finished the season strong, racking up 74 wins, the most the team had managed since 1956. Rookie Jim Nash was 12-1 in 17 starts, Lew Krause went 14-9 with a 2.99 ERA, Jack Aker was probably the best reliever in the league, and Bert Campaneris became a star.

In '67, there was suddenly hope in Kansas City. The starting rotation of Nash, Odom, Lew Krause, Hunter, and Chuck Dobson had an average age of 21.8 years. Rick Monday was ready to play regularly, Reggie Jackson, like Monday, plucked from Arizona State in the amateur draft, arrived, as did another ASU alum, Sal Bando.

Catfish began to flash signs of brilliance. He had four shutouts by mid-June and earned his second All-Star selection, pitching the last five innings in one of the midsummer classic's most memorable contests. Although Catfish gave up a solo home run to Tony Perez in the 15th inning of a 2–1 loss, he impressed everyone with his poise and command.

The A's, however, unraveled as the season wore on. They finished in the cellar again. Discipline on the young squad was sorely lacking. Alvin Dark was more interested in being popular than in cracking the whip. The headstrong boys took advantage, which culminated in a tawdry incident on a team flight from Boston to Kansas City, in which many players were drunk and one player had sex with a stewardess in the bathroom. Finley blew up, Dark was fired, Lew Krause, as a player who was single, was made the fall guy for the illicit airborne dalliance, and Hawk Harrelson, one of the few A's who'd had a good year, was given his outright release. Finley didn't even stop to trade him for something in return. Then Finley made his big move: On October 18, 1967, a week after the end of the stirring Cardinals–Red Sox World Series the owners voted to allow Finley to move the team to Oakland the next year; in a hastily convened second meeting, they agreed that, in two years' time, Kansas City, where attendance had never topped 800,000, would get an expansion team, as would Seattle.

Catfish finished the year 13-17, with a 2.81 ERA and five shutouts.

OAKLAND–ALAMEDA COUNTY Stadium, built two years earlier without a tenant, was a pitcher's ballpark. It was on the small side—330 feet down the lines, 385 in the alleys, 410 to dead center. It had the biggest foul-ball area in baseball, and the cool, damp, ocean air, especially at night, was hard to hit a ball through. The year 1968 was also the year of the pitcher, one that would see the first 30-game winner since 1934 and microscopic ERAs across both leagues, led by Bob Gibson's 1.12. The year was as close as baseball would get to revisiting the dead-ball era of a half-century before. It was also the most domestically tumultuous year in American society since the Civil War.

Racial inequality, legislative empowerment through the Civil Rights Act, the spread of inner-city poverty, and the escalating war in Vietnam had radicalized the streets and classrooms across the country. Martin Luther King Jr. was killed in April. Columbia University was occupied by striking students in May, protesting the school's involvement with the Defense Department. The Students for a Democratic Society were organizing disruptive protests in universities nationwide, the Black Panthers were boycotting and arming themselves in several major cities, from New Haven to Berkeley. Muhammad Ali, stripped of his boxing title for refusing induction into the military, was touring college campuses as a beacon of pacifism. President Johnson declared he would not seek reelection. Nixon was bound for the Republican nomination; Humphrey and Eugene McCarthy were trying to fend off the late entry of Robert Kennedy on the Democrat side. Detroit, which had erupted in flames and looting the year before, was once again a tinderbox; Newark, too, was ready to blow. America's white middle class sensed that revolution was in the air; the children of the middle and upper classes were waving their own flags of protest, through drugs, long hair, and rock 'n' roll music. Nothing, it seemed, was beyond the reach of a new disorder. Not even a tradition as venerable as the Kentucky Derby could avoid controversy, as Dancer's Image was disqualified because a drug—butazolidin—was found in its blood. "That's chaos can you produce chaos? Alice asked," in a Donald Barthelme story of the time that confounded the critics. For a long dark moment in 1968, the country feasted on chaos.

THE BAD-BOY OAKLAND A's hit the Bay Area like some absurd form of theater. Day-Glo uniforms, white shoes, long hair, irreverent nicknames, and lots of youth. They played their first game in front of more than 50,000 people; California governor Ronald Reagan threw out the first ball; Miss California took a turn and Commissioner Eckert made a few remarks; and, in a peculiarly twisted affront to authority, Charley O., Finley's ass, got a police escort. During the national anthem, fireworks burst in the air. During the game, Boog Powell hit a long bomb off Catfish, and the A's lost their first game in Oakland, 4–1.

The team had a 2-6 opening home stand and quickly found themselves playing in front of 6,000 fans. But during the second home stand, in the 12th home game of the year, Catfish would give 6,298 people something to remember.

On May 8, Hunter was exactly one month past his 22nd birthday. He was in his fourth full year in the big leagues, with a lifetime record of 32–38. He was 2-2 for the year. In his last outing, on May 3, he'd pitched a five-hitter in Boston and hit a two-run double in a 7–2 win, helped by three hits by Reggie Jackson. Now back home for their second home stand, the A's had split the first two with the Twins, beating Dean Chance 2–1 on Monday night, May 6, behind a Jackson homer, and losing to Jim Perry the next night, ending a rare A's winning streak—four games. Nonetheless, the A's were beginning to flash the kind of quality pitching, team speed, solid defense, and long-ball power that in a few years would make them the dominant team in the game. For the moment, they were playing .500 ball at 12-12, and facing a team that had lost the pennant in '67 to Boston by one game.

Minnesota had started the season red hot, reeling off six straight wins, but they were struggling when they arrived in Oakland, only one game in front of the A's. The Twins lineup, however, was solid.

Cesar Tovar batted leadoff. The slender 27-year-old Venezuelan had taken over as the regular third baseman for the Twins. He was a tough .270 hitter who could spray the ball to all fields. He would lead the A.L. at one time or another in hits, doubles, and triples. He (like Campaneris) would play every position in a nine-inning game. Over a six-year span for the Twins, he would average 98 runs scored a season. The great Rod Carew, born on a trail in the Panama Canal Zone but raised in New York City, batted second and played second base. He was hitting over .350 early in the season. Harmon Killebrew batted third and played first. He was in his prime, coming off a 44-home-run, 113-RBI, 131-base-on-balls season. At the moment, he was tied with Frank Howard for the league lead in round-trippers at six, and seemed headed for another great year (a hamstring pull in the All-Star Game would end that). Tony Oliva batted cleanup and played right field. Oliva was a superstar, having won the A.L. batting title in each of his first two years in the big leagues. His bad knees had yet to loosen, and in early May he was hitting only .235, though he had knocked in 13 runs, second on the team to Killebrew's 15. Big Ted Uhlaender, a left-handed hitter, was playing center field and on something of a tear himself with 13 RBI and hitting .274. The popular Bob Allison, whose career, like Killebrew's, began back in the '50s, when the Twins were the Senators, batted sixth and roamed left field. A power-hitting three-time All-Star, Allison was coming off a 24-home-run season and was hitting .308 at the time. The one hole in his game was a big one: He struck out a hundred times a year like clockwork. The menace in the Minnesota lineup diminished after Allison, with the light-hitting Jackie Hernandez at short, who split the job with the equally light-hitting Frank Quilici. The Twins were still wondering what happened to Zoilo Versalles, their 1965 league MVP who had about four terrific years, but then, in '67, batted an even .200 in nearly 600 at-bats. He was traded to the Dodgers for Ron Perranoski and John Roseboro, his skills seemingly forever misplaced. Batting eighth was the catcher, Bruce Look, a smallish backstop playing in his only major league season. Roseboro, who would do the bulk of the Twins catching during the season, had the night off. Look, like Roseboro, hit left-handed. Dave Boswell would do the pitching for Minnesota. A tall right-hander with good, hard stuff, Boswell was still learning his craft. He would win 20 games for the Twins in '69, but would retire from the game with only 68 career wins.

For the A's, it was Campy Campaneris leading off and playing short; he was doing what he would do for many years; hit around .260 and steal whatever he could (he had 14 swipes already). Reggie Jackson was in the number-two hole, a reminder of how much speed he once possessed before he bulked up and became the lumbering slugger of his Yankee days a decade later. In 1968, he was lithe and wiry, like a young Hank Aaron, with lots of air in his jersey. He was pounding the ball, hitting .314 at game time with four home runs (he would finish the year with 29, and then bust out completely in 1969 with 47). Sal Bando batted third and played third. He had a hot spring training, hitting 10 home runs to win the starting job. Bando, only 24 years old, was elected team captain, and he proved his mettle in the long run. In the next nine years with the A's, he would play in all but 50 games, hit 192 home runs, and excel in post-season play. Ray Webster, who had but a short career in the bigs, was batting fourth and playing first, giving Danny Cater a night off. The second baseman was John Donaldson, filling in for Dick Green. Donaldson was actually hitting his weight: .165. The veteran Jim Pagliaroni was doing the catching, a duty he shared with the young Dave Duncan, who hadn't learned to hit above .200 yet (by the time he did, Gene Tenace would be ready to strap on the gear). Rick Monday was in center field. Much ballyhooed as the first player chosen in the first-ever amateur draft, and receiving a bonus of more than $100,000, Monday was coming along slowly, but played an elegant center field and had a little pop in his bat.

Rookie Joe Rudi, just recalled the day before from Vancouver in the Pacific Coast League, was starting in left. In spring training, Rudi had been a project of new Oakland coach Joe DiMaggio, who loved the work habits shown by the six-foot-two-inch, 200-pound Californian. Rudi would learn a lot about fielding from Joe D, and a lot from Charlie Lau about hitting, but that was further down the road.

In May 1968, the guy batting ninth for the A's might be a better hitter than Rudi: that would be Catfish, though you wouldn't know it from manager Bob Kennedy. When Catfish showed up at 4:30 to take batting practice, he was shooed out of the cage. Kennedy told him he was "fouling up" the hitters. Hunter didn't say much, as he wasn't one to talk back. But he threw his bat against the cage netting in anger and went back to the clubhouse and began going over the Twins hitters.

Catfish went right to work, breezing through the first inning, getting Tovar to bounce to Bando at third and inducing the tough Carew to pull a slider to right, where Jackson camped under it for the out. Big Harmon was up next, last year's home-run king in the A.L. (in a tie with Yastrzemski, who got to claim the Triple Crown anyway) and the hitter Catfish feared the most. But the Killer took a called third strike.

With the early 6 P.M. start, both Hunter and his opponent Boswell had the advantage over the hitters, at least until darkness truly fell. In the twilight with the lights on at Oakland–Alameda, the seeing wasn't too good. Although Campaneris reached on a single to right field to start things off for the A's, and promptly stole second, Jackson, badly fooled, nubbed one to third-baseman Tovar, who held Campy at second before throwing Jackson out. After a walk to Bando, Webster hit into a 4-6-3 double play to end the inning. The A's wouldn't get as close to scoring again until the seventh.

In the Twins second, Catfish, being too fine with the crafty Tony Oliva, fell behind 3–0. But he battled back to get him swinging. Ted Uhlaender, a fundamentally sound ballplayer, grounded out to Donaldson at second. Bob Allison became Hunter's third strikeout victim.

Monday managed a two-out single in the second, but was out trying to steal.

It was the bottom of the order for the Twins third, and it was a walk in the park for Catfish: weak-hitting Jackie Hernandez rolled out to Campaneris, Look swung through a Hunter slider for the second out, and Boswell twisted one into the air over short for out number three, number nine on the night.

In the A's third, Catfish got to send a little message to his manager: He doubled with one out. But the open base went to Jackson via a careful walk by Boswell, and then Bando fanned. No score after three.

Second time through the order, and the Twins almost broke the Hunter spell. Cesar Tovar jumped on a Hunter offering and nailed it to straightaway left field, where the rookie Joe Rudi was playing. Rudi held his ground, did not charge or retreat, and caught the ball in his tracks, the kind of ball that can eat a rookie up. (Working with DiMaggio was paying off.) Carew then grounded to short and Killebrew went down on strikes for the second time, this time looking.

Boswell was reached for a single and a walk in the A's half of the fourth, and was rescued by another double play, which he started, 1-6-3.

With the game scoreless, the small crowd grew more intense in its attention. This was, after all, the first year of major league baseball in Oakland, practically the first month of it. They were playing one of the best clubs in the league. But on this night, the Twins seemed no match for the 22-year-old country boy. Minnesota went down once again in the fifth—Oliva flying to center-fielder Rick Monday, Uhlaender following with a sharply hit ball that the fleet Reggie hauled in in fairly deep right. Then, the nearest thing to a hit all night against Hunter: Bob Allison hit a hard one-hopper right at Bando, an easy play but for a bad hop. The ball jumped over Bando's left shoulder by his ear but his glove flashed up for the grab. Allison was out easily at first.

Campaneris tried to make trouble in the bottom of the fifth, getting his second hit, then drawing an errant pickoff throw from Boswell, with the slender speedster moving all the way to third. With two out, Jackson took a called third strike, and the game remained scoreless.

There was nothing doing against Hunter in the sixth, as he struck out the side, the seven, eight, and nine hitters. He was as sharp as a brand-new hunting knife.

The A's continued to fall quickly against Boswell, and the crowd grew restless as the game moved into the seventh.

Hunter would later say that reserve outfielder Mike Hershberger began to mutter something in the dugout like, "Didn't somebody get on base in the early innings?" as if to himself. Knowing otherwise, no one moved to enlighten the bench-sitter. Instead, Hunter went out to face the top of the Twins order. Tovar, who had hit the ball on the nose but right at Rudi in the fourth, hit one the other way this time, resulting in an easier chance for Jackson in right. Carew then made a bid to end the evening's perfection when he sliced a line drive the other way, at the nervous left fielder. "I thought it might get Rudi," Catfish would later say. But Rudi did the getting, turning on the ball and making a nice catch going away. Then it was Killebrew again. Although he had struck Killer out in his previous two at-bats, Hunter still worked carefully. The count went full, and Hunter threw what his manager later called the "gutsiest pitch" of the night, a changeup curve. Killebrew took his mighty round rip and was so out in front he lost his bat, which helicoptered out over a ducking Catfish and landed at second base. Strike three, inning over. Twenty-one up and down, still scoreless.

Catfish brought an end to the scoring drought in the bottom of the seventh. After Monday blooped a double to center field and advanced to third on a wild pitch, manager Kennedy apparently didn't trust his pitcher to make good contact. He gave the sign for a squeeze play and Hunter executed perfectly, Monday scored, and Hunter was safe at first because Carew didn't cover: 1–0, A's.

In the eighth, Catfish's mastery was abetted by the nearness, now, of winning. Two more innings and the game would be his. Oliva popped meekly to second. Uhlaender flied to the busy and perhaps slightly traumatized Rudi in left (he later admitted hoping the balls would not be hit to him). Bob Allison grounded to short for out number 24.

Winning became even a greater possibility in the bottom of the eighth, as the A's added three runs, but not without a lot of grinding of the gears from both managers. Bando and Webster hit back-to-back singles to start things off. An attempted sacrifice bunt by Donaldson proved futile, as catcher Bruce Look nailed Bando at third. Pagliaroni then hit one in the hole at short, but Jackie Hernandez dived and made the stop and, from his knees, nipped Donaldson at second. Then Boswell walked Monday to load the bases with two out. Kennedy decided that perhaps the rookie Rudi had had enough excitement for one evening and he pinch-hit for him with left-handed-hitting Floyd Robinson. But when Boswell fell behind 2–0, Twins manager Cal Ermer thought to bring in the lefty Ron Perranoski, prompting Kennedy to pinch-hit for Robinson mid-at-bat with Danny Cater, who worked out a walk, making it 2–0. Striding to the plate, the bases still loaded, was Catfish Hunter. Of course, there was a joke or two in the dugout about Kennedy pinch-hitting for Hunter, but no one thought Kennedy would take such a suggestion. Good thing: Catfish lined a single to right for two more runs and a 4–0 A's lead.

In the exciting ninth, with the meager crowd on its feet, and Hunter's parents, way back in North Carolina, listening to the game on the radio via a phone line from Oakland, Jimmy Hunter faced down imperfection. He knew the enormity of the moment. Johnny Roseboro, who had witnessed (from the bench) Koufax's perfect game three years before, batted for Jackie Hernandez. Roseboro had been on a hot streak with the bat, but he could manage only a grounder to second against the pinpoint delivery of Hunter. Bruce Look went down swinging, which brought up the 27th man, in the person of Rich Reese, a 26-year-old, six-foot-three-inch, 200-pound good-hitting utility man. Accounts vary as to exactly how the last at-bat went, but whatever the version, it was not for the weak of heart. According to Catfish himself, it went like this: fastball, fouled off; fastball for a ball; fastball, "same spot," ball two; fastball swing and miss, 2-2. Then a slider that "knifed through the strike zone, cutting the plate in two," but called ball three by ump Jerry Neudecker. So, on 3-2, the great battle began: five straight fastballs, all of them fouled back by Reese. Then a sixth 3-2 fastball, swung on and missed, and Catfish had it in the bag.

The game accounts in the local papers have it that Reese actually fouled off five straight pitches with the count at 2-2, before Neudecker missed the pitch that cut the heart of the plate, for ball three. Whatever the truth, the at-bat is exhausting to contemplate enduring, as a fan, participant, or umpire. The fact is, Reese swung through a 3-2 pitch and is now part of history.

THE 1968 A'S SQUAD ended up with an 82-80 record, the first Athletics team to finish above .500 since 1952, when they played in Connie Mack Stadium in Philadelphia. Campaneris led the league in hits and stolen bases; Cater finished second to Yastrzemski for the batting title, hitting .290. Catfish was a disappointing 13-13, but had shown that he was capable of absolute mastery of the opposition, and good opposition at that. Nash, following his sparkling rookie year, went 13-13 as well. Blue Moon Odom won 16 and Dobson 12. It would take three more years before the A's put it all together.

In '69, Jackson would hit 37 home runs by the All-Star break, seemingly a threat to Maris's record (he would tail off, pitched around and strained by the pressure, and finish with 47); the A's, in the first year of divisional play, would enjoy a second-place finish, nine games back of the Twins.

Some key trades—Monday for Ken Holtzman, Don Mincher for Darold Knowles—and the discovery that Rollie Fingers didn't belong in the starting rotation but in the bullpen turned things around for Oakland. There was also the development of Rudi into a Gold Glove outfielder who could hit .300 and the arrival of Gene Tenace to anchor the catching position. But it would take manager Dick Williams to put them over the top and make the motley crew a minidynasty in the early seventies. The team that even Catfish lamented was "lacking in baseball discipline" got what it needed in the tough ex-Marine.

Williams arrived in '71, more or less deputized Sal Bando, and won the attention and respect of the ragtag team of potential superstars. Hunter flourished under Williams, wining 21 games that year, the first of five straight 20-win seasons. And Vida Blue would come screaming across the baseball firmament, going 24–8, striking out 301 batters in 312 innings, and pitching eight shutouts. The team would be swept by a tough Orioles team in the American League Championship Series in '71, but in '72, they would finish with the best record in the American League. Catfish would win 21 again and in the postseason the A's would beat the Billy Martin–led Tigers to win the pennant and then brashly go on to upset the Big Red Machine in the Series in seven games behind Tenace, who hit four home runs, and Catfish, who won two games. The Athletics had taken their first World Series since 1930, when Al Simmons and Lefty Grove played in Shibe Park.

They made it two in a row in 1973. Catfish won 21 games for the third straight year, in a row, losing only 5; Kenny Holtzman was 21-13; Fingers had 22 saves and a 1.92 ERA; Jackson drove in 117 runs and hit 32 homers; Billy North took over center field from the departed Rick Monday and hit .285 and stole 53 bases. Catfish's five-hit shutout eliminated the Orioles in Game Five of the ALCS. Down three games to two against the Mets, Catfish outpitched Tom Seaver in Game Six, setting up a Game Seven shellacking of Jon Matlack, giving the A's their second straight world championship. The Series, however, was not without its Finley moment: A's second baseman Mike Andrews's two 12th-inning errors in Game Two prompted the enraged owner to force Andrews to agree that he had injured himself, so that Finley could get him off the roster. Bowie Kuhn had to intercede and reinstate Andrews a day later. Andrews's teammate were so appalled at Finley's action they showed up for Game Three wearing Andrews's number on their sleeves. Finley would worsen the situation by consigning the A's wives to the unfriendly upper deck at

Shea Stadium, while reserving the customary field-level seats for cronies and business contacts. Dick Williams, in the midst of the Series, told his players that he'd had enough and wouldn't be back the next year. He kept his word.

In 1974, it was the return of the Dark Ages, as in Alvin. The A's didn't miss a beat. They brawled and squabbled their way to a division title and an ALCS win, in four games, over the Orioles, with Catfish, who finished the regular seasons with 25 wins, closing out the O's. In the Series, the Dodgers were hardly any opposition at all, falling in five to the mighty A's. Although the games were low scoring and close, the A's always seemed to be ahead, scoring first in four of the five games and then relying on Fingers to close the door. Three straight World Series crowns, and a Cy Young Award for Hunter.

Enter Marvin Miller.

MILLER HAD BEEN on the job as executive director of the Major League Players Association since the vote in Miami in 1966. He had already put together a string of successes for the union, modest from today's perspective, but quite revolutionary in the eyes of players then—increases in minimum salaries, enhancements to the pension plan, and various workplace adjustments. In the negotiations for the Basic Agreement in '73, Miller won the players' right to salary arbitration before an independent arbiter. But gutting the reserve clause remained an elusive goal. Miller's belief was that the infamous clause 10(a) of the standard contract was not renewable in perpetuity. Here's how the clause reads:

"If prior to March 1, the Player and the Club have not agreed upon the terms of the contract, then on or before 10 days after said March 1, the Club shall have the right by written notice to the Player to renew this contract for the period of one year."

Miller felt that there was no reason to read the team option as being renewable year after year. "One year," it said. And Miller was determined to get a judge to agree.

When the 1974 season began, Miller had his eye on seven players who were playing though still unsigned. But none of them played out the entire year—that is, played out their option year, in Miller's view—without signing. Despairing of having lost his chance at a test case of the clause, Miller was delighted to discover, in late September, that Hunter had been in a fierce contract dispute all year with Finley.

Hunter had signed a two-year deal for $100,000 per year, but to ease his tax burden, he was to receive half the money in the form of payments to a North Carolina insurance company. Unfortunately for Finley, this $50,000 in payments for the life insurance annuity could not be deducted as a salary expense, and he balked at making them. Hunter's lawyer, Mr. Cherry of Ahoksie, North Carolina, allowed Miller to file a grievance on Hunter's behalf. All attempts by other owners to get Finley to pay up failed. As the A's beat up on the Dodgers in the Fall Classic, the case was given over to arbitrator Peter Seitz. In December 1974, he ruled that Finley was in default in his contract, and ordered that Finley pay the $50,000 in the manner agreed to and terminate the contract. At Miller's request, Seitz expressly made Catfish Hunter a "free agent," language he had overlooked in writing his first draft of the decision. That's when Catfish got the phone call setting him free.

This was not a case of an ordinary player of certain tenure who is underpaid getting to shop himself to the highest bidder. This is a 10-year veteran at the top of his game ready to vault any team into serious contention for postseason play; this is a serious, hard-working, popular pitcher with a wealth of talent and experience. This is a 28-year-old Cy Young Award winner. This is the fellow who said, "Winning isn't the only thing, but wanting to win is."

Hunter's lawyer, Carlton Cherry, decided that maybe there would be enough interest in Catfish that it made sense for the suitors to come to North Carolina rather than jet all around themselves in December. So down they came, nearly every team sending GMs or managers or players they felt could help make a compelling case for their club's offer. The Indians sent fellow North Carolinian Gaylord Perry, who arrived wearing a feed cap. Everyone stayed at the Tomahawk Motel in Ahoskie, where members of Cherry's law firm heard them out. Mr. Cherry bought up the town's entire supply of baseballs—250—so that Catfish could sign them if so requested by those who'd come all the way to a remote North Carolina town to make Abbott Hunter's boy rich.

Marvin Miller had counseled Cherry not to let Catfish jump at the first big offer, that perhaps no one knew what big could be. At the start of things, doubling Catfish's salary to $200,000 a year seemed ambitious. By the end, the Yankees had soared to the front of the bidding with a $3.75-million offer for five years structured the way Catfish wanted it: a million dollars as a signing bonus, a million in life insurance annuity, the rest in other deferred payments and college funds for his children.

Although the Padres and Pirates offered more, Hunter leaned toward the Yankees and their new owner George Steinbrenner, though the clincher was probably the fact that the Yankees chief scout was the man who had signed Hunter back in 1963, Clyde Kluttz.

Hunter fell in love with playing in New York. Mostly, he loved the players he found there—tough-minded, fun-loving professionals who played to win. At the beginning of the season, he lived at the Sheraton Hotel on Seventh Avenue, as did his new buddies Thurman Munson and Lou Piniella. These three amigos got along so well—in the clubhouse as well as in the night clubs—that Catfish had to order up a house in New Jersey, get out of the hotel, and move his family north. He didn't want to get old too fast, and Mr. Steinbrenner was paying him very well.

Unfortunately for Catfish, he couldn't save himself from a serious case of pitcher abuse. Yankee manager Bill Virdon and his midseason replacement Billy Martin overpitched him. Hunter pitched all but 18 innings of the 39 games he started, finishing with 30 complete games, 7 shutouts, and 328 innings pitched on his way to a 23-14 record. It is the most innings Hunter had ever pitched in a year, and the most he would ever throw. The Yankees faded to a disappointing third place, while in Oakland, the A's won the West division only to lose to the Red Sox in the ALCS.

In 1976, the Yankees returned to a renovated Yankee Stadium after playing in Shea Stadium for a year. The off-season trade of Bobby Bonds to the Angels for center-fielder Mickey Rivers and right-handed pitcher Ed Figueroa put the team over the top. Everybody in the lineup behind leadoff hitter Mick the Quick hit—Munson and Chris Chambliss and Graig Nettles, who led the league in home runs. Figueroa won 19 games. Catfish, however, began to suffer from shoulder pain. For the first time since 1970, he won fewer than 20 games, finishing 17-15. Still, he became only the third pitcher (after Cy Young and Christy Mathewson) to win 200 games by the age of 31. No one has done that since.

Hunter got the Game One start in the 1976 playoffs against the Royals and pitched a five-hitter for the win. The Yankees, on a ninth-inning home run by Chambliss in Game Five, brought George Steinbrenner his first pennant, and the Yankees copped their first flag in a dozen years. But the Reds, still Big and Red, swept them in four games in the World Series. Hunter pitched Game Two, and lost a tough complete-game, 10-hit effort.

In 1977, the straw that stirred the drink arrived. Almost immediately, a very Oakland style of discord enwrapped the Yankees. But still, the team won. Reggie Jackson hit 32 home runs and drove in 110, Nettles hit 37, and

Sparky Lyle was the swashbuckling closer. With little help from the sore-armed Catfish, who had his worst year as a professional at 9-9 with a 4.71 ERA, the Yanks won the division by 2.5 games over both Baltimore and Boston, and defeated the Royals (again) in a five-game series behind great relief work from Lyle and the hitting of Munson, Rivers, and Piniella. Then the Yanks put away the Dodgers in a six-game Series, the first time the two teams had met in postseason play since 1956. Jackson hit three homers in Game Six to secure the legend of Reg-gie. He became Mr. October.

IN THE OFF-SEASON, Catfish was back in his beloved Hertford, working the farm, enjoying the outdoor life. Once again, however, the life outdoors in small-town America proved to be more dangerous than the nightlife of the big city. On January 10, Hunter was up and on the road by 7 A.M. with the town druggist next to him in his truck. They were headed duck-hunting. Then they saw black smoke curling above Hertford and they turned around and headed back to town. Two 30,000-gallon oil tanks had blown at a depot on the south side of town. A building was ablaze. It was five degrees out.

Firemen from Hertford and surrounding towns were fighting the blaze and the cold. Their clothes and gloves were icing up. Catfish sped home and returned to the scene with as much warm clothing and as many pairs of gloves as he could find. Although the fire seemed under control, it was not. Another tank suddenly blew, and a 12-foot-diameter, 400-pound, three-eighths-inch-thick steel plate, red-hot, flew into the air, flipped, came down to earth, rolled, sheared off part of a truck, bounded along a sidewalk and landed on Catfish and two firemen, flattening them. The two firefighters were knocked out; Catfish somehow managed to lift the scalding plate off all of them. He thought he wasn't going to make it, but there he stood. Rescue workers tended to the firemen; Catfish appeared shaken but unhurt. He then ran off, sprinting back and forth, toward town and back. He found his truck and crawled in and didn't move for 15 minutes. Then he drove home. He was in shock.

No one was killed in the Hertford fire, and the damage was contained to the oil depot area. Catfish was unhurt, or so it seemed until six weeks later, on his trip south for spring training. It became obvious as he drove down with Helen and the kids that he had a problem: He was constantly thirsty and every 15 minutes he had to go to the bathroom. Upon his arrival, he talked to the team doctor, who sent him to the hospital for tests. His blood sugar was 500 milligrams per deciliter, about five times above average. The doctor told him that it was a wonder he hadn't passed out by now. Catfish was officially diagnosed a Type I diabetic.

It was the beginning of a physical degradation for Catfish. Although the diabetes was controlled by medication and diet, he developed a swollen ligament in his arm. When the 1978 season began, he could hardly raise his arm above his shoulder. He pitched sparingly and ineffectively. The team played poorly. Billy Martin was drinking heavily, squabbling with Reggie Jackson and the press and Steinbrenner. Finally, Martin got himself fired by insulting his right fielder and his boss ("One's a born liar, the other's convicted," referring to Jackson's theory of truth and Steinbrenner's illegal contributions to the Nixon campaign). But there was relief. Easygoing Bob Lemon replaced Martin, the New York City newspapers went on strike, making the clubhouse writer-free, and a doctor, putting Hunter under a general anesthetic, wrenched his right arm this way and that until something popped. Years of lesions, most likely. When he woke up, Catfish was pain-free.

The Yankees had dropped 14.5 games behind the Red Sox. All seemed lost for the year. But then Catfish, throwing with an ease he hadn't felt since he was with Oakland, went 6-0 in the month of August. No one in the league could touch Ron Guidry, and the Yankees massacred Boston in two successive series and forced a playoff. Bucky Dent hit a home run at Fenway to turn the tide, Reggie hit another to provide the margin of victory, and the Yankees went on to beat the Royals in four and the Dodgers in the World Series in six, with Catfish closing them out in the final game.

Catfish received his fifth World Series ring during a ceremony the following spring. Nineteen seventy-nine would be the last year of his Yankee contract and the last year of his playing career. The Yankees lost their chemistry and then they lost their leader: Thurman Munson died in a crash of his own eight-passenger jet just short of a landing strip in Ohio. Catfish also lost his father and the agent who landed him twice, Clyde Kluttz. On the field, Catfish's skills had vanished. He finished 2-9. Toward the end of the season, when his retirement was a known fact, the Yankees held a Catfish Hunter Day. George Steinbrenner credited the acquisition of Hunter for immediately bringing the moribund Yankees into contention. Indeed, in Hunter's five years in the Bronx, the Yankees were in three World Series, winning twice.

Catfish returned to Hertford at the age of 33, finishing with 224 career wins. He was back to the kind of life he understood best, and where he had developed the baseball skills that made him a rich man. Sadly, the physical woes that had periodically bedeviled him returned. In September 1998, he was diagnosed with amyotrophic lateral sclerosis, the same disease that took Lou Gehrig. After a bad fall shortly thereafter, Catfish was hospitalized. He never came home. He died September 9, 1999, at the age of 53, but the memory of the easygoing, fun-loving country boy pitcher who was a winner wherever he went lives on. Not only immortalized in his own bronze plaque in Cooperstown, but even in the songbook of Bob Dylan, who wrote the blues ditty "Catfish" in 1975, when Catfish hit New York:

> *Lazy stadium night*
> *Catfish on the mound.*
> *"Strike three," the umpire said,*
> *Batter have to go back and sit down.*

> *Catfish, million-dollar-man,*
> *Nobody can throw the ball like Catfish can.*

> *Used to work on Mr. Finley's farm*
> *But the old man wouldn't pay*
> *So he packed his glove and took his arm*
> *An' one day he just ran away.*

> *Catfish, million-dollar-man,*
> *Nobody can throw the ball like Catfish can.*

> *Come up where the Yankees are,*
> *Dress up in a pinstripe suit,*
> *Smoke a custom-made cigar,*
> *Wear an alligator boot.*

> *Catfish, million-dollar-man,*
> *Nobody can throw the ball like Catfish can.*

> *Carolina born and bred,*
> *Love to hunt the little quail.*
> *Got a hundred-acre spread,*
> *Got some huntin' dogs for sale.*

Catfish, million-dollar-man,
Nobody can throw the ball like Catfish can.

Reggie Jackson at the plate
Seein' nothin' but the curve,
Swing too early or too late
Got to eat what Catfish serve.

Catfish, million-dollar-man,
Nobody can throw the ball like Catfish can.

Even Billy Martin grins
When the Fish is in the game.
Every season twenty wins
Gonna make the Hall of Fame.

Catfish, million-dollar-man,
Nobody can throw the ball like Catfish can.

CHAPTER EIGHT

Big Lennie

Len Barker
May 15, 1981

L EN BARKER GOT TO know the streets of several large American cities as a ballplayer would—at night, in the company of male friends, with plenty of cash and a hotel key in his pocket. On the streets of Chicago in May 1981, Barker and his Cleveland Indian teammates were returning by bus to their hotel from a satisfying win over the White Sox. It was near midnight. They were going through the Bridgeport section on the South Side, a once mostly Irish neighborhood now mostly Hispanic, when pitching coach Dave Duncan spotted an altercation on the sidewalk. A car had pulled over and three guys in gold jackets had jumped a young couple. Unmistakably, a baseball bat flashed in the sulfurous lamp glow. The young man was getting the worst of it, while his female companion stood by, screaming. Duncan implored the driver to

stop the bus. Out poured the Cleveland Indians in street clothes. Led by
Duncan, there were Andre Thornton, Joe Charboneau, Rick Manning,
Jorge Orta, Bo Diaz, Duane Kuiper, Bert Blyleven, and Len Barker, all six-
feet-five-inches and 230 pounds of him. The whole team, even the writers, got out. There was plenty of thumping; the guys in gold jackets were
routed. They fled for their lives but didn't get far before Chicago police
put the collar on them. The victim, a 19-year-old Chicagoan named Terry
McKimson, had wandered onto the wrong turf with his girlfriend. Now,
not only were the Indians in first place in the American League West;
they were a force for good in society. "You saved my life," wrote McKimson in a letter to the team.

A year later, on Chicago's State Street, after another game at
Comiskey Park, Barker, the young ace of the Cleveland staff, found himself, this time, on the wrong side of the law, scuffling with two plain-
clothes cops who thought they spotted Barker ditching a marijuana
cigarette. He got arrested, along with a journeyman left-hander named Ed
Glynn; they paid fines. Two years later, along with Charboneau, Brewers
pitcher Mike Caldwell and outfielder Dick Davis, Barker was implicated
in a cocaine investigation. By the time the allegations surfaced, Barker
was no longer an Indian but an Atlanta Brave with a multimillion-dollar
contract, a bad arm, and his own exclusive phalanx of unhappy fans.

Six years after that embarrassment, in 1991, Barker, retired from the
game and running a used-car dealership along a tough stretch of Stewart
Avenue in Atlanta, was talking baseball with a reporter from the *Atlanta
Journal-Constitution*. Baseball had moved out of his life. It was mostly
warranty renewals, credit checks, and counting the cars on the lot.
Barker still cut an imposing figure. His belted blue jeans balanced a considerable roll of flesh in front; tucked in the back of his waistband was a
.45-caliber pistol—"for insurance," he said. The occasion for the interview was the 10th anniversary of a cold Friday evening in Cleveland,
when Barker, in a career otherwise marked by mediocrity and brief bouts
of ignominy, was, for two hours, absolutely perfect. Barker was pleased to
have a chance to talk about the game, but the reporter couldn't help
bringing up the worst trade in Atlanta Braves history, the one that
brought them Barker and six years of bad luck. "It wasn't on purpose,"
Barker felt compelled to point out. "I didn't want that zipper on my arm,
but I had to," referring to a surgical scar. No wonder Barker carried a gun.

———————

BARKER WAS BORN on July 7, 1955, in Fort Knox, Kentucky, where his father was stationed as an Army master sergeant. Three years later, his mother, Emogene, left the life of the Army wife and took Len, his two older brothers, and a young sister north, to Trevose, a blue-collar township, just outside Philadelphia. Trevose was mostly mills and factories and small homes and middle-America street corners. Mrs. Barker got work at the National Biscuit Company plant, divorced, remarried, and the family settled into an unremarkable, stable 1960s way of being. Lennie played the three American sports: He was a hulking blocking full-back on the football team, clearing the way for a couple of all-state half-backs; a center on the basketball team, before breaking an ankle; and, after his freshman year, a pitcher on the Neshaminy High School baseball team.

Barker went undefeated in his sophomore year, winning all six decisions. Well over six-feet and still growing, Barker attracted the attention of scouts in the area, who made notes in their calendars to keep an eye on this boy come his senior year. But when a dozen or so scouts showed up for his last high-school game in the spring of 1972, they found a six-foot-four-inch 200 pounder who hadn't done anything but grow. That day, showing more girth than maturity on the mound, he lost the game; more than that, he lost the interest of the scouts, who started closing up their notebooks in the fifth inning. The riddle of why the promising sophomore of the 1970 season had won only five high-school games since then was now solved: He hadn't improved.

Maybe Barker had become distracted, because, as it turns out, he surely wasn't done improving. The early 1970s in America were certainly full enough of distractions: antiwar protests; Nixon was running for reelection on the promise that "peace was at hand"; violence on the streets of nearby Philadelphia as new mayor Frank Rizzo cracked down. Baseball, too, had its youthful protests, its long-haired radicals preaching personal freedom. And the game had its own recalcitrant, entrenched older generation—the gray-suited owners, who, like Nixon, like Rizzo, sought to reinstate an older order.

In April 1972, baseball ground to halt. The Players Association made its first stand, a strike was called, and the union got what it had asked for: some small enhancements of the pension plan. But soon, the small pension plan issue became a lot bigger. Games were missed, the union held firm, the owners lost, and play resumed. In midsummer, two months after the first work stoppage in the history of American professionals sports, baseball held its first amateur draft. Oakland took Rick Monday. But no one drafted Len Barker, high-school graduate, and he was hugely disappointed.

Since the age of seven, Barker has said, baseball was his dream. He would tell this up front to the football recruiters, trying to discourage them and maybe entice a fence-sitting baseball scout. But the scouts were gone, and football and college did not interest the 17-year-old. So Barker turned to the one baseball guy who had kept close—Harry Startzell, a part-time scout for the Orioles. Not that Startzell had managed to interest the Orioles in Barker. Still, knowing that Startzell managed a team in the All-American Amateur Baseball Association, Barker asked for a tryout.

Pitching for Startzell's Levittown team in the summer and fall of '72, Barker did not lose a game, and the team went all the way to the AAABA World Series. Scouts began to notice again. Barker had filled out a little more and grown an inch, to a full six feet five inches. He was very raw but he threw hard. With proper mechanics, there was a chance he could be a major league pitcher. The brand-new Texas Rangers drafted Barker in the third round of the '73 draft. Barker, acting as his own agent, asked for a $30,000 bonus, was offered half that, said, "No thanks," but then settled for "$16,000 plus $7,500 if he made the majors."

For the next four years, Barker tried to find the maturation that had escaped him thus far as an athlete. He was dominant for Sarasota in the Gulf Coast League in '73, going 7-1 with a stingy 1.37 ERA. In '74, he moved to the Western Carolina League, playing for Gastonia, where he put up winning numbers, 11-7 and a 3.34 ERA. Pittsfield was next, in the tough Eastern League, and though Barker was on the losing end more often than not (7-12), the ERA was again sharp: 2.89.

As Barker was improving, he was also sowing his oats. He would later admit that long before he'd established himself as a player with a future, he would go out "four or five nights a week—sometimes the night before I pitched." The money wasn't bad and the working conditions were good. It was better than an Army base, a biscuit factory, or all-nighters at some state college. Next stop, town of Arlington. But what was the hurry? Baseball had reached a point where it could wait for a Len Barker. Expansion had thinned pitching talent across the board, a thrower with Barker's physical gift was worth the investment of time.

Baker worked his way up. Although the 1976 season began with a lockout of the players in spring training, Barker took advantage of the downtime by showing Rangers owner Brad Corbett that he could actually carry a bar. He lifted one off its pegs in a Pompano Beach club. Corbett was impressed, but somehow, a $7,000 bill had to be settled. Lucky for Barker, he did it for the team, or at least, the team's owner, who paid up the damages.

The antics didn't seem to harm Barker's chances with Texas. He got his first callup later in the year, and made two starts under manager Frank Luchessi and pitched a shutout, but most of his year was spent with Sacramento in the Pacific Coast League. Barker earned a longer look in '77, making 15 appearances but only 3 starts. He pitched effectively, going 4-1, striking out 51 batters in 47 innings. Billy Hunter took over as manager; the Rangers played well, finishing in second place behind strong years from Bert Blyleven, Toby Harrah, and Mike Hargrove—all of whom, along with Barker, would later figure in the sports life of Cleveland. For the time being, however, Hunter saw the big Barker as the future bullpen ace he needed. By '78, Barker was on the squad from opening day. In preseason, manager Hunter was moved to predict, "Barker will be the fireman of the year in baseball this season."

It was not to be. For all his preseason rah-rah, Hunter never gained confidence in Barker. The team was in a pennant race, the starting pitching was strong—Jon Matlack, Fergie Jenkins, Doyle Alexander anchoring the staff. The 23-year-old Barker languished in the bullpen. He says he sometimes went out there without his glove, knowing that the night wouldn't belong to him. His fastball turned on him; it went flat and lost steam. The infrequent work seemed to affect his arm strength. He tried to develop a changeup, but was hampered by his inactivity. The team finished second, and in the off-season Texas traded their unhappy big reliever, in a package with Bobby Bonds, to the Cleveland Indians, for a reliever they would use, Jim Kern, and veteran infielder Larvell Blanks.

Cleveland immediately had ideas for how to handle Barker. "Big as he is," said manager Jeff Torborg, starting his third year as a manager, "Len needs plenty of work and he'll get it. I also want to work with him on his delivery." President Gabe Paul had another suggestion for Barker: Stay away from the beer, lose 10 pounds.

It worked. In 1979, Barker got 19 starts, split 12 decisions, got hit around pretty good, but began to recover the velocity that he'd lost somewhere in the Texas bullpen. The Indians, the very embodiment of mediocrity for years and years, finished 81–80. Barker got trimmer and his fastball got faster.

In 1980, Len Barker the pitcher arrived. The lumbering, easygoing long-haired hurler had managed to stay a step ahead of a reputation for wildness off the field by reining in his wildness *on* the field—he had once thrown a pitch halfway up the backstop at Fenway—and the results were excellent. Barker won 19 games, walked a manageable 92 batters in nearly 250 innings, and led the American League in strikeouts. With Rookie-of-the-Year Joe Charboneau on their side, and Bert Blyleven acquired in an off-season trade, the Indians actually had their eyes set on their first pennant since 1954. Things had not been this good in Cleveland for a long time.

Terry Pluto, in his hilarious book *The Curse of Rocky Colavito*, details the haplessness of the team known in Ohio as "the Tribe": a 26-year-old Rocky Colavito, local idol and budding superstar, already with 123 homers to his credit (he'd hit 251 more) was traded by Cleveland GM Frank Lane in 1960 for 30-year-old Harvey Kuenn, who hit a total of 87 home runs in his 15 years; Lane then tried to make it up to the people of fair Cleveland by reacquiring a 32-year-old Colavito, with three years left in his career, in return for a young Tommy John, who had two wins to his credit, but who would win 286 more with other clubs, and Tommie Agee, who would become Rookie of the Year for the White Sox and a World Series star for the Mets. In between, "Trader" Lane also found time to deal away Roger Maris and Norm Cash. But maybe their Indian luck was changing: The absolutely nutty Charboneau—he ate raw eggs, shell and all, pulled his own teeth with the help of pliers and Jack Daniel's, even sutured a gash with fishing line—seemed like a real player. Dave Garcia was now the manager and was gung-ho: "We will win more than 90 games." The memory of Frank Lane was fading. Ownership was solid: Local trucking millionaire Steve O'Neill was an enthusiastic, hands-off majority owner (he had been a partner with fellow Clevelander Steinbrenner in the Yankees); Gabe Paul was the experienced president, and new GM Phil Seghi had proved adept at developing what seemed to be the team's strength: pitching. Blyleven, Barker, Rick Waits, John Denny, and the recovering Wayne Garland.

The off-season, though, had its own drama, and it involved much more than what was doing in Cleveland. That third collective-bargaining agreement, the one signed in 1976 that codified free agency but tabled the issue of compensation for the team losing a player, was due to expire at the end of the 1980 season. The owners replaced John Gaherin, their chief negotiator and someone they felt Marvin Miller had bloodied enough, with a tough, conservative former GE executive named Ray Grebey, whose expertise was "industrial relations."

As the conservative agenda swept the elections in November and the Reagan era began, Marvin Miller sensed he was in for a huge fight. The owners were going after what they'd lost. Grebey, icy and polished, came out swinging. Miller was right.

By 1981, Marvin Miller had been at the helm of the Major League Players Association for 15 years. He and the players had completed an ingenious dismantling of the reserve clause and introduced into common parlance a term usually saved for philosophy seminars: free agency. He had enhanced the players' pension plan, raised the minimum salary, and wedded salary arbitration with free agency in a way that maximized a player's ability to get his full market value after serving six years. It hadn't been easy. In the 1970s, during each spring training, Miller would read clause 10(a)—the infamous reserve clause—aloud to the player reps; he would cite basketball player Rick Barry's successful challenge of a similar clause in the standard NBA contract. In Miller's view, if a player could sit or play out the "option" year—accepting no pay—then the contract was over and the player was free. In 1974, Catfish Hunter tested the provision, and an arbitration chairman ruled in Hunter's favor. The next year, Miller got two players, Andy Messersmith of the Angels and Dave McNally of the Expos, to play out the year unsigned. Both of them had contract disputes. Both grievances went to arbitrator Peter Seitz, who ruled that indeed clause 10(a) applied for one year only. For all intents and purposes the reserve clause, as it had been interpreted for years, was dead. A team didn't own a player in perpetuity. Greater professional freedom for the player was one result; the other was that the average salary across the majors tripled from 1976 to 1980, to nearly $150,000. The owners had seen enough of emancipation. But they couldn't help themselves.

"Big spenders are ruining the game, baseball has a salary problem," grumbled new Cardinals GM Whitey Herzog, a few months before he signed free-agent Bruce Sutter, who in 1979 made $70,000, to a $3.5-million, 4-year deal. The Indians themselves signed Blyleven for $2 million over 6 years, but the big blow was Dave Winfield, who became a Yankee during the 1980–81 off-season for $13 million over 10 years, a signing that Expos GM John McHale pronounced had a "devastating

effect on salaries." McHale was looking at eight unsigned Montreal players—including his own talented outfield of Andre Dawson, Warren Cro-
martie, and Ellis Valentine. Most everyone was picking Montreal to win
the National League pennant in '81, if only the players would sign.

With teams unable to stop throwing money at newly available talent,
Ray Grebey's plan, developed with ownership, was to make teams pay for
such behavior. Grebey was going for big game: His goal was to make the
signing clubs give up a player from their roster as compensation to the
losing club. He wanted arbitration done away with, replaced by a pay
scale for a player's first five years in the league. The only way Miller
would agree to these things—givebacks of all that had been won in
1976—was if the players collapsed. The owners were ready to wait them
out. They took out a $50-million insurance policy with Lloyd's of Lon-
don that would pay $100,000 per game missed up to 500 games.

THE 1981 SEASON got underway; the labor cloud temporarily scudded
off and over the horizon of ball fans, who instead became entranced with
some truly remarkable things that spring. The Oakland Athletics, under
Billy Martin, and with an awesome starting rotation of Mike Norris,
Steve McCatty, Brian Kingman, and Matt Keogh and the running of
Rickey Henderson, started the season 11-0; rookie Tim Raines of Montreal tore up the league, stealing more than a base a game and hitting .370
the first month; most astounding was the debut of a 20-year-old Mexican
pitcher named Fernando Valenzuela, who won his first eight starts, five
of them by shutouts.

But Cleveland was not a washout, far from it. They broke strong,
winning 9 of 11 games early and, with a 13-7 record, they found themselves in a place that didn't look like Cleveland: first place. Blyleven won
three out of four, including a near no-hitter; Barker was tough, going 2-1
in the early going with an ERA well under two.

Even Joe Charboneau was beginning to hit a little, after a nearly
comatose start. The Tribe returned in mid-May from a successful 5-3
road trip, still in first place. The last game of the trip was a brilliantly
played 16-inning win over the White Sox on a Jorge Orta home run; the
night before that, the team won 3–1 behind Blyleven's pitching and a big
home run from Super Joe, who went 7-13 on the trip to get his average
over .200. That same night, they saved young McKimson from a gang
beating. Was there any limit to what these Cleveland Indians could do?

(Terry Pluto, at this point covering his Indians for the *Plain Dealer*, may be forgiven for thinking that the curse of Rocky Colavito had been lifted.) The Indians were winning at the ballpark and winning on the mean streets of America. Only the fans weren't buying it yet. On Friday night, May 15, 1981, only 7,290 fans showed up to see their first-place Indians play the last-place Toronto Blue Jays. Toronto hadn't scored in its last 21 innings; they were hitting .218 as a team; a second-year man, Luis Leal, was pitching. The high-flying Tribe had their fireballing Len Barker on the hill. The weather was not friendly; a cold mist swept into cavernous Memorial Stadium off Lake Erie; the temperature was in the 40s at game time, and dropping.

Duncan, the Indians pitching coach, could see from Barker's warmup session that he had something special. He told manager Dave Garcia that he was very sharp. He noted that the curveball wasn't breaking much, but it had a lot of velocity and a tight rotation—"almost the perfect curve." Most of the night, it would look like a vicious slider to the Blue Jays.

Former Indian prospect Alfredo Griffin was leading off and playing short for Toronto. Griffin was a speedy switch-hitter; he'd led the league in triples in 1980 with 15. His quickness almost made an ordinary night of it as he squibbed one slowly just past the mound. But Tom Veryzer sped in from short and barehanded the ball, nipping Griffin at first by half a step. Second-year man Lloyd Moseby, the Toronto right fielder, followed. At six-feet-three-inches and 200 pounds, the rangy left-handed hitter would be a principal part of the Blue Jays division-winning teams of 1985 and '89. But at present, with the team destined for its fifth straight last-place finish, he was a 20-year-old in need of seasoning. He rapped out to Veryzer. Rookie George Bell, like Griffin a Dominican, batted third and played left. A solidly built right-handed hitter, Bell would go on to have some huge years, hitting 47 home runs and driving in a league-leading 134 runs in 1987 and finishing a 12-year career with more than 1,000 RBI. Early in this season, he was hitting .288 with three round-trippers. But Barker fooled him with a curveball—Bell slapped it down to Mike Hargrove, an easy out at first.

The Indians put two on the board in their half of the first. Their speedy center-fielder Rick Manning, not hitting a lick so far this year, at .159, served one into left field, in front of George Bell, for a single. Jorge Orta, in his 10th year in the big leagues, grounded out to Griffin, who had no chance to get Manning at second and settled for the out at first. Mike Hargrove, who would go on to manage the Indians in the World

Series in 1997, batted third for the '81 club. A solid .290 lifetime hitter with a good batting eye, Hargrove beat a Luis Leal pitch into the ground, but big John Mayberry, playing first base for Toronto, couldn't come up with it, and Manning moved to third. Andre Thornton, who had sat out all of 1980 with a bad knee, was in the cleanup spot. Struggling to find the form that produced 87 home runs in a three-year span earlier, Thornton was hitting .237 in the early going. But he managed a fly ball to straight-away center field that plated the first run, Manning tagging easily and scoring. Catcher Ron Hassey, coming off a .318 season and with a new three-year contract worth $750,000, lined a single to right, scoring Hargrove with the second (unearned) run. It would prove more than enough for Barker.

John Mayberry was in the next-to-last year of a long, 15-year stint in the big leagues. His best years—spent with Kansas City—were behind him, though he was off to a pretty good start, with four home runs in the first month of play. He could do no better in his first crack at Barker than fist a 2-2 curve into center, where Manning made the catch. Willie Upshaw, the Toronto DH—this would be the first perfect game in the DH era—grounded easily to Duane Kuiper at second. Damaso Garcia, like Upshaw barely hitting .200, wasn't much of a fielder but could hit a little. He would have two All-Star seasons later in the decade, and would retire with a .283 lifetime BA. He almost solved Barker's hard stuff early on. A right-handed hitter, he lined a shot to left-center that Manning ran down in the alley for the third out.

In the Indians second, Garcia muffed a ground ball off the bat of Tom Veryzer, but Leal escaped with no further damage.

Center-fielder Rick Bosetti, hitting a robust .357, led off the third for Toronto. He would play only 25 games for the Blue Jays before being shipped to Oakland and would finish the year below .200. On a 1-2 count, he grounded out routinely to short. Rookie third baseman Danny Ainge, only two months after he thrilled the nation with a full-court dash to score the winning basket for Brigham Young against Notre Dame in the NCAA basketball tournament, and playing baseball with a $500,000 contract, swung at a 2-0 pitch—one of only six two-ball counts on the night for Barker—and grounded out to Kuiper. The catcher Buck Martinez, batting ninth, flied to Manning to give Barker a perfect trip through the order. Two oddities for Barker: no walks, no strikeouts.

In the fourth inning, as the temperature dropped, Barker got even tougher. After Griffin flied to Jorge Orta in right on a 2-2 pitch, Lloyd

Moseby and then George Bell went down swinging. Barker was finding the command that he would later call "awesome." "I could throw anything anywhere I wanted. After a while, they were swinging at everything."

In the fifth, Mayberry swung through a 1-2 pitch for Barker's third straight K. Then Willie Upshaw, in hitting a foul pop-up, would be victimized by the night's first defensive gem: Toby Harrah, the veteran third baseman in his 12th big league campaign, fell into the stands just beyond the Toronto dugout to make the catch. Ainge, his younger counterpart at third, called it "an unbelievable catch." Harrah said, after the game with a perspective he could not possibly have had as he ranged toward the stands under the falling ball, "You've got to dive in a situation like that. You never know if making a catch in the early innings will, or won't, mean something later." In this case, it sent the .208-hitting Upshaw back to the dugout. Damaso Garcia followed with a swinging strikeout on a 2-2 pitch. Barker's fourth.

Meanwhile, Luis Leal wasn't giving much. The six-foot-three-inch, 205-pound Venezuelan had yielded only three hits through five innings. But for Mayberry's error in the first, the game would have been tied.

In the Toronto sixth, the bottom of the order tried to solve Barker. Bosetti, jammed by a Barker fastball, hit a low one-hopper to Kuiper's right. Kuiper, fully recovered from off-season knee surgery, threw him out. Then Ainge and Martinez struck out on Barker curveballs. Barker had struck out six batters in the game, all in the last three innings. It was getting automatic.

The Indians reached Leal for two singles in their half of the sixth, but Charboneau remained in his funk, grounding out to the second baseman.

In the seventh, it was the top of the order again, and again Duane Kuiper's quickness was key. Alfredo Griffin skipped a Barker curveball past Hargrove at first but four quick steps by Kuiper got him to the ball and he nipped Griffin by a hair, with Hargrove scrambling back to cover the bag. Moseby and Bell, as they had in the fourth, went down swinging, strikeouts seven and eight on the night for Barker.

The Indians continued to go down quietly; as often seems the case in a developing perfect game, the hometown crowd and the hometown team both seem in a rush to get their pitcher back out there to continue the run at magic. It remained 2–0 after seven.

The night continued misting. Barker would later credit the wet weather with giving him a better grip on the ball. It certainly wasn't helping the Blue Jays. They'd rather have been indoors, at home. Bosetti, after the game, thought that if the game had in fact been played in Toronto, a few of the balls hit to Kuiper would have been Astroturf base hits.

In the eighth, it was all Barker: Mayberry and Garcia down swinging, around a grounder to that man Kuiper again.

In the bottom of the eighth, Cleveland finally hit a ball well against Leal. Jorge Orta led off with a home run for the evening's final run.

In the ninth, Barker was visibly nervous—Toronto pitcher Mark Bomback said "I thought we had him," when he saw Barker actually drop the ball on the mound. Barker would later admit as much: "My legs were shaking." But with the small crowd making enough noise for a packed house—on the Indian radio call, announcer Herb Score called it "pande-monium"—Barker went to work. Rick Bosetti led off, and got what he called "the best pitch I saw all night . . . he hung me a slider right down the middle." Bosetti fouled it back. Barker then fed him a curveball and Bosetti skied it just foul of the third-base line, where Harrah gloved it for out number 25. Toronto manager Bobby Mattick then sent up pinch-hitter Al Woods to bat for Ainge. Woods was a tall, slender left-handed hitter who'd hit .300 in 109 games the year before. But coming in cold he was no match for the hot Barker, who got him swinging for his 11th strikeout of the evening, all swinging and all since the fourth inning. Down to their last out, Mattick sent up another left-handed hitter, to bat for Buck Martinez. Ernie Whitt, who would end up spending 12 years with the Blue Jays, was looking to make trouble. He later said he consid-ered pointing to center field to try to distract Barker. Thinking better of it, he dug in to hit and swung through a fastball for a strike. He took a curve for a ball and fouled back another to go down in the count, 1-2. Barker broke another tight curve in and Whitt lofted it to center field, such a tame fly ball that Barker immediately began walking off the mound, confident that his buddy, Rick Manning, nicknamed Arch after the great footballer, Archie Manning, would haul it in. He did, camping underneath the ball with his arms spread wide with anticipation. It was over. Len Barker for once in his life was perfect.

Barker was mobbed. He was soaked, as was everyone. The tempera-ture had dropped into the 30s. The game had taken only two hours and nine minutes to play, but must have seemed like a long evening to many, certainly the Blue Jays and no doubt to Barker, too. He greeted his wife, Bonnie, who was in attendance with Len's brother, a contractor who had come in just for the game. In the clubhouse, the route to Barker's locker was already carpeted with towels; on a stool, six bottles of beer in the form of a zero. Owner O'Neill, president Gabe Paul, and GM Phil Seghi came by. Paul announced that Barker had just earned a $5,000 bonus. And then they broke out the champagne.

Back home in Trevose, Pennsylvania, Barker's mother had lost the signal from the Indians station in the eighth and learned later by phone that her son had gone all the way. Her husband, Barker's step-father, had to get in the car and find a spot where the reception was decent. He listened to the game's final outs while parked at a golf course. They weren't able to speak to Barker till the next day: Barker eventually made it home with Bonnie and they had to take the phone off the hook.

Everyone agreed it was Barker's control and his spectacular breaking pitch that did in the Jays time after time. A full 70 percent of Barker's deliveries were curveballs, though the curve's break was so tight and quick, and the velocity so high, that many, like Buck Martinez, called it a slider. But catcher Hassey knew what was what: "Lennie had a great curveball. He threw almost every pitch right where I called for it." Announcer Herb Score, once a pitcher of great promise until a line drive off the bat of Gil McDougald broke his cheekbone, said that the curve "was Barker's bread and butter pitch." Umpire Rich Garcia said the curveball was "out of this world." Barker attributed it all to concentration, something that he'd struggled with for his whole career—Gabe Paul, his general manager, once said, "When I see Barker watching the planes going overhead when he's on the mound, I know he's through." But on this night, Barker said it was "unreal . . . real and yet like a dream. Maybe never before in my life have I concentrated more about each pitch and about controlling myself."

It was a happy Friday night in Cleveland. A perfect night and Cleveland still in first place. One writer had the following exchange with Barker:

"Hey, Lennie, ever heard of Addie Joss?"

"Nah, who's he?"

"The last Indian to throw a perfect game."

"I don't think I saw that one," said Barker, starting work on his third bottle of bubbly.

The Indians lost the next day but swept a doubleheader on Sunday afternoon; the team had the lowest ERA in the league, at 2.39; they were

playing .667 ball at 18-9. The long-suffering Terry Pluto was moved to
pen a story the following Sunday touting the Indians' magic number—
136. But it was not to be.

THE UNION'S STRIKE date approached. A federal court intervened. The
strike date was suspended for two weeks and a mediator, Ken Moffett,
was assigned to help forge an agreement. On June 12, the game shut
down.

Fifty days and 713 games later, Marvin Miller, sensing the desperation in the owners and the rising disgust of the public—a public that
would roundly cheer when President Reagan fired the country's air traffic
controllers for a strike action in the fall, gave in. He had to. It seemed no
one was sympathetic to any disagreements at all between owners and
players. For whatever reason, labor troubles in baseball never inspired
partisanship among the fans. Their high-mindedness reached its apogee
in the precious prose of an Ivy League president, who, in the middle of
the strike, presumed to speak for intelligent fandom in *The New York
Times:* "you play baseball," he chided the players, "so that we may
remember the future we want for our children." He termed the players
"princelings" and the owners "sovereignets," and urged that everyone
"go back to work." Miller was appalled that a smart man like Bart Giamatti, with labor issues of his own at Yale and presumably knowledge-
able about the game's history, would have so little heart for labor politics
up close. He rebuked the future commissioner in his own letter to the
Times. But it was clearly time to settle. Miller agreed to compensation in
the case of premier free agents, though he devilishly proposed a plan
whereby all teams bidding on free agents would have to designate certain
of the roster players as available to a compensation pool, from which
raided teams could select. In this way, teams that lost a player would get
a player in return, but not necessarily from the team doing the signing.
So Miller made a concession. It was one of Miller's last official moves as
executive director of the Players Association. It was a concession that,
soon enough, both parties would detest.

THE ALL-STAR GAME would be baseball's return to the American stage
after a work stoppage. A controversial plan for resuming play was agreed
to: The period before the strike would be a season unto itself; for the sec-

ond half, all teams would begin 0-0. Then, the winners of the two halves of the season, approximately 50 games each, would have a playoff.

The Indians had faded in the last two weeks before the strike. They wouldn't play any better on the other side. The *Plain Dealer* would not write another column about a magic number until late in the century, with Mike Hargrove as manager and the team in a new home at Jacobs Field. But first, Cleveland would get to mark the return of baseball as host to the All-Star Game, with their own Len Barker on the A.L. staff. And to put sweet on the evening, Morganna Cottrell (née Roberts), the buxom blonde who made a habit of strolling onto ball fields to plant a kiss on a handsome player, did so to Barker in front of a packed house and a huge television audience. Walking across the infield with blue shorts on and an extra-large blue-fringed top imprinted with an Indian in full headdress, she laid one on the cheek of Barker, who took it in stride. "Of the 15 players I've kissed," purred Morganna after the game, "this was the most thrilling."

It was all downhill from there for Barker and the A.L., as two home runs by Gary Carter beat them for their ninth straight summer classic defeat. After that, when the second season got under way, the Indians fell apart. They finished one game over .500 for the whole season, their customary spirit level of mediocrity; Barker ended up 8-7, although he did lead the league in strikeouts for the second straight season, with 127.

NONETHELESS, THE next year there was hope in Cleveland—at least early on. Barker started out like a house afire, going 10-5 in the first half. But in August he and Glynn were busted in Chicago and things turned sour. Barker ended the year at 15-11 and his ERA ballooned to 3.90; Cleveland finished tied for last. In early '83, Barker was 27 years old with a big upside. Some teams with either a shot at contention (the Phillies) or absolutely no pitching (the Mets) wanted him, the Phillies offering pitchers Dick Ruthven and George Vukovich and the Mets offering Dave Kingman and pitcher Pat Zachry. If not for Cleveland teammate Bert Blyleven falling off his roof attempting to protect his home from a Southern California brushfire, Barker might have been gone. But he stayed. He filed for salary arbitration, asking for a half-million-dollar raise, to $805,000, while Cleveland countered with an offer of $475,000 total. The arbitrator ruled for the club.

Barker struggled in 1983, and with the Indians out of it early, they traded him in August (he was 8-13) to a pennant-chasing Braves team for players to be named later. Atlanta manager Joe Torre declared himself "glad to be in a position to win this thing." They were hounding the Dodgers, the team they had beaten by a game for the division championship the year before. The Dodgers themselves had just picked up left-handed pitcher Rick Honeycutt for the stretch run, which prompted Ted Turner to pony up the dough for Barker—five years for $5 million—and also give up two good ballplayers, the promising Brook Jacoby and the fleet, good-hitting popular young outfielder with the antebellum name of Brett Butler. In fact, when rumors surfaced that Butler was one of the players to be named later, fans tried to mount a petition-signing campaign to have Turner withdraw Butler from the deal. It was not to be. Barker, with bone chips already biting in his elbow, joined a staff led by Phil Niekro, Craig McMurtry, and Pascual Perez, and he was a bust. The day after the trade, the Braves fell out of first place for the first time since July 3. They never recovered. Barker went 1-3 down the stretch, and the club stumbled and finished three games back of the Dodgers. The Braves wouldn't get to the postseason for another six years.

That marked, more or less, the end for Barker. The next year, his name would surface in a Milwaukee-area cocaine investigation. He would win only 13 more games in his career, which would peter out four years later in 1987 when the Brewers released him.

Barker was exactly the kind of player who might have thrived in an earlier time. Not blessed with the self-discipline of a Bob Feller or a Bob Lemon but given a big horse of a body, Barker would have benefited from do-or-die competition and the realities of making a dollar and watching where—and how—you spent it. Instead, he pitched at a time when the promise of big money was new and talent spread thin. Barker was exactly the kind of fellow who could afford to be patient with himself and get by with what he had. But for his 19 victories in 1980 and his perfect game and All-Star appearance the next year, Barker's was a career distinguished only by legal trouble, an infamous trade, and a kiss on the cheek from Morganna.

The powers gained on the players' behalf at the bargaining table made Len Barker and many another ballplayer rich. However, in the early, heady days of free agency and union strength, such power, protection, and freedom led to serious off-the-field problems for many. After Miller retired, his work done and left to Donald Fehr to protect, the story in baseball became the excesses of ballplayers. Cocaine in the early and mid-eighties was a problem in the country like never before, and ballplayers were not only not immune, they were high-risk—active, wealthy professionals living on the road, away from their families for half the year, working under stress. Barker was not alone in finding trouble. Allan Wiggins of the Padres was arrested in 1982 for cocaine possession; Lonnie Smith checked into a rehab clinic the same year. Dodger pitcher Steve Howe began his lengthy battle with drug addiction, which would eventually lead to eight suspensions. Bob Welch and Darrell Porter both admitted to substance abuse problems in 1983. Kansas City had a huge problem, which surfaced publicly in 1984, when four of its players—Willie Wilson, Willie Aikens, Jerry Martin, and Vida Blue— were convicted of soliciting cocaine and given one-year prison terms. Pascual Perez, Barker's teammate, was arrested for narcotics possession the same year.

In case after case, the union came to the players' rescue. Ferguson Jenkins's suspension by Bowie Kuhn was overturned after the union filed a grievance; Wiggins and Lonnie Smith were guaranteed their salaries during their suspensions; Steve Howe avoided another suspension by paying a fine and having the union insist he be transferred to an inactive list, where, during his rehab, he could accrue service time toward his pension—and free agency. As for the four Kansas City criminals, their jail sentences were reduced to three months; Commissioner Kuhn then suspended them for the entire 1984 season, till a union grievance resulted in their reinstatement in mid-May. Perez refused to cooperate with a baseball investigation into his narcotics possession; his one-year suspension was thrown out by an arbitrator.

The Players Association that Miller built was clearly interested in more than money for its members. It wanted—and won—the right to help run the game, and the lives of its players. Unfortunately, the intercession of agents, managers, and lawyers threatened to abuse those rights, won on the backs of guys like Curt Flood and Dave McNally, Koufax and Drysdale, and the early player reps like Hank Greenberg and Ralph Kiner and Robin Roberts, men who ran the considerable risk of being blackballed for their activities so that future ballplayers could reap the benefits that the Cy Youngs and Eddie Cicottes and Sal Maglies could only dream of; instead, the percentage of players on the disabled list jumped 50 percent during the mid-seventies.

Perhaps it's not fair to thrust Leonard Harold Barker III into this recitation of baseball's labor pains, salary explosion, and drug abuse problems. But it is clear that, during Barker's 14 years in professional ball, from his 1973 draft selection by the Texas Rangers to his unceremonious release by the Brewers after the '87 campaign, the newly liberalized and high-powered game of baseball was more than he could handle. Barker had one good year, one good half-year (wrecked by a 50-day strike), and one great night of untouchable stuff that put him in the unlikely company of guys like Bunning and Koufax and Hunter, guys who handled baseball with perfect élan. Barker made more money than any of those guys, and won 74 games.

CHAPTER NINE

A Sharp Witt

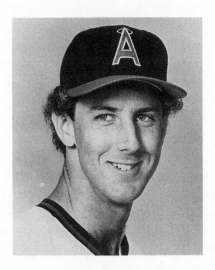

Mike Witt
September 30, 1984

Mike Witt is approaching 44 years of age. He still lives in his native Southern California, where he was born in the summer of 1960. He retired in 1993, after a dozen major league seasons. He does a little coaching now, and a lot of golfing, as his endearingly goofy e-mail handle—"golfndewd"—attests. He talks easily, fondly, of his life in America—as a California teenager of the 1970s and as professional athlete—and harbors no grudges, only good memories, despite his share of tough calls and bad breaks. [The italicized comments in this chapter are from a 2003 interview with Witt.]

I grew up not too far from the ocean, in Fullerton, so summers were the best of times, with picnics, Fourth of July, the beach, stay-

*ing up late, swimming in the neighbor's pool, no school, and just
playing one game after the next. We always had some kind of pickup game going on on the street, be it over-the-line baseball, two-
hand touch football, two-on-two basketball, whatever. In my
high-school years summer was for baseball, almost exclusively, but
it was all fun. The best players played all summer. Southern California is a great place to be a teenager. Girls were a slight distraction,
but only occasionally. I was a laid-back, keep-to-myself kind of guy.
So if they didn't talk to me, then I probably didn't talk to them. You
live and learn.*

*My dad worked for Colgate-Palmolive, and my mom taught
grade school for 30 years at a Catholic school. English was her spe-
cialty. I have five siblings—two older brothers, two older sisters, and
a younger brother. My oldest brother actually taught me how to
throw the curveball when I was 10 years old, at the urging of my
dad. That curveball was with me my whole career.*

*I played basketball and baseball at Servite High School. I loved
to play in front of a packed high-school gym. By the time I graduated, I had a handful of colleges that were willing to let me play both
basketball and baseball. In 1978, I decided that I would attend the
University of Santa Clara. This was based solely on the fact that the
basketball team had UCLA on its schedule. It was a goal of mine to
play basketball at UCLA; this would have been the next best thing. I
figured the baseball would take care of itself, no matter where I
played. But prior to the 1978 draft, I worked out at then Anaheim
Stadium. Larry Himes was a West Coast scout for the Angels and
saw me work out. I had had a great year in high school and, being in
Anaheim, it was probably hard for the Angels to ignore the success I
was having. So they ended up drafting me in the fourth round. After
heavy debate with Mom and Dad, I signed for the—in my mind—
huge sum of $30,000.*

An all-American story, but it just gets more American as time goes
on. Think Arthur Miller's America—or is it David Mamet's? Idealistic
young man with scintillating, natural talent, once a professional, finds
himself playing in a tough game with tough customers. Not so much on
the field, where he can look in the eyes of players in uniform trying to
beat him there, but off the field, in back offices, in front offices, and at
private tables, where he can't see the eyes of businessmen scheming to

get the better of not just Michael Atwater Witt, but all ballplayers. Unbeknownst to them, even the most powerful man in baseball, the so-called protector of the game's integrity, would try to cheat them.

THE MAN IN the sharp power suit moved with the calculated grace of a politician. Planes of glen plaid draped smoothly across his broad athletic build—water polo had been his sport at San Jose State. A nimbus of sunshine accompanied him around the breakfast room—face tanned, brown hair sun-honeyed. A reporter trailed him, too, on assignment for a men's magazine. The man would work the room, reaching across tables to shake hands or pen an autograph on a napkin.

The two men—suit and scribe—were seated at the Park Regency Hotel at 61st and Park Avenue in New York City, just east of Central Park, five minutes from Mickey Mantle's restaurant, with its long bar made of Adirondack ash, and two seconds from the Pierre, where Nancy and Ronald Reagan liked to stay when in New York. It was 1985, so-called morning in America, but this was not the kind of morning most Americans spent.

"A power breakfast headquarters for a host of rich white men who like to take some bran flakes into their day's first meeting," the reporter would acidly observe in *Esquire* a few months later about the morning venue. Richard Ben Cramer was a cool, macho journalist, unimpressed by money or fame but moved to write about it. He had been following the suit around for weeks—he'd been in hotels, airports, airplanes, stadiums, hallways—trying to get a handle on this man who had become the country's most visible crusader for a drug-free America. It was a pretty square idea for the go-go 1980s, but then again, the eighties would come to be known not only for excess but for conservatism. Here was a kind of lay preacher but not a grass-roots one, a Billy Graham with a better job and a better tailor—dressed in a crisply lined bespoke shirt with a gold collar pin, wearing black Italian loafers that gleamed—he could afford in every respect this conspicuousness. He made half a million dollars a year that he didn't need. He had more than money on his mind. His breakfast chat was peppered with talk of "defoliation," "interdiction," and "air strikes." He wanted the National Guard to incinerate hemp plants in his home state of California. He was calling for the federal government to strong-arm any country found to be enabling our citizens to get stoned, high, addicted.

Somehow, this was the commissioner of baseball, Peter Victory Ueberroth. He had work to do.

BY 1984, BASEBALL'S owners had had enough of Commissioner Bowie Kuhn, who with the squeezed voice of a compromised banker and the jug-headed gaze of a country sheriff arriving just too late to the scene, had become a figure of public ridicule. What had really stuck in the craw of the owners was Kuhn's lack of courage during the spring training lockout in 1981 when, bowing to fan pressure, he interceded and forced the camps to open. All had seemed forgiven in the immediate aftermath of what the owners thought was their great win at the bargaining table later that summer—establishment of the player compensation pool. This, the owners felt, would make some owners less willing to buy a free agent, whereas it did nothing of the sort—because the team that lost the player to free agency got to pick from a pool of unprotected talent from around the league. Shortly, it proved to be to no one's liking, especially after Tom Seaver was plucked off the Mets roster by the White Sox as compensation for losing Dennis Lamp to free agency. So, with the three-year collective bargaining agreement of 1981 due to expire, and with Marvin Miller now retired, the owners were ready for another assault on free agency—and they would prefer to do it without Bowie Kuhn in the picture. They hired Ueberroth.

Ueberroth was king of the hill when baseball began courting him. A self-made millionaire in the travel agency business, he had been tapped to run the 1984 summer Olympic Games in Los Angeles. He spent five years making sure the Games turned a profit, and they did. Through an aggressive marketing scheme, he sold every square inch and thin second that the Olympics could claim as its own to sell. At the end of the 16-day event, Ueberroth could claim a $215-million surplus.

By the time Ueberroth arrived on the baseball scene, he'd made a quick study. He knew what the owners wanted. First, he enlisted old pro Lee McPhail to detail how much money teams were losing. McPhail replaced Ray Grebey as head of the Player Relations Committee. It was McPhail's intercession that got the 1981 deal done and helped end the conflict. This time, the owners thought they might like a salary cap, as the NBA had, a kind of self-imposed limit on how much they could spend on players. But they couldn't self-impose any such thing: It had to be bargained with the players.

No agreement was reached. Talks stalled. In February 1985, as Tim Raines was getting a record $1.2-million arbitration ruling, Lee McPhail's study was released. It claimed that major league baseball teams lost $58 million in 1983, and predicted that the loss would be matched, or bettered, in the current year. The players were skeptical. They commissioned a Stanford economist to make an analysis of baseball's health, and he uncovered an arsenal of accounting tricks (such as George Steinbrenner's real estate investments in Tampa entered as club expenses and the Cardinals' hiding concession and parking monies in another subsidiary of Annheuser-Busch). Unfazed, the owners, encouraged by their commissioner, attacked the players on the drug issue. The Dodgers' Peter O'Malley tried to make drug testing a part of the standard player contract. Houston owner John McMullen challenged the players to fire Fehr and his lieutenants for their opposition to mandatory testing. Also in May, Ueberroth sprung a surprise move by announcing that there would be mandatory drug testing, to begin in a month's time, affecting everyone in baseball—minor league players and umpires, major league coaches, managers, trainers, umps—with the rather notable exception of major league players. That, too, would have to be collectively bargained. Editorials across the country came out in support of Ueberroth's move.

Meanwhile, the newspapers were filled with the revelations of prominent major leaguers who were testifying at a narcotics trial in Pittsburgh. In August, the players walked out. Ueberroth then brought his weight to bear—he would not have a lengthy disruption during his first year in office—and the strike was over in two days. It was considered a victory for the owners, featuring the golden boy Ueberroth over Donald Fehr, the overmatched young successor to Marvin Miller. The owners got an extra year before a player could file for salary arbitration, and the compensation pool, for which 700 games were sacrificed in 1981, was scrapped. They also got to lower the rosters to 24 players.

On September 20, 1985, the summer-long drug trial in Pittsburgh came to a conclusion. Former clubhouse caterer Curtis Strong was convicted on 11 of 16 counts of cocaine distribution. Dave Parker, Keith Hernandez, Lonnie Smith, Enos Cabell, Dale Berra, Jeffrey Leonard, and John Milner were among those who testified under immunity. Strong's attorney tried to portray the ballplayers as "junkies." Although the strategy earned the attorney a contempt of court citation, baseball emerged from the trial battered and shamed. Dave Parker admitted to arranging for a dealer to do business with three different teams. Tim Raines was singled out as a guy who would slide headfirst rather than endanger the integrity of the vials of cocaine in his back pocket.

Baseball, however, once again showed its talent for distracting the American public with its charms. Who could keep his mind on drug convictions and work stoppages and union grievance filings when the game had so much else to offer: On September 11, Pete Rose, at 44 years of age, passed Ty Cobb by getting his 4,192nd career base hit, but it was the tight pennant races and a rousing postseason that really stole the show. The Kansas City Royals, but a year removed from the drug convictions of four of its best players, stormed back from a 3–1 deficit against the Blue Jays to take the American League pennant. In the National League, Whitey Herzog's good-old-boy Cardinals (he had traded his cocaine miscreants, Hernandez and Lonnie Smith) beat the Dodgers in six games. In the Series, the Royals managed to lose the first two games at home, but then took two out of three in St. Louis behind great pitching from Bret Saberhagen and Danny Jackson. Back home for Games Six and Seven, their backs against the wall, the Royals swept, finishing off the Cardinals with a scalding 11–0 win in Game Seven, behind Saberhagen's five-hitter. But while fans gloried in the prime-time, "I-70" Series, named after the interstate that connected K.C. and St. Louis, Ueberroth was planning baseball's next move.

In late September, a week after the conviction of Curtis Strong, Ueberroth convened a meeting of the owners in Itasca, Illinois. The topic was ostensibly the cost of player development. Less than a month later, just after the conclusion of the World Series, Lee McPhail, baseball's designated grim reaper, issued a memorandum condemning long-term contracts as bad business. In November, the commissioner expressed his support for the McPhail memo at a meeting of general managers in Florida. When the owners met a month later, at the winter meetings, a list of free agents was distributed. Ueberroth was showing the owners a way to defeat free agency. They would follow him, disastrously, and the way would come to be known as "collusion." But for the time being, no one was the wiser.

I was sent to rookie ball in Idaho Falls, Idaho. I expected the worst, and kind of rolled with whatever was thrown at me for two and half months. I was 17 years old and having the time of my life. I wasn't affected by the 10-hour bus rides, or the sleeping in the racks, or the mosquitoes in Canada, or the college guys who would whine about every little thing. I was there to play ball, and this was good enough for now.

I was promoted to Single A the next spring and spent that season in Salinas, California. It was a very nonproductive year. I was sent back there the next spring, instead of to El Paso Double A. I was devastated, but resolved to let it motivate me. I started off great and eventually was promoted to El Paso for the second half of the year. My confidence was sky high going into major league spring training camp.

Spring training is a great time of year, whether you're a rookie or a veteran. As a rookie in 1981, and being only 20 years old, I had nothing to lose. So, I hustled and had fun and just played off the momentum of my previous year. As it turns out, everything I did was right. They had no choice but to keep me on the major league roster. Fregosi had no pitching and I must have looked heaven-sent to him. I was paid about $27,500 that year plus a $5,000 bonus from my initial contract. Life was good. Single, 20, money, in Southern Cal. Two months into the season we strike . . .

When the young Mike Witt made the club in 1981, the combative local press asked the team's general manager, none other than the legendary Buzzie Bavasi, about whether the Angels were bringing along this promising kid too fast. "I rushed Sandy Koufax, I rushed Don Drysdale, I rushed Carl Erskine," Bavasi somehow said in his defense. "If he can get them out, he can pitch with us." Witt would average 35 starts a year for six years, and virtually be finished by the age of 28.

Pitching coach Tom Morgan was assigned to work with the young, lanky right-hander, and Witt pitched well early. In April, he opened some eyes with a two-hit victory over the Twins. Still, after the strike in the middle of the season, Witt didn't think he'd find himself on the roster, as injured pitchers Dave Frost and Bill Travers were set to return. However, Fregosi was fired two weeks before the strike, and the Angels proceeded to play sharply under new manager Gene Mauch, going 9-4 before the stoppage.

Witt held his job, finishing the strike-shortened season with an 8-9 record and tidy ERA of 3.28. Mauch was happy with his young pitcher, but both he and pitching coach Morgan began to utter that deadly word for young athletes: potential. "If he ever realizes what he has hanging from that right sleeve," said Mauch, "he'll be something special." The young man began to get hammered in the press. Mauch and Morgan were old school—each more than three decades Witt's senior; Mauch had not been out of work as a big league manager since he started, in 1960; Morgan had three World Series rings. Witt would later complain that the stars—he mentioned Rod Carew, Reggie Jackson, Don Baylor, Bobby Grich—were handled with kid gloves by the press, but kids weren't. They were cuffed about. That's old school, too, and the press can be just as old as the coaches.

Mauch, despite the collapse of his Phillies in '64, was respected as an expert strategist and a man who ran a tight ship. The team played fairly well under his stewardship toward the end of the '81 season, and Bavasi made some key moves in the off-season, such as picking up Reggie Jackson from the Yankees. In 1982, with Jackson tying for the league lead in home runs with 39, Brian Downing and Doug DeCinces having good years, Rod Carew hitting .319, Geoff Zahn winning 18 games, Bruce Kison going 10-5, and Tommy John proving to be an effective late-season pickup, young Witt could work on his game. He went 8-6 and showed the occasional dominant flash that proved he belonged. The Angels won their second division title, by three games over the Royals. But despite a two-games-to-none lead over the Brewers in best-of-five ALCS play, Mauch would not find his way to the World Series. He removed Kison after five innings in the final game, with a 3–2 lead, and watched it vanish two innings later on a hit by Cecil Cooper. Witt saw three innings of action, in Game Three, and gave up a damaging two-run homer to Paul Molitor in a 5–3 loss. Morgan said of Witt, "He doesn't retain anything I tell him." Mauch retired shortly after the game. Morgan was gone, too.

John McNamara was named as Mauch's replacement for the 1983 season, and Marcel Lachemann became the pitching coach, but the team's peformance fell off markedly, as they finished 29 games behind the White Sox in the A.L. West, a miserable result for a team that fielded Reggie, Fred Lynn, Bobby Grich, and Rod Carew, and that boasted a pitching staff of Tommy John, Kison, Ken Forsch, and Witt. But Lynn was hurt much of the year, Jackson hit a hard-to-figure .194 in 400 at-bats, and Grich missed 40 games. In the pitching department, Tommy John had an off-year, winning only 11 games in 34 starts, Kison pitched well but sparingly, and Witt suffered the desertion of his curveball and found himself working in long relief for his new manager. He went 7-14. One bit of happiness did lighten the off-season, for Witt at least. In November, he married Lisa Fenn, who had worked as a secretary in the Angels' front office. Shortly thereafter, at Lachemann's suggestion, Witt went to Venezuela and played winter ball. Lachemann told him to just relax, and it worked wonders. Witt, and the Angels, were headed for an exciting year.

McNAMARA WAS A by-the-book manager; he played the percentages, or at least the standard hunches. He platooned, righty/lefty, with the rookie Gary Pettis and Juan Beniquez in center, Rob Wilfong and Bobby Grich at second, and Fred Lynn and Brian Downing in left. Constants in the lineup were Bob Boone behind the plate, Carew at first, DeCinces at second, Dick Schofield at short, and Reggie Jackson as the DH. It was a good lineup that just couldn't ever catch fire. Just about every month the team played .500 ball.

Witt, however, got off to a rocky start, losing 10–1 in his first outing. After another strafing, with his starter's status in peril, he began to see a celebrated Milwaukee hypnotist, Dr. Harvey Misel, and it worked. He then seven-hit the Brewers, four-hit the Mariners, and then beat the Mariners again, 3–1. Three complete-game victories in a row. It would be a year of streakiness for Witt. After his 4-1 start, he dropped six out of seven, pitching poorly at times but more often pitching in tough luck. After beating Texas 2–1, striking out nine, to even his record at 7-7, he found that groove again. On July 23, at home, he was as dominant as he had ever been, striking out 16 Mariners in a five-hit victory. It was his sixth straight win, bringing his record to 11-7. The Angels couldn't get any traction, but in a sluggish division, they remained tantalizingly close to the lead.

By mid-September, the Angels were still hanging in. On September 15, after having lost twice earlier in the season to the White Sox's Tom Seaver, Witt got the upper hand on the future Hall of Famer, with the help of homers by Jackson, Grich, and Lynn, and California moved to within a half game of Kansas City and Minneapolis, who were tied for first place. The Angels were only two games over .500 but one game away from sole possession of first. In his next start, the biggest start of his career thus far, Witt raised his record to 14-11 with a sparkling three-hitter over the first-place Royals in front of 32,000 wildly cheering fans in Anaheim. The Angels were a half-game back with 11 to play. On September 24, the Angels arrived in Kansas City with their fate in their own hands. They were one game back in the loss column and faced a four-game set against the team in front of them. But the Angels let it all go to hell. Bret Saberhagen shut them out on three hits; Danny Jackson tamed them 12–4 in the second game. Witt got doubled to death in game three, won by the Royals in the 12th on a single by Steve Balboni after four innings of shutout ball from reliever Dan Quisenberry. That was pretty much it. When Tommy John lost a heartbreaker in the opener of the season's last and final stop—Arlington, Texas—the Angels, mathematically eliminated, were left to play out the string, two meaningless games.

Except McNamara wouldn't allow it. There was still something to be played for, and more than pride. A second-place finish guaranteed a larger percentage of the play-off pool, and they were fighting the Twins for the honor and the lucre. "We do have some people here who could use it," said Johnny Mac. On Saturday, September 29, the Rangers didn't do much to get in their way. They fell in two hours and 19 minutes, scoring not a run against the Angels' Geoff Zahn. The 4–0 win brought the Angels to within a game of .500, with one game to go.

IT TOOK ALL OF AN hour and 49 minutes. When it was over—both game and season—Mike Witt would say, "Hey, I did that. I mean, to get 27 straight batters out is unbelievable." Thanks to an unearned run—as was the case for Addie Joss and Sandy Koufax—pitching perfection was to be achieved by the narrowest of margins, a 1–0 win. Opposing pitcher Charlie Hough was nearly as brilliant, and pitched to win, despite the utter meaninglessness of the game for Texas. Hough knew early on that Witt had something special going: "He was throwing his curveball on either side of the plate whenever he wanted. His stuff was awesome." In the third inning, according to Texas batting coach Marv Rettenmund, Hough—then 36 years old—was muttering, "The stuff he's got, he's got a chance to do it." In 94 pitches, Witt did it.

Only 8,375 people were present to see Witt's—and Hough's—mastery, on a Sunday afternoon in Arlington.

Hough was in the middle of a great 10-year run in Texas, during which he'd win more than 140 games. Signed as an outfielder by the Dodgers at 18, turned into a pitcher by Tommy Lasorda and taught the knuckleball at Triple-A Spokane, Hough became his generation's Hoyt Wilhelm or Phil Niekro, a pitcher who feasted on the funky, fluttering pitch. He was going for his 17th win of the season, which would be a career high, and he was leading the league in complete games. Facing him was the underachieving Angels lineup—Rob Wilfong was at second, Daryl Sconiers played first, Freddy Lynn, the prodigal son come home only to find injury, was in center and batting third, while Doug DeCinces, another returning Californian, handled third base and the cleanup spot. Brian Downing, one of the first of baseball's devoted body builders—and yet another Southern Californian—played left and batted fifth, while Reggie Jackson, on the downward slope of a great career, was the designated hitter, in the sixth position. Mike Brown, a good field, hit-a-little second-year man, batted seventh and played center, while veteran Bob Boone did the catching; Dick Schofield, a rookie, played short and batted ninth.

Hough wouldn't have much trouble with this outfit—a double play in the second erased DeCinces, who had singled; Mike Brown was stranded at third after his leadoff triple, as Hough induced three consecutive groundouts. Fred Lynn's one-out single in the fourth proved harmless, even after a Hough knuckler clunked to the backstop, wild.

Witt, meanwhile, was mowing down the Rangers with even greater success. Mickey Rivers, the leadoff hitter, who would later claim the Rangers were all thinking about going home, "bags packed," seemed in a hurry himself, striking out on three pitches in the bottom of the first. Second baseman Wayne Tolleson, a switch-hitter, flied out to Downing in left, bringing up the tough Gary Ward, an All-Star the year before, a solid ballplayer with speed and power. Witt went to his first 3-2 count of the day before Ward, a right-handed hitter, cued one off the end of the bat toward first, where Sconiers made the play unassisted.

In the Rangers second, cleanup man Larry Parrish stepped in, playing third base this day but having spent most of the year—a good one—as the DH. Parrish had already gotten his 100th RBI of the year. Buddy Bell, perhaps the best stick on the Texas team and the regular third baseman, had been given the day off by manager Doug Rader. Parrish would come up with no answers all day to Witt's offerings. He began with a weak groundout to Schofield at short. Pete O'Brien, a .290 hitter with some power, batted fifth, but Witt's curveball, taking thinner and thinner slices out of each side of the plate, had him lunging. O'Brien lifted a harmless fly to Lynn in center. George Wright, the Texas center fielder then struck out. In the third, dealing with the bottom of the Texas order, Witt was nearly untouchable—Tom Dunbar, in his second year of a three-year career (lifetime BA: .231), struck out, as did the catcher Donnie Scott, in the second year of a four-year career (lifetime BA: .217). The shortstop Curtis Wilkerson, in the second year of a career that would last him a good 11 years (lifetime BA: .245), tapped to short.

In the Rangers fourth, with the game still scoreless, Mickey Rivers was out on one pitch—a grounder to first, Witt covering. Tolleson then grounded to short, and Ward, getting decent wood on the ball, skied out to Mike Brown in right.

In the fifth, Texas nearly broke through against Witt. Larry Parrish hit a slow chopper toward third. DeCinces—a better hitter than fielder— made the barehanded play to get Parrish at first. Pete O'Brien grounded weakly to second baseman Wilfong for out number two. Then George Wright battled through seven pitches, fouling off three two-strike pitches before striking out, Witt's fifth K through five.

The sixth inning brought the bottom of the Texas order to Witt's cutting table, and again, he diced them up. Dunbar looked at two strikes then grounded out to second. Donnie Scott, who had been the number-two pick in the 1979 draft but was now playing his way out of baseball, struck out; and Curtis Wilkerson did what he had done last time: grounded out. Witt was 18 for 18 at this point. But Charlie Hough was working on a brilliant three-hit shutout.

The Angels finally eked out a run in the seventh. DeCinces, who would finish the year with 20 home runs and 82 RBI, singled to lead off. Then a Hough knuckler got away from catcher Scott for a passed ball. With DeCinces at second, McNamara gave Brian Downing the green light on a 3-0 delivery, and Downing managed to ground the ball to the right side, to Tolleson, allowing DeCinces to advance to third with one out. Reggie Jackson then hit a grounder down to first-baseman O'Brien. With the infield in, the play was at the plate, but DeCinces got such a good jump that he beat the throw. The run, because of the passed ball, was unearned. When Mike Brown doubled, Jackson appeared to have scored, but a fan came on the field in an attempt to get the ball that Brown had hit, and ump Greg Kosc sent Jackson back to third. When he tried to score, as DeCinces had, on a ground ball, he was nailed at the plate. Hough walked Schofield to load the bases, but avoided further damage. But Witt now had a lead.

In the Rangers seventh, it was Mick "The Quick" Rivers again going down on strikes. Kosc punched him out on a close pitch. Rivers looked annoyed as he dragged back to the bench for what turned out to be the last time. It was the final at-bat of his 15-year career. Wayne Tolleson then came close to breaking the string. Witt fell behind 3-0, missing with three straight fastballs. With Tolleson taking all the way, Witt stayed focused and got two good fastballs over to run the count full for the second time during the day. Tolleson then hit the 3-2 pitch to second. That brought up Gary Ward—a hitter Witt was careful of all day ("I wanted to keep the ball away from him"). For the third straight time, Ward made an out to the opposite side—grounding to second.

In the eighth, McNamara made a defensive change—a risky venture for a manager during a perfect game. But Bobby Grich, in the 15th year of what might be a Hall of Fame career, replaced Daryl Sconiers at first. It all seemed academic for an instant when Larry Parrish, the cleanup hitter and the 22nd batter of the day for Texas, rifled the first pitch from Witt toward right field. "I thought it was out of here," Parrish would say later. "The way his breaking ball was working, I knew I had to take it to right and lay off the inside fastball." But Mike Brown was able to move back to the warning track and haul it in. By now, the crowd was aware of what they were seeing. Witt, bearing down now, got Pete O'Brien and George Wright looking. One inning to go.

This game that meant so little seemed suddenly to have meaning. But to guys like Charlie Hough, the game wasn't about someone else's possible perfection. Hough was losing 1–0 and he wasn't giving up. He was no Mickey Rivers—Hough would play 10 more years. He got the first two batters in the top of the ninth, but Mike Brown, having himself an excellent day, got his third hit, a single, to add to his double and triple and his fine running catch in the bottom of the eighth. With Brown on first and two down, Angels manager John McNamara wanted to get Witt another run. He wasn't counting on perfection any more than Charlie Hough was. So Mac sent Gary Pettis, his speedy regular center-fielder, in to run for Brown. Of course, Pettis would stay in as a defensive replacement for the bottom of the ninth, but in the top of the ninth, with two down in a 1–0 game, he was in there to steal second, or so Hough thought. He threw over four straight times, trying to keep Pettis close, or nail him. The first pitch, to Bob Boone, was a pitch-out. And Pettis was running, but not far—he was caught stealing. And on to the bottom of the ninth.

MacNamara moved Fred Lynn to right, Pettis went to center, and Derrel Thomas replaced the muscle-bound Brian Downing in right field. Due up to face Witt was that lowly bottom of the order—Dunbar, Scott, Wilkerson. But after Dunbar struck out on three pitches, Texas manager Doug Rader went to his thin bench for some pinch-hitters. Left-handed-hitting outfielder Bob Jones, stepped in to hit for the catcher, Scott. Jones, whose career in baseball would never involve regular playing time, put up little resistance against Witt, taking a called strike and then grounding out to second. A man named Marv Foley was sent up as Witt's last victim of the day. Another journeyman on a bad team, Foley was about to register his 419th—and last—career at-bat. But he would not register his 95th hit. Witt must have sensed that here was a man whose bête noire was the curveball. Witt sent forth four consecutive curves—called strike, ball low and away, outside ball two, and then the one that resulted in yet another grounder to the busy-as-can-be Wilfong at second, who flawlessly handled his eighth grounder of the day and threw to Grich at first for the final out.

The small crowd saluted Witt as his teammates rushed the mound. Witt's wife, Lisa, standing in a front-row box at the corner of the Angels dugout, was in tears. Witt walked over to her and they embraced. "Couldn't have happened to a nicer guy," she said.

Witt said after the game that he was aware of what he had going as early as the fourth inning, "but up until the seventh, I just wanted to win. After that, I wanted everything." He credited Mike Brown with a great catch on Larry Parrish's eighth-inning drive. Bob Boone said Witt's peformance was no surprise to him: "I think he's the premier pitcher in the league. When he's on, they're not going to hit him. His only hurdle is consistency and concentration."

The Rangers were less than gracious. They blamed home-plate ump Greg Kosc for his wide strike zone. Manager Doug Rader blamed the glare. "No one could see the son of a bitch." Mickey Rivers: "I'm not taking anything away from the pitchers, but for four or five innings, we were only trying to get it over."

The perfect game at the end of the year was simply something that fell into place. I had had a good year up to that point, but getting 15 wins was my goal that day. It was a springboard game and a springboard season for the rest of my career. My stuff that day was definitely a little better than usual. The fastball was a little faster and my curveball was a bit sharper. Most of all, though, my control that day was right on. I went with everything Bob Boone called with the exception of one pitch in about the fourth inning. That pitch was hit pretty hard and it was the last pitch I shook off for the rest of the day.

THE FOLLOWING YEAR, 1985, solidified Witt's credentials, when he went 15-9. He was showing more consistency under the returned manager Gene Mauch, and the team, with 90 wins, finished only one game out of first place. The whole organization looked forward to 1986. It would be Witt's sixth year in the big leagues, making him eligible at year's end for free agency. He could finally be headed for a good payday. He didn't know quite how much he would need it.

In the same week that Peter Ueberroth got to hand down his suspensions and fines for admitted drug users, a California equities firm run by a former sports agent named Harry Stein went bankrupt. Seventy athletes—many of them former Oakland Raiders (Stein was once Dave Casper's agent) had invested with Stein, only to see all their savings vanish. Former Raiders Pete Banaszak, Rod Martin, and Matt Millen lost everything, as did golf great Kathy Whitworth and NBA star Phil Smith. But the biggest loser, reported to be in the half-million-dollar range, was Mike Witt. "Most everything I've got is with them," he said at the time. "It knocked me back about four years as far as my future goes."

Witt turned in a fantastic year in 1986. He went 18-10, pitched 3 shutouts, threw 14 complete games, had an ERA well under 3.00 and struck out 208 batters in 269 innings. He was on the All-Star team. That year, there were no pennant races to speak off. The Mets, behind Doc Gooden, Darryl Strawberry, Keith Hernandez, won their division by more than 20 games, the Astros won the West by 10. In the A.L., a dominant Roger Clemens, and great years from Wade Boggs and Jim Rice, sealed the division crown for Boston in the East; in the West, it was all Angels, led by Mike Witt, along with Grich, Pettis, and rookie first-baseman Wally Joyner, who hit .290.

In the NLCS, the Mets would squeak by the red-hot Astros, four games to two, clinching it with a 16-inning sixth-game victory that is ranked among the greatest postseason games of all time. Boston and the Angels would tangle in a series that would spell heartbreak for Mauch and his team, but only defer the heartbreak for the Red Sox.

Witt would get to challenge the 24-4, 24-year-old Roger Clemens in Game One, and he would come away the victor, pitching a five-hitter, winning 8-1. In Game Four, Clemens entered the ninth with a 3-0 lead, but he and Calvin Schiraldi managed to hand the game to California (Schiraldi hit a batter with the bases loaded), and the Angels took a three-games-to-one lead. Mauch gave the ball to Witt for Game Five at home, to wrap up the series. And Witt pitched well, taking a 5-2 lead into the

ninth. The Angels were only three outs away from the World Series. But
Don Baylor hit a two-run shot off Witt to cut the lead to 5–4. Mauch
allowed Witt to pitch to the next hitter, righty Dwight Evans. Evans
popped out for the second out, but then Mauch made his move. He took
Witt out and brought in the long, narrow lefty Gary Lucas to pitch to the
left-handed-hitting catcher, Rich Gedman, who had worn Witt out
already with a homer, double, and a single. "I'd seen enough of Gedman
against Witt," Mauch would say later. "We needed one out and I thought
my best shot was with Lucas." Lucas plunked Gedman with his first
pitch. Mauch then brought in Donnie Moore, a great reliever the year
before (31 saves, club MVP) but now a man in so much discomfort that
he had taken a cortisone shot to the rib cage the night before. Teammate
Doug DeCinces later expressed his disbelief that Mauch would give
Moore the ball under those conditions. Still, Moore needed only one out.
Dave Henderson was the hitter, a gap-toothed, powerfully built, slashing-
type ballplayer who had come to Boston in a late-season trade but had hit
under .200, and who stood to be the goat in the game, having dropped
Bobby Grich's fly ball—over the wall—for a home run in the seventh. But
Moore served up a fat forkball on a two-strike pitch and Henderson
drilled it over the left-field wall to give Boston a 6–5 lead. The Angels
valiantly battled back for a run in the bottom of the ninth to tie it, but
Henderson, in the 11th, with Donnie Moore still in there pitching, hit a
sacrifice fly for the winning run. Boston would win the next two games
behind Oil Can Boyd and Clemens. The Angels wouldn't see postseason
play again until 2002. Witt would later say of Gene Mauch's taking him
out with a one-run lead and one out to go in Game Five, "He made the
right move."

WITT PLAYED HIS FIRST year in the bigs in 1981 for the minimum
salary, about $32,000. He worked under one-year contracts through the
next three seasons, with his salary rising to just over $200,000 in 1984
when his rights to salary arbitration kicked in, at which point he and his
agent were able to negotiate a three-year deal worth $1.7 million (with
incentives, it was worth about $2.5 million). In 1987, with expectations
now high for the Angels after their disastrous collapse the previous October, Witt was in his final year. He had already been nearly wiped out by
the Harry Stein bankruptcy. A good year would put him in good stead for
his first shot at free agency.

Witt gave it his all; he won 16 and was an All-Star once again, but the Angels fell apart, finishing tied for last place, a full 22 games behind a team that only won 85. Despite Witt's more-than-respectable win total, there were some foreboding signs amid his numbers: He had four fewer complete games than the year before, and no shutouts; while pitching 22 fewer innings than the year before, he gave up 34 more hits, 12 more home runs, 9 more walks, and struck out 16 fewer batters. His ERA jumped from 2.84 to 4.01. He started to hit what one observer called "the six-inning wall." The peaceable, laid-back Witt earned the nickname the Earl of Surl for being touchy with the press. But he was soon to have more to resent than snippy reporters.

Ueberroth's recommended assault on free agency was beginning to take its toll. In 1985, Kirk Gibson attracted no offers at all, after a great year and a great World Series. He re-signed with Detroit. In 1986, Tim Raines got no offers and sat out spring training, unwilling to sign with the Expos; Andre Dawson, similarly abandoned, approached Dallas Green of the Cubs. Wanting to play anywhere but on Montreal's cement-hard artificial turf, Dawson figured, why not the plush confines of Wrigley Field? He offered to sign a blank contract. The Cubs tossed him only $500,000, and Dawson turned in an MVP year. Free-agent Bob Horner, who'd hit 54 homers in two years for Atlanta and was only 29 years old, was so disgusted with the market he went to Japan to play. Witt received no expressions of interest from other clubs and decided to stay at home. He got a two-year deal from Buzzie Bavasi for $3.2 million. A two-time All-Star, ace of the staff, a man who'd thrown a perfect game, beaten Roger Clemens in a playoff opener, struck out 16 Mariners in a game, at the peak of his career and in his prime, only 27 years old, could not find any job security beyond two years. Witt was not happy.

> *I got three offers for the same exact amount of money over the exact same period of time: $2.8 million for two years. Angels, Athletics, Yankees. Autry, Haas, Steinbrenner. No more, no less. I was not aware of the significance of the sameness of the offers. So, all things being equal, I stayed in my hometown.*

Unfortunately for Mike Witt, his best years indeed were behind him. In 1988, his performance continued to trend downward. Although he started 34 games, and pitched one out shy of 250 full innings, his effectiveness seemed to be fleeting, and his ERA rose to 4.15, his record falling to 13–16. The Angels finished 29 games out of first. The next year, with Doug Rader at the helm, was even worse for Witt, as he won only nine games and his ERA edged up toward 5.00. In the off-season, he signed a one-year contract extension, for $1.3 million, but with the team's addition of pitchers Mark Langston and Mike Smithson to a staff that already had Chuck Finley, Kirk McCaskill, and Bert Blyleven, Witt was becoming expendable.

In 1990, Witt found himself in the bullpen. In May, he was traded to the Yankees for Dave Winfield. But it was a new start for Witt, the more so when an arbitrator investigating the collusive behavior of ownership granted Witt "new-look" status, meaning that, despite the fact that he was under contract, he could shop his services to the highest bidder (in the end, nearly 100 players were given such status, and baseball owners were fined a whopping $280 million for their trouble). By this time Witt, trailing an ailing arm, had worked a deal with his new club, the Yankees. George Steinbrenner gave him a three-year deal worth $8 million.

Finally, Mike Witt got his payday. Sadly, his career was virtually over, his arm shot. For their $8 million the Yankees would get eight wins in three years from Mike Witt. On May 22, 1993, at Fenway Park, Witt would go five wobbly innings but get the win—his last win ever—over Roger Clemens.

Baseball gave as much as it took from Mike Witt—it gave a young man a good deal of money; he met his wife through the game; it badgered him at times, outmaneuvered him at times, sometimes illegally. Baseball managed to take credit from him for deeds accomplished; an equities guru made half a million disappear. A teammate, Donnie Moore, in despair over losing a game that Witt had all but won, committed suicide. But no one—not even the commissioner of baseball—can ever take Witt's name from the record books as one of the few men who were perfect enough for one perfect game.

CHAPTER TEN

A Good Bet

Tom Browning
September 16, 1988

THE REDS-DODGERS game was scheduled for 7:35 P.M., but it had been raining most of the day in Cincinnati. Tony Perez, 46 years old, skulked around the Reds clubhouse, ready to get going but teasing the guys about maybe having to play two the next day. He could afford to tease the players; he wasn't one of them. After 2,777 major league games, 23 seasons, 16 of them with Cincinnati, he was now a coach, along with Tommy Helms and Jim Kaat. They all answered to the manager, Pete Rose, a son of Cincinnati and a man who had played more games than anybody else. Together, the four had amassed 86 years of playing time in the big leagues. They'd seen rain before. Rose was in his office talking on the phone.

The 28-year-old Tom Browning was scheduled to be the Reds' starting pitcher. Browning, like Perez, was raring to go; he was a gamer, a pro;

he loved to play. And here he was, suiting up next to the very guys he grew up admiring. As a rabid baseball fan in the mid-seventies, his favorite team was the Big Red Machine. As a Little Leaguer, Browning got to shake hands with his hero, Pete Rose, who played third on those Reds teams and annually got his 200 hits.

It was Rose who had given Browning his first callup to the big leagues and stuck with him through some early arm trouble. Now in his fourth full year, Browning was more or less the ace of the Reds staff. As game time approached, with the rain coming down in sheets, Browning sat alone in the Reds dugout, trying to stay focused. Everyone else had remained in the clubhouse. Through the veil of rain, across the way, he could see a Dodger staring out across the pattering turf. It was the opposing pitcher, Tim Belcher. Browning got up and went inside to play a few hands of cards with the likes of Paul O'Neill, Ron Oester, and his catcher, Jeff Reed.

Browning was having a good year; he had 15 wins with four starts left if he and Rose were willing to push it. In his rookie year, in 1985, Browning had won his final 11 decisions, pitching mostly on three days' rest, to finish at 20-9. Teamwise, the Reds were still in it, but only mathematically. With two weeks to go, they were 8.5 games behind the first-place Dodgers.

At two minutes after 10 P.M., the nearly two-and-a-half-hour rain delay was officially over. The game was to be on radio only back in Los Angeles, no TV; the same for the hometown, with Marty Brennaman & Co. working the mike. By the time the umps came on the field, the paid crowd of 16,591 had dwindled to a few thousand. Rose, as was his custom, stood with one leg up on the top dugout step, he clapped his hands, and the Reds hit the field. Browning hustled out there like any other position player, ready to go. They were close, Rose and Browning. In many ways, they were cut from the same cloth. A quarter-century apart in age, they had fought the same long odds as aspiring ballplayers, been found by the same organization, worked their way through the same system, and now found themselves intent upon the same thing: going out there and whipping the Dodgers, if only for the hell of it.

BROWNING WAS BORN in Casper, Wyoming, on April 28, 1960. He claims to be the second best ballplayer from Wyoming, "after Dick Ellsworth." He had two brothers and two sisters. His mother and father divorced when he was not yet 10, and his mother remarried, to another

Wyomingan, a man named Crause, who worked the power lines. Soon, he was transferred to New York, which was aggressively harvesting the hydroelectric energy along the St. Lawrence River Seaway and stringing it south to the more populous counties of the Empire State. The whole Browning-Crause family moved in 1974 to a small town near Utica, New York, and then further upstate, to the smaller town of Malone, not far from the Canadian border.

Browning's two years at Chadwicks High in Utica were crucial to his development. The competition was stiff and yet the high school and community were of a scale that allowed Tom to fit right in. He also played on a good American Legion team, Clonan Post. When Tom's stepfather got transferred to Malone, Tom reluctantly followed, enrolling at Franklin Academy. Tom dominated for two years, as a batter and pitcher, though there was another pitcher in a nearby town just as good, Jim Deshaies, from Massena High. Deshaies, also a left-hander, was a good three inches taller than Browning, at six-feet-four-inches, and was attracting scouts. During the summer months, after the high-school season, Browning would go back to Utica and play for his old American Legion team. There, a big rangy catcher with a perfect stroke was drawing the scouts, too—Andy Van Slyke. No one noticed Browning.

Browning and Deshaies became fast friends, eventually going to college together, at Le Moyne, outside Syracuse, where they made a dazzling tandem that brought the Le Moyne Dolphins to the Division II World Series twice. Still, no takers for Browning.

Browning didn't complete his four years at Le Moyne. Faced with going to summer school after his junior year in order to maintain academic eligibility, he opted instead to play summer ball in Virginia in hopes of being noticed. It didn't happen. As Browning put it, "It was the summer of the strike in 1981, and they weren't signing anybody, so I finished up at Tennessee Wesleyan." Browning did pretty well there against some of the Division I schools—Tennessee, Kentucky. Eventually, a Cincinnati Reds scout named Chet Montgomery came knocking. The Reds were interested. Indeed, on June 7, 1982, they made Browning their ninth pick of the free-agent draft, signing him for $3,500. The Yankees, meanwhile, ventured upstate where Deshaies was having a great senior season at Le Moyne. Browning and Deshaies—the best pitchers out of upstate New York since Johnny Podres.

BROWNING PLAYED ROOKIE ball in Billings in 1982 in the Pioneer League. He won as many as he lost. The next year he was promoted to A Ball, with the Tampa Tarpons—where Pete Rose had begun to shine more than two decades earlier. In midseason, Browning was promoted to Double-A ball up in Waterbury, Connecticut, and played on a field that had a warning track going through the middle of it, from foul line to foul line. "Used to be a horse track," said Browning. Just before moving to Waterbury, Browning learned a new pitch. A Reds roving pitching instructor named Harry Dorisch "taught me my changeup, or screwball. It was a true screwball," according to Browning. "He told me, 'Get your three pitches mastered and you'll win 20 games.' " Command of the strike zone was what Browning worked on after that. In his half-year at Tampa in '83 Browning, only 22 years old, was 8–1 with a 1.49 ERA; at Waterbury, he posted a very respectable 3.35 ERA.

As a result, Browning was one of five nonroster players invited to camp in the spring of 1984, where he showed only that he wasn't quite ready. Still, he now could say he was at the top of the Reds system, playing at the Reds Triple-A affiliate in Wichita, in the tough American Association. Future major leaguer Lloyd McClendon was Browning's roommate; Eric Davis, Dave Van Gorder, and Paul Householder were on the team, too. Up at the big club, things had changed since Tom was a fan back in upstate New York. Johnny Bench had retired at the end of the 1983 season, Perez was gone, and so was Rose, the Cincinnati Kid.

PETE ROSE HAD PLAYED 16 charmed years in the Queen City: He was Rookie of the Year in 1963, league MVP in 1973, World Series MVP in 1975; he won three batting titles and played on two world championship teams; in 1978, he became the youngest player ever to have 3,000 hits, and he electrified the country in midsummer by running off a 44-game hitting streak. But with free agency a newfangled thing, the great Rose tried his hand at it, and ended up signing with Philadelphia in 1979. For a few weeks at least, Pete Rose could call himself baseball's highest-paid player, getting a $3.2-million deal for four years. The investment paid off for the Phillies. Rose's leadership helped a talented team win a world championship in 1980, with Rose excelling in the postseason. But three years later, Phillies president Bill Giles said of Pete, "I want to be frank. His bat speed is slowing down." Rose's agent Reuven Katz got him a $500,000 deal with Montreal, whose president John McHale felt that

Rose's leadership was just what his young Expos needed to put them over the top. McHale even traded eight-time .300 hitter Al Oliver to open up first base for Rose, who was 201 hits short of Ty Cobb's all-time record. Rose was 42 years old.

But Pete hit poorly in Montreal, and he was relegated to pinch-hitting. He'd never catch Cobb from the bench. Enter Reuven Katz once more—he arranged for Rose to go back home to Cincinnati, as player-manager, prodigal son, for a team going nowhere, for half the money.

On August 17, a Friday night homestand opener against the Cubs, 35,000 filed into Riverfront Stadium to see Pete Rose be a Red once again. They couldn't have been there just to see the Reds, who were 51-70, in next-to-last place in the Western Division. In the first inning, against the Eastern Division–leading Cubs, Rose, batting second, singled to center to drive in a run, moved to second on the throw to the plate, and took third on a throwing error and then scored. He also doubled in a run in the seventh. All in all, a 2-for-4 day for Rose, a 6–4 win for the Reds, and all was well, or at least, better. But the Reds quickly resumed their losing ways, losing 9 of 12, despite Pete's own inspired play—he would hit .365 as a Red for the year.

That September, it was time to expand the rosters and make some changes. Rose had already instituted one change, making good on a promise he had made long ago to Philly teammate Jim Kaat: "If I ever get to be a manager, I'll hire you as my pitching coach." And that turned out to be the good fortune of young Browning, who was then called up from Wichita, where he'd completed his Triple-A season at 12-10 with a 3.91 ERA.

Browning would benefit from several things that September: being around some of his favorite players—Perez, Dave Concepcion, Buddy Bell—as well as being managed by the legendary Rose. "I grew up knowing who Pete was and what he meant to the team and how he played, so it wasn't very hard for me to fall right in line because I just loved to play." And then there was Kaat, the 25-year veteran, winner of 283 games, who had just retired the year before. "He was awesome," Browning said in a phone conversation 20 years later. "He made it very simple. Of course, we were very similar. One, being left-handed, two, we liked to work quick, so we hit it off pretty well."

Anyone would have liked the pitcher that Kaat and Rose saw on September 9, 1984, when young Browning got a surprise start in Los Angeles.

The Sunday day game drew 25,000 fans; Browning was facing another rookie, Orel Hershiser, who'd already won 10 games and pitched four shutouts. The Reds got to Hershiser for two runs in the fourth on singles and groundouts, and added three in the eighth, thanks to a Rafael Landestoy error. Meanwhile, the newcomer was faring well, striking out his first batter, Dave Anderson, giving up his first hit to Pedro Guerrero, and then pitching shutout ball till the ninth, when three straight singles plated a run and brought Kaat and Rose to decide the kid had had enough. Ted Power closed out the 5–1 Reds win, and Tom Browning stood 1-0 lifetime. After that win, the Reds played .500 ball the rest of the way. Browning got two more starts, pitching eight strong innings against the Padres, to no decision, though he did experience his first of many punishments by the great Tony Gwynn, who got three hits. And another seven tough innings, giving up only one run, to the Astros. No decision again, but at season's end, Browning had proved he could get major league hitters (most of them) out. His ERA: 1.54.

The next year was a dream year, for Browning and for Rose. First off, Browning was assured he'd be on the team. His contract guaranteed him $5,000 over the minimum salary, so when the players struck for a few days at the start of the season, and the minimum was negotiated upward by the union, he ended up with a $14,000 raise, to about $60,000, enough to put a down payment on his first house. He had married Debbie Butts from Malone and they had a child on the way. For Rose, he could look forward to managing a team that had responded to him the previous September, even though he had a few problems, one, perhaps, of his own making. Nick Esasky, the former first-round pick for the Reds who was Bench's heir apparent at third base, struck out too much, got moved to first in 1984, only to have the new player-manager Rose supplant him. Esasky ended the season badly—hitting .198 and sitting in Rose's doghouse for his sulking. In 1985, Rose was determined to get his hits and blow by Ty Cobb, so it was back to third for Esasky. In midseason, the Reds traded for Buddy Bell, an All-Star third baseman from the American League. Esasky sat. Pete wanted two things: hits 4,191 and 4,192. So did all of Cincinnati.

They got what they wanted on September 11, 1985, when a packed house watched Rose rap a single to left off San Diego's Eric Show in the first inning. Rose hugged his batboy son, Petey. He received a red Corvette with the license plate PR 4192, which was driven right onto the field. The fans cheered him for seven minutes. Browning was pitching that night, and got the win, 2–0, his 16th of the season.

Browning stayed hot. In late September, he was going for his 11th win in 11 starts; it would give him a 20-win season. A three-run homer by Buddy Bell chased Astros starter Mike Scott. In came reliever Jim Deshaies. Browning got to his old friend for a single before the inning was out. The Reds went on to win, Browning gave up only two runs and pitched into the eighth inning. He was now 20-9, and over the last 11 games had pitched supremely; 77 innings, 76 hits, only 19 walks, and an ERA of 2.99.

The Reds finished in second place. Browning, as the first rookie since Bob Grim of the 1954 Yankees to win 20 games, would have been a lock for Rookie of the Year but for the spectacular debut of Vince Coleman, who stole 110 bases for St. Louis.

By SPRING TRAINING of the 1986 season, Browning, not yet arbitration-eligible since the Basic Agreement of 1985 had extended the eligibility period to three years, was nonetheless treated "pretty good," according to him. He signed a new contract for $180,000. "They've got you by the short hairs till you're arbitration-eligible," he admitted. Down in Tampa, the career-hits-leading manager and his ace expressed their mutual admiration. "I like everything about Tom Browning," Rose told *The New York Times*. "Everything." Browning, taking a page out of Rose's handbook on aggressive play, vowed to "knock somebody down if I have to," and said, "I wouldn't want to play for any other manager."

Nineteen eighty-six was another workhorse year for Browning. Throwing nearly 250 innings but lacking the run support he got in his rookie year, he finished with a 14-13 record, after a miserable 0-4 start. But despite off-season acquisitions of pitchers Bill Gullickson and John Denny, the team faded, finishing 10 games back of Houston. Only Eric Davis, with 27 home runs and 80 stolen bases in 132 games, had a stellar year, looking for all the world like the second coming of Willie Mays. Pete Rose played his last season, and hit .219. After 24 years in the big leagues, induction to the Hall of Fame seemed automatic. He was first-ballot all the way. That's what all the papers said.

What the papers weren't saying was what people close to Rose knew: He had a big gambling problem. There were stories about wild bets—$34,000 on a Super Bowl, $5,000 on Monday Night Football games. Rose took a huge cut in salary in moving from Montreal to the Reds, but he was cashing in on his eclipsing of Cobb's all-time hit record. Everything he touched, or signed, could turn to cash (except betting slips). And if he couldn't get cash, he insisted on checks for less than $10,000, since then he needn't report it to the IRS. His agent told him, "Pete, if you need a million dollars, say so." But Pete wouldn't say so. He'd bet to get even. Or he'd sell his Hickock Belt after dejeweling it, or the Corvette he'd been given.

Nineteen eighty-seven started off inauspiciously for Browning, for Rose, and for the Reds. They were all losing. Actually, the Reds weren't doing so badly. The team went 15-7 in April. Browning, however, went 2-4 for the month, another slow start. And Rose, as would be voluminously detailed two years later in a special report for the commissioner of baseball, was losing big. It was widely known that Rose had been betting for years, but the intensity—and desperation—began to peak in '87. He was in deep trouble. Rose had lost the whopping bet on the Super Bowl in January; he got skunked in the NCAA tournament in March; he was losing $30,000 a week. Then the season began. In April alone, Pete bet more than a quarter of a million dollars; because of his own team's hot start, Rose was down only $21,000 going into May, since he seems to have always backed his team.

The Reds cooled, however, and Rose's luck worsened. On May 9 alone, he lost $19,100; two days later, he lost another $9,000. Two days after that his betting was suspended—he was into the gamblers too much for them to handle his action. He didn't find another guy until May 1, and promptly dropped "ten dimes," or $10,000. Most every night, Rose was betting two grand on his team, and then betting a similar amount on six to eight other major league contests. From the start of the '87 season till July 3, Rose bet nearly a million dollars. He was out of control and in big debt, but Major League Baseball did not yet know the extent of any of it. Pete was still Pete, hustling, seeking an advantage, getting by on guts, and bravado, and reputation.

Rose had begun to run with the wrong crowd—some patrons of his Cincinnati gym were at the center of a cocaine-trafficking investigation, and it turned out one of those investigated was Pete's runner, Paul Janszen. Janszen, when the heat was on, would go to *Sports Illustrated* to tell his story about Rose, who owed him plenty. And a brand-new commissioner, a scholar of Dante and the Italian Renaissance, A. Bartlett Giamatti, would have the task of trying to find out just how far Rose had fallen. Was there proof that Rose was in violation of Major League Rule 21, instituted in 1920 by Judge Landis? The rule says, "Any player, umpire, or club official or employee, who shall bet any sum whatsoever upon any baseball game in connection with which the bettor has no duty to perform shall be declared ineligible for one year." It also says, "Any player, umpire, or club or league official or employee, who shall bet any sum whatsoever upon any baseball game in connection with which the bettor has a duty to perform shall be declared permanently ineligible."

This rule is posted in every clubhouse in baseball.

THINGS HAD TURNED sour for Browning in 1987, too. He had felt twinges running up his elbow in an April start in Atlanta, and he couldn't seem to recover his aggressiveness. Uncharacteristically, Rose screamed at him. Rose wasn't a screamer, he was a talker. He would bark and then talk, as opposed to the unmanly emoting. But during a start in Montreal, Rose felt Browning wasn't using his guts and courage to get through a physical problem. Rose had been outhustling physical shortcomings all his life. Why couldn't Browning? The date was May 13, to be exact. It was the first day of no bets all season for Rose, who couldn't find a way to get around a bookie refusing to take any more of his action.

Browning's problems were real and he was scared, but working on one-year contracts made him keep his physical woes to himself. Browning calls 1987 "my worst year ever. I got hurt and didn't tell anybody and then ended up getting a demotion for it." He was sent to Nashville to find his confidence, which really meant he was sent down to figure out if his arm was sound or not. He got hammered three straight times down there, but then began to find his command and his velocity. He was back after a month, beating Dwight Gooden and the Mets 7–5 on July 5.

Browning struggled to finish 10-13, and his ERA was over 5.00. But he had pitched through what is scariest for a young pitcher: arm trouble. He had found that his arm, apparently, could take it. It could tire and ache and betray him and eat at his confidence, but it could bounce back.

The Reds finished in second place again, behind the Giants. Eric Davis was perhaps the best player in the National League; John Franco had 32 saves. Rose was getting good reviews as a manager, and the team was poised to get past second place in 1988. Browning entered the season older and wiser and stronger. And richer: Finally arbitration-eligible, he compromised with the Reds and signed a one-year deal for $442,500. In the spring, Browning would say, "My goal this season is to pitch 250 innings." That is exactly what he would do, including a string of perfect ones on a rainy night in September. But it would be quite a season even before then.

EARLY IN APRIL, there was a spectacularly wild ballgame, between the Mets and the Reds, that would feature a variety of combatants and would ultimately engage two figures—Rose and Bart Giamatti—in a preview of their great showdown a year later. There would be an odd subplot prefigured, too, featuring a renegade umpire and a ballplayer who hated him.

It was a cold Saturday night when the Mets came to town to square off against the Reds. The world-beating Mets of two years before had begun to unravel due to injuries and drug problems. Despite the raw weather, there was a good crowd of more than 33,000. The Reds were a game above .500, at 11-10, in third place, while the Mets were off to another hot start, having won 14 of their first 20. Working behind the plate—for the umpires would be a major part of the night's unfolding drama—was Eric Gregg, known for his Falstaffian girth and billowing strike zone. At first base stood Dave Pallone, the unloved—he got his job when the unionized umps were on strike in 1973, so he was accustomed to the general scorn not only of fans and ballplayers, but of fellow umps as well. Staid veterans John Kibler and Jim Quick rounded out the crew.

The Mets nicked Browning for a run in the second, thanks to a Tim Teufel single and sacrifice fly by Gary Carter. On a close play at the plate in the third, Gregg called Lloyd McClendon out trying to score on a double by Browning. Rose argued vehemently, to no avail. Browning came across on a single by Barry Larkin to tie the score. A long two-run home run by Strawberry put the Mets up 4-2 in the sixth. In the seventh, the game took a violent turn. With two outs and no one on, Mookie Wilson tripled, the ball deflecting off Eric Davis's glove after a long run. With Teufel stepping in, Browning had to be concerned. Teufel had already collected two hits on the night and was hitting over .500 lifetime against him. As Browning wound to deliver his first pitch, Teufel stepped out of the batter's box. Eric Gregg, however, did not grant time. Browning stopped his delivery. Gregg called a balk. Mookie Wilson strolled in from third to make it 5-2 Mets, and Rose was in Gregg's face before Mookie touched home plate.

Gregg had blown the call. Rule 6.02(b) states that, in this instance, "Both the pitcher and batter have violated a rule and the umpire shall call time and both the batter and pitcher start over from 'scratch.'" But Rose got nowhere with Gregg. Rose looked to Pallone to see if the first-base ump might have some contribution to make to the debate, but the scab Pallone knew better than to presume to overrule Gregg. And he wasn't interested in placating Rose either, for it was Rose who was said to be the source of a rumor that Pallone had visited gay bars in the Queen City.

Rose went to the mound. According to Browning, Rose said, "Listen, this guy hits you like he owns you. There's other things you can do."

He hit Teufel in the back with a fastball. The benches emptied. Strawberry came looking for someone to coldcock, and he was ejected, as was Browning. The tension continued to grow. The Cincy crowd was cold but well oiled. In the bottom of the eighth, their boys rallied. Three singles and two walks tied the score. Then the ninth, and the evening seemed to find its true, appalling heart.

Reds fireman John Franco walked Howard Johnson to start things off. Kevin Elster sacrificed Johnson to second. Franco struck out Barry Lyons for the second out. Mookie Wilson, batting right-handed against the lefty Franco, rapped a grounder into the hole at short. Larkin made a fine play but threw the ball a bit wide of first. Nick Esasky had to stretch to reach it. Mookie was digging hard. Larkin's throw beat him by a hair, but was Esasky pulled off the bag? After a moment's hesitation, the ump, pointing to the bag, shouted "No! Safe!" It was Dave Pallone.

Esasky couldn't believe it. He started jawing with Pallone, by which time Howard Johnson, running with two out, was steaming toward home plate. Esasky's throw was late and the Mets took a 6–5 lead. Rose went wild, and he went right at Pallone. "You stole the goddamn game from us! You waited too goddamn long!" Rose, with his beer-keg chest, pushed Pallone toward second base. He gave him a forearm. No other umps interceded. Finally, Rose was tossed. The boos were cacophonous, the debris aerial and dangerous. Coins, whiskey bottles, batteries, cigarette lighters. When a boom box came arcing down from the upper deck to land near the pitcher's mound, the umps left the field. The public address announcer appealed for calm. Fifteen minutes later, the umps returned, except for Pallone; he wisely stayed in the umpires' room. The Mets corner infielders, Keith Hernandez and Howard Johnson, took the field wearing batting helmets. When Barry Larkin popped to Teufel, the game was over. What had started out as an attempt by one batter—Tim Teufel—to disrupt the rhythm of Tom Browning, turned into a near riot.

National League president Bart Giamatti, who once before had

severely reprimanded manager Rose, slapped him with a huge 30-day suspension and $10,000 fine. Giamatti pronounced the incident "one of the
worst in baseball's recent memory. A tiny minority," he went on to say,
"cannot be allowed to disgrace the vast majority of decent individuals
who truly care for the game." Rose appealed. He wore his best blue
sharkskin suit and, with his lawyer Katz, met with Giamatti in New
York. They came bearing a video purportedly showing that Pallone had
gouged Rose's eye. Pallone contended that the wound was self-inflicted,
in the heat of the moment or for effect. The video was inconclusive,
though Rose had pointedly showed the gash under his eye in the clubhouse after the April 30 melee. Years later, Browning would say, "I
remember Pete coming in and I remember a gash on his face. I don't
remember if I saw it there when he came in or not but eventually he had
a gash on his face."

Giamatti told Pallone not to work the plate the next day, as scheduled. But the umpire's union, as interested in their own sovereignty as in
making Pallone pay for his sins, insisted he do so. And Pallone, no
shrinking violet, called two balks on the Reds, one, outrageously, during
an intentional walk, cashing in a few retribution notes. The game was a
humiliation for Rose and the Reds—Pallone, his team's three errors, the
complete domination by Dwight Gooden, throwing a four-hit complete-
game shutout to bring his record to 6-0. The final: Mets 11, Cincy 0. And
Davey Concepcion steamed ever further. Eight years before, Pallone had
called Concepcion out on a half-swing. Concepcion had taken exception.
They met in the runway after the game, and Concepcion told him, "I'm
gonna get you, Pallone. I'll be in this game longer than you, and I promise
I'll get you."

TOMMY HELMS TOOK over as manager while Rose served his suspension. Browning didn't post his first win till May 10. It was a rough month
all around. Under Helms, the team struggled, winning 12 of 27 games. By
the time Rose returned to the dugout on June 1, things looked dire. Dropping their first three under Rose, to bring their losing streak to six, the
Reds stood at 23-29. But budding star Jose Rijo won his sixth game, besting Orel Hershiser in L.A., 5–2, on a three-run homer by Paul O'Neill in
the ninth. Browning followed two days later with a gem. He carried a no-
hitter into the ninth against the Padres before Tony Gwynn, batting .422
lifetime against him, drilled a single between short and third. The Reds

won 12–0. "No-hitters are mostly luck anyway, so I'll take the win," said Browning afterward.

With Rose now back in the dugout, the Reds started to put it together. In late June, Browning, with the help of a home run by Barry Larkin, beat old pal Jimmy Deshaies 2–1 in Houston for his sixth win. For the July Fourth holiday, the Reds brought their game to Shea Stadium. Fireworks were anticipated, in more ways than one. The Reds were then six games under .500, nine games back of the Dodgers, in fourth place in the N.L. West, while the Mets, in the East, were cruising—23 games over .500, running away with the N.L. East.

But Jose Rijo bested David Cone in the first game, in front of 46,000 partisan New Yorkers, for his ninth win; and Browning the second, in a game packed with tension because of the goings-on back in April, calmly won his sixth straight, 3–1. He didn't hit Strawberry, who had suggested that Browning "didn't have the guts." He didn't hit Teufel, who said after the game, "I really wanted to get him." And Teufel didn't hit Browning, going 0-3. But Browning in the sixth inning did hit shortstop Kevin Elster, who later said of Browning, "He is kind of like we are to the rest of the league. Everybody hates us."

The Reds jelled behind the solid pitching of Browning, Rijo (starting and relieving), and Danny Jackson, who would have a career year, winning 23 games. The bullpen featured John Franco and Rob Murphy, and young Rob Dibble. However, despite playing well over .600 ball from July 1 on, the Reds couldn't overcome the mediocre start and the slide under Helms during Rose's suspension. By mid-September, when the first-place Dodgers came to town, the Reds were barely hanging in there.

SINCE IT WAS LOS ANGELES' last visit of the year to Riverfront, the decision whether to play the game—what with the rain steadily falling—was in the hands of the umpiring crew, a foursome familiar to Cincinnati fans, but with a small difference this time. It was the Gregg-Kibler-Quick crew minus Dave Pallone, who'd been replaced for the Queen City trip by rookie Mark Hirschbeck. Behind this was the hand of Bart Giamatti, who, as president of the National League, was the ultimate employer of the umpires. He ordered a leave of absence for Pallone. The night before, September 15, in Philadelphia, Pallone, a veteran of 15 years as a National League umpire, worked his last game. Although many Cincinnati Reds would cheer that decision, one of them had other things on his mind. On the morning of September 16, Dave Concepcion—along with Rose, baseball's premier Pallone-hater—he who had vowed to outlast the man in the game of baseball and "get" him, underwent career-ending shoulder surgery. As for Pallone, he thought he would work again, but in November, he would be called to New York, and Giamatti, like Pallone an Italian-American Red Sox fan from Massachusetts, would force the umpire's retirement because of the scandals concerning his homosexual activity and his poor umpiring—he ranked third from the bottom of all 36 National League umps. Giamatti had already been named to succeed Ueberroth as commissioner come the following April; he was clearing the desk of messy problems for his successor. Ueberroth, however, would leave a few messes for Bart—namely, collusion, which was just coming down, and the matter of Baseball versus Peter Edward Rose.

"Gosh, it was just a cruddy day," remembers Browning. We'd been right in the hunt all year, but we started kind of fading but were still mathematically in it, and they were in front of us and they were our opponent." That was enough for the competitive Browning. And given the opponent, there was a little added incentive. "Being a Reds fan all my life. . . . Well, I liked beating the Dodgers." You'd have thought they were playing the Mets.

"I was starting to get undressed when a guy comes in and says 'We got a window. We're gonna go at 10.' I thought, ah, cool. I was nice and relaxed, really hadn't thought too much about it and just went out there and got myself ready and just got locked in."

Getting locked in was everything for Browning. Rhythm, release point, game plan, not giving in. If you weren't careful, Browning would be through with you in less than two hours. As Rose said, "That's what Browning does better than anybody in the league. He pitches fast." He also could pitch slow. His one-time catcher Bo Diaz marveled, after coming to the Reds from Philadelphia, how Browning could throw off-speed pitches for strikes. "You don't see left-handed pitchers throw changeups for strikes," he said, "especially when they are behind in the count." Diaz, perhaps giving a few secrets away, went on to say how both Browning and Franco would get behind in the count just to get the hitters sitting on a fastball that would never come, and then the change would get them.

Browning's change of pace was his Harry Dorisch screwball. And on the rainy night of September 16, after a 147-minute rain delay, he wasn't getting behind in the count, and the Dodgers, cruising in first place, and headed ultimately for the World Series, in the midst of a long road trip, were up there swinging.

Alfredo Griffin batted leadoff for L.A. It was his first year as a Dodger, having been acquired in a key off-season acquisition, part of a stunning three-way trade involving L.A., the A's, and the Mets. Unfortunately for the Dodgers, Griffin got hurt early; with Mariano Duncan already on the shelf, they were hard-pressed. With Valenzuela winning only five games during the season, Pedro Guerrero wearing out his welcome and being traded midseason, you'd wonder how the Dodgers were even in contention, much less set to clinch their division (and go on to win everything). But great years from Hershiser, Kirk Gibson, and Mike Marshall did the trick. And Dave Anderson stepped in for Griffin and hit .300. But now it was September, Griffin was back, and he stepped in against Browning hitting barely .200 but with fresh legs.

Griffin was a man to keep off the bases. Bill James calls him the most aggressive baserunner in the 1980s, scoring from second base on infield outs with regularity, going first to third on infield outs, scoring on pop-ups to the catcher. But Browning, with Griffin hitting from the right side, prevailed, inducing a weak fly to center to start the game. Mickey Hatcher, the hulking L.A. first baseman caught in a platoon situation with Franklin Stubbs, was up next. Hatcher was hitting .306, but he'd not had much luck against Browning, going 1-8 against him in two previous games. He would have no luck tonight either, beginning with his grounder to third-baseman Chris Sabo for out number two. Kirk Gibson then strode to the plate. The great hero of all of Michigan, from Pontiac, All-American wide receiver at Michigan State, sprinter's speed, powerful build, drafted by the Tigers, a World Series hero in 1984, and then, the following year, eligible for free agency with his six years in, he ran into the collusive practices of the owners, receiving no offers beyond what Detroit was offering. He stayed, but was awarded second-look free agency, just as Mike Witt and others were, and signed with Peter O'Malley and the Dodgers for three years and $4.5 million. Coming into the game, Gibson was hitting .301, with 25 home runs, 72 RBI; he had also stolen 30 bases in 34 attempts, despite his deteriorating hamstring. Gibson had feasted on Tom Browning's stuff, going 7-10, with three homers and a double. Only five days earlier at Dodger Stadium, he'd taken Browning deep, for number 25. But not this night. Gibson ended Browning's first inning of work with a fly ball to Kal Daniels in left.

Big Tim Belcher came out for the Dodgers. Belcher was the number-one draft pick in all of baseball back in 1983. He was 4-2 in a brief stint in 1987, but blossomed in '88. Coming into the game he was 10-4 (Belcher would have his best year in a 14-year career in '89, hurling an astounding eight shutouts—no one has thrown more than five since).

For the Reds, Barry Larkin batted leadoff, hitting .285, with some pop (11 HR) and lots of speed (37 stolen bases). Rookie sensation Chris Sabo, the third baseman who replaced Ray Knight, batted second and was hitting a solid .275; he was even faster than Larkin, having stolen 46 bases. And he could handle the hot corner with nerdy aplomb (he wore an unflattering set of goggles on the field). Batting third was Kal Daniels, an underrated outfielder with power, speed, and a good eye. He was hitting .285 and was on his way to an 18-home-run year, with 27 stolen bases. However, Belcher dispatched all three of these fellows with ease—groundout, pop-up, strikeout, to match Browning through one inning.

Mike Marshall, the towering, six-foot-five-inch Illinois native who tore up the Pacific Coast League in the Dodger organization, batted cleanup. His best years behind him, Marshall, at 28, was still a tough out for Browning, since he covered so much area with his long arms, and Browning got right-handers out with pitches away, out of reach. Marshall had homered earlier in the year off Browning, but, leading off the top of the second, he grounded out to Sabo at third. John Shelby, a fleet-footed switch-hitter, traded to the Dodgers the previous year after seven seasons with the Orioles, was having an up-and-down time with National League pitching. Suddenly becoming a power hitter in the fastball-dominant N.L., he also became a more frequent strikeout victim. He went down swinging for the second out of the inning, and he would go down swinging in all three at-bats on the evening. Jeff Hamilton, tall and rangy, batted sixth, played third. With little speed, little power, Hamilton was having the kind of year that would have him out of baseball after a few more seasons. Here, he lifted a fly to O'Neill in right for the third out.

In the bottom of the second, Belcher issued his only walk of the night, to the Reds' best player, Eric Davis. Davis was leading the league in a statistical category now no longer kept, game-winning hits. At 26 years of age, he was in the fifth year of what looked like a Hall of Fame career. He was a Gold Glove speedster with power to all fields. He was the first National Leaguer to hit 20 home runs and steal 80 bases in a season, and in 1988, he was having another sparkling year, hitting .277 with

25 homers and 90 RBI, and having stolen 34 bases in 35 attempts. Unfortunately for Davis, a series of injuries, including a lacerated kidney suffered when diving for a ball in the World Series, was topped off by a battle with colon cancer, so he can no longer put Cooperstown on his itinerary. But for four or five years, he might have been the best player in the National League. So when Belcher walked him, it wasn't a bad move. With the defensively fierce Rick Dempsey behind the plate, Belcher was able to keep Davis close at first. Paul O'Neill, not yet the hitter he would become as a Yankee, tried to advance Davis by pulling the ball behind him, but merely skied to right-center. Nick Esasky, hitting only .243, followed and struck out, bringing up Jeff Reed, the Reds catcher, a guy who would play for 17 years in the big leagues. Splitting the catching duties with Bo Diaz, Reed was hitting .229 (10 points better than Diaz!); he grounded out to second to end the second.

The bottom of the Dodgers order wasn't much more formidable than the Reds', what with Dempsey, second-baseman Steve Sax, and the pitcher Belcher due up. Dempsey, a lifetime sub-.250 hitter in his 19th year who even resorted to switch-hitting for a year, was still no automatic out. He had a good eye and could hit a mistake. Later, his counterpart Jeff Reed would say, "The only guy who gave us trouble all night was Rick Dempsey." Although Reed and Browning were attacking the Dodgers with first-pitch fastballs, Dempsey went up there looking for such a pitch, and leading off the third that's what he got and he hit it hard to Sabo's left, but the third baseman deftly turned it into an out at first. That brought up Steve Sax, a Rookie of the Year in 1982. Only two years before, Sax had collected 210 hits and batted .332, but he was now a hitter with a hole in his swing and limited range at second base. Lasorda had dropped him down in the order to the eighth spot. Sax hadn't had a hit off Browning all year, and he kept it up, popping to Oester at second. Up came Belcher, a pitcher who hit one home run in his career, struck out about half the time, and was a .143 lifetime slugger. He grounded out weakly to Esasky at first, Browning covering.

Nine up and down for Browning. And after Belcher put down Oester, Browning, and Larkin in order in the bottom of the third, there was a double no-hitter going through three. The game was clipping along.

Browning was like a machine, doing it all by himself. He had the hitters so off-balance that, other than Sabo's stab of the hopper by Dempsey, the only defensive play mentioned in the game reports came in the fifth, when Mike Marshall hit a high chopper over the third-base bag only to have the scrappy Sabo, backing up, make a backhand grab and nip the lumbering one by a step. Otherwise, through five, it was 15 Dodgers down in a row and, but for the walk to Eric Davis in the second, the same for Belcher.

"Timmy took a no-hitter with me into the sixth, so the game was just flying," Browning would recall 15 years later. "We must have had the first five innings over in probably 40 minutes. As it wore on, you could just sense something. I was locked in. It didn't matter to me, I was just trying to throw strikes."

In the sixth, Browning got Dempsey again, although the first-pitch fastball was tagged pretty well. Kal Daniels hauled it in. Sax followed, and hit one the other way, to O'Neill for out number 2. Belcher then fanned.

In the Reds sixth, the team got a run for Browning, and it would be all he'd need.

With two out and nobody on, Larkin rifled an 0-1 pitch on a line into the right-field corner for a double, breaking up Belcher's no-hitter. The crowd, what there was of it, leaned into the moment. The spunky Sabo was up, but his grounder to third seemed to spell the end of the threat. However, Larkin, running on contact, passed in front of third-baseman Jeff Hamilton a second before the ball reached him. Unnerved, Hamilton bounced the throw to Hatcher, who got a glove on it but couldn't hold on. The ball squirted away and rolled toward the Reds dugout as Larkin swept around third and scored—throwing error on Hamilton. Like the lone run in the Koufax game, like the lone run in Mike Witt's game, like the lone run in the Addie Joss/Ed Walsh game, the run was officially unearned.

Browning recalls the Sabo grounder as taking a "fluke bounce," which perhaps, added to Larkin's moving screen, made for Hamilton's undoing, and ultimately the Dodgers'. In any event, Browning finally had the advantage, and he tried to press it home. "From that point on," he says, "I took one hitter at a time and tried to make every pitch an out pitch. And essentially, I got away with it."

Helped by a good curveball and what his catcher called perfect control—"He was a painter, painting the corners," said Reed—Browning had but one more time through the order to go to join an exclusive club. Teammate Ron Robinson had come as close as one can get earlier in the season, in Montreal, getting within one out, within one strike of a perfect game, before a fellow named Wallace Johnson doubled on a 2-2 pitch.

It often seems the case in perfect games that the home-plate umpire gets into the spirit of things, seeing history unfold quite possibly before his discerning eyes. Jim Quick was calling the balls and strikes on this night (Pallone's replacement was working first base). After Browning dispatched Alfredo Griffin on a grounder to second for the first out (with Griffin perhaps déjà-vuing: he'd gone o-for-3 with Toronto against Len Barker seven years earlier), and then induced Hatcher to pop up, Kirk Gibson stepped in.

Gibson would later complain that Quick's strike zone was "huge . . . ridiculous." Being even-handed, Gibson observed that both pitchers understood the established zone and "utilized it." But when Quick brought the Dodger seventh inning to a close by calling Gibson out on strikes, Kirk couldn't find the equanimity in himself to keep quiet. He palmed his helmet and then bounced it. He argued with Quick and got the thumb. Browning now had six batters to go.

Mike Marshall led off the eighth for L.A. Browning's ball was darting and moving, and he began to believe. Still, he was starting to rush. Rose instructed catcher Reed to slow him down. "I started feeling a little antsy," Browning said after, recalling the eighth. But, working the fastball in and the change away, he got Marshall to loop one to right, where O'Neill hauled it in. John Shelby was up next, and for the third straight time he went down swinging, for Browning's sixth K of the night. Hamilton then walked to the plate with goat horns already crowning his head for his sixth-inning throwing error. Looking for redemption, he could only pull a curveball to Larkin at short for out number 24 on the night.

"It's just rhythm, just timing," recalled Browning. "You know, I didn't waste a lot of time, so I was able to stay in rhythm. I remember guys like Pedro Guerrero, who'd step out, try to kill my timing off, but for the most part if I was locked in it didn't matter. I would wait for them to get ready and I'd go. . . . I just had good command that night. If Jeff called for fastball low and away I threw it low and away; or inside up and in, that's where I put it. Any mistakes I made they either fouled off or didn't swing.

Browning didn't go to a three-ball count on anyone all night. When he came to the plate to hit in the bottom of the eighth, with Ron Oester aboard via only the second hit off Belcher, the crowd roared as loudly as a few thousand can roar. Browning, a proud hitter, struck out to the most praise he would ever hear for doing so.

Top of the ninth. Reds 1, Dodgers 0. It was 11:47 in the evening. In six minutes, Browning would be at the bottom of a dogpile. But here came Rick Dempsey. Having started Dempsey off with fastballs his first two times up, and having had Dempsey hit them pretty well, Reed called for a changeup. Dempsey unfooled, fouled it off. Browning then zipped a fastball in at the hands, but too far inside; ball one. Back to the changeup. Again, Dempsey waited on it; he slammed it well the opposite way, but O'Neill was able to drift back on the warning track and make the catch. Then came Sax, hacking. He hit the first pitch right back up the middle past Browning. But the very quick Larkin scooted behind second and nailed Sax easily for out number 26 on the night. Lasorda of course sent up a pinch-hitter for Belcher, who received a nice hand for his stellar effort. Up walked Tracy Woodson, a right-handed-hitting second-year man who would only get about a season's worth of plate appearances in his five-year career.

There was no use looking for a walk against Browning tonight. Woodson, the 27th man up, became the 21st batter to get a first-pitch strike, fouling off Browning's fastball. He then took a fastball inside for a ball, then a changeup away for ball two. Browning, not wanting to go 3-1, came in with a fastball. Woodson fouled it back over the L.A. dugout. With the count even, he went to the fastball again, with even a little more mustard. As he tells it, "It was forehead high. I didn't know what to think." But Woodson jumped at it and missed. It was over. Browning shortly was to disappear in a mess of Reds teammates, from the field, from the bullpen, from the dugout. The game, which took less time to play than the rain delay that preceded it, was over. The ebullient rookie Sabo enthused, "We're going to Cooperstown!" Well, the scorecard did, and Browning's hat did, too.

Johnny Bench sent over a case of champagne, owner Marge Schott gave Debbie Browning a mink coat. But there were no more highlights for the Reds in 1988. In a sense, it was the end of a good run that wasn't good enough, under Rose. The Reds finished their customary second, to the Dodgers, who beat the Mets for the N.L. pennant and then, behind Kirk Gibson's only at-bat in the World Series, beat the Athletics for all the marbles. For the Reds, the off-season offered some challenges: to sign Danny Jackson (23-8) and Browning (18-5) and Eric Davis, who had another great year. The team, long in the making, had continued to improve under Rose, who signed a new two-year contract at season's end, saying, "I'm the right man for the job because I care about the Reds more than anybody on God's little earth."

THE MONTHS after the team cleared out its lockers we can now guess were the last months of contentment for Pete Rose, for in the winter the noose began to tighten. The FBI, in the course of their cocaine investigation in the Cincinnati area, turned up Rose's name, in connection with gambling as well as income tax evasion. They decided to hand over the income tax irregularities to the IRS and drop the gambling issue. But somebody called Major League Baseball, and Commissioner Ueberroth, in his last weeks in office, called in Rose. He asked Rose questions, Rose dodged, Ueberroth more or less said the issue was closed.

It wasn't. When Bart Giamatti became baseball's seventh commissioner in the spring of 1989, he arrived at his Park Avenue office with a huge problem on his desk. He and his deputy Fay Vincent called in Rose and his attorneys. Neither cared at all for Rose's arrogance. Giamatti hired a mob investigator, John Dowd, to do an investigation and write a report. A day later, on February 23, Dowd was interviewing the former bodybuilder Paul Janszen, a part-time flunkie/part business partner of Rose's. Janszen turned over his betting records, detailing Rose's daily lay-down, as it was Janzsen who would call the bets in to a series of willing bookies. Dowd and his men then paid a visit to restaurateur Ron Peters, another bookmaker, who testified to even deeper gambling activity on Rose's part. In April, two weeks into the season, Dowd had his draft ready and Rose sat for an eight-hour interview to hear and answer the allegations. It was not only baseball gambling, and it was not only Peters and Janzsen. There were horse-track schemes, money-laundering procedures, cocaine pickups, firearms, and under-the-table card-show payments. There was Tommy Giosa, an orotund, steroid-addicted gofer who befriended Pete's son and became part of the Rose retinue. There were guys from Staten Island and threats and cars and souvenir bats sold for cash. On May 11, the final report was received by the commissioner. Before Giamatti discussed the report, he put in a good word—unwisely, in writing—to a federal judge praising the cooperation of Peters, who was facing serious drug trafficking charges. Rose's team filed for an injunction, claiming that Giamatti couldn't possibly be objective if he already believed the testimony of Peters, so much so that he could ask a judge to be lenient with him. On August 23, at a jammed press conference at the Hyatt Regency in New York, Giamatti rendered his decision to banish Rose from baseball, which fate Rose had accepted as part of the settlement. The language of the settlement, for all its politesse, was fraught with ambiguities, if not out-and-out contradictions. "Peter Edward Rose acknowledges that the Commissioner has a factual basis to impose the penalty provided . . . and hereby accepts the penalty . . . and agrees not to challenge that penalty in court or otherwise." The penalty, in its full dress: "Peter Edward Rose is hereby declared permanently ineligible . . . and placed on the Ineligible List." The agreement goes on to say that Rose had the right to apply for reinstatement within a year, and that "nothing in this agreement shall be deemed either an admission or a denial by Peter Edward Rose of the allegation that he bet on any Major League Baseball game." So, there was a "factual basis" for a penalty but not a finding. . . . Finally, there was a clause stipulating that both parties would refrain from making any public comments that would contradict the agreement. Giamatti blew that one right away, saying at that very press conference that he thought Rose did bet on baseball.

A week later, Giamatti, hoping to relax at his Martha's Vineyard summer home, ran an errand—to buy a wedding gift for Bud Selig's daughter—when he felt chest pains. He then succumbed to a major coronary at home. He was 53 years old; he'd been commissioner only five months. Rose banished, Giamatti dead. Fay Vincent, commissioner.

AND TOMMY HELMS, once again, the Reds manager. But it was already a lost year for the team. The season stacked up as a huge disappointment after four successive second-place finishes. A 7-19 July took the air out of the season, and the Reds finished in fifth place, 17 games behind the division-winning Giants. Browning pitched well, going 15-12, but Danny Jackson hurt his arm and dropped from 23-9 to 6-11. The team played listlessly most of the year in front of churlish crowds, unhappy that their hometown hero was being pilloried in New York for being what he'd always been: a gambler.

Good times, however, would finally visit the Reds and their fans. Lou Piniella became the manager in 1990, and all the talent on the team suddenly jelled. It was as if Rose, dragging too much baggage, and no doubt a distraction even to himself, just couldn't bring them over the top. But Piniella brought a new fire. With the key addition of Mariano Duncan and another 15-win season from Browning, the Reds won the division and then beat Pittsburgh for the National League pennant. They then went on to register one of the most decisive upsets in World Series history, sweeping the heavily favored Oakland A's of Mark McGwire and Jose Canseco and Dave Stewart in four straight. Tom Browning rather infamously disappeared from the bullpen in Game Two—to take his wife to the emergency room: She was in labor. But he showed up for Game Three, and got the win, fulfilling his dream of one day playing at the top of his profession in the top game.

Browning had a World Series ring, a growing family, and he was making seriously good money. After his perfect-game season, he settled on a contract for $1.2 million or so, and then, facing free agency in 1990, he signed a four-year deal worth about $12.5 million. Unfortunately, his body would betray him. A knee injury ended his 1992 season in midsummer, and in 1994, in the last year of his contract, the humerus bone in his left arm—the bone that runs from the shoulder socket to the elbow—snapped as he was making a pitch. "I just felt like I had been shot," he said.

Browning was out for the remainder of the year, and the Reds exercised a buyout clause for the following year. Browning caught on with Kansas City for the '95 season, pitched 10 innings, and retired.

Browning now lives just across the Ohio River, in Kentucky, where his congressman is Jim Bunning—"a perfect-game guy," as Browning puts it. He knows Bunning, and likes him.

Browning has five kids, all with first names beginning with "T." He has a grandchild. Golf has filled his need for competition. He remembers fondly his years with the Reds, and looks on a little sadly at what Pete Rose is going through, trying desperately to get the game to take him back.

"In the Hall of Fame?" asks Browning. "Absolutely. He needs to be there. He's got more hits than anybody. I mean, these laws that were set down by Kenesaw Mountain Landis were set down in 1919 and we are in 2003 now, there has been a lot of things that have taken place in the game of baseball, and they've addressed the steroid issue and somewhat the drug issue, and gambling has always been there—you're not allowed to bet on the game of baseball." Browning remembers some of the hangers-on in the clubhouse who were later connected to Rose's gambling—"It never crossed my mind that they might be doing something like that, but, you know they could've been, and they probably were, from what I have been told."

Browning, for his part, is deeply respectful of what Rose accomplished, and grateful for what Rose did for his own career. He also is grateful for another terrific player who is not in the Hall of Fame but whose contribution to the game is not lost on players of Browning's era.

"They opened this facility here called Champions of Baseball Academy, and they have these letters that Curt Flood wrote to Bowie Kuhn, and they have Kuhn's response. It was really neat, about how Curt thought he should be able to say where he goes. I'd never seen that stuff before. But I did have a chance to thank Curt Flood just before he passed. I happened to see him in San Diego one day and I just walked to him and said, 'Thanks, man.'"

CHAPTER ELEVEN

El Presidente

Dennis Martinez
July 28, 1991

O
N APRIL 15, 1947, Jack Roosevelt Robinson of Pasadena, California, ran to his position at first base at Brooklyn's Ebbets Field
and broke baseball's "color barrier." He went 0-for-3 against the Braves'
Johnny Sain that day, but that's hardly a measure of the impact of his
play. The barrier had been in place since the dawn of major league ball.
All of a sudden, it was gone.

Technically, there had never been anything stopping an owner from
fielding any player of any color, or of any sex, for that matter. There was
never an official rule against integrated play. It just wasn't done. Not that
it hadn't been tried once or twice. As long ago as 1884, a black man
named Moses Fleetwood Walker, a graduate of Oberlin College, played 42
games and caught for Toledo of the American Association. His younger

brother, Welday, got into five games, too; but when Cap Anson's Chicago team refused to play on the same field with men of dark skin— "chocolate-covered coons," he called them—the Walkers were released. But on a lovely spring day six decades and two world wars later, in front of packed house—with half of the patrons being black—the barrier was high-hurdled by the four-sport star athlete from UCLA.

It is important to note that the reason the Walker brothers were playing at all back in 1884 had to do with money, not enlightenment. In this case a rival league, the Union Association, was threatening to steal players and drive salaries up. Anything that increased the demand for talent was bad for business, from the owners' perspective. So some of them looked for other talent streams—and why not Negroes? But the reaction of Anson—an Iowa-born graduate of Notre Dame and a future Hall of Famer—was typical of the white players everywhere who felt their jobs were at risk; there was also ownership's fear that the predominantly white fans, including white women, would not feel comfortable seeing black players on the field, or black fans at the ballpark. So, despite the temptation to find salary relief by opening baseball to blacks, the game resisted, for still other financial reasons, until a Bible-reading, sharp-eyed businessman named Branch Rickey threw caution to the wind, signed several black ballplayers, put them on the Brooklyn Dodgers farm team in Montreal, and waited for the right moment, and the right player, which was 1947, and Robinson.

Of course, Rickey wasn't the first executive who ever tried to gain a competitive edge at a cheap price. Before 1947, with baseball apartheid in effect, a few owners looked to the Negro Leagues for talented, light-skinned blacks. What they found was evidence that baseball had already become an American export to another world, a world with a Latin face speaking another language.

Even before Fleet Walker had his aborted run as the first black major leaguer, a Cuban named Esteban Bellan was a player in the National Association, a league that historians rank now as a bona fide major league. You can find "Steve" Bellan's career stats in *Total Baseball*—three years (1871–73) with the Troy (New York) Haymakers— a short, stocky third baseman who apparently was rather porous at the position, his lifetime fielding average being .671. Born in Havana, Bellan had come north to attend Columbia University, and fell in love with the game of baseball. He was good enough to earn a paycheck for three seasons, after which he returned to his homeland. In 1874, he organized the first formal contest in all of Cuba. Within four years, there would be a professional league, and over the next few decades, Cuba would serve as the principal ambassador of baseball to the Caribbean.

On February 15, 1898, a tragedy in Havana harbor—the U.S. battleship *Maine* exploded, killing 260 men—precipitated the commencement of a 112-day war and a decades'-long U.S. military presence in the Caribbean basin. It also gave a boost to baseball. Cuba would rather quickly gain a coambassador for the game of *beisbol*—American GIs.

The United States, choosing to construe the explosion aboard the *Maine* as a terrorist act, declared war on Spain. It then invaded Cuba and bombarded Puerto Rico. It was the start of a 35-year period that would give popular currency to the terms "gunboat diplomacy" and "banana republic," as the United States positioned itself as protector of freedom and democracy in the Western Hemisphere. During that time, the Marine Corps made nearly three dozen landings in 10 different countries; Spain was forced to cede Cuba, Puerto Rico, Guam, and the Philippines; the Venezuelan navy was seized; the Panama Canal Zone was annexed; there were landings in Honduras, Vera Cruz, Santo Domingo; there was a U.S.-engineered ousting of the Nicaraguan president in 1909, with a new man put in his place. Nicaragua became a quagmire. Large fruit company interests, once intense, began to wane. The constant Marine presence that had been required to ensure the stability of the little country and the safety of U.S. investments slowly became redundant. In 1933, American forces finally withdrew—there was the Depression at home and dark clouds of war over Europe. Nicaragua was left to its own feuding militaries. In the following year, in the absence of American forces, General Antonio Somoza of the National Guard invited General Augusto Sandino to a meeting. Sandino, who had vehemently opposed the occupation by U.S. forces, did not survive the conversation. Somoza consolidated his control of the military and of the country, with the United States' blessing. The Somozas would rule Nicaragua for the next 46 years, when insurgents, named after Sandino, would force the reigning Somoza— Anastasio Somoza Debayle—to flee.

The period from the sinking of the *Maine* till the Marines' departure from Nicaragua is often referred to as the "Yankee years." Teddy Roosevelt's "walk softly but carry a big stick" strategy for the home hemisphere was Yanqui, all right—righteous, ambitious, patronizing, aggressive. It was also Yankee as in baseball, big stick as in bat. The Marines brought their own equipment; what they found in port town after port town and far into the tropical inlands was baseball, already implanted, teeming with players who knew the game.

With baseball booming in popularity in the Caribbean basin and in Mexico, it's no wonder talent there flourished. No wonder, too, that from these impoverished countries good talent looked to *el norte* to make a living. Wages were better up north and there was no color barrier into the Negro Leagues. And the barrier into the major leagues could be hurdled if your color wasn't too dark.

DOLPH LUQUE WAS the first prominent Latin American to play major league ball. Born Adolpho Domingo De Guzman Luque in Havana in 1890, the five-foot-seven-inch, 160-pound right-handed pitcher signed with the Boston Nationals in 1914 and finished with the New York Giants in 1935. He won 194 games during his career, pitched in the infamous 1919 Series for Cincinnati (five scoreless innings), went 27-8 four years later, with a league-leading ERA of 1.93. In that same year, the pale-faced Cuban with a cold stare and chiseled face, tired of the racial ribbing he was getting from Casey Stengel, charged the Giants dugout and clocked Stengel on the jaw. He later returned, wielding a bat, but was restrained. Ten years later, in 1933, while playing for John McGraw's New York Giants, Luque made it into one more World Series; in the process, he played a part in opening wider the major league door to Latin talent. In Game Five, with the scored tied 3–3 between the Giants and the Washington Senators, Luque entered the game. He pitched four innings of shutout ball, and got the win when Mel Ott homered for the Giants in the 10th. The Giants won the World Series, four games to one. Legend has it that Senators' owner Clark Griffith, disappointed at the defeat, strapped for cash, and unhappy with his team's talent anyway, needed nothing more than the sight of this durable Cuban finishing off his boys in order to get an idea. He dispatched a scout, Joe Cambria, to Havana in search of more ballplayers like Luque.

Cambria, an Italian, owned a team in the Negro Leagues; he was familiar with—and friendly with—many Latin ballplayers. Over the next

25 years, Cambria signed more than 400 Cubans to play ball, including Bobby Estalella, Camilo Pascual, Tony Oliva, and Pete Ramos (Cambria had one prospect turn him down—a pitcher named Fidel Castro). After Jackie Robinson made it through the barrier, no color was too dark for baseball, and the flow of players from the Caribbean suddenly increased. Being a pale Latin was no longer key. With the onset of the Korean War, Caribbean players—who after all, were not Americans—became all the more attractive as they would not have to answer the call to military service.

Enter Branch Rickey, in the late 1950s an executive with Pittsburgh after a power struggle with Walter O'Malley in Brooklyn. He sent a young scout named Howie Haak to Puerto Rico to check out a young man actually signed by Al Campanis of the Dodgers for $10,000 but left unprotected. A rule in effect at the time, meant to constrain spending, stipulated that any player signed for more than $4,000 had to be on the major league roster at season's end or be draftable by another team. The Dodgers had no room for the young Roberto Clemente in their outfield in 1954–55—who was he going to replace, Duke, Skoonj, Sandy Amoros? The team also had reached its unofficial limit of "five blacks." The Dodgers tried to hide Clemente as much as they could; the Dodgers were most concerned the rival Giants didn't see how good this kid was. But Haak knew what he was seeing, even if the Dodgers did play Clemente when he was banged up, sat him when he turned hot, and hinted disparagingly about his attitude. Haak recommended to Rickey that the last-place Pirates draft the wiry, talented Clemente. As Peter Bjarkman succinctly put it in his *Baseball with a Latin Beat*, "The event would play no small role in dismantling a baseball powerhouse [Brooklyn] in the fifties and jump-starting another [Pittsburgh] in the sixties." Haak went on to sign many other players for the Pirates, not only from Puerto Rico (Julian Javier, Rennie Stennett, Omar Moreno, Tony Armas) but from Panama as well (Manny Sanguillen).

In Clemente, baseball in the Caribbean had its greatest ambassador. He was not only a Puerto Rican ballplayer who made good, he was a star. When the Pirates upset the great New York Yankees in the 1960 World Series, Whitey Ford—who noticed how hard young Clemente played in even the big blowout games of that Series—was not alone in seeing the 26-year-old as the Pirates' heart and soul. All of Puerto Rico already thought so, too, as did young boys from Santo Domingo to Mexico City.

The next year, Clemente hit .351. By the late sixties, as Willie Mays's career wound down, Clemente was probably the best player in the National League. He proved it to everyone in the 1971 World Series, when he carried the Pirates to the championship, hitting .414, with 12 hits, two doubles, a triple, and two home runs in the seven games. There were other great Latin players making a name—Orlando Cepeda, Juan Marichal, and Tony Oliva—All-Stars all. But Clemente was the super-star. In 1972, events would conspire to raise Clemente to a level beyond baseball, a level reserved for martyrs and saints.

The season would be an injury-plagued one, but Clemente would still finish at .312. On the last day of the season in New York, he would get his 3,000th career hit, putting him in an exclusive club with only 13 members. For Clemente, already with 18 years under his belt, 11 All-Star selections, a dozen Gold Gloves, and four batting titles, eventual induc-tion into the Hall of Fame seemed assured. Little did the season-ending crowd at Shea know that they would be the last to see the great Clemente play in a regular-season game. Wintering, as he always did, in his home town of Carolina in Puerto Rico, Clemente heard the news that Managua, the capital city of Nicaragua, had been struck by a devastating earthquake. It was three days before Christmas. Six thousand people were presumed dead, with tens of thousands left homeless. Clemente immediately began raising money, pleading for donations and supplies; he helped pack and load boxes for shipment, working 16-hour days. In Nicaragua, President Somoza's leadership consisted of urging survivors to flee the city so as avoid infection from the decaying dead. Rumors began to spread that relief supplies weren't making it to the right people, and that cash was proving to be particularly perishable. On New Year's Eve, Clemente took matters into his own hands. He leased an old DC-7 cargo plane for $4,000, packed it full—perhaps too full—with medicine and food, and left San Juan airport bound for Nicaragua.

January 1, 1973, was a terrible day in Puerto Rico and throughout the baseball world, as news of Clemente's death spread. The plane had gone down in the Caribbean, shortly after takeoff, leaving no survivors.

All of his Pirates teammates flew down for the funeral. Inauguration ceremonies for the new president of Puerto Rico were canceled. Clemente, who in his stirring baseball life had been a great ambassador of the game across the breadth of Latin America, in his death became a bea-con of principled charity and selflessness. Baseball's Hall of Fame would do what it had only done once—for Lou Gehrig: suspend the five-year waiting period for eligibility. Clemente became the first Latin American major leaguer to enter Cooperstown.

"I WAS IN BED AND I suddenly felt the house and the bed shaking. I started screaming, 'Mom, Dad, where are you?' I went outside and found everyone there."

Jose Dennis Martinez Emilia was 17 years old when the earthquake cracked through the western part of Nicaragua on December 22, 1972. It was centered near the capital of Managua, but the effects in the town of Granada, 30 miles to the southeast, where Martinez was born and raised, were profound, though not deadly. The small clapboard and plywood homes rattled and fell; foundations of the larger buildings, churches, and schools cracked. Windows, where there were windows, splintered into the muddy streets. Into the streets also spilled round rolled socks stuffed with once-sopping cardboard—makeshift baseballs given up for lost on roofs and in gutters, now put back in play. The kids were happy to get them back. The parents knew there was just more trouble, more deprivation, ahead.

Out on the street stood Martinez's father, Edmundo—"the quietest, most lovely drunk I ever saw," said his son years later—and his mother, Emilia, the family's guiding counsel. Dennis was the youngest (by 10 years) of seven children. Also standing in Hospitale Road on that December 22, 1972, was the girl he fancied from across the street. "What are you doing out here like this?" she shyly inquired. Martinez looked at himself. He had no clothes on. He and Luz were married the next year.

At the time, Dennis was enrolled in an engineering course at National University in Managua. He was interested in building things— the country was a tangle of bad roads; you drove through, or waded through, streams for lack of bridges; drinking water was threatened by sewage; hospitals were needed, as were schools. Whatever had come to Nicaragua in the way of American and international aid had somehow not made it past the government. The buck, it seemed, stopped at Somoza.

Martinez was tall, slender, athletic, and handsome, but at 120 pounds, he was a little too slender to seem to have any chance at playing ball professionally. He played third base—he had a strong arm—but he found himself on some bad teams in a motley Nicaraguan league, and ended up on his hometown team, the Tiburones (the Sharks). Loosening up on the sidelines before a game one day, the manager spotted Martinez goofing off with curveball—the thing broke three feet. He had Martinez pitch a week later against the Nicaraguan national team in an exhibition game, and the skinny kid threw a one-hitter.

By 1973, Martinez was on that national team, and pitching in the championship game of the amateur World Series against the team from the United States. He lost a tough one, 1–0 in 10 innings. However, a couple of scouts from the Baltimore Orioles were in attendance. The Orioles already had some key Latin players—Mike Cuellar, a Cuban, had won 85 games in Baltimore in the last four seasons, and Elrod Hendricks, of the Virgin Islands, was his catcher. Although the scouts were there to sign Martinez's teammate Tony Chevez, they ended up trying to talk Emilia Martinez into allowing her youngest son to leave school and go to America to play ball. He signed a contract then and there; the captain on his team decided they should celebrate. The young Martinez, still only 17, wanted to show his older teammates he was one of them; he drank rum till he passed out.

IN THREE YEARS, Martinez advanced through the tough Orioles system, which was heavy on teaching and fundamentals and prided itself on its development of pitchers. Cuellar, for example, had been only a so-so pitcher till he came under the wing of pitching coach George Bamberger and manager Earl Weaver, where he blossomed. In Miami, where Martinez was to play for the Class-A Marlins, he benefited right away: minor league pitching coach Ray Miller told him to throw more from over the top and drop his head, and as a result the fastball popped. He won 15 games that year and the Marlins won the Florida State League. In their first year away from home, Luz and Dennis had found the right thing: success and a welcoming, Spanish-speaking Latino community in Miami. The road would get tougher, though baseballwise things went smoothly. Two years later, Martinez was at Baltimore's Triple-A affiliate in Rochester, their top minor league team, and he was Pitcher of the Year. But Martinez began to feel not only the pressure of success building, but a kind of isolation settling in with it, both cultural and linguistic. Rochester, New York, can do that to a 21-year-old *campesino*. He turned to drinking.

From his pitching, you wouldn't know Dennis Martinez didn't feel right at home after his arrival in Baltimore. He won 14 games his rookie year, 1977, while losing only 7. The Orioles had finished second in the division the year before to the Yankees, who had acquired Catfish Hunter, and now, again, they had just chased the Yankees, who had acquired Reggie Jackson (then of the O's) as a free agent, and they'd come up a couple of games short. Martinez was holding his own on one of the best pitching staffs in baseball, led by the veteran Jim Palmer, and flanked by the young lefties Mike Flanagan and Scott McGregor. But while the press flocked around the imperious and handsome Palmer and the two Irish-American lefties, both quick with a quip, Martinez was off to the side, proud, fiery, but wary of being able to make himself understood.

Unfortunately, the baseball school that was the Baltimore Orioles didn't respect this kind of reticence, and made the assumption that Martinez was being either stubborn or stupid. In any event, in 1978, while Martinez continued to improve, making 38 starts and winning 16 games, he began to have trouble. His catcher Rick Dempsey pulled a fit when Martinez shook his signs off and they actually had a shoving match on the mound. Martinez sulked; he drank; he feuded. But he continued to pitch well. In 1979, he won 10 straight decisions, had 14 wins by early August, and seemed headed for his first 20-win season, and the Orioles were in first place. But in the private world of Dennis Martinez, things were not so rosy. In late July of that year, the Sandinistas had thrown Somoza out of office; the deposed leader fled to Miami as the rebels appropriated the Somoza family properties and moved in on the seven or eight other families that had all the country's wealth. Chaos ensued. For the next two and a half months, Martinez would not be able to reach his parents by phone.

Martinez, an emotional man, was affected. He won only one more game the rest of the season, and finished 15-16. As if he were deaf to private counsel, some of the Orioles took to talking to Martinez through the press. Dempsey called Martinez's pitch selection "poor." Their relationship had deteriorated so much that Weaver didn't allow Dempsey to catch him. Coach Elrod Hendricks said simply, "He doesn't know how to use his four pitches," and added, "You don't see Palmer lose a game because he throws the wrong pitch." But Flanagan won 23, Ken Singleton had a huge year for the O's, and the team won 102 games and took the Eastern Division by eight games over Milwaukee.

Martinez got the start in Game Three of the playoffs against California. But Don Baylor hit a home run off a Martinez slow curve—a pitch he says he was told to get Baylor out with even though he doesn't have one. The Orioles lost the game but took the series three games to one. When Weaver announced the starting pitchers for the World Series against the Pirates, Martinez was not among them. Unfortunately for Martinez, Game One was snowed out, and Weaver couldn't go with Flanagan/Palmer/McGregor. Martinez got the Game Four start, in Pittsburgh, with the Orioles up two games to one. Martinez didn't make it out of the second inning, giving up four runs on six hits, including a home run to Willie Stargell. Baltimore lost the Series in seven.

The next year, his zeal to play winter ball in Puerto Rico had taken a toll—he came up with a sore arm. Martinez started the regular season on the Disabled List, and got only a dozen starts, working mostly out of the bullpen. Steve Stone stepped in and had his Cy Young year, going 25-7. Martinez moved one notch further down in the pecking order on the Baltimore staff. General manager Hank Peters challenged Martinez to "make a contribution" if he didn't like the bullpen. Weaver weighed in with a call for Dennis to "grow up." He finished 6-4 on the year. With McGregor winning 20, the Orioles stayed in contention late, but finished in second place.

Martinez bounced back in the strike-shortened 1981 season, tying for the league lead in wins with 14 and showing the kind of mettle and rubber-arm qualities that, in the end, would give him a 23-year career. With free agency an option, Martinez opted instead for a five-year deal during the off-season for $2.5 million. In an Orioles press release, Martinez was quoted as saying, "Both my wife and I wanted to stay here. We're very comfortable in Baltimore."

And perhaps they were. Dennis continued to pitch well, winning 16 games in 1982 in 39 starts. But he was pitching in trouble constantly, giving up more hits than innings pitched, his ERA going over 4.00. And in '83, something caught up to him. On nights he wasn't pitching, he would drink before the game. During the game, he would think about the bottle of wine he had chilling in his hotel room. After the game, there would be the wine, and then his favorite liqueur, Grand Marnier—"I would have five or six a night." His performance suffered terribly. By the second half of the year he was once again in the bullpen. He finished the season 7-16, his ERA at 5.53. The Orioles won the division crown, the American League pennant, and then the World Series in five games over the Phillies. The new kids on the block were Mike Boddicker and Storm Davis. Martinez didn't appear at all in postseason play. In the jubilant

Orioles locker room after McGregor blanked the Phillies in Game Five, Martinez was so obnoxiously drunk that a *New York Times* reporter called him out on it the next day.

During the winter, Dennis and Luz, now with children in school, stayed in Baltimore. Martinez's arm could no longer take the wear of winter ball, and he didn't need the money. Returning from a trip to the gym in early December, he stopped in a bar to watch a football game and have a few drinks. He blew off a dinner date with his wife and closed the bar at 1:30. On his way home, he skidded off the Beltway and was arrested—DWI, resisting arrest.

Martinez checked himself into an eight-week rehab center outside Baltimore. Upon his release, he went to 90 consecutive AA meetings—in Sarasota and Vero Beach, and, once the 1984 season began, in places like Kansas City, Boston, and of course, Baltimore. As a pitcher, he continued to struggle; he won only six games. In 1985, he was hit hard again; although he posted 13 victories, for the third year in a row his ERA was over 5.00. He seemed finished, at the age of 30. In 1986, in the last year of his contract, at the trading deadline, he was moved to the Montreal Expos, where he was ineffective. His record on the year in total: 3-6. Having played out his contract, he was a free agent. Understandably, there were no takers. Added to that, it was the second year of the owners' collusive tactics. "It was a very scary winter," Martinez said later.

Martinez approached the Miami Marlins, the team with which he first played professional ball 13 years earlier, and he signed a one-month contract. In May, the Expos, in need of pitching, signed him to a contract worth $162,500. Martinez, his seven years of heavy drinking now cleansed from his body, could pitch again. He beat Pittsburgh in his Montreal debut, 4–3; he beat Dwight Gooden and the Mets, 4–0. He won seven of his first eight decisions and finished 11-4, with an ERA of 3.30, and he quickly became a favorite in Montreal. Martinez had found that one of the ways for him to maintain sobriety was to express himself. With his English improved, and a clear head, he did just that. He was gracious to the Orioles, thanking them for insisting he get help. He chastised himself for blaming Dempsey and the Orioles coaches for his problem. And as the Expos would find, they had an outspoken veteran on their team, a spokesman for himself and for fellow Latin ballplayers. When Tommy Lasorda passed over Martinez for the All-Star team in 1989, despite Martinez's 9-1 record and ERA of 2.83, he claimed prejudice. When Montreal sent a slumping Cuban catcher named Nelson Santovenia to the minors

Martinez spoke up and said they'd never do that to a white player. "The Latin player," he said, "better be way, way better than the black or the white guy. Because, black or white, *they're* American."

But the Montreal front office seemed not to mind the fiery pronouncements. They treated Martinez with respect and signed him to a two-year deal worth $1.5 million; he was the ace of their staff. Martinez responded, and won 15 games in '88 and 16 in '89 for good Montreal teams that just couldn't get over the hump. He had the company of some fellow Latins on the team, Andres Galarraga, the Venezuelan, and the Dominican Pascual Perez, who was trying to work his way back from his own addiction problems.

The 1990 season began with a lockout. The owners were intent on eliminating salary arbitration. But in light of the whopping settlement in the collusion case, there was not much backbone for a fight. The season got under way a week late but all games were made up. Although Martinez pitched well during the season, the team struggled, especially, it seemed, when he was pitching. Despite a sparkling ERA under 3.00, he won only 10 games. The Expos scored only 16 runs in his 11 losses, and finished the season a distant third.

After the 1990 season, Martinez was rewarded with a two-year, $6.7-million contract, though he and his agent Ron Shapiro had wanted a three-year deal. Instead, they got the promise of a $500,000 payout if the Expos were to trade Martinez before July 31, 1991, at which point his 10-5 clause (10 years in the majors, 5 with the same club) was due to kick in. After that, Martinez could veto any trade. Martinez was happy with the deal. He understood that the Expos, under new ownership, felt they must institute a policy whereby no pitcher would be signed to more than a two-year pact.

At the turn of the year, prospects for peace brightened at last in Martinez's homeland. After years of war between the ruling Sandinistas, who had deposed Somoza, and the Contras, a force secretly funded by the Reagan administration, an election was held. To the surprise of many, Daniel Ortega, the Sandinista leader, lost to Violetta Chamorro, the widow of an assassinated newspaper editor. She possessed no political experience whatsoever—Nicaraguans, it seems, had had enough of politicians. Although Martinez took no sides in the election, he was clearly relieved that there was indeed a democratic process. "People deserve to have choice," he said.

MARTINEZ PITCHED WELL in 1991, making the All-Star team, but by midsummer, the Expos were already out of it. In July, they made a West Coast road trip. On July 28, a sunny and hot Sunday afternoon, Martinez, with a record of 10-6 and a league-leading ERA of 2.17, was set to face Mike Morgan, 9-5, with a good ERA himself at 2.70. The Dodgers, winners of seven straight at home, the last two—as shutouts—over the Expos, were six games in front of Cincinnati in the N.L. West. The Expos, losers of 8 of their last 10, were 19.5 games behind the Pirates in the N.L. East. Two nights before, the Expos' Mark Gardner, in front of a packed Friday night house, had pitched a no-hitter through nine innings. Trouble was, Orel Hershiser of the Dodgers gave up only one hit—and no runs—and the game went into extra innings in a scoreless tie. Gardner, a 29-year-old native of Los Angeles, lost his no-hitter in the 10th on an infield single by Lenny Harris, who later scored the winning run. The Dodgers won on Saturday, too, 7-0. The Expos, without spirit or prospects, and averaging only 14,000 fans per game at home, were rumored to be pondering a salary dump. They had three days to do it before the trading deadline passed. Martinez, injured slugger Andres Galarraga, and the recently acquired Ron Darling were high on the list.

It was camera day at Dodger Stadium, with fans allowed to mill on the field before game time and take pictures of their favorite players— Darryl Strawberry (an L.A. boy), Brett Butler, Eddie Murray, Hershiser, manager Tommy Lasorda, and pitching coach Ron Perranoski. The game was a sellout, with attendance announced as 45,560.

Mike Morgan looked sharp in the first inning—he would be very sharp all day—and when he closed out the Expos one, two, three, it was the 33rd consecutive shutout inning pitched by the Dodgers staff. Vin Scully, calling the game on Dodger radio, immediately pointed out that the team record was 38 consecutive innings, set from September 9 to 12 in 1966—by a combination of Koufax, Drysdale, Claude Osteen, Don Sutton, and Bob Miller. Suddenly, 25 years of Dodger history was on the line.

Before Martinez threw a single pitch, he had the crew chief Bruce Froemming inspecting the mound. There was what Scully called "a carpet of damp" going from the rubber right down to the front of the hill, and Martinez was finding it too muddy. He dug and scuffed at it with first his right shoe then his left. In half-circles, he swung his cleats, spreading a little dry clay from the side of the mound across the front. Then El Presidente, as he was nicknamed, was ready to go.

With four pitches—three of them superb curveballs—he struck out leadoff hitter Brett Butler, who didn't strike out much. Butler was third in the league in hits and the leader in runs scored. With 23 stolen bases already in the year, he was a good man to keep off the paths. Juan Samuel, the Dodger second baseman, was hitting .300, and he was second in the league in base hits, though he had been on a skid lately. Samuel swung at the first pitch and grounded to the Montreal shortstop Spike Owen, who threw him out. Eddie Murray, the switch-hitting future Hall of Famer, stepped in. Murray was in his third year as a Dodger, after a dozen years in Baltimore. Although he had hit .330 the year before, this year was the beginning of his gradual decline, which will see him play with five different teams in his last six years. Like many a batter on this day against Martinez, Murray tried to pull the outside fastball, and Delino DeShields, a shaky second baseman at best, got the first of his nine ground balls.

In the Dodger second, Strawberry, on a 13-game hitting streak, and having hit a two-run homer the night before, reached for the outside fastball, as Murray had, and gave DeShields another assist. Kal Daniels, the Dodger left fielder, batting fifth and hitting .268 on the season, just didn't seem to have a clue against Martinez, who so far was mixing curves in and out with fastballs away. Daniels, hot of late (.350 over the last couple of weeks), took three pitches, all fastballs, and was down in the count 1-2. Martinez gave him the first rising fastball of the day, and Daniels swung through it, chin high, for strike three. Lenny Harris, the Dodger third baseman, tried his luck. A good fastball backed Harris off the plate but it caught the corner for a strike. Then, Martinez threw his first changeup of the game, and Harris was way out in front. Probably thinking curveball, Harris then looked a three straight fastballs, the last of which was a called strike three. A neat, 10-pitch inning for Martinez.

In the Expos top of the third, they again went one, two, three, making Mike Morgan perfect through three. But Expo catcher Ron Hassey got to see the home-plate ump's strike zone from the batter's box rather than the catcher's box. Hassey was called out by Larry Poncino on a pitch clearly off the plate. But Hassey just nodded and uttered no complaint.

Big Mike Scioscia was first up in the Dodger third. At 32 years of age, the Upper Darby, Pennsylvania, native was in his twelfth year with L.A.; he would retire after the following season and move on to a career in coaching and managing. Scioscia went the way of the overeager Murray and Straw—tapping out to second. Alfredo Griffin, the Dodger shortstop hitting .255, and a guy who had faced Len Barker during his perfect game 10 years before and Tom Browning during his in '88, stood in left-handed against the right-hand offerings of Martinez. Griffin, a Dominican and an almost exact contemporary of Martinez, swung over a low fastball, fouled another fastball back, fouled a curveball off, and then tapped another breaking ball weakly to Larry Walker at first. Pitcher Morgan strolled to the plate. The crowd at Dodger Stadium seemed barely awake. Martinez fell behind the pitcher, and then Morgan did him a favor—swinging 2-0, fouling it back. The next pitch—another fastball—was grounded to Delino Reliable for out number three. Through three innings against Martinez, no Dodger had gotten the ball out of the infield.

The L.A. crowd roused a little in the fourth inning; they could read the scoreboard—neither team had a hit. And with Scully tuned in on the transistors, they knew too that no one of any stripe had reached base in any way. When Juan Samuel stabbed DeShields's one-hop liner and threw him out, fans were aware of what was saved: Morgan's chance at perfection. Scully, however, was concentrating on the mounting scoreless-inning streak, which reached 36 innings as the Expos went quietly in the fourth.

The crowd got animated at the half-inning change by the video replay on the Mitsubishi scoreboard of Kevin Mitchell grabbing a long fly ball at the wall with his bare hand at Candlestick Park. Meanwhile, Martinez, oblivious, set to work on the top of the order. Butler again: lollipop curve high for a ball; fastball missed low; third-baseman Tim Wallach playing in against the bunt. On 2-0, Martinez confounded Butler with a curve, for a swinging strike, then followed that with a fastball that Butler flicked at, late, for the count to even at 2-2. Butler fouled another fastball back and then Martinez missed by a hair inside, making the count full. On the seventh pitch of the at-bat, Martinez's 33rd pitch of the game, he got his 10th out, as Butler rapped the fastball to Owen at short. Juan Samuel followed with the first real bid to get a hit off Martinez, hitting a 1-1 fastball right at Tim Wallach's feet at third. Wallach hung in there, stayed low, and got it on a very short hop and threw to first for the out. Eddie Murray got a fastball low and away, right where Ron Hassey—who was the catcher for Len Barker's perfect game back in '81—was positioned. It was a set-up pitch for Martinez's second changeup of the day. Murray, way out in front, swung through it. He then was late on a fastball to fall behind 1-2, and Hassey and Martinez were working him perfectly.

But then Martinez called time. He squatted right on the mound. He stood up, surrounded now by his infielders. His pitching coach, Larry Bearnarth, came running out to check on his pitcher. Tom Runnells, the manager came out, too. Martinez grabbed his lower right back. He slowly windmilled his right arm. The home-plate ump paid a visit and agreed to let Martinez have a couple of warmup pitches. After some conferring with Runnells and Bearnarth, Martinez pronounced himself okay. On the very next play he had to make a maximum effort: Murray hit a smash to Walker at first; the ball skipped up and hit Walker on one hop on his right forearm; the ball bounded away to Walker's right; he scampered after it, as Martinez darted off the mound, sprinting to cover first. He got there in time to handle Walker's soft toss and Murray was out. A lengthy 14-pitch inning for Martinez, but he escaped physical harm and still no one had reached base against him.

Morgan's luck almost ran out in the top of the fifth, as the heart of the Expos order started getting the ball up in the air. Ivan Calderon's fly ball was caught; Tim Wallach's long drive to right was hauled in by Strawberry; and Larry Walker's laser to left field was snagged by Kal Daniels just as he crashed into the wall for out number three, making it 15 in a row for Morgan. Scully reminded the Dodger faithful that the scoreless-inning streak was now 37 innings, one short of the team record.

In the Dodgers fifth, Straw, Daniels, and Harris gave Martinez the kind of quick inning he needed: Strawberry hit 1-1 two-hopper to Walker for an easy out; Daniels topped a 1-1 pitch to DeShields, who made things interesting by nonchalanting the play, but got the runner by half a step; and Harris fouled out to Calderon down the left-field line on the first pitch.

Scully had to admit that "one part of the bubble has burst" when Ron Hassey ripped a single to center leading off the Montreal sixth. The perfect game was over, for Mike Morgan at least. But when Montreal failed to score, Scully got to intone about the glory of Dodgerdom: "Not bad, when you can put your name in the book next to Koufax and Drysdale and Regan and Sutton and Osteen and Miller." The six innings of shutout ball made it 38 straight for the club, tying the 1966 record.

In the Dodger sixth, bottom of the order, Martinez had another brief inning—three outs on nine pitches. Scioscia grounded to the busy DeShields; Griffin did the same on a 2-2 pitch, though Delino almost overran the play, throwing erratically to Walker, who saved the day with a nice scoop. Mike Morgan, who had swung at a 2-0 pitch his first time up, hacked this time at an eye-high 1-0 fastball and hit it to deep left-center, where Marquis Grissom, playing shallow, hauled it in. Eighteen in a row but still no score. (Shades of two nights before, Hershiser dueling Mark Gardner in a scoreless drama.)

But it wouldn't stay scoreless for long. Alfredo Griffin let Dave Martinez's slow ground ball run up his arm for an error. Ivan Calderon, Montreal's cleanup hitter, was asked to bunt by manager Runnells, and he did, perfectly. With Dave Martinez in scoring position, Wallach hit a sharp grounder to Griffin—a busy guy this inning. Griffin threw to second—behind Martinez—who just got back, and second-baseman Samuel took the throw and fired to first to get Wallach, a strange 6-4-3 putout. With two out, the tough Larry Walker stood in. Walker worked the count to 2-2. Morgan just missed with a fastball low and away, bringing the count full. Walker hit the next pitch on a line into the gap in right-center, scoring Martinez with the game's first run, ending the consecutive scoreless-inning streak one strike shy of a club record, and making Tommy Lasorda very mad. He was all over ump Larry Poncino for the 2-2 call on Walker. Another muffed grounder by Alfredo Griffin, off the bat of Hassey, brought Walker home, making Lasorda even more dyspeptic. Tough luck for Morgan, pitching a beautiful game, but trailing 2–0 thanks to two unearned runs and a tainted triple.

For Dennis Martinez, it was one more time through the order, one through nine, and immortality would then be his, baseball speaking. He knew his wife, Luz, back in Florida, was watching the game via satellite dish, and was probably on the phone to his mother with the play-by-play, *en español.*

The tough, picky Butler led off the Dodgers seventh, and he wouldn't offer at a fastball. Martinez put another one in, right under the hands; Butler tried to yank it to right field but fouled it off. A fastball was low, 2-1. Martinez went to the rising fastball and Butler got a piece of it, straight back, 2-2. Martinez then went with a curve, after four straight fastballs, and Butler cut at it, spinning it foul in the dirt. Still 2-2, Martinez twirled another curve up, Butler hit it in the air, foul, over third, and Wallach ranged over and grabbed it just before stepping into the Dodger dugout. Then came Samuel, who bunted down the first-base line, but Martinez was there in a flash, barehanded pick-up, falling across the grass, but his throw to Walker got Samuel by a couple of steps.

Martinez had been careful with Eddie Murray all day, and it worked again. Murray didn't nibble at two wide breaking balls, and Martinez had to figure out, with Hassey, what to throw him on a 2-0 count. They decided fastball, for a strike on the corner. Now what? Another fastball, or a curve? Martinez came up with his third changeup of the game; Murray took it, but it was a called strike. A huge, gutsy pitch that evened the count at 2-2. Once Murray stepped back in, Martinez threw a fastball up and in, which Murray took for a ball as the count went full. Martinez made a wide circle around the back of the mound, rubbing hard at a new ball, spitting, rubbing, spitting some more. He walked up the hill, buried the ball in his glove, touched his right-hand fingers to his pants leg, to his cap, bill and back of the cap, looked in for the sign. Breaking ball, over the plate, and Murray tapped it weakly to Delino. Twenty-one men had failed.

In the eighth, poor Dennis Martinez walked to the plate to hit with a perfect game going, and received almost no acknowledgment from the Dodgers fans. He then had the misfortune to have his weakly hit ball make it through the right side of the infield, putting him on base. DeShields followed with a single and Dennis found himself on second base. A passed ball brought him chugging to third. He was stranded there, and at inning's end walked very slowly to the Expos dugout, trying to catch a breath and a piece of history as he headed out for the bottom of the eighth.

It would be Strawman, Kal Daniels, and Lenny Harris. Strawberry, who didn't seem comfortable all day, hit a 2-2 fastball to—who else?—Delino DeShields, for out number one. Daniels got four fastballs and found himself with the count even at 2-2. Martinez sensed a moment. He walked around the mound again. He decided on a curveball to Daniels. What Scully called "a little crinkler" bent down near the outside corner, but Larry Poncino called it a ball. Count full. Martinez then went to his bread-and-butter and threw a 3-2 curveball for a strike—a very hittable pitch—and Daniels missed it. The crowd at last was into it, there were cheers at Daniels's failure. Harris tapped the ball back to Martinez who fielded it to his left, tossed to Walker, and just kept sprinting off into the dugout. Twenty-four down. More cheers.

TRAINERS TOWELED OFF Martinez between half-innings. He was wearing his Expos jacket, but his face was steaming with heat and sweat. On the radio, Vin Scully mentioned the date and the time and Luz Martinez and the Martinez children. Scully knew history when he saw it coming down the road. He'd seen Don Larsen's perfect game; he'd seen Sandy

Koufax's, thrown right in this ballpark, 26 years before. He'd seen Tom Browning's three summers back.

Leading off the bottom of the ninth, Mike Scioscia, not yet born when Larsen beat Maglie, not yet seven when Koufax bested Bob Hendley, took a curveball for a strike on the inside corner, the corner that Poncino had been giving all day. The fastball away, something he hadn't called much for strikes, was skied to Calderon. There was one out.

It had been a bad day for Alfredo Griffin. He'd grounded out and grounded out and made two errors that cost two runs. After his second error, Mike Morgan had given him a glare. His day was finally over. Stan Javier stood in for him, a switch-hitter batting left who had been 0-for-17 in that capacity theretofore. Javier nonetheless gave a good account of himself. He hacked at a curveball and missed; he watched a fastball stay low, to even the count at 1-1. Against untested hitters, Martinez and Hassey liked the curveball, and Javier got one here, under the hands, and he swung and missed. The hometown crowd began to root for Dennis Martinez, despite themselves. Scully remarked on the radio that Martinez "has come too far, he has journeyed too long, to drop it." Javier fouled off another curveball, and the count remained 1-2. Hassey called for the fastball next, and suddenly Martinez was overthrowing. Hassey tried to frame the moving pitch, but Poncino would have none of it. Ball, 2-2. Back to the breaking ball, and Javier swung right over the pitch, for Martinez's fifth strikeout of the day.

Another pinch-hitter was sent up by Lasorda, Chris Gwynn, younger brother of Tony Gwynn, in his fifth year with L.A. Chris was a carbon copy of his brother—batted left, threw left, six feet even, 200 pounds. Any Gwynn up there looking like that was to be feared. Martinez started him off the way he'd pitched all the guys he respected in this lineup— Murray, Strawberry, Daniels—fastball away. Ball one. Sensing that, even pinch-hitting, a Gwynn will be taking, or at least looking fastball again, Martinez and Hassey bent a curve over to even the count. They followed with a fastball, and now Gwynn was a little behind it. He hit the ball solidly—he later said he "smoked it"—and it skipped a foot foul outside the third-base bag and rattled around down the left-field line. The crowd noise swelled, with the count now 1-2. Martinez then threw a bad pitch—Hassey set up low and inside, calling for a fastball. Martinez, tiring, got the ball up—it sailed. It looked good to Gwynn, he socked it high and deep to center. Marquis Grissom, playing Gwynn to hit the opposite way, had a pretty long run, but the ball stayed up and Grissom put it in his glove. The 27th straight out, and Martinez had done it. He was mobbed by his teammates at home plate. He left the field, weeping.

"There was nothing we could do but sit and take it," said Eddie Murray, his former teammate in Baltimore, after the game. Martinez was in complete control, inducing 17 groundouts, striking out five, going to three-ball counts only three times. Hassey, who had been there before, with Len Barker, helped keep Martinez loose and the Expos focused. "I don't buy that stuff about not talking to a guy," said Hassey. "In the seventh, I was walking up and down the dugout, going 'We got us a perfect one going, boys. Everybody stay sharp.' "

Martinez had struggled for so long against some disbelieving management, the spectre of his homeland's problems, and his own demons, that his tears must have been tears of relief as much as of joy. His game was the ultimate triumph. "I know I talk about my drinking a lot," he said the next day. "But I haven't had a drink in seven years and I know there are people out there now who are dying, who are reaching out for help and not getting any. They can look at me. They can look at me and say it's never too late." Tears of thanks as well.

IN THE END, THE DODGERS faded, and lost the division by a game to Atlanta. The Expos, too, continued to plummet. But team ownership no longer considered trading their perfect-game ace and leader, who survived the trading deadline.

The next year, 1992, Martinez continued to pitch brilliantly. It was as if he had a second career, one with Baltimore, the second, north of the border. In Montreal, he admitted, he was able to enjoy himself again. "The people in Canada understand me," he said. He won 16 games again in '92 and another 15 in '93, under a new, one-year contract that paid him close to $3 million. He was now 38 years old and, again, a free agent.

After eight years in Montreal, Martinez signed with the Cleveland Indians, a young team coming into its own. And there he would have a great impact, going 23-11 over a two-year period and then, in 1995, memorably pitching Cleveland into their first World Series since 1948 by besting Randy Johnson 4–0 in Game Six at the King Dome in Seattle.

As Martinez passed his 40th birthday, he began to think of his legacy and his future. He was approaching Juan Marichal as the all-time leader in pitching wins by a Latin American. His nickname, El Presidente, was now being bandied about as a possibly apt moniker for a man who could easily run for the presidency in his homeland and win. There was no one more popular or revered. During the elections in 1996, while he was pitching for Cleveland, both political parties in Nicaragua offered him the post of minister of sport. But Martinez had his eyes set on the Marichal record. When his $12-million three-year contract expired at the end of '96, he caught on with Seattle, but he hung up his spikes midyear, two wins short of Marichal's 243 lifetime wins.

However, Martinez enjoyed another surge of energy and ambition, and he went to Puerto Rico during the winter to see if the layoff had rejuvenated his arm. Some said he looked like the Dennis Martinez of old. The Atlanta Braves took note and signed him to a minor league contract. In spring training, manager Bobby Cox liked what he saw. "He's still got it."

Grandfather Martinez, for he now had a three-year-old grandson, began the season with Atlanta with high hopes. But he didn't really figure much in the Braves plans, as it turned out. Still, on June 2, he shut out Milwaukee 9–0 for his 243rd career win, tying Marichal. Two months passed, and a good deal of ineffectiveness, until he was able to get his next win, thanks to one inning of perfect relief in a game against Marichal's old team, the Giants. When Chipper Jones ripped a two-run single in the ninth, Martinez had win number 244. On the opposing side was Melvin Bernard, the sixth and latest Nicaraguan to play in the major leagues, who, admitting to taking pride in Martinez's achievement, said, "He was the first to make it. They don't call him 'El Presidente' for nothing."

Martinez retired at the end of the year, for good, with a record of 245-193. He won more than 100 games in each league. He kept his family together, himself together, and even helped unite his people throughout decades of political strife. His name is still mentioned as presidential material in Nicaragua, and from time to time Martinez appears open to the idea. For the moment, though, he is following in the footsteps of the great Clemente. The Dennis Martinez Foundation, based in Miami, raises money for disaster-relief projects throughout Latin America, where, like Clemente, he remains a hero to his people.

CHAPTER TWELVE

Strawberries

Kenny Rogers

July 28, 1994

KENNY ROGERS WAS an easygoing, bright, handsome kid when he decided he'd have a go at playing baseball in his senior year in high school. He had a look—blue-eyed, square-jawed, with a slightly turned-up nose—that suggested he could do anything he wanted to, if he cared to. However, his folks ran a large strawberry farm among the many strawberry farms in Plant City, Florida, a town then of about 20,000, named not after the agriculture that dominates its commerce, but after Henry B. Plant, who ran a railroad through in 1884. In Plant City, strawberry is king—chances are three in four that your midwinter strawberry is from there. In fact, the town has played host every February since the 1930s to the Florida State Strawberry Festival, now a four-day affair featuring livestock tents, lamb shows, tractor pulls, and most recently, Bobby Vinton. Year after year, that was some big excitement in Plant City, a kind of between-ways town on the way to Tampa. The strawberrry patch was a world unto itself.

Even playing a spring of baseball required young Rogers to get a special dispensation from his father, who had come to expect his son's extracurriculars would be played out on the farm, not the ball diamond. Plans were that he'd continue working there after graduation. Agribusiness was a good enough living for most of the people they knew, and it was Kenny's likely future.

Rogers had played Little League ball for a while, but then seemed to lose interest. The standard pursuits of teenagerhood in the warm Florida clime proved to be recreation enough. But Kenny was sprouting toward six feet in height, and blessed with a natural athleticism, and the traipsing about in a uniform and a cap and shagging flies and driving the ball seemed like an attractive idea; not to mention it just might cut mercifully into his farm time a little. The family agreed to do without Kenny's chore duties for the spring months of 1982.

Although slender, at only about 130 pounds, Rogers could rifle the ball and was fast in the field. Before a game with a Tampa high school, he broke a lace in his glove and had to trot in from the outfield to get it laced up. On the sideline, his coach was chatting with a man he introduced as Joe Marchese, a scout employed by the Texas Rangers who usually worked the upper Midwest. Marchese was in Florida, as most of the scouts were, for organization meetings and a little sunshine, and also to take another look, as many scouts had been doing of late, at one Stanley Broderick, a load of a ballplayer from Tampa. Marchese invited the Rangers' assistant farm director, Joe Klein, to come along. For some reason, Marchese took a liking to the kid Rogers, who said a polite hello as he worried over his mitt. Michael Lewis, in his insightful book *Moneyball*, takes the measure of many an old-time scout. He notes their peculiar anatoromancy, reading potential in physique—long arms, narrow hips, broad shoulders, high calves. And the face. From "The Good Face," as they put it, these scouts could divine character. Kenny Rogers had that good face, serene, clear, and naturally set, determined. "He took a liking to me," is all Rogers would say. "I also made a couple of good throws from the outfield that day." And Joe Klein, who today is executive director of the Atlantic League, agreed with Marchese's assessment. "I could see he had a strong arm."

Marchese sought the kid out after the game. "You're going be a pitcher, that's what you're gonna be," he declared.

"Are you sure?" asked the kid.

IN 1982 BASEBALL was becoming a more lucrative profession; not that it hadn't always been an attractive one since its inception more than 100 years before. But now, with free agency in place since 1976, the risk of skipping other pursuits while toiling to make the major leagues had more reward to it; and the perpetual servitude to owners' wishes, once the rule of the land, had been mightily liberalized. The average salary for major leaguers had tripled since 1976, to more than $150,000. (That's a lot of strawberries.) So the kid with the good face and the strong left arm, when selected by the Texas Rangers in the 39th round of the amateur draft, signed. He got a $10,000 bonus.

But getting anywhere near the average salary meant making it to the big time; becoming a free agent required six years of service at the major league level. Even becoming eligible for salary arbitration, in case of a salary dispute—whereby both the player and the team would submit a one-year salary figure and an arbitrator would choose one or the other—required three full years of service. If you didn't make it to the major leagues to start this clock running, first, toward arbitration eligibility, and then to free agency, the team that drafted you could own you for four minor league seasons, and another three if you were put on the 40-man roster, after which you could become a minor league free agent. They could pay you the minimum minor league salary and make you take buses everywhere; and you might not eat well, living with a bunch of guys your age; and forget about trying to have a romance or build a family, or keeping one intact with the squalid temptations of the minor league circuit's night life. In the year previous, baseball had endured a 52-day strike so the players, for the most part, could preserve these rights. There was a lot to look forward to as a professional ballplayer, but it could be a long haul through rookie leagues, Class-D ball, Class-C ball, and the three levels of A, Double-A and Triple-A ball. Signing up was either a big commitment, or a complete lark.

Rogers was committed. He would spend a full seven years in the minors, starting out in the Gulf Coast League, a rookie league, where he pitched only three innings the whole season. Six years later he was at Double-A ball, a reliever with a promising arm, but still learning his craft. In seven seasons in the Texas system, he hadn't once sipped at the proverbial cup of coffee up in Arlington with the big club.

And the big club hadn't exactly had a streak of success. In fact, the Rangers had not won anything since Bob Short moved the team there from Washington, D.C., in 1972. They came as close as second place several times, under managers who ranged from Ted Williams to Whitey Herzog to Billy Martin to Doug Rader. By 1989, George W. Bush, having managed a successful presidential campaign for his father, was looking around for something else to do. A certain sporting quality ran through the family—his father had played first base at Yale. Bush the Younger was also looking around for a good investment. He decided on baseball, and Bush led a group that bought the Rangers that year for $80 million. They brought in a Texas-sized attraction, one Lynn Nolan Ryan, to get the turnstiles rolling every five days—and it worked: The team drew two million in 1989. It was in that year that Kenny Rogers got his start.

IN HIS SEVEN YEARS in the minors, Rogers had never won more than six games in a season. But the Ranger organization saw something in him. It was the organization's job to develop skills, knowledge, and maturity—those things that come from experience. Pitching-coach Tom House, a former pitcher himself, remarked in later years of the young Rogers: "He was as skinny as my son . . . a real skinny kid with great athletic ability. He was the quickest in all our running, all our drills."

In '89, the Rangers were looking to rebound from a next-to-last-place finish in the American League West, 33.5 games behind Oakland. Rogers made the team, and made his first appearance in Arlington Stadium on April 6. In a tie game in the seventh inning, with two out and a man on first, Bobby Valentine brought him in to get out a left-handed hitter, Matt Nokes. Rogers walked him, and was taken out. But two days later, he got his first career win, entering in the ninth inning after the Blue Jays' Pat Borders doubled with nobody out. Toronto was up 2–1. Rogers got behind 3-0 on his first batter, but then whirled and picked Borders off second base. He went on to retire the next two hitters. In the bottom of the ninth, Rafael Palmeiro doubled and Ruben Sierra homered for the 3–2 victory. The box score read Rogers W (1-0). That first 10 days of his major league tenure stands almost as a microcosm of what was to follow: indifferent, lightly worn failure followed by modest effectiveness mixed with carelessness saved by stunning skill and redeemed, as often as not, by luck. By season's end, Rogers had made appearances in 73 games, all in relief. He finished with three wins, four losses, and only two saves. Although his ERA was a sharp 2.93, he would often give way in crucial situations to Jeff Russell, a big, right-handed Ohioan, a starter the year before but now the closer. He pitched as often as Rogers but was used differently, and got the big stat: a league-leading 38 saves and selection to the All-Star team. At season's end, Rogers, who was making $68,000 as a rookie, got a raise for himself, not that he had any leverage whatsoever, but he had proven himself to be injury-free and versatile if not spectacular. He was now married; he and Becky wanted to have a family, so he gladly accepted a doubling of his pay for the next year, to about $140,000, not without noticing that the guy who was around at the end of games, Russell, made $480K for the year, and was in for $1.16 million in 1990.

During the off-season, talks were under way toward a new collective-bargaining agreement. The owners were determined to see salary arbitration scrapped in favor of a wage scale for one-, two-, and three-year players. Some were troubled, though, by the new commissioner, Fay Vincent, who seemed to them awestruck by the great Marvin Miller.

In the spring of 1990, the owners locked the camps for 32 days. When the lockout ended, the players had triumphed once again; arbitration was even enhanced. But the shortened spring training—everyone rushed to start the season only one week late—worked to the disadvantage of some players. Jeff Russell got hurt early and Rogers found himself where any reliever hoping to make a real good living would want to be—in the game in the ninth inning. But Rogers wasn't quite ready: in 66 relief appearances he managed 15 saves, but blew 9 opportunities. Behind good years from Palmeiro, Julio Franco, Pete Incaviglia, and Ruben Sierra, the team finished at four games over .500, but far behind the Oakland A's.

Things were going to be different for Rogers in 1991: He was going to get to start, or so said Valentine during the off-season. "I'm happy," said Rogers. "I think I can do it and make us a better team." When it came time to talk money again in February, the Rangers were dealing with a man headed for their starting rotation. Rogers gladly accepted another doubling of his pay. He headed off to the Florida Instructional League to work on his stamina.

It didn't pan out. Rogers was 0-3 after his first three starts in 1991, with an ERA over 13.00. He was bumped to the bullpen. Valentine gave him another try in midsummer, but Rogers remained ineffective. Said pitching coach Tom House: "He always had the pitches to be a starter but he didn't seem to keep his focus for more than one or two innings. Relieving seemed to suit him."

The Rangers were starting to round into form as a team. Juan Gonzalez arrived with a bang, and drove in 102 runs, Sierra drove in 116, and Palmeiro rapped out 49 doubles. On the pitching side, though, it was a lot of mediocrity: Jose Guzman won 13, Ryan 12, and system product Kevin Brown still wore the sign "potential" on his back, suffering wild spells, hitting batters (a league-leading 13), and winning only 9 games. Jeff Russell returned as the saver, and got 30. Rogers was in no-man's-land: 10-10 record, 9 starts, 54 relief appearances, a dreadful ERA. The Rangers finished 10 games back of the Twins. Because now he could, and because the Rangers were not interested in giving him anything more than a one-year deal, Rogers filed for salary arbitration—he lost, but still ended up with a $620,000 contract.

In 1992, Rogers pitched in relief only—no starts—just as in his rookie year. He made a league-leading 81 appearances, pitched 79 innings, won 3 games, saved 6. It was a disastrous year; Valentine was fired in midseason. Once gain, Texas finished in the middle of the pack, way out of contention.

At the end of the '92 season, Rogers wasn't happy. It was arbitration time again, and Rogers had made it clear through his agent that he wanted to be looked at as a starter for the '93 season. And he had a new manager to tell it to—Kevin Kennedy, who was getting his first managing job. "It's not like there's five Cy Young Award winners out there," Rogers acidly observed about the Texas rotation. Of the outcome of the previous year's arbitration hearing, he said, "It made me realize that my job wasn't that important. That's pretty much what they said. If it's not an important job, maybe they should get someone who's not important, because I feel I am important." But things didn't go any better. Rogers filed again, asking for $1.5 million, the club offered an even million, and they won.

Kennedy, today an ESPN analyst, wasn't thinking about any of this. He had spent nine years as a coach in the Dodgers organization before becoming Montreal's farm director and then Felipe Alou's bench coach. He was invited to interview for the Texas Rangers job. "The president hired me," recalls Kennedy, marveling a little at the fact that the statement is true. "George W. did the second interview, for about four hours, with a few others, and he put the stamp on me. He knew some baseball. Sure did." (Make a note: A Bush and a Kennedy see eye to eye.)

Kennedy says he had heard "through the grapevine" that Rogers might be interested in a starting role. And on a caravan trip promoting the club during the winter—making stops in places like Paris, Texas, Wichita Falls, and Austin—Kennedy talked to Rogers, and then talked to Sandy Johnson, the assistant GM. "Johnson thought Kenny had the stuff to do it," says Kennedy. "And I mean the *stuff* stuff: a good curveball, the fastball of course, a good changeup, and everything was there. He had the arsenal for a starter. So we decided—myself and Sandy Johnson and Kenny, who was on that particular trip, and of course GM Tom Grieve and Claude Osteen, my pitching coach. We said, 'Let's just give him a shot.' "

Rogers did get into Kennedy's starting rotation, and Kennedy and Osteen looked like geniuses early on. Rogers got off to a blazing start in '93, going 3-1 with an ERA around 2.25. But just as quickly, he began to struggle, enduring a handful of rocky starts. Kennedy began to sense some insecurity.

"I don't think he knew how good he might be," says Kennedy, "and everybody in the media was saying I was going to put him back in the bullpen"—as Valentine had done in 1990. "It was a Sunday afternoon, and Kenny was due to start on the following Wednesday. He'd been really struggling, after that good start. He had complained that maybe his arm was sore, but the doctor said there was nothing wrong. So I said, Kenny, there's such a thing that's called fear of failure, but there's such a thing that's called fear of success. You've got to decide. I feel like you woke up and looked up and all of sudden you're leading the league in earned run average and you're 3 or 4 and 1 and you say to yourself, Am I really this good? You've had three or four bad starts in a row, but I'm not gonna take you out of the rotation. You come in and tell me tomorrow if you want to start, then on Wednesday the start's yours. If you don't want to start, you want to go back to the pen, I'll put you in the pen. The decision is yours. I felt like that meeting, for us anyways, was kind of a turning point. Because he came in the next day and he was chatting with the guys and was having fun in the clubhouse and never came into my office. So I called him in and I said, 'Hey, what did you decide?' He says, 'Oh, I want to start.' Just like it was nothing." This is the side of Kenny Rogers that would later exasperate a few teammates and managers, but also shows the kind of pluck he had to carry him through adversity, which might be why he's still drawing major league pay 21 years after Joe Marchese spotted him in Plant City.

ROGERS SETTLED IN AND went 16-10 for the season, which saw Texas finish in second place in the A.L. West, eight games back of the White Sox. Palmeiro led the league in runs, Gonzalez led in home runs, Tom Henke had 40 saves, and Kevin Brown won 15. The Rangers drew 2.5 million fans, and said good-bye to Nolan Ryan, who retired. The Rangers were a young team on the rise.

Rogers's fortunes were finally on the rise, too. Facing arbitration once again in the winter between the '93 and '94 campaigns, he asked for $2.5 million, and the team offered $2 million; they agreed to settle on $2.3 million before the case went to an arbiter. It was the 13th consecutive one-year contract signed by Rogers and the Rangers organization. He was 29 years old. But he had hoped for something more, something in the way of security for his family and his own piece of mind. He wanted a three-year contract, the Rangers would offer only two, so he settled for one. At least he'd be a free agent the next year—he'd have his six years in.

Kennedy called upon some old friends within the Dodger organization to give him a hand. Osteen, of course, who also had a connection (once removed) to the Rangers via his time with the Senators; and Sandy Koufax, who came on as a pitching consultant in spring training of '94, specifically to help Rogers. The hitting was not a problem—and the addition of Will Clark in a $30-million deal would only make the lineup more productive. On the pitching side, there was hope, too. The addition of Jay Howell and the arrival of the Stanford star Rick Helling promised an improvement to complement the continued blossoming of Kevin Brown and the late blooming of Rogers. The Rangers, said *The Sporting News,* were sure to "bludgeon opposing pitching" in 1994 and were the favorite to win the West. Kennedy was not afraid to sound cocksure himself: "With the new stadium, the realignment, and the guys we added, there are no excuses. We should win." Bold, for a second-year manager to raise such expectations for his club. But his boss Mr. Bush, and the people of Arlington, who had paid for the team's new stadium, expected nothing less.

THE OPINIONS OF *The Sporting News,* Kevin Kennedy, various pundits, and George W. notwithstanding, the dynamic Texas Rangers of 1994, all tricked out in their new Ballpark at Arlington, squibbed like a wet rocket.

First Brown (five innings, 10 hits) and then Rogers (three innings, eight runs) got hammered in the season's opening-game losses at Yankee Stadium; Rogers pitched poorly in losing the home opener a week later. Brown started off 0-3, Rogers 0-2. By May, the Rangers were four games under .500 in the new three-divisional play, grouped in the West with Oakland, Seattle, and Anaheim—a small, undernourished division if there ever was one, but still, they were in first place. Will Clark, who had his worst year as a pro the year previous, liked the big money and the small new ballpark, and liked hitting .384. Jose Canseco, after a long off-season of physical rehab, was over .300 and hitting with power. Juan Gonzalez had not gotten untracked yet, but was warming up; and the squat, powerful young catcher, Ivan Rodriguez, was looking like a star in the making, hitting in the .270s and gunning people down from behind the plate.

Despite the offensive numbers, and their place in the standings, Kennedy didn't like this team. "We gave up," he said frankly after one bad loss. "Guys who are scared I don't want in this organization," he said after another defeat. It gets worse: "I want guys trying to play with pain." Kennedy moved David Hulse out of the leadoff spot for having one of the league's lowest on-base percentages for a top-of-the-order guy; he replaced him with Oddibe McDowell, who had faster feet, a better eye, and an infinitely cooler name. He platooned him in right field with the irrepressible Chris James, while Hulse proceeded to lose his center-field job altogether to a kid Kennedy brought up in May, Rusty Greer, out of Fort Rucker, Alabama, whose game he just loved. "I saw him in Arizona in the winter and I liked him; Rob Ducey made the club in the spring, but I called Rusty up after about three weeks and the rest for him was his-tory—he was a great steady player, a solid player."

Rogers started to come around, and got to 7-3 by June. Brown, mean-while, started getting nicked by injuries and was hit solidly around the league. The team endured a backache from Tom Henke, the closer, and a 13-game RBI drought from "Juan Gone," who had driven in 329 runs in the previous three years, and yet the team could still claim first place, at 42-45. Rogers was leading the pitching staff with a 10-4 record. The Rangers were a successful bad team. It was turning out to be that kind of year.

While owners and the players were at an impasse, and talk of strike was in the air—there was no longer a commissioner, Fay Vincent having been forced out—the air was filled by baseballs flying out of the stadiums like never before. And people poured into the ballparks in record numbers, despite the strike talk. At the All-Star break in July, Matt Williams had 33 homers, as did Frank Thomas, who was hitting .329. Junior Griffey had 32 home runs, and was hitting a whopping .383, with 78 RBI.

As the summer wore on, the owners argued among themselves over what measures were needed to take care of the small-market teams; the large-market teams had a different notion of who should help whom and by how much. Basically, they wanted the players to accept a salary cap tied to a fixed percentage of TV revenues. In clearly its most desperate attempt to control player costs, ownership wanted to altogether eliminate salary arbitration, which had been a player's right since 1973, predating free agency itself. Talks were fruitless; they didn't even begin in earnest till just before the season began. In Congress, a committee headed by Senator Howard Metzenbaum (D., Ohio) was considering repealing or amending baseball's antitrust exemption. But the owners would not be swayed from their course. Seeming hell-bent on forcing a strike and hoping to wait out the players till the union cracked, the owners fired yet another salvo at Donald Fehr and the membership when they withheld a $7.8-million scheduled payment to the players' pension fund. The players nearly voted to strike then and there, in July, but Donald Fehr reminded them that as long as they played, they got paid. So they played on, and people kept coming to the ballparks, hoping against hope for some kind of miracle. And a miracle of a sort happened on July 28 in front of a packed house in Arlington.

IT WAS DRY AND HOT, the temperature, even at 7:35, game time, 88 degrees. The Angels were in town to start a four-game series. A light breeze out of the northwest tried to cool things, but everyone at the jammed ballpark was aware of the ill wind blowing from the northeast, up in New York. At around 5 P.M., Donald Fehr, the executive director of the Players Association, in receipt of the owners' flat rejection of the players' latest proposal, set a strike date of August 12.

The Rangers were, of course, in first place, although playing under .500 ball. They had dropped the game the previous night, 1–0, and their lead over Oakland was down to a game and half. With the strike date set, it had just begun to dawn on writers in the press box that there was now a two-week sprint till what could end up to be the final standings.

Assuming dollars and sense prevailed, there would be an agreement just in time for the postseason, where the big television money was. The mood in the Texas clubhouse was both anxious and relaxed. A local reporter, Jim Reeves, of the *Fort Worth Star-Telegram*, said the team was "as loosey-goosey" as he'd seen them all year. After all, a lot of teams would look at the impending strike and say, "We're out of it."

No one had given the Angels much of a chance in the preseason—too young. And yet when you look at their lineup with 10 years' perspective, you wonder how bad could they have been: Chad Curtis, Spike Owen, Jim Edmonds, Chili Davis, Bo Jackson, J. T. Snow, Tim Salmon, and Harold Reynolds; the pitching staff had Mark Langston, and Chuck Finley. But they were already 18 games under .500. Buck Rodgers had been fired in May after the slow start; Marcel Lachemann—passed over for the Rangers job in favor of Kennedy—took his place. Their biggest problem was offense: The Angels were last in the league in runs scored. Part of the problem walked up to the plate to start the game.

Chad Curtis, a decent outfielder with good speed and some pop in his bat, had broken in with the Angels two years before. He'd hit .285 in his second year, and Buck Rodgers made him the leadoff man in '94. It wasn't working out. Curtis came to the plate batting .257. Although he had 10 home runs, he wasn't getting on the base paths enough; his on base percentage stood at .313.

Rogers got his first pitch of the night, a fastball, in for a called strike. Curtis watched a curve go in the dirt for a ball, and another, low again, followed by a fastball below the knees. Curtis, against type, was looking for a walk. He took another fastball, right at the knees, for strike two, which brought the count full. Then Rogers, shaking off his catcher, fired a fastball in the mid-90s at the knees and Curtis went down looking. He never swung.

Spike Owen was next. A one-time first-round draft choice for Seattle, the small, switch-hitting Texan had developed a reputation as a defensive specialist, a shortstop with good range and great hands. He was instrumental in the Red Sox drive to the World Series in 1986, but had bounced to Montreal, the Yankees, and now the Angels. This year, the lifetime .250 hitter was seeing the ball well, hitting .302. Owen took the opposite tack from Curtis, swinging at the first pitch, fouling the fastball back. Then he hit a neat two-hopper to Esteban Beltre at short, who threw him out easily. Twenty-four-year-old Jim Edmonds batted third for the Angels, and he was not yet the player he would become. Temperamental, given to emotive displays, he was playing second fiddle to another young-ster who had a little more seasoning, the 1993 Rookie of the Year Tim Salmon. If Salmon hadn't been hurt (hamstring), Edmonds, a left-handed hitter, wouldn't have been starting against a tough lefty like Rogers. He took a fastball high for a ball. Edmonds, hitting .286 with five homers, took another fastball high to make it 2-0, before Rogers nipped the out-side corner for a strike, or so said home-plate ump Ed Bean, a minor league arbiter called up to spell a major league ump on vacation. Edmonds gave the green ump a scowl. Rogers then blew a fastball at the letters right by Edmonds, a sign that Rogers had powerful stuff going for him; he then missed with a curve to bring the count to 3-2 once again. With his 15th pitch of the inning—a rather inefficient start—Rogers caught the outside corner again. It looked below the knees to Edmonds. But Ivan Rodriguez framed the pitch for the ump, whose arm shot up in the air. Pudge rolled the ball back to the mound as Rogers mincingly walked off, his first inning of work done.

Opposing Rogers was a 21-year-old left-hander, tall and skinny with a nervous-looking Adam's apple, making his second major league start. Andrew Lorraine, a year before, had been pitching in Boise, in the rookie leagues, but had vaulted up to Triple A this spring at Vancouver, where he was 9-3 with two shutouts.

First up for Texas was one Wallace McArthur "Butch" Davis, out of Martin County, North Carolina, who was now on his fifth team in eight years in a career that would be over and done with in two weeks. Kennedy made the call to the Wichita club after the previous night's game, asking that Davis, who was hitting .297, report immediately. The Rangers were a little banged up, and short of right-handed-hitting out-fielders. Davis gave Lorraine his first out, rapping a ground ball to short. Ivan Rodriguez, batting second, and hitting an even .300, with 13 home runs, 51 RBI, came to the plate, hot off his first All-Star start. Rodriguez hit a high fly that drifted toward the wall in left, but Jim Edmonds hauled it in. And big Jose Canseco, having a terrific year with 27 home runs already, stepped up. Crouching as much as a muscle-bound man with swagger can, Canseco swung at a 2-2 pitch and put it about one row into the left-field stands, to give the Rangers a 1–0 lead, a homer so poorly hit that Canseco hung his head on the way to first and inspected the handle of his bat. Will Clark stood in, his facial expression—big eyed and with a tobacco chaw distending his features—making him look absolutely appalled at everything around him. In fact, he looked like he wanted to hit a baseball hard somewhere just to feel better. He was hitting .331, but was in no great mood of late, going 9 for his last 50. He drew a full-count walk. Up came Juan Gonzalez, having an off-year for him, hitting .278 with 16 home runs and 75 RBI, but he ripped a shot on a line between short and third and moved Clark to second. Dean Palmer, yet another thumper in the Rangers lineup but also in a slump, then rapped a low fastball into center field for an RBI single, and Rogers now had more than enough for his night's work. Kennedy's favored rookie Rusty Greer, hitting .309, skied out to Bo Jackson in right, and after one inning, it was two-zip.

Charles Theodore "Chili" Davis, from Kingston, Jamaica, a six-foot-three-inch, 215-pound switch-hitting All-Star, began the day hitting .332, with 21 home runs and 71 RBI. Never being fast afoot, Chili, at 34, was a confirmed designated hitter. He jumped on Rogers's down-the-middle fastball but hit it to straightaway center field, where Greer hauled it in. Chili never fooled around at the plate: he saw it, he hit it. It was why he would become a potent pinch-hitter toward the end of his career, with the Yanks, where he would exit a winner.

Batting fifth for the Angels was a man who would be a gigantic American legend were it not for a debilitating hip injury suffered as a pro football player. Vincent Edward "Bo" Jackson, out of Bessemer, Alabama, won the Heisman Trophy in 1985, playing for the Auburn Tigers. At an oak-solid six feet one inch, 225 pounds, he was drafted to be a running back by the Oakland Raiders and to be an outfielder by the Kansas City Royals. He did both, and did both very well. He was also a marketing juggernaut, a steaming urn of burning brand—if it was Bo, it was cool. But by 1994, his hip, injured at the goal line in a playoff game for Oakland, had been replaced. And so had Bo as Madison Avenue's favorite human billboard. And, even though he had broken a bat over his thigh, bare-handed a carom off the outfield wall and thrown out a runner, "walked up a wall" after making a catch in order to slow his momentum, and hit humungous home runs, Jackson was near to being through as a baseball player. His numbers were fading. With 12 home runs and a .271 average, he did what he always did a lot of: struck out, this time on three pitches, all fastballs, the last one blown right by him.

J. T. Snow, born Jack Thomas Snow, the son of a famous Notre Dame and L.A. Rams wide receiver, was staggering under the weight of having pedigree and potential. A graceful fielder, Snow was still in trouble at the plate, especially right-handed (he later would return to batting only lefty, his natural side, in 1999). Hitting .227 with only six home runs, he popped up a Rogers fastball, and third-baseman Dean Palmer gloved it.

In the Texas half of the second, the second baseman, Manny Lee, who hailed from the shortstop-rich San Pedro de Macoris in the Dominican Republic, batting right-handed against the lefty Lorraine, led off. He hit one right down the first-base line and Jack Snow dove and made the stop and threw him out, Lorraine covering. Esteban Beltre, the shortstop for the Rangers, skied to fairly deep center. As the top of the order came up, in Butch Davis, it looked as if Andrew Lorraine could at least handle the bottom of the Texas order. Davis too, who popped out to second.

The bottom third of the Angels lineup began with Rex Hudler, who had debuted as a Yankee back in 1984, but then made stops in Baltimore, Montreal, and St. Louis before landing with the Angels. He platooned at second with Harold Reynolds, who was in his last year—he too would not play again after the strike. Hudler drew his pay in Japan the previous year, where he did well. And he seemed to have returned to the stateside game with more confidence, hitting .301. But against Rogers he looked at a called-strike fastball, check-fouled the next, also a fastball, and then leaned, stared, and groaned at a huge curveball from his eyeballs to his shoe tops through the strike zone for strike three. Rogers's stuff was growing extremely sharp.

The catcher Chris Turner was up next, hitting only .233, in his second year. After falling behind to Rogers, 1-2, he looped one weakly to Juan Gonzalez in left, who loped in for the grab. Slick-fielding Gary Di-Sarcina, out of Malden, Massachusetts, stepped in, batting ninth but hitting a not-so-anemic .261—better than the guys around him, Turner and Curtis. After looking at a slider on the corner for a called strike and then laying off a slow curve to even the count, he hacked at a slow curve. The ball hit the dirt in front of home plate, the hard, baked ground, and it shot toward the hole between third and short, but Dean Palmer, playing even with the bag, cut to his left and short-hopped it on the edge of the grass and got the fleet DiSarcina by a step to end the inning. It was the night's first tough play.

The Rangers, in their half of the third, finished off their scoring, and seemed to make their best effort at convincing Andrew Lorraine that he should have finished up at Stanford, which he left after his junior year. Two home runs, a line drive 20 rows back in left by Pudge Rodriguez, and a shot from Canseco that made it over the fence by a foot or two, made it 4-0 Rangers.

It was back to the top of the order for Rogers, who had gotten his nine outs on only 30 pitches, mixing fastball and slider with the occasional wide changeup to right-handed hitters. He threw half those pitches—15—to the first three hitters, being careful with the top of the order, but also, it seems, finding his rhythm. With a 4–0 lead, it was time for him to ride that rhythm.

Curtis, who had struck out without taking the bat off his shoulder to start the game, took a fastball low on his second time up, and then flied to center. Pesky Spike Owen took a fastball strike, but then laid off another fastball as well as the dying changeup off the plate. With the count 2-1, Rogers came straight down the middle—no use running to three balls on the number-two hitter when you are up four runs. And it was a good fastball, moving laterally, and Owen lifted a little flare to short left that shortstop Beltre ran down easily. Jim Edmonds, who would see more pitches from Rogers than anyone else this night, got the big hook for a called strike, watched a curveball just miss the corner, stayed away from high outside heat, but then pulled a grounder to Hudler at second. Twelve in a row for Rogers.

In the bottom of the fourth, Lorraine started to show some of what must have gotten him to the big club, fanning Rusty Greer on sweeping curves, getting Manny Lee to fly routinely to right field, and busting Beltre in on the hands, inducing a slow roller to short.

In the fifth, after a Desenex commercial on the Home Sports Network, viewers in Texas got a look at a pair of flaming red baseball shoes, tongues of real fire licking from them as they sat on the cement dugout floor. The red dye appeared to be melting out of the leather. Within a minute word got to the press box that these were Jose Canseco's shoes, set afire by prankster Chris James. Although there was speculation between the Ranger TV broadcasters that it was Canseco's two home runs already that inspired the conflagration—as in, He's hot!—the explanation that emerged was more pedestrian and reasonable: The spikes stank to high heaven. The club was loosey-goosey all right. Kevin Kennedy must have been reminded once again that he wasn't in the classy Dodger organization, but he really didn't seem to mind. As he would say years later, "So they were having fun. It was a tough year, the strike was coming. Kenny was throwing well; we had a lead. It wasn't an easy night, but a loose night."

Fortunately, Kenny Rogers was not in the dugout to witness the hijinks, but out on the mound, his face set grimly in anticipation of the upcoming number-four, -five, and -six hitters. Chili Davis, cleanup man, took a changeup wide for a ball, with Rogers and Rodriguez opting to stay out of Chili's wheelhouse. The second pitch was the same as the first, and Davis swung mightily but could manage only a weak ground ball to Palmer at third. One out.

Bo Jackson was next, and Rogers was careful with him too. He started him out with a slider down for a ball, and then a fastball in a perfect spot, low and away, and Jackson swung right through it. Rogers then threw the same pitch, but spotted it down and in, and Jackson, looking outside, bent over it and didn't offer. Ump Bean called it a strike, Jackson spun away and gave Bean the business. He talked and muttered and took to grooming the batter's box with his cleats, still chattering. Bean kept his peace. The fifth pitch to Jackson strayed wide but he flailed at it, for strike three. Rogers's third K.

Jack Snow just about made it an ordinary night, with the help of Rogers, who missed with a curve twice and then brought in a fastball too high, for the night's first 3-0 count. But Rogers got the fastball in for a called strike, high and on the corner, and hit the spot again, at 3-1, and Snow lifted it to straightaway center field, to Rusty Greer.

Lorraine—who would go on to have a six-year career, topping out at 3-1 in 1997 with Oakland—faced the top of the Texas order. He got Davis on a grounder to third, Rodriguez, who had earlier homered, rapped out to third, and Canseco, he of the gone shoes and the two home runs already, worked the count to 3-0 before hitting a line drive to medium center field for the third out. Lorraine had, all of a sudden, put down nine Rangers in a row. Rogers, though, had put down 15, and was back for more.

It was the bottom of the order in the top of the sixth. Last time, Rogers had gotten through them in 10 pitches. This time, it took 7. Hudler looked at a fastball low for a ball to get ahead in the count, and then swung at another fastball—Rogers seemed determined not to fall too far behind on any count, and to rely on his fastball to see that he didn't—it was fouled back. Hudler then lunged futilely at a curve to fall behind 1-2 and then jumped at an eye-high fastball, lining it to left-center, where Gonzalez ran it down. Catcher Chris Turner popped a 1-0 fastball in the air, and when it came down, Will Clark had it. Two out. DiSarcina hit the first pitch, a fastball, right back to Rogers, who made a clean pick and throw to first. Eighteen in a row, 59 pitches. The crowd sensed something. Rogers walked off to expectant, hopeful, can-it-be cheers.

Rogers was in the dugout, seeming to pick sleep dust out of his eyes. He was there in a world of his own. No one talked to him; no one sat near him. He watched Lorraine try to get out Will Clark, who was 0 for 2 with a walk and a run scored. Clark went down on the slider away, Lorraine's second strikeout. Ten straight Rangers retired. But Gonzalez ended that with a line shot up the middle on the first pitch. Palmer was next, with a single and RBI already to his credit. Swinging wildly, he popped out to the infield. On three pitches, Lorraine got Greer to retire the side.

Rogers walked out for the seventh inning. It was Chad Curtis, who had struck out in the first and flied to center in the fourth. Again, Curtis showed patience, but not quite so much as he had managed his first time up. He took a huge cut at Rogers's slider to get in the hole 0-1, but then watched a curve stay high. Another curve was too tight, and Rogers found himself behind in the count, 2-1. Time for a fastball, time for Curtis to think fastball; it's what Rogers had been doing since the early innings not to fall too far behind, but Curtis looked at it, and the count went 2-2. Another fastball, inside, caught Curtis looking outside, but he got out of the way; it just missed, bringing the count full. The crowd was on the ump; they were on Curtis for standing up there and looking at pitches. Rogers and Rodriguez appeared to be at odds as to what to throw on the full-count pitch. Rogers, looking in at Rodriguez's single, downward-pointing finger—fastball, low—swiped his own glove across his letters, meaning, "run through 'em again." Rodriguez stopped, looked down. He then gave Rogers the sign he figured he wanted—and Rogers, not giving in, threw the pitch he wanted—fastball on the outside corner, which Curtis tried to pull, only to ground to third for an easy out.

Rogers ended up going full to the next hitter as well: After shaking off Pudge's call for a fastball inside on a 2-1 pitch in favor of a slider, Rogers missed, but came back with a fastball for a called strike. On the 3-2 pitch, Rodriguez called again for the low inside strike and it was perfectly placed, but Owen got around on it and drove it in the gap in left-center. Juan Gonzalez hauled it in at a jogging pace. Then Jim Edmonds came up—not accustomed to playing against left-handers that much, he was nonetheless having better at-bats as the game went on, even with what looked like Rogers's precision stuff. Despite getting behind 0-2 in the count, Edmonds resisted a slow curve, then flicked another curve foul. He let a fastball zip by a little bit high to even the count, and then laid off a fastball, waist-high, that ump Bean called a ball. For the third time in the inning, the count was full. This time,

Rodriguez signaled for the breaking ball, and the slow slider was swung at and missed.

In the Rangers' half of the seventh, that peculiar, half-eager, half-squelched rhythm of the conflicted sets in, whereby hometown fans wish to hurry their own through their tries at the plate in order to return to the improbably gorgeous vanquishing their pitcher is laying on the opposition. The 4–0 lead is unquestionably enough. A pitching change by the Angels dragged things out for the fans in the bottom of the seventh. Rogers, though, tried to conserve himself in the dugout, and took care to wrap his left arm in a towel. Will Clark sat down next to him, but looked more like a bodyguard than an interlocutor. They didn't speak.

It then went to the eighth, and the heart of the order for the Angels—Chili, Bo, Snow. Rogers, on his 79th pitch, got a slow curve over for a called strike to Davis, and the crowd erupted. He returned to the curve. Davis, who was 6 for 14 lifetime against Rogers, hit it well, on a line to left, but Gonzalez was quick to move in and catch the sinking liner. Jackson stepped in, looking menacing, walking with swagger. But Rogers looked unaffected, unintimidated, unreachable. Then he missed with two sliders down and, after 22 outs, he found himself making a 2-0 pitch to a tough hitter. However, Jackson was not as quick through the strike zone as he once was; Rogers threw a fastball that Jackson was barely able to flick at, late. Rogers and Rodriguez cleverly followed with a changeup, off the plate. Jackson was way out in front and swung over it, to even the count. Rogers's 85th pitch was a fastball—capping a beautiful sequence of pitching—and Bo swung and missed. Snow, who had hit Rogers pretty well in a small sampling (6 hits, 11 at-bats), quickly got ahead, 2-0, as Rogers continued to pitch carefully, not afraid to be too fine, to get behind, and pitch from there. As with Jackson, Rogers came in with a 2-0 fastball; like Jackson, Snow hit it foul. Rather than following with a change of pace on the 2-1 pitch, Rogers (and Rodriguez, of course) came in with a biting slider, down and in, and Snow went for it. The ball skipped up chalk on the third-base line about 75 feet away and veered in the air over the bag. Dean Palmer lunged into foul territory and gloved it, off-balance, and made the long throw, in time, yet the third-base umpire, Tim Tschida, signaled foul, revoking what looked like out number 24. The crowd booed. Rogers remained composed; waited for Snow to get back in the box, then served up a tumbling waterfall of a curveball and Snow just looked at it for a called strike three.

Clark, Gonzalez, and Palmer had to run it up to the plate and back in the bottom of the eighth. With Clark batting, Canseco assumed his spot next to Rogers, fending off fools who might rush in with some jinxing words. Rogers's brow was furrowed; he looked worried and tense. Clark had a good at-bat and ripped a shot down the first-base line, but Snow made a sensational leaping grab for the out. Gonzalez reached out and hit the proverbial can of corn to center for out number two. Palmer stepped up there hacking, fouling off the first pitch, swinging through the next, before popping out to second.

The three guys set to face Rogers for the ninth had not had much luck against him careerwise, going a collective 1-25. Rex Hudler was first. The big hook started him off for strike one, called. Hudler had struck out and flied out in his previous times up. Rogers gave him the curve again, this one outside, and Hudler couldn't touch it, strike two. Rogers looked stricken, forlorn, scared. Rodriguez called for a fastball, outside part of the plate. It was a good pitch but Hudler slammed it on a line toward right-center. It was sinking. The crowd watched the arcing ball and two fielders, Greer from center and Butch Davis from right, speedily converge in hopes that one would intercept the flight of the ball before it hit the ground. And Greer, the rookie, the redhead in the red hat, made a headlong dive, reaching to full extension, gloving the ball a foot off the grass, across which he slid for 15 feet. The crowd was staggered by it all. Delirious. Rogers remained cool. In two pitches, Chris Turner had grounded out routinely to short. And then Gary DiSarcina strode to the plate, 0-16 lifetime against Rogers. He swung at the absolutely unhittable big Rogers hook. The next pitch, number 98 on the night, was a high fastball, the same pitch that Hudler almost put safely in the gap. And this one again headed toward center. Greer came in a step, went back a step, seemed frozen in indecision but was actually holding his ground to get a read on the ball. He was a good outfielder, he's still a good outfielder nine years later. Greer drifted back three or four steps, saw it, and made the catch. It was over.

Long past is the dignified walk toward the dugout with only Yogi Berra across your lap. It was bedlam, mayhem, mosh pit. Rogers recovered and was typically gracious. In the dugout, though, before the headset interview that fans could see on the scoreboard, before the family gathered round, before any of that, he bent over at the waist and deeply breathed.

MILLING ABOUT IN THE dugout, Rogers hugged his catcher, and they had words back and forth. Rodriguez was still young, still developing, and, despite his obvious talent, had been getting his share of criticism in the Texas press. But together, they called a great game. Rogers had his preferences on occasion, which he made known. At game's end, he complimented Ivan on the game he called, and said, "We both learned something tonight."

Kennedy contends that Rogers had only "his normal stuff" that night, but you have to wonder what he was seeing. It's not normal to walk no one, it's not normal to have a three-and-a-half-foot breaking curveball that you can throw for strikes low and inside and on the outside corner; it's not normal to have a moving fastball that stays at the knees every time. Rogers had all of these, and the Angels could only swing.

Hudler thought his drive in the ninth was going to drop in; Greer, who came running in full speed, thought he had no chance; they were both wrong, perhaps as wrong as Kennedy about Kenny's stuff.

That week's *Sporting News* cover pictured Rogers in the arms of Will Clark and Ivan Rodriguez, the first players to reach him after the last out was recorded; inset next to the happy Rangers were grim passport-looking photos of Richard Ravitch and Donald Fehr, the two men who represented the labor-management impasse. The headline said it: "The Ecstasy and the Agony."

In two weeks, agony won, the players walked. Although fans and some players and the press seemed to hold out hope for a settlement, for a postseason, Kennedy was told differently by George W. Bush. "He told me to tell the players that if they strike the season will be over; the owners were serious about that. After the meeting, I remember Chris James saying, 'Skip, see you in two weeks.' I said, 'I don't think so, guys.'" Too bad for Texas—they were still in first place on August 12. Too bad for the White Sox, the Yankees, the Reds, the Dodgers, and Montreal, all in first place, too, in baseball's first year of three-division play. Very much too bad for the Expos, 34 games over .500 at 74-40, the best record in baseball. Not good, either, for Matt Williams, who had 43 home runs with 47 games left on the schedule; for Tony Gwynn, who was hitting .394; for Frank Thomas, having a Triple Crown year, at 38/101/.353. Too bad for the fans, who had been coming to the ballparks in America in record numbers.

In September, the owners canceled the season and the postseason, while America had to content itself with 10 nights of Ken Burns's *Baseball*, which debuted on public television. In December, the owners unilaterally—as they thought was their right—reimposed the work rules in place under the former contract. A court thought otherwise. The owners also, while they were at it, broke off talks with the umpires union, and were determined to play ball in 1995 with replacement players and replacement umps. And despite a variety of things that might've weakened player resolve—from high-profile drug problems (Gooden, Strawberry) to a rumor that Latin American players were about to flee the union—the union held firm. In April, there was one game actually scheduled to be played—with replacement players—between the Mets and the Marlins. But it was canceled, and an agreement was announced the next day. Baseball was back; the owners collapsed.

Baseball might have been back, but it has yet to be restored. The Montreal franchise never recovered from the blow; no one will ever know what level Frank Thomas's game might have reached by year's end, or if kids might now be hearing that Tony Gwynn was the last man to hit .400. Where are those fans who 10 years ago hoped it would be so?

It took Cal Ripken's consecutive-game streak to reignite fan and advertiser interest in the game. Attendance is still recovering from the fatal disfiguring of the game that occurred in 1994—no September pennant runs, no postseason, and, for the first time since John Brush refused to field his team against Pittsburgh in 1904, no World Series.

Kenny Rogers suffered another personal injury as a result of the strike—he needed the full season of service time to earn his free agency. So it was yet another one-year contract with Texas for 1995, during which he had his best year as a pro—17 wins, 7 losses, and a 3.38 ERA, but Texas finished in third place. By then, Kevin Kennedy had moved off to Boston.

Kenny Rogers got his long-awaited payday when he signed a four-year deal with the New York Yankees for $20 million. The Bronx, though, was not a happy experience. Granted, Rogers got to the postseason, but pitched ineffectively in the '96 playoffs and World Series, giving up 15 hits and 11 earned runs in 7 innings of work. The Yankees were unhappy with Rogers's effort; they traded him, along with Mariano Duncan, to San Diego, for Greg Vaughn, only to have Vaughn fail the physical. After Rogers went 18-15 in 61 games over two years for the Yanks, they finally did trade him, to Oakland, which traded him back to New

York—the Mets, this time—during the Mets run for the flag in 1999. And Rogers helped them, going 5-1 in 12 starts, but when he walked in the winning run with the bases loaded in Game Six of the League Championship Series against Atlanta, he walked off the field with a shrugging calm that Mets fans have never forgiven.

There's no accounting for style. By all accounts, Kenny Rogers is a caring, humble fellow who put in his time in the game of baseball, expected his just desserts, and had always played hard. Kevin Kennedy would allow as to how "Kenny had too much stuff sometimes to be so fine. He didn't go and get it," a lack of aggression that may be suited to life on the farm, or in baseball's second division, but was a bad show in New York.

Still, Rogers's deliberate, careful style of pitching, and his full repertoire, has him still working at the age of 39. In 2000, he returned to the Rangers, for whom he had a 31-28 record over the next three years. Having finally made his money, and earned the luxury of working how and where he wants, he turned down a two-year, $10-million offering from the Rangers in the spring of 2003, an amount that he considered an insult on a club paying a shortstop at $25 million per. So he was out of work, until Eric Milton, a left-hander for the Twins, went down with a season-ending knee injury, prompting Denny Hocking, the Twins' player representative, to call Rogers. They spoke for 10 minutes, and shortly thereafter Rogers instructed his agent Scott Boras to accept the Twins $2-million, one-year deal. "I'm not a guy who spends a lot," said Rogers.

He went on to help the Twins to a division title in 2003, going 13-8, but was not in the starting rotation in the playoffs, where the Yanks beat them in four games. In the off-season, Texas called, as it had more than two decades ago, and Rogers answered: $6 million for two years—home to Arlington, where he had his greatest day, back in 1994.

CHAPTER THIRTEEN

New York, New York

Davids Wells and Cone

May 17, 1998   •   July 18, 1999

THEY WERE BORN in the same year, 1963—David Brian Cone in Kansas City, two days into January, and David Lee Wells, five and a half months later, in Torrance, California, on May 20. They were working class all the way—Cone's father fixed machinery in a meat-packing plant, while his mother worked as a teacher; Wells, a rung or two down the social ladder, lived in a small bungalow with his mother, Annie, the mother of five kids to four different men. Wells was the youngest and more or less grew up with his mom and his still-at-home sister Jeannie. None of the dads who once romanced the woman called Attitude Annie were around.

For Wells more than Cone, baseball was a ticket out. Where Cone would have the variety of options that a stable upbringing, private-school education, and broad athletic achievement afford, Wells, content to remain part of a brawling, endearingly fractious family of ne'er-do-wells, bikers, and restaurant workers, would only be rescued, ironically, by something of a higher standard, something as pure and fun as baseball. Whatever it was, it had to be fun. And it couldn't be bullshit.

The tall, skinny, long-haired kid got his wish: At the age of 19, after graduating from Point Loma High, Wells was taken in the second round of the amateur draft by the Toronto Blue Jays. He got a $50,000 signing bonus and reported to pitching duty to a place called Medicine Hat, in western Canada. According to his spirited autobiography, Medicine Hat for Wells was a goodly spell of beer-drinking—on the roof of the hotel where the players lived, looking at the stars, and listening to trains come and go from the nearby rail depot, and in the honky-tonks of the American upper Midwest. Wells moved south the next year, getting promoted to A Ball in the Carolina League in '83, where he pitched fairly well and racked up a lot of innings and had just as good a time. The following year, however, came his first physical trouble: He tore an elbow ligament at Double-A Knoxville. He rehabbed over the winter in his own inimitable fashion—strict regimens of his favorite hops beverage and junk food—then blew out the elbow again the next year. Enter Dr. James Andrews, who performed surgery on the damaged ligament—the Tommy John surgery, unheard of 10 years before, when Dodger physician Frank Jobe pioneered it, and undreamed of 10 years before that, when Sandy Koufax, out of medical options, tired of regimens of aspirin and cortisone, quit the game. Now it was something available to a 21-year-old Double-A pitcher.

Wells took the year off from baseball and summered as a busboy and a shopping cart jockey back home in California, where he lived in a friend's Chevy Suburban. There, he had a dream that his real father, whom he'd never known, lived on a tree-lined street in West Virginia. When David reported his dream to Annie, she gave him a slip of paper with a phone number. The man lived in West Virginia. Before the 1986 season commenced, Wells found David Pritt, who had left Annie Wells just before little David's first birthday. Father and son have been close ever since.

Restoring a connection that had been cut seemed to help Wells; his arm was healing, too. The Toronto organization, headed by GM Pat Gillick, eased him back into competition, and Wells was, if not a new man, a new pitcher. He rocketed from low A Ball to high A Ball to Double A to Triple A in the course of the season—Florence, South Carolina, to

Ventura, California, to Knoxville to Triple-A Syracuse. In September, the big club called him up, but Wells, nursing an aching shoulder, made a smart move: He declined. Time to go see Dr. Andrews for an opinion— had Wells reinjured himself? Andrews reassured Wells that there was nothing wrong with the reconstructed elbow. That was the good news. The bad new was that his rotator cuff and labrum were torn. More knife work.

Andrews cleaned things up inside the shoulder, and within weeks Wells was feeling better. Back at Syracuse the following spring, he was unhittable, throwing nearly 100 miles per hour and racking up an ERA of 0.87. He got the callup again, this time in midseason; he debuted against the Yankees, a starting assignment against Ron Guidry. It didn't go well, and before long, Wells found himself back in Syracuse. Maybe he *should* be a reliever, as some old-timers were counseling. But to Wells there was no money in it, no fun in it. It was bullshit.

Still, Wells developed into a pretty good middle-innings guy, but had to watch from the bullpen in 1989 as Toronto lost in the playoffs, four games to one against Oakland. The next year, injuries to 38-year-old Mike Flanagan and Al Leiter—both lefties—got Wells into the starting rotation, where he pitched fairly well, finishing the year 11-6 with an ERA of 3.14. In '91, Wells was tabbed as the fourth starter, behind Dave Stieb, Jimmy Key, and Wells's minor league drinking pal Todd Stottlemyre. Wells pitched streakily through the year, cold in April, on fire in May, collapsing in June, and finally, coming undone in July, arguing on the mound with his manager Cito Gaston—who had decided to call Wells's pitches—and refusing to give up the ball. When Gaston insisted, in colorful language, that Wells hand it over and head for the showers, Wells told him to "Go get it," and promptly heaved the ball into the stands down the right-field line, and stomped off. By the time Toronto won their division, Wells was back in what he calls that "little cyclone-fenced kennel"—the bullpen. Or doghouse. The Jays got clobbered, four games to one, by the Twins. Wells pitched effectively but in vain in four of the contests. The Blue Jays, though, were a great success at the gate, drawing more than four million fans. The next year, 1992, the fans would get their reward.

With the Toronto brass feeling that it was now or never, they made a trade for a player on the verge of free agency, David Cone. This happened in late August, just in time for Cone to make the postseason roster. Wells, who had been in and out of the starting rotation, found himself "bitch-slapped back to the pen one more time" to make room for the new guy. Wells hated Cone immediately, but not for long. As he says in *Perfect I'm Not*, "You can't hate Coney. It's impossible, he's too cool, too funny, too much fun to goof off with. . . . We quickly laid the groundwork for a great, enduring solid friendship."

The Jays handled Oakland this time, in six games, and moved on to play Atlanta in the World Series. Behind the pitching of Jack Morris, Jimmy Key, and Cone, and with timely hitting from the unlikely Ed Sprague (a game-winning homer), and the unlikelier Candy Maldonado (a crucial bloop single), the Jays won it all in six games. World Series champs; World Series ring promised in the spring. Wells contributed little, though. In fact, he'd contributed his last to Canada, at least for the time being. And so had Cone.

During the off-season, Cone went home—signing a three-year deal with Kansas City worth $18 million. Jimmy Key left before he got his ring, too, in his case to the Yankees, where more rings would be won. The Blue Jays shopped in the market themselves, and lured the accomplished and severely game-faced Dave Stewart up north. Wells watched it all, sensing that it was more kennel time ahead for him. But it would turn out worse than that. The off-season passed without incident, and spring training at Dunedin got underway smoothly enough. Wells felt fine, working his way into shape. But five days before the season's opener, Cito Gaston, not exactly Wells's greatest admirer, ordered Wells to a meeting with Gillick and owner Gord Ash. Wells knew this was not good. They gave him his unconditional release. In baseball terms, he was fired. "We tried to trade you . . . but there was no interest, nothing," is how Wells reported management's cold good-bye.

But Wells's agent, Greg Clifton, got to work. There was always need for pitching, Wells was a veteran now, he could start and relieve. So Wells told Clifton that money wasn't as important as staying out of a middle-inning mopup role. As everyone knew, there was no glory in that, and less lucre. Wells wanted to start. The Mets were interested, the Dodgers were interested, but both were interested in "the reliever David Wells." Then old friend Cecil Fielder—they'd roomed together in Venezuela years before—told him in no uncertain terms that Tigers manager Sparky Anderson was going to call him and Wells was going to accept an offer from Detroit. You don't say no to Cecil and, as Wells had heard, you didn't doubt Sparky's word. Wells was guaranteed the fifth spot in the Tiger rotation. He took it and a $900,000 offer. It was a cut in pay, but Wells was not complaining. He was out of the doghouse and into Detroit.

WELLS LOVED THE TIGERS. The atmosphere was relaxed but businesslike, the treatment fair. Anderson ran the ball club, the players played. As Wells put it, "no cliques, no weigh-ins, no clubhouse politicians." And nobody second-guessed the manager. Wells was allowed to play his boom box in the clubhouse with his own heavy metal music blaring—but only on the days he was pitching. Sparky knew how to open his office door and he knew when to close it.

Wells spent two and a half enjoyable, stress-free years in Detroit. That's not to say the team accomplished much—it didn't—or that Wells was injury-free. He wasn't. He suffered his first back injury and did a 21-day stint on the disabled list in '93 and then, in the spring of '94, looking at a stiff, swollen left elbow, he availed himself once again of Dr. Andrews, who removed a cackle of bone chips. But Wells learned a lot about pitching during that time, which he attributes to Sparky's straightforward approach to working hitters and long, off-season conversations with two very good hitters—Kirk Gibson and Alan Trammell. Holed up in duck blinds waiting for unsuspecting water fowl to wheel by, Wells got guided tours of a hitter's mind and expectations, especially from Gibson. By 1995, the 32-year-old Wells was reaching a level he had not sustained before. He made the All-Star team for the first time, won five straight after that, and then, watching ESPN one night, heard Peter Gammons tell him he was now a Cincinnati Red.

He hated Reds owner Marge Schott and her cheap ways and her dog and his crapping on the ball field—but he liked playing for the easygoing Davey Johnson and his "golf-friendly work ethic," and he liked playing with solid guys like Benito Santiago, Hal Morris, and the superb young Barry Larkin. In Cincinnati, Wells began to pitch with a veteran's confidence. And he also began to pitch regularly with pain management on his mind. After three straight early-season complete-game wins, the bad back was back. And as Wells says in his book, cortisone became "my new best friend." Wells got along with his new friend well enough. Pitching in August and September for the Reds, he won 6 of his 11 starts and threw three complete games (combined with his Tigers' numbers, Wells was 16–8 on the season). The Reds won their division by nine games over Houston, and then swept the Dodgers, with Wells winning Game Three.

The powerful Braves were next, but it was no contest. This time, it was the Braves who swept in four, with Wells losing Game Three. Season over. Wells also would lose Davey Johnson as manager.

Wells had earned his first shot at free agency going into the 1996 season, his second with Cincinnati, but he agreed to a deal with the Reds rather than test the market. He and his agent weren't alone in sensing there would be major labor trouble during the season, which turned out to be true. When Johnson was fired and replaced by Ray Knight, Wells looked for a contract extension. Knight told him it wouldn't be a problem. Marge Schott, pennywise heir to her husband's car dealership, thought differently. Or so Wells found out, this time via a newspaper headline on the day after Christmas 1995. He'd be rejoining Davey Johnson in Baltimore, traded for two unknowns named Curtis Goodwin and Trovin Valdez. Wells couldn't figure out how his value had dropped so, but took solace in the fact that maybe Davey and the new Orioles GM— Pat Gillick again—had gotten one over on the owner of Schottzie the dog. Whatever the stratagems, Wells was once again on a good team—Alomar, Bonilla, Mussina, Ripken, Zeile, Surhoff, Erickson, Palmeiro—and back in the American League.

The Orioles played erratically under Johnson, hot streaks followed by cold spells guaranteeing them a fairly consistent hover around .500 baseball. A 5–13 home record in the month of July seemed to bury the team's chances; Wells and Bonilla were struggling dramatically, and there was no joy in Baltimore. But, as has often been the case with Davey Johnson clubs, the veterans gradually got around to playing better. The Orioles went 35-22 in the last two months and closed on a floundering Yankee club. New York won the division, but the Orioles qualified as the wild card. Wells was badly aching; his back again, then his foot in a first-time attack of gout. He began to plan his life and his pitching around his cortisone shots.

Wells, 11-14 on the year, was named the Game One starter against Cleveland. The Orioles had spent the last several weeks enduring teammate Roberto Alomar's ignominious tour from town to town as the guy who had spat on an umpire. Alomar's act earned him a suspension, but the league allowed the games to be served the following season. It would prove to be too bad for Cleveland.

Wells, rested and with a fresh shot of cortisone, won Game One easily, 10-4. He pitched well again in Game Four, with the O's up two games to one, but left the game trailing by a run. Robby Alomar—"spit boy" in

Wells's book—tied the game in the ninth with a single and then, in front
of a roaring, taunting Cleveland crowd, hit a 400-foot home run in the
12th to win it. The Orioles took the best-of-five series, 3–1. It was on to
New York and a place Wells already loved and revered—Yankee Stadium—to play for the American League pennant. After Game One was
rained out, Davey Johnson juggled his rotation. Wells would face his
"great, enduring solid" friend David Cone, at the House that Ruth Built,
in Game Two.

LIKE WELLS, DAVID Cone was the youngest of the litter—he had two
older brothers and a sister. Unlike Wells, there was only one father and
he was present and accounted for, big time. Ed Cone worked across the
Missouri River in a Swift's meat-packing plant. The family lived in the
northeast part of Kansas City, on the Missouri side, a mostly Irish-
American neighborhood—Catholic, union, Democrat. The house was
large, and so was the backyard, where Ed Cone installed floodlights to
facilitate late-night ballgames. All his kids were athletic, but none as
fiercely so as David. In a drama played out in families all over America,
the young son was recruited as a late, fresh substitute in the fading athletic dreams of the father. Ed Cone had been a promising pitcher with a
sidearm delivery not unlike the one his son would make famous years
down the road. But Ed's game languished, and he was overtaken by better
competition. After a falling-out with his own dad, who had operated profitably as a cog in the Pendergast political machine in K.C., Ed was left to
work in steel mills and factories. He went out and married Joan Curran,
had a family, and became a tireless baseball coach in the area youth
leagues.

Ed and Joan Cone took care to educate their kids as best they could—
they stretched to the very limit to send all their kids to private Catholic
schools all the way through. David was a star football, basketball, and
baseball player at Rockhurst, a Jesuit academy for boys located in the
suburbs south of the city. He also played in the Ban Johnson League,
named after the first president of the American League. It was a show-
case mostly for college-bound players. David, with the help of his father,
got into the league when he was only 15. He played for a team called
Boyle's Corned Beef, fielded by a local sponsor who saw fit to provide uniforms featuring shamrocks across the chest and leprechauns upon the
sleeves. Cone played in the league for three summers. Scouts couldn't

help but notice the fireballing, fiery youngster. In the third round of the amateur draft in 1981, at the age of 18, Ed Cone's youngest kid was drafted by the hometown Royals. The signing bonus was $17,500. Ed Cone's youngest took off for Florida and rookie ball.

Five years later, Cone got the callup to the big club. He had worked his way through the system—Sarasota, Charleston in the Sally League, Fort Myers, Double A Ball at Memphis, and finally, two seasons at Triple-A Omaha. The only bump in the road for Cone was a badly torn knee, injured in a collision at home plate, which forced him to undergo surgery and to rehab for the entirety of the 1983 season. Lucky for him, he got to rehab at home and hang out with his homeboy Royals. At 20 years old, he was out partying with George Brett and his pitching hero Dennis Leonard. And his eyes got opened to the darker side of the party life by the spectacle of the cocaine abuse on the club, which led later that year to arrests and prison terms for four prominent Royals. But Cone was loving baseball—the talk, the competition, the camaraderie, the wild, free life.

He pitched a little in 1986, about 23 innings. Some of his minor league buddies were already on the club—Mark Gubicza, Danny Jackson. He went off and had a great season of winter ball in Puerto Rico; he also met his future wife there, a woman named Lynn DiGioia, who was vacationing with her folks. With everything flying high for the young Cone— his career, his love life, his prospects in general—it all came crashing in a single morning. In spring training, Kansas City general manager John Schuerholz called Cone in and told him he was a New York Met.

Today, it is up there with the worst trades in history: Met rookie catcher Ed Hearn (who'd labored eight years in the minors), plus pitcher Rick Anderson and a minor leaguer, for Cone and a minor league outfielder named Chris Jelic. Legend has it that K.C. scouts, on the lookout for a solid catcher, saw Hearn on a Met West Coast trip, playing for an injured Gary Carter, who'd twisted a knee. It was August, and the Mets were 15 games up in the N.L. East. They roared through the Dodgers, the Giants, and the Padres, hardly breaking a sweat, winning eight of nine on their western swing. Hearn got seven hits in 26 at-bats. He looked like a winner; he looked like he could handle pitchers. Of course, he was handling Gooden, Darling, Ojeda, Fernandez.

Unfortunately for the Royals, Hearn would wreck his shoulder and play only 14 more games in his career after the trade. Unfortunately for Hearn, he would struggle with kidney failure and cancer in his postbaseball life. Fortunately for the Mets, they got a young talent poised for stardom in the Big Apple. As for Cone, he was devastated at first—finally ready to play for his hometown team and he's traded. But the survivor instinct that would later come to characterize Cone came to the fore almost immediately. He arrived at the Mets camp intent on staying on the club—no more Triple-A Ball. He blew everyone away with his pitching speed, his ball movement, his ballsy attitude. He seemed to fit in with the cocky and arrogant Mets, who swaggered with success up and down the Upper East Side of Manhattan. His new girlfriend, from nearby Connecticut, squired him around a city he would come to own.

The Mets were coming off their spectacular 1986 success—winning 108 regular-season games, running away with their division, taking the Astros in a dramatic six-game series, and then, against the Red Sox . . . Mookie, Buckner, etc. World champs.

Heading into the 1987 season, the Mets looked like a dynasty. Young Cone, 24 years old, was jumping aboard at just the right time. He earned his stripes early, getting unmercifully strafed in an April game against the Astros but taking it manfully, showing almost a veteran's hidebound confidence. In May, however, he smashed a finger in what can only be called a bunting mishap at Candlestick, and missed 10 weeks. The Mets, under the dynastic pressure, began to unravel—Gooden went into drug rehab—and the team lost the division late in the year to the Cardinals. Cone on the year went 5-6.

THE NEXT YEAR, 1988, would be perhaps Cone's finest overall as a pro, but would also feature his greatest professional embarrassment. He won 20 games, lost only 3. The Mets won their division handily, by 15 games over Pittsburgh, and faced the Dodgers for the pennant, a team they had lost to only once all year. The Mets were cocky, Cone was young and invincible.

Heading into Los Angeles for the opening of the series, Bobby Ojeda versus Orel Hershiser, Cone agreed to write a column after each game. He would come to regret it. A New York beat writer ghosted it, and one notable column featured some high-schoolish taunting words from Cone, ridiculing Hershiser and Dodger reliever Jay Howell after the Mets eked out a Game One victory. The next day, there was an uproar when Cone's column reached the Dodger dugout; Cone was visibly distraught as he stood on the mound, his face, literally, red, as if with shame. The verbal abuse at Dodger Stadium rattled him; he lasted only two innings, the

Mets lost 6–3. Although Cone later pitched a gutsy complete-game five-hitter to force a game seven, the Mets couldn't overcome his Game Two meltdown and Kirk Gibson's 12th-inning homer in Game Four (following Mike Scioscia's ninth-inning game-tying shot off Gooden). The favored Mets went down.

Roger Angell, in his warmly avuncular and insightful book about Cone, says the incident established Cone as a stand-up gentleman; he could have sidestepped embarrassment by exposing the folly of player-bylined articles in the tabloids, but he didn't. He didn't talk about the column being based on a quick phone conversation with the reporter. Cone didn't point out the obvious to save his skin, and everyone inside the Mets organization and inside sports journalism admired him for it. There's such a thing as taking one for the team, but Cone took one for the whole enterprise that baseball is—an entertainment pretending to be news.

After the disappointing early ouster of the talented '88 club, the Mets slowly went to hell. Cone pitched well and a lot, posting three consecutive 14-win seasons, with good ERAs—3.52, 3.23, 3.29—and leading the league in strikeouts in '90 and '91. Cone soldiered on. He prowled Manhattan, talked to the press intelligently, patiently; managed to dust himself off from a few scrapes with sex scandals—an alleged rape at the end of the 1991 season in Philadelphia (the charge was later dropped; Cone struck out 19 Phillies the night he was expecting to be arrested); a charge that Cone exposed himself to two women while in the bullpen, which surfaced in 1992, and which Cone adamantly denied, and which came to nothing; and then the bizarre implication that Lynn DiGioia was the unnamed woman who had filed a rape complaint in Florida against Dwight Gooden, Vince Coleman, and Daryl Boston. Bottom line, base-ballwise: two second-place finishes for the Mets, followed by two fifth-place finishes. For Cone, the steady, powerful, and improving pitching won him three consecutive salary arbitration hearings: His pay went from $332,000 in '89 to $1.3 million in '90, his first arbitration win, to $2.35 million the next year, to $4.25 million for 1992. If only the Mets could return to their winning form.

On August 27 of that year, the Mets were languishing, 14 games behind the Pirates. Cone, still pitching well and leading the league in strikeouts again, was due to become a free agent at the end of the year. He and his agent Steve Fehr (brother of Players Association executive director Don Fehr, all of them Kansas Citians) had turned down a $17-million, four-year deal from Met GM Frank Cashen. So Cashen worked a trade—and Cone, just like that, was gone. To Toronto, for Jeff Kent and Ryan Thompson, two blue-chip prospects. Cone—knocking David Wells out of the rotation—would win four games for Toronto down the stretch, and be very much a part of the team's postseason. In the end, the world championship would be theirs, Blue Jays over Atlanta, with Cone holding the Braves to one run in six innings in the clinching game, won by Toronto in the 11th thanks to a two-run double by Dave Winfield. A ring for Cone, but Cone, now a free agent, would move on, forever after to be known as a gun for hire, this guy who was loyal to his Royals till Ed Hearn beckoned, loyal to the wild Mets till Cashen closed his checkbook. Now he'd earned the right to shop his services.

Cone and Steve Fehr entertained interest from the Yankees, who were also courting Greg Maddux. When Fehr was able to get Ewing Kaufman to match the Yankee offer of $18 million for three years but also front-load the contract, in anticipation of a work stoppage, Cone went home. For a moment, he was baseball's highest paid player.

Going home helped Cone in many ways: Personally, he escaped the party grind of New York; he was able to reconcile things with his long-suffering girlfriend Lynn, after their relationship had foundered; and he spent a lot of time with his father. Professionally, after years of challenging hitters at every instant with a dizzying variety of stuff, and reaching some of the highest pitch counts in the modern era, including a legendary 166-pitch game just before being traded to Toronto (it was a 1–0 shutout win over the Giants), Cone was hearing a different, gentler tune from his manager, Hal McRae, and pitching coach, Bruce Kison. He was counseled to pitch more economically. "At first," said Cone, "it was very difficult. When I went out on the field in a Mets uniform, I felt strikeouts were expected of me, and therefore I ran the counts deep." It was a change of pitching philosophy that may have staved off physical disaster.

Cone pitched in bad luck in 1993, going 11-14 with hardly any run support, but with an ERA of 3.33. In 1994, of course, the strike finally hit, as Steve Fehr had anticipated. Still, Cone had a tremendous year. He won 16 of 23 starts, lost only 5, and had an ERA under 3.00. The Royals won 14 straight as the strike date approached, and closed in on the White Sox in the Central Division. But then it was over, the strike was called, the players walked.

During the long dark days of the player strike, from August 1994 through April '95, baseball fans saw a lot of Cone, in his role as American League player representative, wearing a suit jacket and open-necked shirt, either standing next to Don Fehr along with N.L. rep Tom Glavine, or answering questions on courthouse steps about what had or had not gone down in the latest meeting. Of his union activity, Cone observed, "I guess it kind of stemmed from my father. He was a union guy, and I guess it was just in my blood."

By Cone's own reckoning, as relayed to Roger Angell, his most crucial contribution was toward the end of the strike, at a player meeting in Florida. With defections among some prominent players rumored, and minor leaguers being courted as replacements, he took the podium at a packed hotel ballroom in Tampa, turned his back to the audience of major and minor leaguers, bent over, grabbed his ankles, and told the assembled in locker-room language just what the owners wanted to do to them— "without Vaseline." Solidarity among the rank and file was maintained. When the 234-day strike was settled, and play resumed, Cone was still a Kansas City Royal. Within a week, however, the A.L. player rep, Kansas City's favorite son, the Cy Young Award–winning David Cone, was traded, back to Toronto, for three guys named Stynes, Medrano, and Sinnes.

CONE SPENT BUT HALF a season with the Blue Jays, who thought they had a chance to return to the form that had produced A.L. East titles in four of the past six years and two world titles. But when late July found them in last place, they moved Cone and his salary to what had become Cone's second home—New York—in this case, to the Yankees, in return for three guys named Gordon, Janzen, and Jarvis. The Yankees were tied for second place with Baltimore, and nipping at the heels of the Red Sox.

Cone would win 18 games combined for the '95 season, itself shortened by 18 games because of the late strike settlement. With the Yankees, Cone went 9-2 in his 13 starts. For the first time since 1981, New York made it to the postseason, as the wild card entry in the American League playoffs. It was a sentimental struggle, as Yankee fan favorite Don Mattingly was playing in the last season of a career that lasted exactly as long as the Yankee postseason drought. This was Donnie Baseball's one chance. The team almost made it. Facing the young, hungry Seattle Mariners team of Ken Griffey, Edgar Martinez, Tino Martinez, Randy Johnson, and Luis Sojo (playing shortstop ahead of rookie Alex Rodriguez), New York won Game One despite some rocky pitching by Cone, and Game Two thanks to a 15th-inning Jim Leyritz homer. When the series moved to Seattle, Yankees up 2–0, Randy Johnson struck out 10 before a wild Mariners crowd—

there had never ever been a postseason game in Seattle—to take Game
Three, and Edgar Martinez, who would hit .571 for the series, slugged a
grand slam in the eighth inning of Game Four to force a fifth and deciding
game. In the end, Randy Johnson would be called from the bullpen by
manager Lou Piniella, on just one day's rest, as would the Yankees' Jack
McDowell. They would be the pitchers of record when Edgar Martinez hit
a two-run double in the 11th to win it for Seattle, 6–5. Not lost in the hero-
ics by any means was the stirring effort by Cone, the Yankees' fifth-game
starter, who, on his 147th pitch, walked in the tying run in the eighth
inning. It was his last pitch of the year. Mattingly retired, having seen his
first and only postseason series (he hit .417 with four doubles and a home
run), and George Steinbrenner showed manager Buck Showalter the door
and brought in a replacement who was derided in the New York papers as a
loser—Brooklyn's own Joe Torre. "Clueless Joe," read one of the New York
tabloids.

Of course, 1996 would be magic for the Yankees. Tino Martinez was
picked up from Seattle, in exchange for Russ Davis; they added Cecil
Fielder and Mariano Duncan and pitcher Jimmy Key. They picked up a
perfect-game pitcher named Kenny Rogers.

Cone got a big contract—three years, $18 million—and then found
himself off to a hot start, with a 3-1 record and a league-leading ERA, but
also a growing numbness in the fingers of his pitching hand, something
that had been bothering him since spring training. The Yankee physician,
Dr. Stuart Hershon, grew concerned. Cone missed a start in late April, his
first in nine years, and underwent an angiogram. When his ring finger and
pinkie turned purple after his next start (a complete-game victory over the
White Sox), the situation grew more grave. The angiogram had shown
clots in Cone's hand and wrist, but no one knew where they came from.
Medicine had balked in the early innings of Cone's circulation problem,
and let the man pitch. A follow-up test, however, showed an aneurysm
under the shoulder, and it was life-threatening. A team of top vascular
surgeons and orthopedists convened to chart a course. In the end, they
decided to remove the arterial section, deep in Cone's armpit, where the
offending aneurysm was parked, and replace it with a one-inch vein graft
taken from his left thigh. The operation took three hours. It was May 10.
The Yankees were in first place, 2.5 games in front of Baltimore. Cone was
33 years old. Many assumed his career was over. How could he possibly
subject a grafted artery in the armpit to the rigors of major league pitching? How could he risk a clot running into his brain, his heart?

When Cone returned in September—he had been counted out by many, at least for the rest of the season, if not his career—he proceeded to put what Angell calls "the Conean imprimatur" on the event, his signature mix of athletic prowess, human frailty, personal pride, and emotional rawness. It was evident in almost everything Cone did, and blazingly so in rare, unsurpassable instances like that September night. Cone, with his father making a surprise appearance at the ballpark, pitched no-hit ball against the Athletics for seven innings; Torre took him out, his pitch count at 85. "If I leave him in and he throws 105 or 106 pitches and wakes up with a sore arm tomorrow, I'd never forgive myself," said Torre. Cone didn't argue. He was happy to be back, and to see his father. "I can't remember a major league game where I could make eye contact with my dad. I kept wondering if he was going to yell at me for hanging a pitch or something."

The Yankees won their division and played Texas in the championship series. Cone was rattled around in Game One—Torre as much as paid homage to Cone's season of rehab by giving him the start—but the team bounced back and took the series in four games. The Orioles, having vanquished Cleveland in four, were next. The best-of-seven for the American League pennant would open at Yankee Stadium, the O's Scott Erickson versus Andy Pettitte; Game Two would be David Wells for Baltimore, David Cone for New York.

GAME ONE WAS MADE famous by a 12-year-old kid from New Jersey named Jeffrey Maier, who leaned over the railing and grabbed a fly ball hit by rookie Derek Jeter just before it had a chance to plop into the glove of Orioles right-fielder Tony Tarasco. Umpire Rich Garcia called it a home run; the Orioles argued, to no avail. It allowed the Yankees to tie the game at 4–4 in the eighth, and Bernie Williams ended it with a legitimate home run in the 11th. In Game Two, David Wells, 11–14 on the season, got nailed for consecutive singles by Jeter, Tim Raines, and Williams and was down 2–0 after 10 pitches. Cone, who loaded the bases on walks in the first before escaping, gave up a two-run homer to Todd Zeile in the third, and Wells settled down and blanked the Yankees. The Orioles prevailed, 5–3, to even the series. But then again, the series was over—behind Jimmy Key and Andy Pettitte and big home runs by Darryl Strawberry, the Yanks swept the three games in Baltimore to take the series. Wells went home to California. The Braves came to town.

Two days later, the Yankees were happy to get out of their own town. Scoring only one run against Smoltz and Maddux in Games One and Two at the Stadium, the Yanks arrived in Atlanta in trouble. Torre handed the ball to Cone, who was set to face Tom Glavine, a 15-game winner that year with an ERA under 3.00 Cone pitched beautifully, holding the Braves to one run and four hits over six. Strawberry and Williams provided the run support and the Yanks got back in the series with a 5–2 win. When Kenny Rogers, a complete dud since the Yankees signed him to a lucrative contract and a target for fan derision, gave up five earned runs in two innings, it looked as if Atlanta was back in charge in Game Four. And that didn't change, till the eighth inning, when Jim Leyritz, following a botched double-play grounder by Rafael Belliard, hit a three-run home run off Mark Wohlers to tie the game. The Yanks then scored two in the 10th to win it, tying the series at two games apiece. Two pitching masterpieces—one by Andy Pettitte in Game Five, and the other by Jimmy Key in Game Six, back in New York, gave the Yankees their first World Series title since 1978.

WELLS WAS A FREE AGENT after playing out his one-year, $3.2-million contract with Baltimore in '96. He was in the driver's seat now. He liked what he'd seen of the Yankees, liked the players there—Cone, Fielder, Jimmy Key; and the Yankees liked what they'd seen of him. Good left-handers are always important in Yankee Stadium—to keep left-handed hitters from becoming too intimate with the short porch in right. Gomez, Ford, Guidry, Righetti—now Key and Pettitte. Why not Wells? But Wells's agent asked too much money of Yankee GM Bob Watson. The Yankees didn't even make a counteroffer, according to Wells's recent book. But then Jimmy Key took off for Baltimore and $35 million and suddenly Wells looked like an affordable left-hander. And he was dying to play for the Yanks.

When longtime Red Sox Roger Clemens hit the market, and three big clubs in the A.L. went after him—New York, Cleveland, Toronto—Wells was sure he would be a well-compensated consolation prize for any team losing out on the Rocket. Thing was, the Yanks made the best offer for Clemens, but Clemens opted for the Blue Jays, for less, while Wells got a second-best offer from the Yankees (Toronto's was better), and he opted for New York.

Three years, $13.25 million, the good fortune of playing in pinstripes, and then, on a Sunday morning in January, the bad that comes with the good: In a Tampa supermarket, Wells, loading a shopping cart with NFL play-off game-day provisions, doubled over in pain, went white. Three thousand miles away, his mother Annie was stricken with a heart attack. Soon, his pager would ring. It was his wife, Nina: Come home right away.

Wells made the trip to California for his mother's funeral, but ended up in a roadside brawl and broke his left hand throwing a haymaker at some guy he contends took his car keys (they were under the seat). So Wells didn't get off on his best foot with the Yankee brass—in fact, he developed gout in his left foot in spring training, but the team had other discontents among the malcontents—Fielder, Wade Boggs, Charlie Hayes. At this point in Wells's autobiography—at the start of the '97 season—he took a breath and offered "one quick paragraph on David Cone."

"The guy's a monster . . . he's a lot like me . . . he just gets way better press. Don't let the 'smart guy' stuff fool you. . . . Don't let the 'student of the game' stories turn your head. Coney is without question every bit the rabble-rousing, ball-busting, beer-drinking goofball that I am."

WELLS HAD AN up-and-down year in 1997 as a Yankee, going 16-10. His ERA was high, he gave up a lot of hits, he pitched well enough to win a lot but had long stretches of ineffectiveness or, as he puts it, "sucking eggs." Andy Pettitte, following his 21-win season of the year before, led the staff again, with 18 wins against 7 losses. Not to be overlooked, however, was the effort of David Cone, still making a nimble recovery from his vein graft surgery. Cone won 12 and lost 6, pitched 195 innings and struck out 222 batters, third in the league; his ERA was 2.82, also third in the league, but he broke down in August with tendinitis in his pitching shoulder and spent a month on the disabled list. By season's end, his arm would be killing him.

There were other problems. The team was squabbling; Boggs asked to be traded, the club tried to unload an ineffective Kenny Rogers for Greg Vaughn of San Diego, the whole club resented the money paid to Japanese pitcher Hideki Irabu, and the team was stuck at .500 ball in late May. Riding Pettitte and Wells in midsummer, the Yankees roared into contention; they stalled toward the end and had to be content with a wild card showing. In the playoffs against Cleveland, nothing was meant to be in Yankee blue. Cone opened the series and was down 5–0 after the first inning, his shoulder throbbing. Wells pitched a marvelous third game, a five-hit complete game, but the Yankees couldn't get the clutch hit throughout the series, and Cleveland, it seemed, could, and the Indians moved on in five games. Season over—the Yanks did not repeat as world champs. They would have to regroup and retool to get back to where they felt they belonged—with champagne pouring in late, late October.

BASEBALL HAD A LEAP year in 1998; it leaped from 28 teams to 30, with the addition of Arizona and Tampa Bay, its second expansion in five years. The season also saw some hallowed records being grandly assailed and even taken down; it was the year of McGwire and Sosa. It was also the year of the Yankees, who won 114 regular-season games, breaking a 44-year-old American League record. Around both leagues, it was a year of great achievement, both on the field and at the box office. But it was also a year of ignominious failures. There were no pennant races—the six divisions were won by wide margins: 22, 18, 12.5, 9.5, 9, and one narrowish one, the 3 games that separated Texas and Anaheim in the A.L. West, baseball's worst division. And while the attendance growth overall of seven million customers was impressive, it was owing to the new franchises and their new ballparks, and a few other improved turnstile performances (thanks to Yanks and the home-run race), while Montreal, Pittsburgh, Cincinnati, and the Chicago White Sox, not to mention the five-year-old defending world champion Marlins, who had gutted their team to make ends meet, saw attendance decline significantly. Why such achievement in the presence of such failure? Is there a connection between record-setting performances and competitive imbalance? Economist Andrew Zimbalist, in his recent book *May the Best Team Win*, puts forth a theory: He contends that expansion—particularly the four teams added in the 1990s—was responsible for the extreme performances. He attributes it to "talent compression."

Until 1998, most of baseball's modern-day individual records were set between 1910 and World War II—Rogers Hornsby's .424 average in 1924, Hack Wilson's RBI record of 190 set in 1930, Babe Ruth's 177 runs in 1921 among them. Is it because players of that time were better than today's? Zimbalist says no—he contends that baseball statistics "are the product of competing forces and reveal little about the absolute quality of the players."

Talent compression has to do with the distribution of baseball skills in the population; it follows a normal, bell-shaped curve. The more people selected to play ball relative to the population, the greater the difference between the best and the worst players. That is to say, if major league baseball had 100 teams instead of 30, and fielded 2,500 players instead of 750, Barry Bonds would be standing in there against more bums than he is now. However, if the population grows and the number of major league teams remains the same, as if did from 1903 to 1961, when the population jumped from 80 million to 181 million and baseball fielded the same 16 clubs, the distribution of talent becomes more compressed. Willie Mays was playing against much better competition than his godson Barry Bonds, which is a truism regardless of the question of how good Mays is compared to Bonds. In the 1940s and 1950s, Zimbalist points out, baseball began to accept black and Latin American players, which only accentuated the compression. By this measurement, major league baseball was at is most competitive in 1960, the last year before the first expansion. Since then, there has been a continuous talent decompression; today, thanks to four decades of expansion, adding 14 teams overall, the ratio of major league players to U.S. population is about what it was in the 1930s, when those many individual performance records were set. Does this explain why there were four perfect games before 1960, and 10 since? Might it explain why there were four in the decade of the 1990s? It probably does explain the numerical heights reached by sluggers Sosa, McGwire, Rodriguez, and Bonds, though weight training and steroids might have something to do with it. But don't pitchers pump iron, too?

TALENT COMPRESSION OR NO, the Yankees, having sipped from the championship cup in '96 and then watched the lowly Marlins beat the Indians in seven games in '97, began an ingenious retooling heading into '98, which started with the pickup of Scott Brosius to play third, finally putting an end to the unsightly Charlie Hayes–Wade Boggs squabble. They threw big Yankee dollars at a Cuban defector, Orlando Hernandez—a mystery wrapped around an enigma and a leg kick. And, unhappy about heading into another season with Andy Fox and Rey Sanchez sharing second base, they shipped four players to Minnesota for Chuck Knoblauch, a four-time All-Star who had hit as high as .341. The team let Cecil Fielder go and added Chili Davis. Sprinkle Jeter, Bernie Williams, Paul O'Neill, Tino Martinez, and Jorge Posada into the lineup, and you have a powerful club.

And they showed their stuff nearly from the get-go. After dropping three in a row to start the season, in Anaheim and Oakland, with Pettitte, Wells, and Cone taking the losses, the team got very hot, winning 20 out of 22 at one stretch. Quickly, the Yankees made a mockery of the A.L. East race and of all competition. In the middle of May, they were playing .750 ball. Cone had bounced back from last season's shoulder fatigue, Pettitte was sharp, even Irabu was mowing them down. Hernandez—El Duque—was still rounding into form in Tampa, not to arrive till June. Wells, for the most part, was pitching well, but for a meltdown in Arlington on May 6 that led to an ugly confrontation with Torre. Wells had blown a 9–0 lead and stomped off the mound, flipping the ball over his back to the manager. A tense meeting with Torre later managed to clear the air. Torre assured Wells he had confidence in him; Wells seemed unsure. Wells assured Torre he wouldn't quit when things didn't go his way, and Torre accepted that, and the Yankee ship sailed on. When the Minnesota Twins came to town for a weekend set in May, the Yankees' record stood at 27-9. Cone was 5-1, Wells 4-1.

Minnesota stunk. They were 18–23 going into the May 17 matinee, and would be worse if not for the expert, never-say-die managing of Tom Kelly. The batting averages of their starting lineup read thus: .239, .123, .255, 256, .269, .253, .211, .234, and .220. The Twins, a small-market team, were depending on home-grown prospects, journeymen, and a prodigal son come back to St. Paul, where he was born.

IT WAS COOL AND overcast in New York, 59 degrees, the sky one white glare. The Yankees had won the night before, 5–2, behind the four-hit pitching of Ramiro Mendoza and Mariano Rivera; Jeter went 4 for 5 with three runs scored and two RBI, on his way to his best year. There were 35,000 fans on hand. For Saturday's game, the place was nearly packed, almost 50,000 people there to see the red-hot Yankees. And to get the latest in novelty giveaways, a Beanie Baby—white with a red heart on the chest. It had a name: Valentina.

Boomer Wells took the mound for the Yankees, with a 9-5 lifetime record versus the Twins. Manager Tom Kelly had stacked his anemic lineup with right-handed hitters, except for the leadoff man, Matt Lawton. Lawton was a fleet young center fielder, hitting .245, in his fourth year, out of Gulfport, Mississippi. He was playing regularly since Otis Nixon had his jaw broken early in the season. Wells got right to work for the 1:05 start. Fastball high, fastball called strike, breaking ball low. Ahead 2-1, Lawton then lofted a fly to left off an outside fastball, and Wells had his first out.

Lawton was followed by good-field, no-hit Brent Gates, playing second base instead of the promising Todd Walker, whose good stick was what had emboldened the Twins to trade Knoblauch to the Yankees. But Walker batted left and was on the bench on this day. Gates, a star college player at the University of Minnesota, drafted by Oakland, was in his fifth year. He was hardly hitting his weight, which was 180 pounds, but he was a switch-hitter, so he got the start. Wells followed the same pattern—two fastballs, a curve, and another fastball—with the same result: a shallow fly, this time to left-center where Bernie Williams hauled it in. Up third for the Twins was sure-fire Hall of Famer Paul Molitor, out of St. Paul, Minnesota, playing his last year. He would finish his career with more than 3,000 hits and more than 500 stolen bases, something only four other players have done (that puts him in an exclusive class—with Lou Brock, Ty Cobb, Honus Wagner, and Rickey Henderson). But this season he was hitting .255. On one pitch Molitor was out, nubbing a grounder to Chuck Knoblauch at second—but as Yankee fans would come to know, that wasn't necessarily automatic. The night previous, Knoblauch had made two errors, his third and fourth of the year (he would finish the season with 13, make 26 the next year, and end up a left fielder in Kansas City). With Molitor running steady-hard to first, Knoblauch kept moving as he threw the ball and it tailed. Only a high stretch by Tino Martinez saved the play. Three out.

The Yankees would be looking at LaTroy Hawkins on the mound, a rangy right-hander with live stuff but just learning the trade. He was 2-3 on the year with an ERA over 5.00. The lights came on at the Stadium. Hawkins put New York down fairly quietly—Jeter, after singling, was stranded.

Marty Cordova, the Twins right fielder in his fourth year in the big leagues, started his long day (his longest inning will come with his glove on). In his first at-bat, the right-hander tapped back to Wells after falling behind 1-2. Ron Coomer was up next. A versatile player, solid hitter, playing first base this day, Coomer was one of the toughest hitters in the lineup for Wells, 8-13 against him lifetime. And he almost got Wells right there in the second inning. Wells started him off with two breaking balls—knowing Coomer has owned him. Then he threw a fastball in the dirt. With the count 2-1, Wells tried to slice the outside corner with another fastball and Coomer lined a shot down the right-field line that went into the stands, but just short and to the right of the foul pole. It was nearly a home run, nearly a double rattling around in the corner. Instead, it was merely a strike. Wells then fanned him. Alex Ochoa, playing right field, billed as a five-tool player when in the Baltimore system, was missing at least a couple, not hitting much for average (.253) or power (2 HRs). Once traded to the Mets with Damon Buford for Bobby Bonilla, he had come to the Twins in return for one Rick Becker. He popped to catcher Posada.

The Yankees gave Wells something to work with in their half of the second, thanks to Cordova, who turned twice on Bernie Williams's opposite-field liner. It went over his head and Williams ended up on second with a double. After he advanced to third on an out, a wild pitch got Williams in for the first run of the game.

Wells seemed to be getting into a groove. He struck out the side in the third, as he began showing the big, slow curve, 10 to 4 in sweep (from 10 o'clock on the dial to 4 o'clock). Rookie third-baseman Jon Shave looked at it for strike three, rookie catcher Javier Valentin had the day's best at-bat versus Wells, a nine-pitch affair that ended with a fastball at the letters, called strike three. Pat Meares followed. In his sixth year with the Twins, the utility man with the pretty good bat struck out on Wells's first changeup of the afternoon.

The Yankees went quietly in their half of the third, as young LaTroy Hawkins showed his good stuff, getting easily through Brosius, Knoblauch, and Jeter. (Hawkins, five years later, in 2003, would bedevil the Yankees in a relief role in Game One of the Division Series playoffs.)

In any perfect game, there are two turns on the trip through the 27 outs. In the fourth, Wells made the first—facing leadoff man Matt Lawton for the second time. He had flied to left in the first, but here found Wells momentarily at a loss—two fastballs sailed way high and a curveball stayed up, too, and Lawton was looking at a 3-0 pitch. Wells nipped the corner for a strike. On the next pitch, Lawton popped up to Jeter. Brent Gates stepped in and struck out on an 0-2 curveball. Then it was Molitor, who seemed to be looking curveball, and got it, but Wells had taken a little off and it was pulled foul, hard. Wells then threw his second changeup of the day, fooling the veteran, who swung over it and missed. Molitor then hacked at a high fastball and flied out to Chad Curtis in medium left field. Twelve up and down.

In the Yankee fourth, Bernie Williams, from his wide crouched stance, hit a low line drive into the seats in right field to give Wells a 2–0 lead.

In the Twins fifth, the strike zone of Tim McClelland began to be a factor, this during a period of the greatest umpire abuse. It was only the year before that Eric Gregg foisted his own private, floating strike zone on an unwilling public during the Indians-Marlins World Series. McClelland's calls on this May afternoon raised not a single argument, but would not be tolerated today by the QuesTec System and image-conscious Bud Selig. Poor Marty Cordova: He took a fastball at the knees, or below, for a strike; fought off a fastball in on the hands; and then went down looking at a fastball six inches wide of the plate. He dragged his lumber. Wells trudged back up the hill of the mound and scanned the outfield; he lifted his bare, meaty left arm into the air as if reaching for something, but really just stretching it, and then jackknifed it at the elbow and with his fingers tugged at his jersey around his neck. The ball popped back into his mitt from Tino, and he was ready to go. Next was Coomer. Wells got the curve over for a called strike, then delivered a fastball tight to even the count. He then offered up the big slow curve, which dropped in the dirt, but McClelland called it a strike, and the crowd, aware now of what could be happening, roared its approval. Wells came back with the same pitch—why not?—and again it broke into the dirt, but Coomer took a half-swing, defensively, and missed and was called out. Up stepped Alex Ochoa, and Wells fell behind immediately, 2-0. Suddenly, he couldn't get the breaking ball over, and McClelland wasn't helping him. He went back to the fastball and missed, but McClelland had a heart, maybe—he called it a strike. Ochoa swung right over a breaking ball in the middle of the plate to even the count and then chopped a breaking ball at Knoblauch for out number three. A neat inning for Wells—12 pitches, and 68 through five innings.

Nursing the 2–0 lead into the sixth, Wells seemed to be in a hurry. He looked excited but serious on the mound, and he worked quickly. Rookie Jon Shave struck out on four pitches—three fastballs and a curve foul-tipped and held by Posada. Valentin was next, and he too went down on four pitches, the last being the slow curve, Wells's ninth strikeout. Pat Meares, number nine in the order, managed to put the ball in play—a weak pop to Bernie Williams in short center field. Another 12-pitch inning for the cruising Boomer.

The Yankees went quietly in the bottom of the sixth. Fortunately, with the day cool, Wells didn't need to be spelled by long home at-bats. He hustled back to work. Through the order once again, for the third time.

Pesky young Lawton stepped in. A small strike zone. Wells overthrew the fastball; Posada stood up to catch it. A fastball low and away put Wells in the hole. After running through an order of almost all righties, Wells seemed lost as to where to bite the strike zone against a lefthander. But Lawton showed how green he was, or how bold, swinging at a 2-0 pitch. He hit a soft out to Williams in center. Then, a tough out: Throwing all fastballs to the second-baseman Brent Gates, Wells found himself with a full count after missing in the dirt on a 2-2 pitch. The crowd grew restless. Wells peered in. Gates hit a one-hop shot to Tino's right, but Tino was there and made the play unassisted, although Wells was there to cover.

The Yankees secured the game, to this point a rather taut 2–0 contest, with two runs in the home half of the seventh. Twins right-fielder Cordova turned out to be a big help. Playing Bernie too deep, he let a routine single turn into a hustled double. And then Strawberry, in a 1-for-22 slump, hit a high fly down the left-field line. Cordova, who'd been playing in the gap, ran a long way, leaped at the wall and banged his face into it as the ball missed his glove and caromed back into the playing field. Cordova threw up his hands as if to say there was fan interference. But there was no Jeffrey Maier, only a Yankee fan who missed the ball by more than Cordova did. Strawberry pulled into third and it was 3–0. Curtis doubled him home and the Yanks led 4–0 going into the eighth.

Doesn't it always seem that the guy who made a great defensive play leads off the next inning? About as often as a guy who blunders out there is the first up. Cordova: fastball low; fastball fouled back to even the count; changeup from Wells stayed high. Then Cordova grounded a fastball to Jeter for out number 22. The tough Coomer was next. Wells started him off with fastballs—missing for ball one, but then getting a foul back to even the count. An inside slider made it 2–1. Then, a low outside fastball rocketed right at Knoblauch and hopped up, a nasty face-high hop, and Knoblauch knocked it down and scurried to his right, turned, and made the perfect throw. Two down. The hapless Ochoa was next and Wells was out to mix the kid up, starting with a curve high for a ball, then a changeup that Ochoa stared at, 1-1. A fastball sailed wide. Wells got the next one in a little closer and Ochoa popped to first.

By now the lore has been established: David Cone kept David Wells loose by suggesting he debut a new pitch—a knuckler—thereby breaking the tension with the loose enough Wells, who by late in the game appeared to have overcome whatever form of half-drunkenness or hangover he may have had (the galleys and the final version of *Perfect I'm Not* disagree on his condition). On television, Cone was visible in the dugout with a dark blue warmup jacket zipped and pulled up over his nose and with sunglasses and Yankee cap on, hiding the emotions that no doubt swarmed over his always readable face.

It would be the two rookies—Jon Shave and Javier Valentin—followed by Pat Meares, standing between Wells and the 13th perfect game of the modern era. The crowd of 49,820 roared its collective anguish as the first pitch to Shave was high. But good cheer returned at an even higher volume as Wells's fastball was fouled back. No one wanted a walk to stand in the way of a perfect game, a lonely walk. It had happened to Milt Pappas in 1972: After Pappas had retired 26 in a row, rookie ump Bruce Froemming called two close pitches balls, and pinch-hitter Larry Stahl worked out a walk. (Pappas is still mad.) Shave, who had already struck out twice, took a slider for a strike on the inside corner and was behind, 1-2. He then fouled off the big 10–4 curve. Wells, working deliberately now, missed inside with another slider. He and Posada decided to go back to fastballs. Shave popped one foul, out of play. But the next was lofted to right-fielder Paul O'Neill. Two outs to go.

Valentin, also a double strikeout victim, watched the big loopy Wells curve miss inside. A fastball on the outside corner—an unhittable pitch—evened the count. Wells loaded up the big curve again, figuring these rookies couldn't hit the curveball, and he was right again, as Valentin swung a foot from a ball that ended at his ankles. Then a fastball went right through Valentin's bat for strike three. Posada dropped the ball but Valentin was done and didn't run to first and was tagged out standing there.

Up came Pat Meares. The crowd noise was deafening. Wells tugged at his shirt. His paunch stood proudly over his belt, looking, in pinstripes, athletic somehow (Wells looked fatter in the road gray uniform). Meares was up there swinging. He fouled a fastball back to the screen. Just as the tension mounted again, as Wells wound, and delivered, it was over—an even louder expression of relief thundered forth; Wells looked up expectantly as Meares's fly ball lifted with no hint of menace down the right-field line where Ol' Reliable Paul O'Neill glided over, all assurance in his

long-haunched stride, and hauled it in—after all, he'd been part of a perfect game before, with the Reds a decade ago. Wells pumped his left arm
once, twice, three times. And was mobbed and carried off the field, waving his Yankee hat to the fans, his face in a broad smile.

   Though there would be much ado in four years' time about what
Wells did the night before his perfect game, let the record show that on
May 17, 1998, Wells's work day was done at about 3:30 in the afternoon,
and the Yankees had the next day off. And Wells and Cone went out until
the wee hours became less wee—East Side, West Side, all around the
town; they were still up for the morning rush hour, or so says the unreli-
able Boomer. We do know he made it to *Letterman* later that night,
whether he remembers it or not.

AND WE KNOW THAT the Yankees' year continued just as magically.
While the national fandom became entranced by the Sosa-McGwire
home-run race, by the specter of Roger Maris's family deporting themselves with a kind of prairie-home grace, the Yanks just kept pounding
the daylights out of the opposition, and Yankee fans had themselves a
gluttonous summer of easy wins. Cone was nearly untouchable, on his
way to an astounding 20-7 season; Wells would finish 18-4. The two ran
down the August and September stretch by rooming together on the
road, paying for big suites together where they could entertain the other
guys (ahem). The world was their oyster, for sure. Although the club lost
its focus for a while in September, it was really more in the way of a
breather. They won their division by 22 games. And Wells was awesome
in the postseason, beating Texas in the opener, 2–0, and Cone closed
them out in Game Three, a Yankee sweep. The Indians, who had eliminated New York in '97, were next, and Wells was given the ball twice,
getting wins each time, striking out 18 in 16 innings. Behind him they
took the opener at the Stadium, 7–2. But things got tougher after that. In
Game Two, Knoblauch chose the 12th inning to inspire the morning
tabloid headline "Blauch-Head!" The Yankee second baseman argued a
call down the first-base line as the go-ahead run, in the person of
Enrique Wilson, flopped across the plate in the extra-inning, 4–1 loss.
Cone pitched expertly and with his usual verve, but left the game in the
eighth with the scored tied at 1–1, having matched with Indians right-
hander Charles Nagy. The Yanks' magical season seemed ready to go up
in smoke when young Bartolo Colon put the Indians up two games to

one, with a masterful four-hit complete game in Game Three. Then, El Duque saved the team, and the season. As Darryl Strawberry tried to inspire the team from his hospital bed (he had just been diagnosed with colon cancer), El Duque just went out and outsmarted the Cleveland hitters in a 4–0 shutout to tie the series at 2–2. And then Wells got the Yankees back on top, notching his second win of the series, pitching into the eighth inning of a 5–3 win. Cone uncharacteristically—although as a pitcher gets older, his characteristics change—almost blew a 6–0 lead in Game Six, but the Yankees hitters responded. And, speaking of the uncharacteristic, Indian shortstop Omar Vizquel made a key throwing error in a three-run Yankee sixth, and it was back to the Fall Classic for New York.

WELLS FOUND OUT in the joyous clubhouse that he had been named MVP of the series. He celebrated in his own fashion, vigorously strafing the man who paid him, George Steinbrenner, with expensive champagne. Everyone loves a winner, even a Boomer.

The San Diego Padres came to New York. No one gave them a chance: Wells beat them in Game One, Hernandez in Game Two, Cone gave up only two hits in six innings, but the Yanks had to rally in the eighth to win Game Three. Andy Pettitte shut them down in Game Four, 3–0, with the help of Jeff Nelson and Mariano Rivera, and the Yankees were world champions for the 24th time. As the celebration in the clubhouse wound down, as it sank in that the Yankees had, incredibly, won their 125th game of the year, Wells led the entire team out onto the field to savor the moment. San Diego, after all, was his town; he was the host; they toasted themselves and smoked cigars.

It was a fun winter for the Yankees. But for Wells, it ended in late February. Reporting for spring training, he got called into Torre's office and was told that he'd been traded, along with Graeme Lloyd and Homer Bush, to Toronto, for Roger Clemens. Although heartbroken, Wells had been through too much—remember Medicine Hat, Cito Gaston, Marge Schott—to be surprised. He had a long hug and chat with Steinbrenner, who told him it was the one deal that he, as general partner, abstained from voting on. "Too personal." So Wells went back to his apartment; Cone joined him later for four hours of beer drinking and spiritual advice. Coney counseled a few days of golf.

THE 1999 CAMPAIGN got off to a dramatic start. There was Joe Torre's announcement that he had prostate cancer, Darryl Strawberry's drug arrest in the spring, the reported deal to make Albert Belle a Yankee, and the courting of free-agent Bernie Williams by Boston. But Belle changed his mind 15 minutes after agreeing to a $52-million Yankee contract, and the Yankees then decided to keep the home-grown Bernie for another seven years at $87.5 million. They also signed Cone to a one-year, $8-million deal.

Clemens was admitted into the Yankee circle, but not without a few messages being sent. The Rocket had always been known as a head-hunter—he'd plunked several Yankees during his time—and Knoblauch and Jeter stepped into the cage against him in spring training sporting full riot gear—shin guards, chest protector, catcher's mask, arm guards. It broke the tension, at least for the Yankee batters. Clemens had a rougher time getting comfortable in his new stripes. He had won 41 games and two Cy Young Awards in his two years in Toronto (after 13 years in Boston). But in those two years, the Blue Jays finished a total of 48 games behind New York. With the Yanks, he managed only 14 wins, had an ERA of 4.60—he looked the same as when the Red Sox figured he was fin-ished. Meanwhile, Wells went to work in Toronto, gave them 17 wins and seven complete games—one more than Clemens—but in the end, the glory would be in New York, not Ontario. The Yankees finished 4 games ahead of the second-place Red Sox, and 14 games ahead of Toronto. Another grand year for the powerful Bombers, but, in a way, the last hur-rah for warrior David Cone.

ALL OF THE FOREGOING comes to nothing—or would come to noth-ing—were it not for the ways in which baseball reaches into people's lives. The exploits of Cy Young or Don Larsen, of Koufax and Catfish and Dennis Martinez, would really amount to less, in the public mind, than the games of jacks played on porch fronts over the decades if not for the endurance of the institution of baseball. Today's Little Leaguers are at least the seventh generation to be following box scores in their local papers, and to have baseball to talk about with their elders. Baseball is America's great perennial, shooting up every spring and blossoming in the summer and ripening in resplendent drama in the fall for every new class of citizen since before the Civil War.

True, libraries are groaning under the weight of paeans to baseball, its

American character, its importance to fathers and sons. And for good reason. It is a wonderfully absorbing sport that has managed to appeal to an
American's sense of fair play. It has become a democratic game, but not
an idealized one. A little corruption, cheating, exploitation, and chi-
canery are an accepted part of the game; still, it is a mite cleaner than
most ventures, and its greatest gift is hope. There's always next year.
There's always, from April till October, a chance to see something amazing, even something perfect, however long the odds might be. And if it
doesn't happen, well, it's really nothing more than a game.

July 18, 1999, was a hot and heavy Sunday morning in the city of
New York—hot from the accumulated heat of a week or more of temperatures in the 90s, and heavy, in an emotional sense, from the fact that
John Kennedy Jr.'s plane had disappeared into the Atlantic Ocean some-
time late Friday night—not that the world was grief-stricken, but in New
York, it was a very intense local story. I had spent an hour that Sunday
morning with the television on, alone in the living room, standing there
with my running clothes on, my wife and kids still asleep, watching live
footage of the Kennedy family compound at Hyannisport, of the Coast
Guard clippers scouring the ocean area off Martha's Vineyard, looking for
signs of survival. Teddy had survived a plane crash some 35 years ago,
someone pointed out. It looked like a beautiful day was assembling itself
in the famous summer resort island, the haze of morning brightening
into sunshine, the slow rollers breaking softly on the shore, but a sense of
doom hung in the air, the dispirited-looking Kennedys shuffled sadly,
arm in arm, along the beaches; the ocean in the distance huge, and silent,
giving up no secrets.

I'd read enough about John and his wife, Carolyn Bessette, to know
that they had an apartment on North Moore Street; that they used to
drink screwdrivers at a bar called Walker's; that John kept a kayak at the
boathouse on the Hudson River and was often seen biking around the
neighborhood or strolling with Carolyn, these two forming the Royal
Couple of young New York. It felt pointless to care about their rumored
marital problems or Carolyn's supposed drug use—these were Kennedys,
and I had grown accustomed to blinking past flaws to the signature mix
of glamour and mystery that lay beyond. So I turned off the television
and took my run. I ran down through the West Village, down Greenwich
Street and around and up across North Moore, and there, on a stoop, was
the first bouquet of flowers. In the next week, those steps would be
engulfed in them.

As I ran by I couldn't suppress a panged cry. A young cop heard me, and was wise to it. I noticed his name, Gilmartin. I'm sure Gilmartin thought somewhat like I did. I'm now older than President Kennedy was in 1963, older than Bobby in '68, and always older than young John. Now to think they all are gone. For me, the situation refreshed the pain of my own departed parents, whose lives, like the lives of so many Americans, and particularly of Irish-American Catholic Democrats of a certain age, were vividly marked by the deaths of Kennedys. The cobblestones on North Moore were damp, and the street was still in early morning shadow. I then slapped my way down Church Street into the sunlight. It was some consolation that I had a ballgame to go to that afternoon with my son. The Expos (a sentimental favorite of mine) were in town, and it was to be Yogi Berra Day. And we decided, for the first time, rather than ride the D Train to the Bronx, we'd take the Yankee Clipper, a boat, from the South Street Seaport in lower Manhattan, up the East River, along the Harlem River, to our port of call: 161st Street and River Avenue in the Bronx.

When Sunday rolled around, it was just what I needed: the comfort and company of my eight-year-old and 40,000 strangers enjoying the celebration of a Yankee legend, the inimitable treasure that is Yogi, and then, turning to the matter at hand, the beautiful game of baseball itself. David Cone, the ace of the staff (9-4), on the mound for the first-place Yankees.

Gabriel, my son, was no stranger to Yankee Stadium. I had been taking him to games since he was four years old; a few weeks earlier, on his birthday, my wife and I had taken him and four of his friends to the Stadium for a birthday treat. While the Yankees got unaccountably crushed by the Tigers that day, it turned out that one of the boys knew how to keep score, which challenged Gabe to try to learn. So, after our glorious boat trip, and the picking up of our tickets at the Will Call window and our official Chase-sponsored Yogi Berra pin at the turnstile, I forked over another five bucks for *Yankees Magazine*, to have its scorecard. The little Yankee golf pencils were free of charge. Then, by dint of a long switchback of ramps, we arrived at our seats in the loge area way around near the left-field foul pole; just in fair territory, above the Yankee bullpen, section 540, row A, seats 5 and 6.

Though the game was slated for a 1:35 start, someone forgot to factor in the Yogi factor. It was too late to start that early, as Yogi might say, for the festivities were lavish, with Yankee radio voice Michael Kay leading the on-field ceremonies. Old-timers were introduced first, then the Berra family; jokes were told. Yogi entered the Stadium through a gate in right field, perched atop the back of the backseat of a white '57 Thunderbird convertible. The car made a slow tour along the warning track; on the Spectra Vision in center field, a video montage of Yogi highlights flickered to the accompaniment of Louis Armstrong singing "What a Wonderful World." The crowd's sustained ovation peaked when the Yogimobile arrived near home plate. Yogi, with his gift for making the figurative literal, said, "Thank you for making me feel right at home," which was where he was.

Joe Torre presented Yogi with a 1998 World Series ring, which made it 11 in his possession, and a genuine American League pennant from 1955 (when a team wins the pennant, they actually *win* a pennant, which flies above the home field). After the dignitaries and the folding chairs and the podium with its spray of mikes were cleared from the field, former Yankee Don Larsen, who had pitched the only perfect game in World Series history from this very mound, threw out the first pitch to the man who had caught his gem against the Brooklyn Dodgers in 1956. It was a strike, and Mr. Berra, in his gray slacks and Yankee-blue blazer, with a mitt borrowed from Yanks catcher Joe Girardi, handled the pitch nicely.

Cone, 36 years old, at that point had compiled a 32-7 record at Yankee Stadium; the Yankees were once again looking invincible, while the Expos were curled up in the cellar in the National League East—though the team was young and with promise. Cone, who entered the game with an ERA of 2.98, roared through the early innings with great dispatch—the first inning, three up and down (though not without a nifty sliding catch in right by Paul O'Neill) on 8 pitches; the second inning in 11. The Yankees put five runs on the board in the bottom of the second on a moon shot home run by Ricky Ledee into the upper deck in right, and a three-run blast lasered over the left-center-field wall by Derek Jeter. Only a third-inning rain delay, which was mighty welcome to the broiling crowd, could slow the Yanks. Gabe and I sat happily in the drizzle. I noticed the steam coming off people.

As the innings passed and the scorecard on the Expos' side neatly filled itself with the expense of very little pencil lead—Ks, and 6–3s and 9s—the crowd would not be seated. As we guiltily wished the Yankees through their at-bats—their 5–0 lead seemed as cleanly delivered, and as deadly, as a knife to the heart of the Expos—in order to get to the historic moment we both hoped for and doubted, the tension grew. I kept reminding my son that these things seldom happen, there are so many ways a perfect game can go wrong (Knoblauch!) that you shouldn't be disappointed when it goes away. Just give Cone a good hand, and we can all sit down. But when the seventh inning was over, I did sit down and thought, "Only six more outs?" I ordered myself a Bud Lite.

I wanted to talk. I kept stealing glances over my shoulder at other dads, in order to share a nod or a wink or a "Can you believe this?" But no one was biting. I suppose it was the old superstition about jinxing a pitcher by talking about it. So I talked to Gabriel, too young for superstition, I hoped. Of course he was! I told him about the perfect games I could remember: Jim Bunning against the Mets on Father's Day in 1964. I told him how the press made such a huge deal out of it because Bunning had so many kids; and Koufax against the Cubs, a game in which Koufax's Dodgers were one-hit by Bob Hendley; and David Wells's game of just the previous summer, on a Sunday, too, I recalled. And of course, Larsen. Isn't it amazing, I said to him, that Don Larsen is here today. Wouldn't that be something? Yea, said Gabe, pounding his mitt. And it's Joe Torre's birthday, he added.

When Knoblauch, who hadn't handled a ball all day, raced behind second to backhand a hot grounder with one down in the eighth, set his feet, and, hesitating for an instant's focus as if saying a silent prayer, turned and whipped a bullet to first to nip Jose Vidro, I really started to believe. The crowd went absolutely wild, wild with excitement, yes, but more so, I think, with a suddenly clarified belief, a faith. And I remembered suddenly what Yogi had said about two and half hours earlier: that his mother loved two buildings in the world—St. Peter's in Rome and Yankee Stadium in the Bronx. The basilica of baseball—we were in it, praying for a miracle of grace.

Looking at the scorecard, which now was a mixture of my handwriting and my son's, I rushed ahead, as I had counseled my son not to do, rushed ahead through the remaining Expo batters, wiping them away in my mind, to arrive at a moment I wanted to savor in advance. I would want to call my father but of course could not; not in the conventional way, with a quarter or on a cell phone, because he'd been dead eight years. I thought of the four-year-old John-John, waving a small flag and saluting, but turned back to baseball, the here and now.

After an excruciating delay in the bottom of the eighth while the Yankees added a slow-developing and absolutely redundant run (O'Neill double, Williams single, Martinez RBI single), we moved to the ninth.

The bottom of the order, of course, for Les Expos—a team that began in 1969, to the delight of my father and my friends in upstate New York, because major league baseball would then be only an hour away. I seldom found myself rooting against the Expos, but had to now. The poor Expos—interleague play, expansion, and free agency were taking their toll this day: The much-traveled hired gun, Cone, was facing a very young team, and not a single player in the lineup had ever faced him before. And it showed.

It could be easy, I thought, getting the last three outs in succession, knowing that it could be hard, too—a fluke, an error, a bit of wildness, *a hit batsman.* I hadn't thought of that all day! So much could ruin what we were so close to possessing. My son kept assuring me that it could happen, it could happen *because* it had happened to Wells a year ago, whereas I found myself arguing that for precisely that reason it could not happen again, not so soon. And for a moment, I despaired at such clear evidence of what I must've learned since I was eight: that if something most certainly can happen it somehow won't. May my son's optimism be proven right, and my pessimism vanish, I thought. Luckily, I was snapped out of such solemn reveries by the following: After Expos catcher Chris Widger struck out to lead off the ninth, third-baseman Shane Andrews lofted a fly to left, right at us, high up, and right below us, Yankee left-fielder Ricky Ledee advanced shakily on the ball now descending, we could see it, a bright white dot falling, then grayed by shadow as it plummeted, and, at the last instant, Ledee flinched—he'd lost sight of the ball!—and then he jerked his glove in front of his face, and grabbed it, somehow, for the out, lots of ball showing, lots of hearts in the crowd being swallowed back. The assembled slowly erupted with relief, grateful that the delicate young Ledee would not have to spend a lifetime haunted by the fly ball he dropped in the ninth inning of what was, till then, a perfect game in front of 40,000 people in his hometown. Thank you, Lord.

Then the last batter, or I should say, then what we most fervently hoped was the last batter.

There came a Shepard, Bob, the Yankee public address announcer for the last half-century, and he intoned in his deep bass ouzo voice the name of the 27th batter: "Orlando Cabrera, the shortstop, batting ninth." In his two previous at-bats, Cabrera had struck out and bounced back to the mound. And before we could ponder disaster, it was over. A pop-up in the infield, which Cone helpfully seemed the first to spot, pointing his right index finger at it, with third-baseman Scott Brosius drifting in a few steps. Cone raised his hands to about ear level with disbelief as the ball, we all know, will be caught by the steady Scott. And then Cone was on his knees and he was mobbed. The crowd was in ecstasy; my son asked, "Why are you crying, Dad?"

THE LONG SLOW BOAT ride back, from Yankee Stadium all the way down the East River to South Street Seaport, wasn't long enough or slow enough. We were savoring being stunned. The day remained beautiful, the sun would set late in the evening. We saw Yogi boarding another New York Waterway boat, heading down toward Montclair. The city itself looked like a miracle crafted out of geometry and imaginary materi- als, as fantastic in its way as what we had just seen.

For days I pondered the whole event, took sweet care of the Yogi pins, ticket stubs, and the scorecard, with the fabulous line on Cone, in both Gabe's hand and mine: 9 0 0 0 0 10—nine innings, no hits, no runs, no earned runs, no walks, 10 strikeouts. Cone had not gone to a three-ball count on any hitter; he threw only 88 pitches. His fastball was low and moving and his slider swept like a scimitar, slicing the smallest corner of the plate or sailing way outside. It was a pitch that Vladimir Guerrero couldn't lay off, and couldn't touch. Only two balls were hit well by the Expos all day, both in the first inning—O'Neill made a sliding catch in the alley on Terry Jones's drive, and Ledee went to the warning track in left-center to haul in a blast by Rondell White. Somehow, in the excite- ment, we lost Gabe's mitt. Fair price. We made a videotape of the game when it was replayed on local TV a few days later. And then we went to the library.

What we had seen had happened only 14 times in more than 150,000 ball games in the modern era, since 1903, once every 10,000 or so games. Ten in the American League, only four in the National. Before expansion in 1961 there were only four perfect games pitched in six decades (a span of about 74,000 games), and there have been 10 pitched in the four decades since (more than 80,000 games). Mostly very good pitchers have thrown them, Cone, Wells, Martinez, Bunning, Hunter; a few great pitchers, Young, Joss, Koufax; and a few mediocre pitchers having good years, Barker, Browning, Witt. And then you have Larsen, Robertson, Rogers. Why not other mediocre pitchers, why not other great pitchers? Why not Bob Gib- son, Pedro Martinez, Randy Johnson, Tom Seaver, Lefty Grove, Christy Mathewson, Walter Johnson, Warren Spahn? Why not Kenny Rogers again, who came within two batters of doing so for the second time in 2002?

No rhyme or reason. Bill James has pointed out that all the perfect-game pitchers, but for Larsen, were better than the league average in keeping runners off base. But that's not much of a distinction. James will allow as how "skill is a factor." But James (in a private correspondence), after fooling with a pitcher's OOBA (opposition's on-base average) and his team's fielding average, concluded that we are left standing at "the gateway to a vast statistical swamp." His final blessing: "It is my opinion that *nothing is more foolish than to pursue the illusion of precision when dealing with an issue which is incapable of precise measurement.* It's a waste of time."

James, of course, is right. There are no factors you can isolate that will even begin to suggest what might affect the probability of perfection. But in the case of David Cone's enormous day, one can't help but suggest two things, one rational, one perhaps not.

The rational explanation is payroll discrepancy—the Yankee payroll for the '99 season was $85 million, while the Expos' entire team made about $16 million, or as much as Bernie and Cone. The Expos were in last place in the other league, 21.5 games out; the Yankees were Kings of the Hill. The Expos' starting lineup had guys hitting .233, .222, .217; they were starting a 22-year-old pitcher who the year before had tied a club record for losses with 15. The Yankees, on the other hand, had the American League's leading hitter in Derek Jeter at .374; Williams was at .335, O'Neill at .296; Chili Davis, Tino Martinez, and Rickey Ledee were all hitting .275 or better. The team was solid. And David Cone was pitching, of course, looking for win number 10 against 4 losses, with an ERA under 3.00.

But Cone had been bombed his last time out—six earned runs—and hadn't pitched in 11 days. The festivities—Yogi and Larsen—must have fired him up. As he walked toward immortality of a sort in the later innings, who's to say he didn't make a silent deal with his God to help him go the final distance. For after this game, David Cone was virtually finished as a pitcher.

Consider this: After the game, his record stood at 10-4 with an ERA of 2.73, but he won only two games the rest of the year and had an ERA over that period of 4.69. In true rise-to-the-occasion Cone fashion, he pitched beautifully in two postseason appearances, beating Seattle and Atlanta in dominating seven-inning stints. With another World Series ring coming to him, Cone signed the ultimate in free-wheeling contracts—a big payday of $12 million for just one year. But Cone was indeed washed up. In 2000, he had his worst year in the big leagues, going

4-14 with a gigantic ERA of 6.91, suffering a harrowing-looking separated left shoulder diving awkwardly for a ball, but coming back once again. He managed to add to his New York all-time warrior status by coming in to get one big out in the Subway Series, retiring the Mets' Mike Piazza on a pop-up in the final game.

Cone got a congratulatory call from Wells in the clubhouse right after the game. They couldn't party together this night. Wells would make it back to the Yankees and put on the pinstripes once again, in 2001. But Cone would be gone.

Cone's decamping for the Red Sox in 2001 seemed a little tawdry for someone with such style, but when he got off to a 6-1 start it just seemed that the fire and the gift had returned and that the Yankees, unaccountably, lacked the faith. But Cone's mastery abandoned him for the last time—he faded badly, and finished with another fat ERA and a 9-7 record. A year of retirement in 2002 didn't sit so well with Cone, who succumbed to the entreaties of John Franco and Al Leiter in the winter of 2003 and signaled to the Mets he wanted to try a comeback. Tendinitis in his hip ended the experiment in late May, before a June subway series with the Yanks could bring a wonderful matchup with Wells.

In his 17-year career, Cone pulled down about $65 million in salaries. He and his wife have three homes, flashy cars, and no children. Always determined, Cone was able to conjure the luck he needed to navigate his way to perfection on a day that seemed to require such a thing—in the presence of Yankee greats on Yogi Berra's day; he gave heart and soul and perhaps more to do it. Roger Angell speculates in his book that Cone is now well prepared for a career in politics. A history of throwing curves to the opposition and speaking straight to your own kind might be good training. And he's already dealt with a few skeletons. But life without baseball might be his biggest hurdle.

Unlike Cone, David Wells made it through his 17th major league season, intact but to the very end, winning 15 games for the Yankees during the regular season before wearing down, and out, in the postseason. Wells's back operation after the 2001 season of misery with the White Sox (5-7, only 100 innings pitched) had rejuvenated him for a time, but as the Yankees moved down the stretch, holding off the Red Sox and winning the division, he was once again relying on cortisone shots to get by. Wells pitched very effectively for a time in the postseason, clinching the American League Division Series with a strong effort in Game Four against the Twins, giving up one run and eight hits in 7²/₃ innings for an

8–1 win, which brought on the much-anticipated Yankees–Red Sox series for the American League pennant. With the series tied at two games apiece, Game Five in Boston was as tense as any ballgame in recent memory. In Game Four, Yankee coach Don Zimmer had gotten rolled to the ground by Pedro Martinez and two Yankees had pummeled a Fenway security employee in the bullpen. But in the acrimonious atmosphere of Game Five, Wells coolly tamed the Sox over seven innings, giving up only one run—a homer to the hot-tempered Manny Ramirez—and the series went back to New York. The Yankees would prevail in Game Seven on an 11th-inning home run by Aaron Boone off a Tim Wakefield knuckler.

It was on to the Fall Classic for the Yankees, against the surprising mix of intrepid youth and septuagenarian wisdom in the figure of manager Jack McKeon. As they had in the previous two series, the Yankees lost Game One, but seemingly gained control of their fate with wins in Games Two and Three. However, a 12th-inning home run by Florida shortstop Alex Gonzalez off reliever Jeff Weaver tied the series at two games apiece. And when Wells took the mound for the crucial Game Five, he couldn't fight through back spasms, despite five cortisone shots. Torre lifted him after one scoreless inning in favor of Jose Contreras, who was hammered around in the second inning, eventually taking the loss. When Josh Beckett blanked New York on five hits in Game Six, it was the Marlins celebrating in the House That Ruth Built, and the Yankees looking at an off-season filled with tough decisions.

Shortly after the Series, the Yankees declined to pay Wells $6 million for the 2004 season, and instead bought out his option for five million dollars less. Wells consented to back surgery in January, claimed that his relationship with George Steinbrenner had gone sour, and signed for the 2004 season with San Diego. Wells came back home at last. Whether either David ever makes it back to the New York stage, their exploits will outlive their actual presence in uniform. Certainly, their afternoons of pitching perfection will.

APPENDIX I

PERFECT-GAME CURIOS

What is a perfect game? Since 1991, Major League Baseball has insisted that it is a game in which a pitcher pitches a complete game victory that lasts a minimum of nine innings and in which no opposition runner reaches first base. This rules out several games once thought perfect: the five-inning rain-shortened, 15-up and 15-down wins by Dean Chance in 1967 and David Palmer of the Expos in 1984; the 12 perfect innings thrown by Harvey Haddix in 1959, and the nine full innings from Pedro Martinez in 1999, because those games were either not victories (as with Haddix) or were not complete games (as for Martinez). At one time, Boston's Ernie Shore was credited with a perfect game, though he actually came in in relief, retiring 27 straight batters after starting pitcher Babe Ruth walked the first guy, argued balls and strikes, and was ejected. The definition of a perfect game does allow for one instance of imperfection—an error can be committed if it does not lead to a runner reaching first base: a dropped foul pop, for example, extending an at-bat, earning the fielder an error, but with the at-bat ending in an out.

Many have come very close, down to the 27th out before losing it: Hooks Wiltse of the New York Giants hit the opposing pitcher with two out in the ninth inning in 1914; the Tigers' Tommy Bridges gave up a single to pinch-hitter Dave Harris in 1932 in a 13-0 rout of the Senators; in 1958, Ed Fitz Gerald doubled with one out to go for Billy Pierce of the White Sox; Milt Pappas, in 1972, had rookie ump Bruce Froemming call a ball four on what woulda/shoulda been strike three on the 27th and last batter; in 1983, Detroit's Milt Wilcox's bid was ruined by a Jerry Hairston single; Dave Stieb and Brian Holman, both in 1988, gave up clean hits to their 27th batter, as did the Reds' Ron Robinson, who was reached for a hit by the Expos' Wallace Johnson with only one out to go. The same happened to Mike Mussina in 2000 on Labor Day in Fenway Park—Carl Everett, two-strike pinch-hit single. There will surely be more.

Two perfect games were thrown before the modern era, and these are often included in the official count. J. Lee Richmond and John Montgomery Ward, one pitching for Worcester, the other for Providence, retired 27 men straight in games only five days apart in the summer of 1880. The rules were different then—batters asked for a high or low pitch, it took eight balls to walk a guy, pitching was underhanded, and the distance from mound to home was 45 feet. However, in a link to the modern era, Richmond, like Larsen in 1956 and Wells in 1998, was up nearly all night the night before his game. It was Class Day at Brown University, and Richmond was seen at 5 A.M. with a champagne bottle. Problem was, he was in Rhode Island; his game was later that day in Massachusetts. He made it, and was the first of the perfect-game pitchers.

	DATE	H/A	D/N	SCORE	ATTENDANCE	TIME	AGE	NUMBER OF PITCHES
Cy Young	May 5, 1904	Home	Day	3–0	10,267	1:23	37	NA
Addie Joss	Oct. 2, 1908	Home	Day	1–0	10,598	1:29	28	74
Charlie Robertson	Apr. 30, 1922	Away	Day	2–0	25,000	1:55	26	90
Don Larsen	Oct. 8, 1956	Home	Day	2–0	64,519	2:06	27	97
Jim Bunning	June 21, 1964	Away	Day	6–0	32,026	2:19	32	90
Sandy Koufax	Sept. 9, 1965	Home	Night	1–0	29,139	1:43	29	113
Catfish Hunter	May 8, 1968	Home	Night	4–0	6,298	2:28	22	107
Len Barker	May 15, 1981	Home	Night	3–0	7,290	2:09	25	103
Mike Witt	Sept. 30, 1984	Away	Day	1–0	8,375	1:49	24	94
Tom Browning	Sept. 16, 1988	Home	Night	1–0	16,591	1:51	28	102
Dennis Martinez	July 28, 1991	Away	Day	2–0	45,560	2:14	36	95
Kenny Rogers	July 28, 1994	Home	Night	4–0	46,581	2:08	29	98
David Wells	May 17, 1998	Home	Day	4–0	49,820	2:40	34	120
David Cone	July 18, 1999	Home	Day	6–0	41,930	2:16	36	88

APPENDIX II

PERFECT-GAME BOX SCORES

CY YOUNG

May 5, 1904 (D) at Huntington Avenue Grounds, Boston

									R	H	E
PHIL (A)	0 0 0		0 0 0		0 0 0				0	0	1
BOST (A)	0 0 0		0 0 1		2 0 x				3	10	0

PHILADELPHIA A'S	AB	R	H	RBI	PO	A
Hartsel lf	1	0	0	0	0	0
Hoffman lf	2	0	0	0	2	1
Pickering cf	3	0	0	0	1	0
Davis 1b	3	0	0	0	5	0
L. Cross 3b	3	0	0	0	2	0
Seybold rf	3	0	0	0	2	0
Murphy 2b	3	0	0	0	1	2
M. Cross ss	3	0	0	0	2	2
Schreckengost c	3	0	0	0	7	0
Waddell p	3	0	0	0	0	1
TOTALS	27	0	0	0	22	6

BOSTON PILGRIMS	AB	R	H	RBI	PO	A
Dougherty lf	3	0	1	0	1	0
Collins 3b	4	0	2	0	2	0
Stahl cf	4	1	1	0	3	0
Freeman rf	4	0	1	1	2	0
Parent ss	4	0	2	0	1	4
LaChance 1b	3	0	1	0	9	0
Ferris 2b	3	1	1	0	0	3
Criger c	3	1	1	1	9	0
Young p	3	0	0	0	1	0
TOTALS	31	3	10	2	28	7

PITCHING PHILADELPHIA	IP	H	R	ER	BB	K
Waddell	8	10	3	2	0	6

BOSTON	IP	H	R	ER	BB	K
Young	9	0	0	0	0	8

ADDIE JOSS

October 2, 1908 (D) at League Park, Cleveland

									R	H	E
CHI (A)	0 0 0		0 0 0		0 0 0				0	0	1
CLE (A)	0 0 1		0 0 0		0 0 x				1	4	0

CHICAGO WHITE SOX(A)	AB	R	H	PO	A
Hahn rf	3	0	0	1	0
Jones cf	3	0	0	0	0
Isbell 1b	3	0	0	7	1
Dougherty lf	3	0	0	0	0
Davis 2b	3	0	0	1	0
Parent ss	3	0	0	0	3
Schreckengost c	2	0	0	12	1
Shaw c	0	0	0	2	0
Tannehill 3b	2	0	0	0	0
Walsh p	2	0	0	1	3
White	1	0	0	0	0
Donahue	1	0	0	0	0
Anderson	1	0	0	0	0
TOTALS	27	0	0	24	8

CLEVELAND NAPS	AB	R	H	PO	A
Good rf	4	0	0	1	0
Bradley 3b	4	0	0	0	1
Hinchman lf	3	0	0	3	0
Lajoie 2b	3	0	1	2	8
Stovall 1b	3	0	0	16	0
N. Clarke c	3	0	0	4	1
Birmingham cf	3	1	2	0	0
Parent ss	2	0	1	1	1
Joss p	3	0	0	0	5
TOTALS	28	1	4	27	16

PITCHING CHICAGO WHITE SOX	IP	H	R	ER	BB	K
Walsh	8	4	1	0	1	15

CLEVELAND	IP	H	R	ER	BB	K
Joss	9	0	0	0	0	3

CHARLIE ROBERTSON

April 30, 1922 (D) at Navin Field, Detroit

				R	H	E
CHI (A)	0 2 0	0 0 0	0 0 0	2	7	0
DET (A)	0 0 0	0 0 0	0 0 0	0	0	1

CHICAGO WHITE SOX	AB	R	H	RBI
Mulligan ss	4	0	1	0
McClellan 3b	3	0	1	0
Collins 2b	3	0	1	0
Hooper rf	3	1	0	0
Mostil lf	4	1	1	0
Strunk cf	3	0	0	0
Sheely 1b	4	0	2	2
Schalk c	4	0	1	0
Robertson p	4	0	0	0
TOTALS	32	2	7	2

DETROIT TIGERS	AB	R	H	RBI
Blue 1b	3	0	0	0
Cutshaw 2b	3	0	0	0
Cobb cf	3	0	0	0
Veach lf	3	0	0	0
Heilmann rf	3	0	0	0
Jones 3b	3	0	0	0
Rigney ss	2	0	0	0
Clark ph	1	0	0	0
Manion c	3	0	0	0
Pillette p	2	0	0	0
Bassler ph	1	0	0	0
TOTALS	27	0	0	0

PITCHING

DETROIT	IP	H	R	ER	BB	K
Pillette	9	7	2	2	2	5

CHICAGO	IP	H	R	ER	BB	K
Robertson	9	0	0	0	0	6

DON LARSEN

October 8, 1956 (D) at Yankee Stadium

				R	H	E
BKLYN (N)	0 0 0	0 0 0	0 0 0	0	0	0
NY (A)	0 0 0	1 0 1	0 0 x	2	5	0

BKLN DODGERS	AB	R	H	RBI	PO	A
Gilliam 2b	3	0	0	0	2	0
Reese ss	3	0	0	0	4	2
Snider cf	3	0	0	0	1	0
Robinson 3b	3	0	0	0	2	4
Hodges 1b	3	0	0	0	5	1
Amoros lf	3	0	0	0	3	0
Furillo rf	3	0	0	0	0	0
Campanella c	3	0	0	0	7	2
Maglie p	2	0	0	0	0	1
Mitchell ph	1	0	0	0	0	0
TOTALS	27	0	0	0	24	10

NY YANKEES	AB	R	H	RBI	PO	A
Bauer rf	4	0	1	1	4	0
Collins 1b	4	0	1	0	7	0
Mantle cf	3	1	1	1	4	0
Berra c	3	0	0	0	7	0
Slaughter lf	2	0	0	0	1	0
Martin 2b	3	0	1	0	3	4
McDougald ss	2	0	0	0	0	2
Carey 3b	3	1	1	0	1	1
Larsen p	2	0	0	0	0	1
TOTALS	26	2	5	2	27	8

PITCHING

BROOKLYN	IP	H	R	ER	BB	K
Maglie	8	5	2	2	2	5

NY YANKEES	IP	H	R	ER	BB	K
Larsen	9	0	0	0	0	7

JIM BUNNING

June 21, 1964 (D) at Shea Stadium

										R	H	E
PHILA (N)	1 1 0	0 0 4	0 0 0	6	8	0
NY (N)	0 0 0	0 0 0	0 0 0	0	0	0

PHILADELPHIA PHILLIES	AB	R	H	RBI
Briggs cf	4	1	0	0
Herrnstein 1b	4	0	0	0
Callison rf	4	1	2	1
Allen 3b	3	0	1	1
Covington lf	2	0	0	0
Wine ss	1	1	0	0
Taylor 2b	3	2	1	0
Rojas ss-lf	3	0	1	0
Triandos c	4	1	2	2
Bunning p	4	0	1	2
TOTALS	32	6	8	6

NEW YORK METS	AB	R	H	RBI
Hickman cf	3	0	0	0
Hunt 2b	3	0	0	0
Kranepool 1b	3	0	0	0
Christopher rf	3	0	0	0
Gonder c	3	0	0	0
Taylor lf	3	0	0	0
Smith ss	3	0	0	0
Samuel 3b	2	0	0	0
Altman ph	1	0	0	0
Stallard p	1	0	0	0
Wakefield p	0	0	0	0
Kanehl ph	1	0	0	0
Sturdivant p	0	0	0	0
Stephenson ph	1	0	0	0
TOTALS	27	0	0	0

PITCHING

PHILADELPHIA	IP	H	R	ER	BB	K
Bunning	9	0	0	0	0	10

NEW YORK METS	IP	H	R	ER	BB	K
Stallard	5.2	7	6	6	4	3
Wakefield	0.1	0	0	0	0	0
Sturdivant	3	1	0	0	0	3

SANDY KOUFAX

September 9, 1965 (N) at Dodger Stadium

										R	H	E
CHI (N)	0 0 0	0 0 0	0 0 0	0	0	1
LA (N)	0 0 0	0 1 0	0 0 x	1	1	0

CHICAGO CUBS	AB	R	H	RBI
Young cf	3	0	0	0
Beckert 2b	3	0	0	0
Williams rf	3	0	0	0
Santo 3b	3	0	0	0
Banks 1b	3	0	0	0
Browne lf	3	0	0	0
Krug c	3	0	0	0
Kessinger ss	2	0	0	0
Amalfitano ph	1	0	0	0
Hendley p	2	0	0	0
Kuenn ph	1	0	0	0
TOTALS	27	0	0	0

LA DODGERS	AB	R	H	RBI
Wills ss	3	0	0	0
Gilliam 3b	3	0	0	0
Kennedy 3b	3	0	0	0
W. Davis cf	3	0	0	0
Johnson lf	2	1	1	0
Fairly rf	2	0	0	0
Lefebvre 2b	3	0	0	0
Tracewski 2b	0	0	0	0
Parker 1b	3	0	0	0
Torborg c	3	0	0	0
Koufax p	2	0	0	0
TOTALS	24	1	1	0

PITCHING

CHICAGO CUBS	IP	H	R	ER	BB	SO
Hendley	8	1	1	0	1	3

LOS ANGELES	IP	H	R	ER	BB	SO
Koufax	9	0	0	0	0	14

CATFISH HUNTER

May 8, 1968 (N) at Oakland-Alameda County Coliseum

										R	H	E
MIN (A)	0	0	0	0	0	0	0	0	0	0	0	1
OAK (A)	0	0	0	0	0	0	1	3	x	4	10	0

MINNESOTA TWINS	AB	R	H	RBI	PO	A
Tovar 3b	3	0	0	0	1	2
Carew 2b	3	0	0	0	5	1
Killebrew 1b	3	0	0	0	4	0
Oliva rf	3	0	0	0	3	0
Uhlaender cf	3	0	0	0	2	0
Allison lf	3	0	0	0	0	0
Hernandez ss	2	0	0	0	2	4
Roseboro ph	1	0	0	0	0	0
Look c	3	0	0	0	7	2
Boswell p	2	0	0	0	0	1
Perranoski p	0	0	0	0	0	0
Reese ph	1	0	0	0	0	0
TOTALS	27	0	0	0	24	10

OAKLAND ATHLETICS	AB	R	H	RBI	PO	A
Campaneris ss	4	0	2	0	1	3
Jackson rf	4	0	0	0	3	0
Bando 3b	3	0	1	0	0	2
Webster 1b	4	1	2	0	7	0
Donaldson 2b	3	0	0	0	1	2
Pagliaroni c	3	1	0	0	11	0
Monday cf	3	2	2	0	1	0
Rudi lf	3	0	0	0	3	0
Robinson ph	0	0	0	0	0	0
Cater ph	0	0	0	1	0	0
Hershberger lf	0	0	0	0	0	0
Hunter p	4	0	3	3	0	0
TOTALS	31	4	10	4	27	7

PITCHING

MINNESOTA	IP	H	R	ER	BB	K
Boswell	7.2	9	4	4	5	6
Perranoski	0.1	1	0	0	0	0

OAKLAND	IP	H	R	ER	BB	K
Hunter	9	0	0	0	0	11

LEN BARKER

May 15, 1981 (N) at Cleveland Stadium

										R	H	E
TOR (A)	0	0	0	0	0	0	0	0	0	0	0	3
CLE (A)	2	0	0	0	0	0	0	1	x	3	7	0

TORONTO BLUE JAYS	AB	R	H	RBI	PO	A
Griffin ss	3	0	0	0	2	1
Moseby rf	3	0	0	0	4	0
Bell lf	3	0	0	0	2	0
Mayberry 1b	3	0	0	0	4	1
Upshaw dh	3	0	0	0	0	0
Garcia 2b	3	0	0	0	2	2
Bosetti cf	3	0	0	0	3	0
Ainge 3b	2	0	0	0	1	0
Woods ph	1	0	0	0	0	0
Martinez c	2	0	0	0	5	1
Whitt ph	1	0	0	0	0	0
Leal p	0	0	0	0	1	1
TOTALS	27	0	0	0	24	6

CLEVELAND INDIANS	AB	R	H	RBI	PO	A
Manning cf	4	1	1	0	4	0
Orta rf	4	1	3	1	0	0
Hargrove 1b	4	1	1	0	9	0
Thornton dh	3	0	0	1	0	0
Hassey c	4	0	1	1	11	0
Harrah 3b	4	0	1	0	2	0
Charboneau lf	3	0	0	0	1	0
Kuiper 2b	3	0	0	0	0	5
Veryzer ss	3	0	0	0	0	3
Barker p	0	0	0	0	0	0
TOTALS	32	3	7	3	27	8

PITCHING

TORONTO	IP	H	R	ER	BB	K
Leal	8	7	3	1	0	5

CLEVELAND	IP	H	R	ER	BB	K
Barker	9	0	0	0	0	11

MIKE WITT

September 30, 1984 (D) at Arlington Stadium

				R	H	E
CAL (A)	0 0 0	0 0 0	1 0 0	1	7	0
TEX (A)	0 0 0	0 0 0	0 0 0	0	0	0

CALIFORNIA ANGELS	AB	R	H	RBI	PO	A
Wilfong 2b	4	0	0	0	0	8
Sconiers 1b	4	0	0	0	10	1
Grich 1b	0	0	0	0	2	0
Lynn cf, rf	3	0	2	0	1	0
DeCinces 3b	4	1	2	0	0	1
Downing lf	4	0	0	0	1	0
Thomas lf	0	0	0	0	0	0
Reggie Jackson dh	4	0	0	1	0	0
M. Brown rf	3	0	3	0	2	0
Pettis pr, cf	0	0	0	0	0	0
Boone c	3	0	0	0	10	0
Schofield ss	2	0	0	0	0	3
Witt p	0	0	0	0	1	0
TOTALS	31	1	7	1	27	13

TEXAS RANGERS	AB	R	H	RBI	PO	A
Rivers dh	3	0	0	0	0	0
Tolleson 2b	3	0	0	0	4	5
Ward lf	3	0	0	0	0	0
Parrish 3b	3	0	0	0	0	3
O'Brien 1b	3	0	0	0	13	0
G. Wright cf	3	0	0	0	3	0
Dunbar rf	3	0	0	0	1	0
Scott c	2	0	0	0	4	3
B. Jones ph	1	0	0	0	0	0
Wilkerson ss	2	0	0	0	2	4
Foley ph	1	0	0	0	0	0
Hough p	0	0	0	0	0	2
TOTALS	27	0	0	0	27	17

PITCHING

CALIFORNIA	IP	H	R	ER	BB	K
Witt	9	0	0	0	0	10

TEXAS	IP	H	R	ER	BB	K
Hough	9	7	1	0	3	3

TOM BROWNING

September 16, 1988 (N) at Riverfront Stadium

				R	H	E
LA (N)	0 0 0	0 0 0	0 0 0	0	0	1
CIN (N)	0 0 0	0 0 1	0 0 x	1	3	0

LA DODGERS	AB	R	H	RBI	PO	A
Griffin ss	3	0	0	0	0	4
Hatcher 1b	3	0	0	0	10	0
Gibson lf	3	0	0	0	1	0
Gonzalez lf	0	0	0	0	0	0
Marshall rf	3	0	0	0	2	0
Shelby cf	3	0	0	0	2	0
Hamilton 3b	3	0	0	0	0	1
Dempsey c	3	0	0	0	7	0
Sax 2b	3	0	0	0	2	2
Belcher p	2	0	0	0	0	2
Woodson ph	1	0	0	0	0	0
TOTALS	27	0	0	0	24	9

CINCINNATI REDS	AB	R	H	RBI	PO	A
Larkin ss	3	1	1	0	0	4
Sabo 3b	3	0	1	0	0	4
Daniels f	3	0	0	0	3	0
Davis cf	2	0	0	0	1	0
O'Neill rf	3	0	0	0	4	0
Esasky 1b	3	0	0	0	10	1
Reed c	3	0	0	0	7	0
Oester 2b	3	0	1	0	1	1
Browning p	3	0	0	0	1	0
TOTALS	26	1	3	0	27	10

PITCHING

LOS ANGELES	IP	H	R	ER	BB	K
Belcher	8	3	1	0	1	7

CINCINNATI	IP	H	R	ER	BB	K
Browning	9	0	0	0	0	7

DENNIS MARTINEZ

July 28, 1991 (D) at Dodger Stadium

				R	H	E
MON (N)	0 0 0	0 0 0	2 0 0	2	4	0
LA (N)	0 0 0	0 0 0	0 0 0	0	0	2

MONTREAL EXPOS	AB	R	H	RBI	PO	A
DeShields 2b	3	0	1	0	0	9
Grissom cf	4	0	0	0	2	0
Dave Martinez rf	4	1	0	0	0	0
Calderon lf	3	0	0	0	2	0
Wallach 3b	4	0	0	0	1	1
Walker 1b	4	1	1	1	17	0
Hassey c	3	0	1	0	5	0
Owen ss	3	0	0	0	0	2
Dennis Martinez p	3	0	1	0	0	2
TOTALS	31	2	4	1	27	14

LA DODGERS	AB	R	H	RBI	PO	A
Butler cf	3	0	0	0	1	0
Samuel 2b	3	0	0	0	1	3
Murray 1b	3	0	0	0	8	2
Strawberry rf	3	0	0	0	4	0
Daniels lf	3	0	0	0	3	0
Harris 3b	3	0	0	0	0	0
Scioscia c	3	0	0	0	5	1
Griffin ss	2	0	0	0	4	4
Javier ph	1	0	0	0	0	0
Morgan p	2	0	0	0	1	2
Gwynn ph	1	0	0	0	0	0
TOTALS	27	0	0	0	27	12

PITCHING

MONTREAL	IP	H	R	ER	BB	K
Dennis Martinez	9	0	0	0	0	5

LOS ANGELES	IP	H	R	ER	BB	K
Morgan	9	4	2	0	1	5

KENNY ROGERS

July 28, 1994 (N) at The Ballpark in Arlington

				R	H	E
CAL (A)	0 0 0	0 0 0	0 0 0	0	0	0
TEX (A)	2 0 2	0 0 0	0 0 x	4	6	0

CALIFORNIA ANGELS	AB	R	H	RBI	PO	A
Curtis cf	3	0	0	0	3	0
Owen 3b	3	0	0	0	0	4
Edmonds lf	3	0	0	0	2	0
Davis dh	3	0	0	0	0	0
Jackson rf	3	0	0	0	2	0
Snow 1b	3	0	0	0	8	1
Hudler 2b	3	0	0	0	3	0
Turner c	3	0	0	0	4	1
DiSarcina ss	3	0	0	0	1	2
Lorraine p	0	0	0	0	1	0
Springer p	0	0	0	0	0	0
TOTALS	27	0	0	0	24	8

TEXAS RANGERS	AB	R	H	RBI	PO	A
Davis rf	4	0	0	0	0	0
Rodriguez c	3	1	1	1	8	0
Canseco dh	4	2	2	2	0	0
Clark 1b	3	1	0	0	8	0
Gonzalez lf	4	0	2	0	4	0
Palmer 3b	4	0	1	1	1	3
Greer cf	3	0	0	0	5	0
Lee 2b	3	0	0	0	0	1
Beltre ss	2	0	0	0	1	2
Rogers p	0	0	0	0	0	1
TOTALS	30	4	6	4	27	7

PITCHING

CALIFORNIA	IP	H	R	ER	BB	K
Lorraine	6.2	6	4	4	2	4
Springer	1.1	0	0	0	1	1

TEXAS	IP	H	R	ER	BB	K
Rogers	9	0	0	0	0	8

DAVID WELLS

May 17, 1998 (D) at Yankee Stadium

				R	H	E
MIN (A)	0 0 0	0 0 0	0 0 0	0	0	0
NY (A)	0 1 0	1 0 0	2 0 x	4	6	0

MINNESOTA TWINS	AB	R	H	RBI	PO	A
Lawton cf	3	0	0	0	2	0
Gates 2b	3	0	0	0	0	1
Molitor dh	3	0	0	0	0	0
Cordova lf	3	0	0	0	5	0
Coomer 1b	3	0	0	0	6	1
Ochoa rf	3	0	0	0	2	0
Shave 3b	3	0	0	0	1	2
Valentin c	3	0	0	0	6	0
Meares ss	3	0	0	0	1	0
Hawkins p	0	0	0	0	1	1
Naulty p	0	0	0	0	0	0
Swindell p	0	0	0	0	0	0
TOTALS	27	0	0	0	24	5

NEW YORK YANKEES	AB	R	H	RBI	PO	A
Knoblauch 2b	4	0	0	0	0	3
Jeter ss	3	1	0	1	1	1
O'Neill rf	4	0	0	0	2	0
Martinez 1b	4	0	0	0	8	0
Williams cf	3	3	3	1	3	0
Strawberry dh	3	1	1	1	0	0
Curtis lf	3	0	1	1	2	0
Posada c	3	0	0	0	11	1
Brosius 3b	3	0	0	0	0	0
Wells p	0	0	0	0	0	1
TOTALS	30	4	6	3	27	6

PITCHING

MINNESOTA	IP	H	R	ER	BB	K
Hawkins	7	6	4	4	0	5
Naulty	0.1	0	0	0	1	0
Swindell	0.2	0	0	0	0	1

NEW YORK	IP	H	R	ER	BB	K
Wells	9	0	0	0	0	11

DAVID CONE

July 18, 1999 (D) at Yankee Stadium

				R	H	E
MON (N)	0 0 0	0 0 0	0 0 0	0	0	0
NY (A)	0 5 0	0 0 0	0 1 x	6	8	0

MONTREAL EXPOS	AB	R	H	RBI	PO	A
W. Guerrero dh	3	0	0	0	0	0
Jones cf	2	0	0	0	1	1
Mouton cf	1	0	0	0	0	0
White lf	3	0	0	0	4	0
V. Guerrero rf	3	0	0	0	2	0
Vidro 2b	3	0	0	0	1	5
Fullmer 1b	3	0	0	0	9	0
Widger c	3	0	0	0	3	0
Andrews 3b	2	0	0	0	0	0
McGuire ph	1	0	0	0	0	0
Cabrera ss	3	0	0	0	4	1
Vazquez p	0	0	0	0	0	2
Ayala p	0	0	0	0	0	1
TOTALS	27	0	0	0	24	10

NEW YORK YANKEES	AB	R	H	RBI	PO	A
Knoblauch 2b	2	1	1	0	1	1
Jeter ss	4	1	1	2	0	0
O'Neill rf	4	1	1	0	4	0
Williams cf	4	0	1	1	2	0
Martinez 1b	4	0	1	0	4	0
Davis dh	3	1	1	0	0	0
Ledee lf	4	1	1	2	3	0
Brosius 3b	2	1	0	0	1	2
Girardi c	3	0	1	1	12	0
Cone p	0	0	0	0	0	0
TOTALS	30	6	8	6	27	3

PITCHING

MONTREAL	IP	H	R	ER	BB	K
Vazquez	7	7	6	6	2	3
Ayala	1	1	0	0	0	0

NEW YORK	IP	H	R	ER	BB	K
Cone	9	0	0	0	0	10

BIBLIOGRAPHICAL NOTES

Baseball has attracted writers since its inception. It's a game with a pace and strategy conducive to the kinds of observations made in words. Since Henry Chadwick invented the box score, it has been a game, too, that provides solid, quantitative runways for flights of prose. In the writing of 27 Men Out, several books served as general background, authoritative reference and informing spirit. Let me start with the latter.

I read Daniel Okrent's *Nine Innings: The Anatomy of a Baseball Game* before I took a single step in the direction of preparing to write about the perfect game. Okrent showed that from a single game one can see, as through a prism, a much larger world. Jules Tygiel's collection of essays, *Past Time: Baseball as History*, showed that through the large window of American history one can clearly see baseball. Lawrence Ritter's classic oral history, *The Glory of Their Times*, reminded me that the language of ballplayers is where much of the game's magic and charm inheres. David McGimpsey's *Imagining Baseball* is an underappreciated reading of baseball in literature and culture. Finally, Eliot Asinof's *Eight Men Out*, in its clear-eyed look at how the imperatives of the businessman can contribute to the ultimate corruption of a ballplayer, provided the encouragement to dig more deeply into the player-owner relationship over time. My book's title is an acknowledgment of that debt.

As for authoritative reference, I depended on the many wonderful essays in the fourth, sixth, and seventh editions of *Total Baseball*, edited with such care by John Thorn, Peter Palmer, and Michael Gershman. I also relied almost solely on *Total Baseball* for player stats and year-end standings. The magnificent Retrosheet Web site run by Dave Smith allowed me to look at day-by-day box scores and team standings around the perfect games, saving me a hundred hours in the library looking at microfilm. Two other Web sites were invaluable in this regard: BaseballLibrary.com and Baseball-Reference.com, which provided easy access to player stats and pointed me in the right direction for further reading on several occasions. Doug Pappas, on his Web site, The Business of Baseball, offered brilliant summaries of baseball's labor history, access to such documents as Basic Agreements between players and owners, and posted regular updates on new agreements dealing with everything from stadium bond issues to licensing deals. The daily appearance in my e-mailbox of the SABR Listserv kept me assured that baseball mattered to so many good and smart people. Throughout, I turned to the *Sporting News*, especially for late nineteenth- and early-twentieth-century game accounts and news about teams and player movement. And for each perfect-game pitcher I had handy copies of the player files located at the A. Bartlett Giamatti Library at the Hall of Fame in Cooperstown, N.Y. In addition, I often looked to the *Biographical Dictionary of Baseball* and Burt Solomon's *Baseball Timeline* and Jim Charlton's *Baseball Chronology*. Two previous books about perfect games—Ronald Mayer's 1991 *Perfect* and James Buckley Jr.'s *Perfect!* (2002)—were also a helpful resource.

For the general history of the game, I found Harold Seymour's two-volume *Baseball* to be unfailingly comprehensive. For the history of the business of baseball, Robert F. Burke's *Never Just a Game: Players, Owners & American Baseball to 1920* and *Much More Than a Game: Players, Owners, & American Baseball Since 1921* were extremely rich resources, however partisan the tone. Charles P. Korr's study of the Player's Union, *The End of Baseball as We Knew It*, was also helpful, especially with respect to the early years of Marvin Miller. G. Richard McKelvey's *For It's One, Two, Three Strikes You're Out at the Owners' Ball Game: Players versus Management in Baseball* offered extremely cogent analyses of labor negotiations and settlements over the years.

SELECTED BIBLIOGRAPHY:

Alvarez, Mark, *The Perfect Game: A Classic Collection of Facts, Figures, Stories and Characters from the Society of American Baseball Research* (Taylor, 1993)

Anderson, David W., *More Than Merkle: A History of the Best and Most Exciting Baseball Season in Human History* (University of Nebraska Press, 2000)

Angell, Roger, *A Pitcher's Story: Innings with David Cone* (Warner Books, 2001)

Asinof, Eliot, *Eight Men Out: The Black Sox and the 1991 World Series* (Henry Holt, 1977)

Barzilla, Scott, *Checks and Balances, Competitive Disparity in Major League Baseball* (McFarland, 2002)

Bjarkman, Peter C., *Baseball with a Latin Beat* (McFarland, 1994)

Browning, Reed, *Cy Young: A Baseball Life* (University of Massachusetts Press, 2000)

Buckley, James, Jr., *Perfect: The Inside Story of Baseball's Sixteen Perfect Games* (Triumph, 2002)

Bunning, Jim, *The Story of Jim Bunning* (Lippincott, 1965)

Burke, Robert F., *Never Just a Game* (University of North Carolina Press, 1994)

———., *More Than Just a Game* (University of North Carolina Press, 2001)

Charlton, James, *The Baseball Chronology* (Hungry Minds, 1991)

Cherry, Thomas L., *Good Ol' Country Boy* (Pierce Printing)

Condon, Dave, *Go-Go Chicago White Sox* (Coward-McCann, 1960)

Daley, Arthur, *Times at Bat: A Half-Century of Baseball* (Random, 1950)

Dolson, Frank, *Jim Bunning: Baseball and Beyond* (Temple University Press, 1998)

Drysdale, Don, *Once a Bum, Always a Dodger* (St. Martin's, 1990)

Fischer, David Hackett, *Albion's Seed: Four British Folkways in America* (Oxford, 1991)

Golenbock, Peter, *Bums: An Oral History of the Brooklyn Dodgers* (Contemporary Books, 2000)

Gordon, Peter, *Diamonds Are Forever: Artists and Writers on Baseball* (Chronicle, 1987)

Helyar, John, *Lords of the Realm* (Random House Value, 1995)

Jackson, Reggie, *Reggie* (Ballantine, 1985)

James, Bill, *The New Bill James Historical Baseball Abstract* (The Free Press, 2001)

Kahn, Roger, *The Era: 1947-1957, When the Yankees, the Giants and the Dodgers Ruled the World* (Ticknor & Fields, 1993; University of Nebraska Press, 2002)

Korr, Charles P., *The End of Baseball as We Knew It* (Univ. of Illinois, 2002)

Larsen, Don (with Mark Shaw), *The Perfect Yankee* (Sagamore Publishing, 2001)

Leavy, Jane, *Sandy Koufax: A Lefty's Legacy* (HarperCollins, 2002)

Levy, Alan H., *Rube Waddell: The Zany, Brilliant Life of a Strikeout Artist*

Lewis, Michael, *Moneyball* (W.W. Norton, 2003)

Libby, Bill, *Catfish: The Three Million Dollar Pitcher* (Putnam, 1976)

Longert, Scott, *Addie Joss: King of the Pitchers* (SABR, 1998)

McGimpsey, David, *Imagining Baseball: America's Pastime and American Culture* (Indiana University Press, 2000)

McKelvey, G. Richard, *For It's One, Two, Three Strikes You're Out at the Owners' Ball Game* (McFarland, 2001)

Mantle, Mickey, *My Favorite Summer, 1956* (Doubleday, 1991)

Martin, Billy, *Billyball* (Doubleday, 1987)

Mayer, Ronald A., *Perfect* (McFarland, 1991)

Miller, Marvin, *A Whole Different Ballgame: The Sport and Business of Baseball* (Birch Lane, 1991)

Nemec, David, *The Rules of Baseball* (Lyons & Burford, 1994)

Okrent, Daniel, *Nine Innings: The Anatomy of a Baseball Game* (Houghton Mifflin, 2000)

Pallone, Dave, *Behind the Mask: My Double Life in Baseball* (Viking, 1990)

Pluto, Terry, *The Curse of Rocky Colavito: A Loving Look at a Thirty-Year Slump* (Simon & Schuster, 1994)

Reston, James, Jr., *Collision at Home Plate: The Lives of Pete Rose and Bart Giamatti* (HarperCollins/Edward Burlingame Books, 1991)

Romig, Ralph H., *Cy Young, Baseball's Legendary Giant* (Dorrance, 1964)

Seymour, Harold, *Baseball* (Oxford, 1971)

Solomon, Burt, *The Baseball Timeline* (DK, 2001)

Tunis, John, *The American Way in Sport* (Duelle, Sloane and Pearce, 1958)

Tygiel, Jules, *Past Time: Baseball as History* (Oxford, 2000)

Ueberroth, Peter, *Made in America* (Horizon, 1988)

Veeck, Bill, *Hustler's Handbook* (Putnam, 1965)

Vincent, Fay, *The Last Commissioner: A Baseball Valentine* (Simon & Schuster, 2002)

Wells, David, *Perfect I'm Not* (William Morrow, 2003)

Westcott, Rich and Lewis, Allen, *No-Hitters: The 225 Games, 1893-1999* (McFarland, 2000)

Zimbalist, Andrew, *Baseball and Billions* (Basic, 1994)

———, *May the Best Team Win: Baseball Economics and Public Policy* (The Brookings Institution, 2003)

ACKNOWLEDGMENTS

I want to thank my agent, John Wright, for his patient advice during the conception of this project, and for his steadying hand throughout its execution; my editor, Luke Dempsey, for his helpful line edits and cheerful counsel; friend Dermot McEvoy for alerting me along the way to many relevant books and countless anecdotes, and for being a continuous source of ideas and correctives from first to last. Tim Wiles and the good people at the A. Bartlett Giamatti Library in Cooperstown were unfailingly gracious to me as I researched from home and on visits to the Hall. Bill Burdick, overseer of the photo archives there, was a savior when it came to finding illustrations for the book. Bruce Markusen, an expert on the Athletics, helped steer me away from some chronological potholes in my Catfish chapter, and Dave Smith and Jane Leavy each gave a read to an early draft of my Sandy Koufax chapter—all my thanks. Jim Charlton came to my aid more than once, as did Will Carroll with his sage advice about arm injuries and surgical interventions. I thank Mike Quinlin for running down some Cy Young clippings for me at the Boston Public Library. I would also like to thank anyone who has ever given any money to the New York Public Library. The reading room at the main branch became my second home.

At *Publishers Weekly*, managing editor Robin Lenz stepped in to cover for me when a book deadline loomed, for which I am very grateful. And thanks to all my colleagues there who lent encouragement and advice.

Finally, I want to thank my family, which hung in there through trying times as I labored away at the library and made baseball seem an endless season. My only hope is to repay at least a portion of what they gave to the book.

PHOTO CREDITS

INDEX